The Collected Works of John Brandane:
The Full-Length Plays

The Collected Works of John Brandane

The Treasure Ship and other Full-Length Plays
The Glen is Mine (1923)
The Treasure Ship (1924)
The Lifting (1925)
The Inn of Adventure (1932)
Heather Gentry (1932)

Rory Aforesaid and other One-Act Plays
Glenforsa (1921) *with Alec Wilson Yuill*
The Change-House (1921)
Rory Aforesaid (1928)
The Happy War (1928)
The Spanish Galleon (1932) *with Alec Wilson Yuill*
Man of Uz (1932)

Three Novels
My Lady of Aros (1910)
The Captain More (1923)
Strawfeet (1930)

The Collected Works of John Brandane
Volume 1

The Treasure Ship
and other Full-Length Plays

The Glen is Mine (1923)
The Treasure Ship (1924)
The Lifting (1925)
The Inn of Adventure (1932)
Heather Gentry (1932)

John Brandane

Kennedy & Boyd

Kennedy & Boyd
an imprint of
Zeticula Ltd
Unit 13,
196 Rose Street,
Edinburgh,
EH2 4AT

http://www.kennedyandboyd.co.uk
admin@kennedyandboyd.co.uk

First published:
The Glen is Mine (1923)
The Treasure Ship (1924)
The Lifting (1925)
The Inn of Adventure (1932)
Heather Gentry (1932)

This edition Copyright © Zeticula Ltd 2022
First published in this edition 2022

ISBN 978-1-84921-155-0

All rights reserved. No part of this publication may be reproduced, stored in a retrieval system, or transmitted in any form or by any means, electronic, mechanical, photocopying, recording or otherwise, without the prior permission of the publishers.

Contents

Introduction *by Ronald W. Renton*	vii
Glossary of Gaelic Words	ix
Glossary of Scots Words	xi
The Glen is Mine	1
The Treasure Ship	69
The Lifting	179
The Inn of Adventure	243
Heather Gentry	345

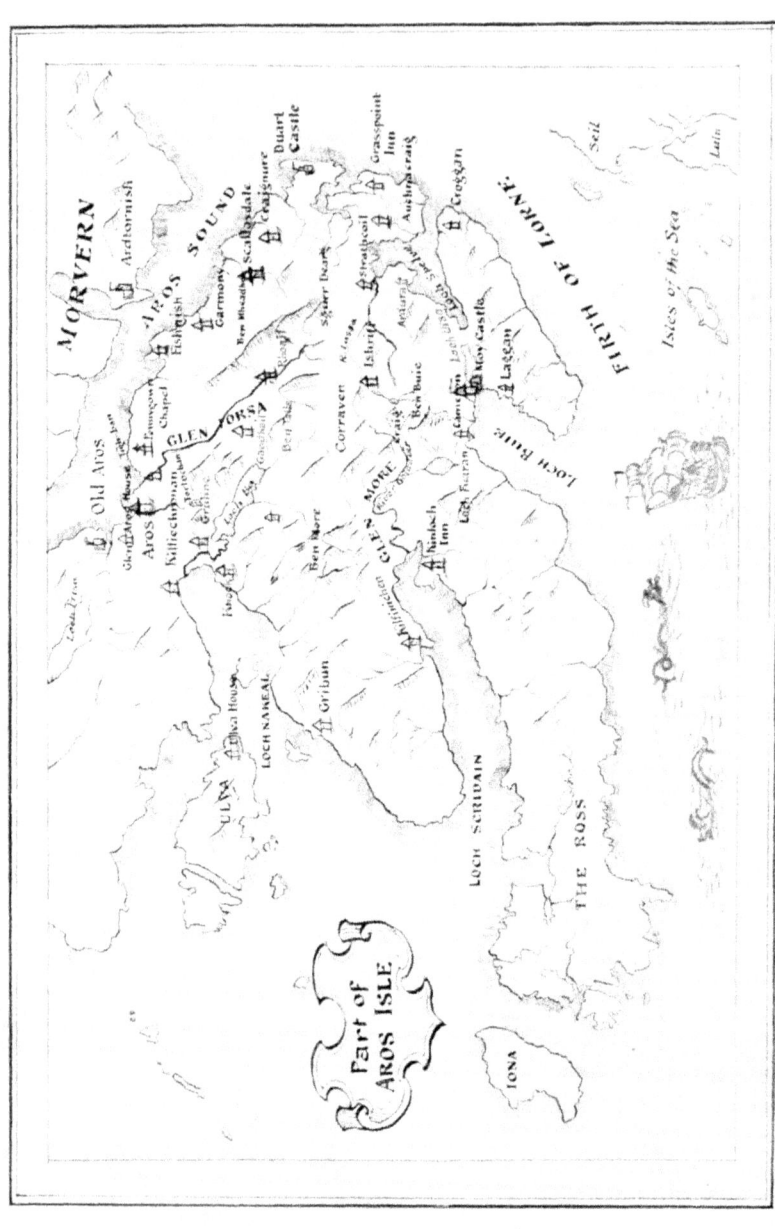

Map used by Ian Fraser in his Journeyings in the Isle of Aros, A.D. 1759

Introduction

John Brandane (1869-1947)
dramatist and novelist

John Brandane (the pen name for Dr John MacIntyre) was arguably Scotland's best known resident dramatist in the 1920s before the emergence of that other great doctor/dramatist James Bridie (OH Mavor).

He was born in Rothesay on the Isle of Bute on 14th August, 1869. His family moved to the Bridgeton area of Glasgow and as a boy he worked in a Glasgow cotton mill and between the ages of 15-27 was employed as a clerk in a warehouse. During his latter years in the warehouse he took up the study of medicine at Glasgow University. In 1901 he graduated and while specialising in surgery at Glasgow Royal Infirmary he met and became a friend of Bridie. Since he had not taken a holiday for six years, for the sake of his health he obtained his first medical post in a rural practice on the Island of Mull and remained there until 1908.

His first known venture into literature is a long short story called "In Aros Isle" which he wrote in 1905. With advice on its plot and characterisation and praise for its "zest" from Neil Munro this developed into the novel *My Lady of Aros* which was published in 1910. Its setting is the location for almost all of Brandane's later work -Eilean Aros or Aros Isle, a thinly disguised Island of Mull. Like Neil Munro's *Shoes of Fortune*, it deals with the abortive Jacobite Rising of 1759 and treachery -in this case the treachery of the heroine's double dealing spy brother Norman.

From 1908 until 1912 Brandane moved to England and was a general practitioner in a rural area in the Thames Valley. While there he paid occasional visits to London where performances by the Abbey Theatre Players from Dublin turned his mind towards writing drama. In 1912 he returned to Glasgow and remained in general practice in the Hyndland area until 1935. During WW1 he served as surgeon in a hospital in the French sector of the Western Front at Arc-en-Barrois near Verdun.

When he returned to live in Glasgow he was to become deeply involved in the city's theatrical life. He renewed his acquaintance with A W Yuill and together they pushed the cause for a native Scottish drama and began writing for the Scottish National Players. His first one act play (with Yuill) *Glenforsa* (1921) portrays a spirited and drunken quarrel between two friends, Glenforsa and Oskamull, the gambling away of Glenforsa's Mull properties and the romantic entanglement of the two men with two sisters. This was followed by another one act play *The Change House*. In 1922, when he was 53 years old, he became a founder member of the Scottish National Players and in effect their in-house dramatist since almost all of his plays were performed by them.

1923 saw the performance of what is probably his most important full length play *The Glen is Mine*. This work has good characterisation and a strong theme, the future of the Highlands: are industry and progress preferable to the destruction of the old Highland way of life? The ending, however, shies away from a bold resolution and opts for a safer, more sentimental conclusion. In 1923 he also published the novel *The Captain More*, a re-working and extension of the ideas of his play *Glenforsa*.

1924 saw the performance of the full length romantic comedy *The Treasure Ship* with its background of the salvaging of treasure from a Spanish galleon supposedly sunk in Tobermory Bay. In 1925 *The Lifting* (an extension of the one act *The Change House*) a full length play full of irony and coincidence set in the south of Mull near Lochbuie goes back to the period of 1745 Jacobite Rising. It demonstrates the honour and decency of the hero Iain in sacrificing his life to protect the friend whom he had inadvertently implicated in the killing of an "enemy" before the beginning of the play.

In 1926 Tyrone Guthrie directed Brandane's one act comedy masterpiece *Rory Aforesaid* with its wily elderly protagonist. This was followed by the grim and ironic one act *The Happy War* (1928) set in war-torn France, the full length comedy *Heather Gentry* (1932), the historical one act *The Spanish Galleon* (1932) (again co-authored with Yuill) which deals with the sinking of the galleon in Tobermory Bay and *The Inn of Adventure* (1932), a stage adaptation of the novel *The Captain More*. His final play, *The Man of Uz* (1938), is his dramatic representation of the suffering of Job.

Perhaps, outside his plays, the most interesting achievement of his later literary work is his third and final novel *Strawfeet* (1930). This deals with the First World War and is set partly on Mull and partly in France on the Western Front. Like *My Lady of Aros* it deals again with espionage and betrayal but this time in contemporary life. Brandane is one of the few Scots to have written a novel dealing with the First World War. And he dedicated it to Neil Munro, "Master of those who know the Gael".

In 1935 he found the demands of medical practice in the city and authorship too heavy. He returned to the Highlands to rural practice in Lochgoilhead in Argyll. He died there on 17th October, 1947.

Glossary of Gaelic Words

Aghmhor	happy
Albainn	Scotland
Amadan	fool
An Gillie Dubh	The Dark-haired lad
Beannachd leat (singular)	Blessing on you, goodbye
Beannachd leibh (plural))	
Beag	little
Bodach	old man
Caileag bheag	little girl
Cailleach	old woman
Cailleachean	old women
Canach	wild cotton
Canntaireachd	chaunt
Cas-chrom	plough
Cibeir	shepherd
Ceilidh	story-telling, gossip, folk tales
Clachan	a group of cottages
Cladh Phobuill	The Burying Place of the People (or Tribe)
Clarsach	Highland harp
Cnoc-na-croiche	Gallows-Hill
Co tha sin?	Who is there?
Cogadh no Sith	War or Peace
Creach	spoil, plunder
Crodh Chailein	Colin's cattle
Crotnag	shepherd's crook
Cuach	cup, wooden bowl
Cuarain	foot-covering of the raw hide
Dhia!	God!
Direach sin!	Just so!
Drammach	meal and water
Dubh	dark

Duin'-uasal	gentleman
Eilean	isle
Eilean Dhia	isle of God
Feasgar math!	Good evening!
Fin McCoul	Legendary Gaelic hero
Fleurisch	Flint and steel
Garron	Highland pony
Ghaol mo chridhe!	White love of my heart
Gillie	a lad, a Highland commoner
ille!	lad
Iorraman	boat-songs
Laochain	my hero
Maam	a round, steep hill
Mainnir nam Fiadh	The Playground of the Deer (a hill)
Marbh phaisg ort!	Death-wrapping be on thee!
M'eudail!	My treasure!
Mallachd ort!	Curse on you!
Mo chridhe!	My dear!
Mo thruaigh!	My sorrow!
Mogain	footless stockings
Och, ille, ille	Oh, lad, lad!
Och, ochan!	Alas, alas!
Och, ubh, ubh!	Oh, dear, dear!
Oidche mhath!	Good night!
Ruapais	The Careless One, the Rigmarole
Sassenach	Southerner
Seanachaidhean	story-tellers, bards
seilisders	sedges
Sgalag	ploughman
Sgian dubh	black knife
Slainte mhath!	Good health!
Slainte mhor mhath!	Great health!
Slan lea!	Farewell!
Suas e ... suas e	up with it ... up with it
Taghairm	invocation (of spirits)
Tearlach	Charles
Tearlach Og	Prince Charlie
Thoir an aire!	Look out!
Tir-nan-Oig	Land of the Ever-Young
Tonnag	a small shawl

Glossary of Scots Words

Airt	direction
Bannock	scone
Bawbee	halfpenny
Body	person
Bouman	cowman, or crofter
Breaking	bankruptcy
Brock	beast
Causey	causeway
Cogie	wooden bowl
Craig	throat
Cruisie	metal lamp
Deave	deafen
Doer	agent
Ettled	intended
Fleeching.	scolding
Girning	complaining peevishly
Gowff	gust
Greetin'	bewailing
Hamesucken	assaulting a person with violence in his own house.
Haud	hold
Haud till't!	Hold on!
Howe and corrie	hollow and height
instrument o' sasine	An attestation by a Notary Public certifying the bargain.
Jalouse	surmise
Jo	lover
Lave	remainder
Loon	fellow
Maun	must
Mirk	dark
Oxter	armpit

Scunner	disgust
Scrape, the	the 'Forty-five Rising
Shaw	thicket, plantations
Skirling	shrieking
Smeddum	spirit
Snood	a ribbon for the hair
Soumings	allotments
Spate	flood
Spier	enquire
Spring	lively tune
Stravaging	wandering
Tacks of land	portions of land
Tacksman	a lessee of land who sublets to crofters
Thrapple	windpipe
Tinchel	hunt
Tocher	marriage portion
Trusty	secret agent
Tyke	dog
Wadset	a pawning of land
Warlock	wizard

The Glen is Mine

A Comedy in three Acts

ACT I
The Farm-Kitchen at Ardsheilach.
A day in early August, 1920.

ACT II
The Farm-Kitchen at Ardsheilach.
Six weeks later.

ACT III
The Living-Room of the Croft at Coillemore.
A week later.

JOCK GALLETLY	*Farmer at Ardsheilach.*
MRS. GALLETLY	*His Wife.*
ANGUS MACKINNON	*Odd-man at Ardsheilach Farm and Crofter in Coillemore.*
MORAG	*His daughter.*
MURDO MACKAY	*Odd-man at Torlochan Hotel.*
COLONEL MURRAY	*Former Proprietor of Ardsheilach and Coilliemore.*
CAPTAIN CHARLIE	*His son.*
DR. MORRISON	*Doctor in Eilean Aros.*
STOCKMAN	*Mining Expert from London.*
DUGALD **MACPHEDRAN**	*Village Merchant.*
MRS. **MACALLISTER**)	*Crofter Women.*
MRS. DUNCAN)	

The Glen is Mine was first produced by the Scottish Theatre Society at the Athenaeum Theatre, Glasgow, on 25th January, 1923, under the direction of Andrew P. Wilson, with the following cast:

Mrs Galletly	Nell Ballantyne
Angus MacKinnon	Archibald Buchanan
Colonel Murray	W. McD. Honeyman
Jock Gelletly	W. Levack Ritchie .
Dr. Morrison	David Russell
Captain Charlie	W. Graham Dow
Stockman	Alexander McGregor
Murdo Mac Kay	Donald Robertson
Morag MacKinnon	Meg B. Buchanan
Dugald MacPhedran	Andrew P. Wilson
Mrs. MacAllister	Belina Miller
Mrs. Duncan	Elliot C. Mason

ACT I

SCENE.—*The kitchen of the farm-house of Ardsheilach in* EILEAN AROS. *In back wall, midway, is fireplace with peat-creel and peats. On mantelpiece is a set of cast-iron ornaments, "Burns at the Plough". Above mantelpiece, a coloured bust portrait of Gladstone. Flanking it, on walls, are two chromo-lithographs from the illustrated weeklies, tacked carelessly to plaster. At back also, to left of fireplace is a dresser with household vessels. On top of it are two pathetic white china dogs of large size, and some brass candlesticks. To the left of fire is an armchair and small wooden stool; to right of it an ordinary chair of kitchen type. The window, which has its lower panes of opaque glass, and draped by cheap lace curtains, is on right wall at back. Further forward on same wall is main door. A table is set towards right corner, with an enamelled basin containing potatoes ready for peeling. In left wall at rear is the back door leading to yard and stables. In same wall near front is another door leading to a little room.*
Sounds of bagpipe practice, which finally break into the air of the pibroch known as "The Glen is Mine" from little room on left. MRS. GALLETLY—*a typical Ayrshire farmer's wife—enters from main door. She is a sturdy, steerin', sharp-tongued woman of fifty, with high colour and high cheek-bones, gat-toothed. Her dark hair, greyed a little, is parted plainly in the middle, and gathered behind in a flat roll, tightly plaited. She is trig and trim, and her dress includes a shortgown shewing bare arms, a drugget skirt, and a blue apron.* SHE *goes to door of little room, and at sound of her approach the piping ceases.* SHE *opens door.*

MRS. GALLETLY
Ye're at the pipes again, in spite o' a' the doctor's orders.

VOICE
Och, it was only a little practice.

MRS. GALLETLY
Come oot o' that, and let me get yer bed tidied.

(SHE *enters room and reappears, assisting* ANGUS MACKINNON, *a Crofter. He has a lame leg and walks on crutches with difficulty towards chair beside kitchen fire.* ANGUS *is dressed in the plain, well-worn clothes of the peasant. He is about sixty, and has a shrewd humorous expression of countenance and a twinkling eye. His bearded face is sun-tanned.*)

MRS. GALLETLY
Canny noo.
(SHE *assists* ANGUS *cautiously to the chair.* HE *subsides slowly on it, and stretches himself.*)
There ye are.

(SHE *returns to little room and comes to its door banging pillows and bolster in turn, disappearing at times: she is evidently making a bed.* ANGUS *produces matches and pipe and lights up, puffing contentedly.* MRS. GALLETLY *reappears, sniffing.*)

Ye've been smoking in yer bed, again!

ANGUS

Just a puff or two.

MRS. GALLETLY

Ye'll ha'e the place burnt doon! I declare I wish ye were hame oot o' this. And here—set ye up—are yer pipes!

(SHE *flings out a very ancient set of bagpipes, with faded tartan covering them.*)

Playing the pipes, and you wi' broken ribs on ye! Could ye no' ha'e left them in the bothy?

ANGUS

(*Reaching to the pipes and fondling them.*) You'll be breaking them with your flinging them about!—Och! the ribs are not that bad.—Wait you! I'll be giving you the fine tune some of these days : "Castle Donnan" or "The Praise of Mary" or "The Glen is Mine" maybe.

MRS. GALLETLY

Ye'll wait till ye're up at yer ain hoose then—fower miles awa'. Ye'll dae nae piping here. Fower miles is my distance for the pipes.

ANGUS

What can have come over the Doctor at all, at all, Mrs. Galletly?

MRS. GALLETLY

Aye, he's late. But dinna you lippen ower muckle on the doctor, ma man. Put you your faith in a Higher Power.—Keep aff the drink, and trust in Providence.

ANGUS

Providence!—When the cart-wheel went over my leg, look you, Providence did nothing at all, at all!

MRS. GALLETLY

Whit a thing to say!

ANGUS

A leg and three ribs broken, and you'll be talking of Providence!

MRS. GALLETLY

It's the Loard's mercy ye hadna twa legs broken, ye heathen!

ANGUS

Heathen, is it?—Well, well! I'm not like some people, trying to be better than I was meant to be.

MRS. GALLETLY

Is it me ye're hinting at?—I'll—Och! I wish ye were oot o' this, and up the Glen at yer ain hoose. *(Knock at main door.)*

Here's yer great Doctor at last, and muckle guid may he dae ye!

(**SHE** *opens main door, and* **COLONEL MURRAY** *enters. He is an elderly man of sixty-five, dressed in sporting suit of Harris tweed, knickers, leather shoulder pads, etc. He wears a monocle. His air is military, and his address consequential, yet familiar.)*

Oh, it's the Laird!—And me thinking it was the Doctor, Colonel.

COLONEL

(Shaking hands.) How are you, Mrs. Galletly?—And your husband?

MRS. GALLETLY

Oh, we're a' fine, thank ye.—Jock's juist oot, taking a look at the queys.

COLONEL

Good!—I only dropped in to ask for Angus.—Having a tramp, y'know.—Six miles out and six back—not bad for an old chap, eh? Well, Angus, getting on? *(Shaking hands.)* Leg any easier?

ANGUS

Thank you, sir. I'm juist wonderful.

MRS. GALLETLY

Wonderfu', did ye say? Aye, wonderfu' that ye were spared ava! Drinking a' day at Torlochan, and then coming back fou', wi' a heavy cart, ower they wild Hielan' roads. What else could ye expect but broken banes?

ANGUS

(Sighing.) Och, I'm wishing I was home, out of this.

MRS. GALLETLY

There's mair than you wishing that, ma man.

ANGUS

The croft will be going all wrong, look you, sir. I'm wishing I'd never left it at all, at all, to be doing this dirty farmwork!

COLONEL

Oh, your croft's all right, Angus. Morag is managing beautifully. I had a walk over the hill that way yesterday, and I saw she had the hay all in. Good thing, too, before this broken weather came.

ANGUS
She's the fine daughter to me, is Morag.—She must have had the sore work getting that hay in.

MRS. GALLETLY
And she'll ha'e the sair wark keeping you sober, aince she gets ye hame.

COLONEL
Oh, you're not used to Highland ways yet, Mrs. Galletly. The dram's a great institution here. But it's what I've always said—drink and politics—drink and politics—the ruin of the working man. Now, Angus here *(rallying him)* was quite a decent chap until he took up with the Hotel Bar and all this Radical stuff about the land for the people.

ANGUS
(Meekly.) So the Colonel is always telling me.

COLONEL
(Smiling.) Telling you for your good, you rascal!
(**JOCK GALLETLY** *enters from door at back, a black-avised, hirsute individual of about forty, not over-clean. His rough clothes are well-patched.*)

COLONEL
(Shaking hands.) Ah, Galletly! Glad to see you looking so well and so industrious. I've just been telling your wife that you'll soon get used to our ways in the Highlands—the drams and all that—a bit queer at first, eh?

JOCK
(Blankly.) Queer! Oh, aye, tastes a wee thing o' peat, ye ken—but a dram's aye a dram, ye see.

MRS. GALLETLY
(Bitterly.) You and yer drams! It's the Hielands the Colonel's talking aboot.

COLONEL
Yes, yes. How do you like these parts, Galletly?

JOCK
Oh, no' bad—no' bad. A bit wat, ye ken, a bit wat for the arable.

COLONEL
But for dairy work, all right, eh? Ah, but I daresay you'll be home-sick for Ayrshire for a little while.

JOCK
Oh, aye—aye—A wadna wunner. Oh, aye, it's no' bad land doon Carrick way.

COLONEL

You know, Galletly, I've often puzzled my brains as to what it was attracted a South-country man like you up here. Whatever made you leave Carrick?

JOCK

Ma faither.

COLONEL

Your father?

JOCK

Aye. He ses to me ae day "Time ye were mairrit, Jock." Ses A, "A wadna wunner". Ses he, "You get mairrit and A'll get ye a fairm."

COLONEL

Well?

JOCK

So A got mairrit. And this is his idea o' a fairm.

COLONEL

You're a trifle hard on him, I fancy.

JOCK

Oh, A wadna say that. But, ye see, he got stock and plenishing cheaper hereaboots than doon yonder. Oh, it's no' a bad fairm—in a kin' o' a wey it's no' bad.

MRS. GALLETLY

No' bad? What about the barn, Jock?

COLONEL

Oh, yes—that barn. Needs quite a lot of repairs, I understand. Something omitted from the lease, wasn't there? But we'll see to that. Must start a new tenant fair. Can I have a look at it now? We'll repair, of course.

MRS. GALLETLY

I'm gled to hear't. For your factor tell't me yesterday he wadna dae a hand's turn till't.

COLONEL

Oh, you mustn't mind him. That's the way of factors, Mrs. Galletly.

MRS. GALLETLY

Just whit I said till him. But he said he had Captain Charlie's orders to haud aff a' repairs on the estate.

COLONEL

Charlie's orders?

MRS. GALLETLY

Aye—your ain son's orders, Colonel.

COLONEL

(*Perturbed.*) Oh—ah—yes—Charlie said that, did he? Well, let's have a look at the barn, Galletly. (*Looks out of window.*) Oh, we'll be able to—ah—arrange—ah—something, I daresay.

GALLETLY

This wey, Colonel.—Through the yaird, ye ken. (**GALLETLY** *and the* **COLONEL** *go out by back door.*)

ANGUS

(*Smiling.*) That's your death-duties for you.

MRS. GALLETLY

Whit are ye havering aboot noo?

ANGUS

I'm saying—that's the death-duties.

MRS. GALLETLY

Ach! You and yer poaliticks!

ANGUS

I'm telling you it's the death-duties. The Colonel's not the Laird here any more. It's Captain Charlie who is the Laird now.

MRS. GALLETLY

And if the Colonel's no' the Laird noo, whit wey is he steying on at the big hoose?

ANGUS

He can surely be staying on with his own son. There are only the two of them left now, anyway. But the Estate is not the Colonel's any more. And that is why they're both giving different orders about your barn. It's the death-duties. And that's one way of saving the money.

MRS. G*ALLETLY*

Saving money! Tell me aboot that, man.

ANGUS

It's this way. If a man has much land and money, and he dies, the Government comes up and says, "We are needing money very badly.—Be giving us some of that." And off the Government goes with their sporrans full of pound notes. And that's what they call the death-duties.

MRS. GALLETLY
There's Government for ye! There's poaliticks! The big thiefs!

ANGUS
But if a man has a great deal of land and money, and he doesn't want the Government to get too much of it, he gives the land and the money to his son or his daughter or one of his friends, and he says, " Be you taking that now; and when I'm dying, I'll have no money for them to be lifting their dirty death-duties out of, and this greedy Government will never smell a penny of that, if I can help it."

MRS. GALLETLY
And isn't that clever noo! Dod, I maun tell Jock aboot this! They Governments are the perfect villains!

ANGUS
And that's what the Colonel has been doing, look you.

MRS. GALLETLY
Isn't he the wyce auld man!

ANGUS
But the Colonel has not got used to not being the Laird any more. And so he'll be giving one order, and Captain Charlie will be giving the other order. And that's your repairing of the barns, look you.

MRS. GALLETLY
Well, you're the great scholar, Angus. But whaurever did ye hear a' this?

ANGUS
Och! everybody has heard about it. Wasn't the prize bull at the last Cattle Show put down in Captain Charlie's name? And haven't the butler and the servant maids been talking? And Torlochan Post Office did the rest. You'll be knowing what a Post Office is for spreading the news, Mrs. Galletly? Och, yes, it's true enough!

MRS. GALLETLY
Aye, true eneuch, nae doot, for I noticed he was gey camflustered like, when the Captain's name was mentioned. Man, man! what a warld o' deception, Angus! *(Knock at main door.)* Here's your Doctor at last.
  (**DR. MORRISON** *enters, a young, fair-complexioned hearty man of thirty-five. He brings forward his professional bag.*)

DR. M.
Good day, Mrs. Galletly. How are you, Angus? Getting along? How's the leg? Ribs any better?

ANGUS

Oh, the ribs are fine now, and I'll soon be at the piping, look you! And the leg's not bad, at all, at all. I can be moving my toes now without the great pain.

DR. M.

(Testing bandages and splints.) Good! Let's see, eight weeks since the accident. Other two, and you'll be able to put some weight on it.—Well, you're more comfortable here than in that awful bothy next the stable. Pneumonia sure for you, if I'd let Mrs. Galletly keep you there.

MRS. GALLETLY

'Deed, and he was juist fine yonder, Doctor. And a dale less bother than here.

DR. M.

Broken ribs sticking into a man's lung, and you'd keep him in a stable, Mrs. Galletly!

MRS. GALLETLY

(Lifting peat-basket from fireside and going to door with it.) Tach! he was fine in yonder. And ye ken, Doctor, oor Loard was born in a stable.
(Goes out hurriedly by back door on left.)

DR. M.

(Scratching his head.) Well, I'm dashed—

ANGUS

(Chuckling.) There's no knot on yon one's tongue!
(**DR. MORRISON** *goes on with his examination of leg, and* **COLONEL MURRAY** *and* **JOCK GALLETLY** *enter by back door.*)

COLONEL

How do, Doctor! *(Shakes hands.)* Angus getting on? Breaking his heart to be back on his croft, though. Wishes he'd never started carting on the big farm.

DR. M.

(Smiling.) Aye. No carts in the Glen, Angus, eh?

ANGUS

'Deed no, Doctor. No more carts for me.

COLONEL

By the bye, Doctor—hope you don't mind my asking— but whatever are your friends doing out on the hill there?

DR. M.

My friends!

(**MRS. GALLETLY** *returns with peat basket filled, and sets to renewing the fire. Later she peels potatoes, stopping at times to listen to the conversation.*)

COLONEL

Yes, those two fellows you brought down in your trap. I saw them get off at the main road, when I was at the barn with Galletly. *(Looks out of window.)* They're all over the hill now. Must be fond of climbing surely! And aren't they just scaring the young grouse no end! Too bad, y'know, and it so near the Twelfth.

DR. M.

But, dear me, Colonel—

COLONEL

(Still at window, and now furious.) Hang it, sir! What the devil are they after? There go the birds! Getting up around them everywhere! There! Look at that! The shooting spoiled on that side of the hill for a week to come! Please call them in, Morrison! If they're waiting for you, can't they do so indoors, instead of messing my game about?

DR. M.

But it's your own son, Colonel, and a friend from London, and it's their trap, not mine—a hire from the hotel at Torlochan. Knowing I was coming down, they kindly gave me a lift.

COLONEL

Charlie! Whatever is he doing here? I thought he was in London.

DR. M.

He's just straight up from London, sir. And he's brought one of those haematite fellows with him to prospect the ground.

COLONEL

Haematite?

DR. M.

Yes. This iron ore business. They say Ben Creach's chock full of it.

COLONEL

Minerals! I never heard a word of this. Good Heavens! They're not talking of mining here, are they?

DR. M.

Sorry if I've put my foot in it, sir. I thought you knew all about it.

COLONEL

I? Never heard a syllable!

DR. M.
They were talking quite freely as we drove down, and I couldn't help chipping in. It seems there's unlimited mineral wealth in the Highlands.

COLONEL
But it's desecration, Doctor! Mining in Eilean Aros.

JOCK
Aye, it'll be a puir look-out for the black-faced sheep trade then. (*Looking out of window.*) The Captain's turning back down the hill again.

COLONEL
I must see Charlie about this. Mining! — Good heavens!
(**HE** *goes out by main door hurriedly.*)

JOCK
There'll be a rare collieshangie atween them. A maun see that.
(*Goes out after the* **COLONEL.**)

ANGUS
(*Chuckling.*) There's your death-duties again for you! The Colonel will not like them to be spoiling the forest.

MRS. GALLETLY
The forest?

ANGUS
The deer-forest. He's the great one for the deer and the grouse. But, see you, the young one's for making money from the bowels of the earth. *Ochanoch!*[1] Didn't I tell you the death-duties was the queer thing?

DR. M.
Oh, I see. I've heard of that. The Colonel transferred the Estate to Charlie so as to get rid of the death-duties didn't he? And now his troubles are beginning, poor man!

ANGUS
Yes, yes. Nothing now for the poor Colonel, but trouble and trouble!

DR. M.
They say it's as good haematite as the Swedish stuff. And, of course, they'll capture the market, for they'll save the freightage across the North Sea. Well, I suppose the Captain will want all the cash he can get, for he's been making the money spin in London, I hear.

ANGUS
And isn't he the foolish one, now?

MRS. GALLETLY

Time he was mairrit—and settled down, I'm thinking! Was there no' some talk o' him and yin o' thae Mirlees women?

DR. M.

Oh! The people who had the shooting here last season?

ANGUS

Just that! Miss Alice—a fine lass! And too good for the Captain, as I'm seeing it. Tach! Him and his haematite!

MRS. GALLETLY

Whit was that ye ca'd it?—Haud-me-tight?

DR. M.

No, no. Haematite—a fine kind of iron.

MRS. GALLETLY

Iron? I see nae sense in a name like that for iron.— If they're thinking o' advertising it, haud-me-tight would be faur better.

ANGUS

Ach, let them alone with their haematite and their foolishness. I well believe no one in Eilean Aros will be any the happier for all their mines! But the Doctor came to see my leg and not their nonsense. Would the Doctor like to see me on my stilts?

DR. M.

Yes, to be sure. I'd quite forgotten about them.

ANGUS

(*Rising slowly to his crutches, walks a few steps.*) Look at that! I'm thinking I could be getting home quite soon now.

DR. M.

You'll never walk four miles up the Glen on crutches, Angus. If there was a decent cart-track, we could get you up in a wagonette, but there isn't.

ANGUS

But Morag will be killed with all the work on the croft and the hay—

MRS. GALLETLY

The hay's a' in, Doctor. Ne'er heed him.—And noo, if ye're feenished wi' his bad leg, maybe ye'll tell me whit to dae wi' mine.

(**ANGUS** *goes back to couch.*)

DR. M.

Sorry to hear you have a bad leg, Mrs. Galletly.

MRS. GALLETLY

No' a bit o' ye! It's anither fee in your pooch. I needna bother showing it to ye, for ye'll ken a' aboot it. It's verra coorse veins. Is rubbing ony guid?

DR. M.

Very coarse veins? Oh, yes, I see. Rubbing? Well, no. An elastic bandage is the thing.

MRS. GALLETLY

But is rubbing ony guid? Tamson, the tea-traveller, tell't me to rub them doon the wey. (SHE *demonstrates*.)

DR. M.

Oh, never, Mrs. Galletly! No, no. If you must rub, rub gently upwards. Aids the circulation, you know.

MRS. GALLETLY

The like o' that! And me rubbing a' wrang! Wait till I get Tamson!

DR. M.

I'll post you an elastic bandage.

MRS. GALLETLY

A' richt.—But here's anither thing I maun ask ye. (*Goes to window.*) Whaur's Jock, I wunner? (*Comes back from window.*) It's this. Whit's guid for indigestion in the throat?

DR. M.

Never heard of it there.

MRS. GALLETLY

Weel, that's whaur oor Jock has it, onywey.

DR. M.

Nonsense!

MRS. GALLETLY

Indigestion! Whaur should he ha'e't then?

DR. M.

Here. (*Places his hand over his stomach.*)

MRS. GALLETLY

Aye, man, aye. He has pain there sometimes. A wee thing to the left, maybe. Aye, juist here. What ha'e we hereaboots, Doctor? (*Holds her hand on left side.*)

DR. M.
(*Mischievously solemn.*) Cardiac end of the stomach, tail of pancreas, spleen, splenic flexure of colon, left kidney, left suprarenal capsule, and left suprarenal sympathetic plexus.

MRS. GALLETLY
Guid be aboot us! — A' that!

ANGUS
Just fancy you!

DR. M.
Yes. — You know, Mrs. Galletly, we're fearfully and wonderfully made.

MRS. GALLETLY
(*Excitedly.*) That's it Doctor — that's it. — By a Higher Power — a Higher Power! Whit I'm aye telling Angus.

(*Noise of voices outside. She goes to window.*)

Whatever's this noo! Keep me! Here's the hale jing-bang o' them back. And the Colonel that puffed oot wi' anger, juist like a bubbly-jock.

(*The main door opens and the* COLONEL *enters with his son,* CHARLES, *a young man of thirty-two, slightly stooping, and lackadaisical in manner, his speech drawling.* STOCKMAN, *the mining expert, accompanies them — a dark-complexioned alert man of forty. He keeps in the background and is diplomatically silent.*)

CAPTAIN
Finished, doctor? (DOCTOR *nods.*) Well then, we're for the road again, I suppose. Hullo, Angus! Leg mending?

ANGUS
Thank you, sir, yes. I'm hoping the Captain is well.

CAPTAIN
Oh! I'm all right, thanks. Well, Doctor — ready?

COLONEL
But Charlie, you're not going back to Torlochan, surely? Why not walk home with me — you and Mr. Stockman? I want an evening with you — a little talk, you know.

CAPTAIN
Sorry, dad, but I have to be in Edinburgh by to-morrow to see about things. I'll have to stay at Torlochan tonight, so as to get the early mail-boat.

COLONEL
Well—but I must have a word with you here, then. Mrs. Galletly, may we go into your parlour for a moment? Sorry to trouble you.

MRS. GALLETLY
The paurlor? Och, it's a' reel-rail. We've been cleaning it. And there's nae fire there. But juist you bide here, and I'll tak' the Doctor and this gentleman roon to the new patent kirn and shew them hoo it works. And Angus can gang intil his ain wee room there.

COLONEL
Oh! Sorry. Afraid we're a bother, you know, but—
(ALL *go out except* COLONEL *and* CHARLIE.) Well, Charlie. Not very nice for me to hear the first of this from a stranger, eh?

CAPTAIN
A little rough on you, I admit, dad. I intended writing you as soon as I got things settled somewhat tomorrow in Edinburgh.

COLONEL
Iron-mines here?

CAPTAIN
Yes. I knew you'd not see eye to eye with me, but I had to close with Redfern's offer, or he'd have got some other show in the Highlands for his money. There's haematite in plenty all up the West Coast here.

COLONEL
But couldn't you have let me have word of this before you went so far?

CAPTAIN
I was rushed. There was really no time, dad. And, besides, I knew you wouldn't take a business view of the matter.—I mean one that would have left out sentiment.

But it just comes to this. There's money in that old hill; so why shouldn't we have it?

COLONEL
And you're Highland, and can say that! Ben Creach! The deer-forest! Rubbish heaps and mineral waggons all over it! The river with oily scum in it! Labourers slouching about! You should have consulted me first of all, Charlie!

CAPTAIN
I tell you it was a big chance—hit or miss. The London people were keen. Redfern offered a good price. I had to snap at it or let it go. Besides, the thing will be but a flea-bite in a big countryside like this.

COLONEL

More like a plague that will spread!

CAPTAIN

I think that's a bit savage, dad. Look here! You're Tariff Reform, aren't you? Protection of home industries, and all that? Well, here we are! Sweden has the monopoly at present of this ore. We've got stuff in Ben Creach and elsewhere in the Highlands, quite as good as theirs. And we'll bust their market in this country quite easily. Redfern offers good money, and I need it.

COLONEL

Need?

CAPTAIN

Need's the word, dad. Sorry, but you may as well have the truth now as later. I've been let down by some rotten speculations—South African stuff. And five figures is what it runs to.

COLONEL

Good heavens, Charlie!

CAPTAIN

Yes; it's bitter to hear of your money going in such a foolish fashion, I know. But there's wisdom enough in this haematite deal to make up for all that.

COLONEL

You might have asked my advice about retrieving before—this—

CAPTAIN

There was my trouble. I did think of you. But a time-limit was set—and there was no chance of getting into touch with you soon enough. We've got to catch the early market. It was all slap-dash, y'know.

COLONEL

But—Oh, it's no use talking! But the Highlands, Charlie! Is this to be the beginning of the end of them? Are the old hunting, pastoral days to go—the wild free open life?

CAPTAIN

Sentiment, dad! Really now, it's nothing else.

COLONEL

Sentiment's a great power, lad, and not to be sneered at, as we Army folk should know well.

CAPTAIN

You talk of the old life going. I don't know. But I tell you what *will* go, dad, if we start a decent industry here— the huckstereven of letting deer forests and grouse moors to a lot of scabby profiteers. Aye, and the lairds' genteel poverty will go! And these lazy crofters will go! That's what it amounts to.

COLONEL

The lairds! Well, we're maybe not all we should be. But think, man, think! Blast furnaces, smoke, coal-dust, in Eilean Aros? Think of the men you'll breed under those conditions!

CAPTAIN

But who's talking of coal? Why, we've water power in the Glen sufficient to drive a dozen Ben Creachs into the sea. We're going to dam at the head of the Glen—at Coillemore.

COLONEL

At the larachs?—You'll never do that. There's still a holding there: Angus MacKinnon's croft—the broken-leg fellow in the room here.

CAPTAIN

Oh, every man has his price, father. We'll buy him out all right.

COLONEL

Sentiment is a greater power than money with the Highlander, I tell you! And Angus will stick to his croft because of it.

CAPTAIN

He'll give us no bother, I'm certain. Plenty of drams is all he wants! Whisky will beat sentiment any day with these chaps.—But I'll have him in and shew you how we can work this.

COLONEL

No need. We're wandering from the main point. Can nothing be done to stop this mad scheme before it goes further? I'm opposed to it, root and branch

CAPTAIN

You'll see things differently once the dividends begin to roll in. No, we can't stop now. I'm committed by all kinds of legal flummery already. But just to shew you about Angus—let's ask him in.

COLONEL

Oh! don't bother!—I'm sick of all this sorry business.

CAPTAIN

But just to shew you.—*(Going to door of little room, opens it).* Can you spare me a moment, Angus?

(**ANGUS** *hobbles in on crutches and seats himself on couch.*)

Oh, about that croft of yours, Angus. You're getting up in years now. Won't want to stay on there all your life, eh?

ANGUS

(Cautiously.) Oh, there's nothing wrong with the croft, sir, even for an old man.

CAPTAIN

Well, but that bad leg of yours will trouble you for some time, I fancy, eh? Now what price?—I mean—how much would you take to move out, supposing we wanted the croft for—ah—purposes of our own, y'know?

ANGUS

That will be for the mines that the Doctor was speaking about.

CAPTAIN

(Softly.) Damn! *(Then aloud.)* Oh! I see you know all about it.—Well, supposing now—

ANGUS

I could be conseedering, sir.

CAPTAIN

Yes—but supposing—

ANGUS

Och! I would have to be conseedering.

CAPTAIN

Well now, two hundred, Angus.

ANGUS

It's a good croft, look you, and—

CAPTAIN

Three hundred, then.

ANGUS

The Captain is very kind. But I'll have to be going back first of all and seeing to the hay and things—

CAPTAIN

(Bluffing.) Well, y'know, if the Government wants to make a water-power dam there, they'll take it at their own valuation, and that will be a good deal less, I'm afraid, than what I'm offering.

ANGUS

The Government will have more sense, I well believe.

CAPTAIN

More sense than to take an interest in a—a—a scheme that will benefit the whole countryside?

ANGUS

(*Slyly.*) Och, no!—I have more manners than to be saying anyone will have more sense than the Captain when it comes to doing good. No—no—! But the Government will have burnt its fingers too often on the Crofters' Act for them to try forcing a poor crofter out of his holding hereabouts, look you.

COLONEL

(*Chuckling.*) Didn't I tell you, Charlie?

CAPTAIN

(*Chagrined, but pretending to take the matter humorously.*) Well, you are an old pirate, Angus, I must say!

ANGUS

But I will be conseedering—

CAPTAIN

Well, we'll leave it at that. Time I was away, though, father. You walking home? (**COLONEL** *nods.*) Come and see me off, then. And be sure there's no need for worrying, dad. Think it over. (*Goes to main door.*)

COLONEL

(*Following him.*) Well, I'm afraid I can have only one opinion, Charlie. The whole thing's a mistake, and—
(**THEY** *pass out talking.* **ANGUS** *starts humming a Gaelic air.* **DR. MORRISON** *enters by back door to collect his impedimenta.* **MRS. GALLETLY** *comes in with him.*)

DR. M.

Well, goodbye, Angus. Now, rest, man—rest! And take the splints off every second day and rub the leg well. What's that air you're humming? Seems familiar.

ANGUS

It's well seen you're not Highland, not to know that tune. It's old, and it's Gaelic, and it's called "The Glen is Mine." (**HE** *hums a stave of it.*) But never mind that. Is there no way at all, at all, Doctor, I could be going home to the croft, think you?

DR. M.

Not unless they take you up on a shutter. There's no trap or cart could go up those awful glen roads without shaking you to bits.

ANGUS

A shutter?

MRS. GALLETLY

(*Eagerly.*) Aye, a shutter. Wi' a blanket or twa, ye'd be quite joco.— Whit's to hinder Jock and the ploughman and the twa herds taking ye up, if we get a dry day? The day efter the morn wadna be too sune, Doctor, wad it?

DR. M.

But that's a Sunday!

MRS. GALLETLY

A Sawbath, ye mean.

DR. M.

Well, a Sabbath. Work on a Sabbath, Mrs. Galletly?

MRS. GALLETLY

Well, Doctor, ye ken oor Loard wrocht on a Sawbath.

DR. M.

(*Slyly.*) Aye, and you'd lose no farm-work from your men on a Sabbath, eh?

MRS. GALLETLY

Ach! gae wa' wi' ye!

(**SHE** *goes out by back door.*)

ANGUS

On a shutter be it then.—I'm for the croft— Sabbath or no Sabbath! (**MURDO**, *the driver of the Torlochart hotel-trap, appears at the main door. He is a young dark-complexioned man, with a thoughtful face and brooding eyes.*)

MURDO

The Captain says he wants to go up the hill again with Mr. Stockman, and could the Doctor wait half-an-hour more?

DR. M.

Oh, bother! I want off.

MURDO

I think the Colonel being here cut their inspection short. And now that he's off, tramping home, they'll be wanting to finish going over the ground.

DR. M.
Very awkward for me!

MURDO
And I was to say that if the Doctor cared to go over the ground with them they'd be pleased.

DR. M.
They'll want me to take shares, of course! *(Goes out grumbling.)*

ANGUS
Come you in and warm yourself, Murdo. You'll be cold and wet with the drive down.

MURDO
I am that. (He *sits down by fire.*) Is Morag come yet?

ANGUS
Not yet, lad.—*(Rallying him.)* But isn't it the strange thing now, that you and Morag always turn up here on the same day?

MURDO
(Uncomfortable.) Oh, she'll know the days the Doctor comes, and she'll be wanting to see the Doctor and hear what he says about you.

ANGUS
I'm thinking, maybe, she'll be wanting to see the Doctor's driver, and hear what he says about herself.

MURDO
(Roused.) And what though?

ANGUS
Now, now, lad! It's you are the fiery one. I was but joking. She's a good lass; and you are a decent lad.— And I'll say no more. *(He lights his pipe and puffs a bit; then changes the subject cheerily.)* Great ploys nowadays on Ben Creach, Murdo! You would hear the talk on the way down, and you driving them?

MURDO
I did that.

ANGUS
They're saying there's great money to be got out of Ben Creach.

MURDO
(Bitterly.) Och, money! money! And is that all your thoughts are on? Is that all that's in it?

ANGUS
You'll be thinking, maybe, that they're after spoiling Eilean Aros with their mines and their waterworks? It's what I'm for thinking myself.

MURDO
(Fierily.) No, no. They're bringing life to our very doors, man! What foolishness will you be talking?

ANGUS
(Annoyed.) Foolishness, is it?

MURDO
Just that. Isn't it myself has been hungering for the South and the great things there this many a day? Science! Discovery! And here they come to our very doors, I tell you.

ANGUS
Aye, you were always the ambitious one, lad.

MURDO
And I am still! I ken I'm fit for something better than an odd-man's job at Torlochan Hotel. Driving—fencing— sheep-shearing—peat-lifting. Tach! the life of a slave!

ANGUS
You're the great one for the pretty learning, Murdo. But there will surely be no harm in making a little money as well?

MURDO
You're right! Money brings power—power to give us knowledge. Oh, Angus, they'll be reading the rocks up there like a book! Geology! Chemistry! It's like a romance of the Feinne,[1] man!

ANGUS
Well, well, it's the strange world! If anyone had told me this morning that they could be lifting pound-notes out of Ben Creach—
(Main-door opens and **MORAG MACKINNON** *enters. She is a girl with dark hair, clear skin, and laughing eyes. Her dress is of crofter type.)*
And isn't it Morag herself that is in it! We were just talking about you, lass!
*(***MORAG** *kisses* **ANGUS**, *and shakes hands with* **MURDO**, *glancing shyly at the latter.* **HE** *also is embarrassed, and it is clear from their manner that they are lovers.)*

MORAG
And how are you, father? Fine? *(***ANGUS** *nods.)* And is it all the ends of the world are at Ardsheilach this day? Here's Murdo. And I met the Doctor, and Captain Charlie, and a stranger with them, and they going up the mouth of the Glen just now.

ANGUS

Aye, and there will be a hundred here before long for every one you've seen this day, let me tell you.

MORAG

Whatever kind of talk is that, you droll man? And how is the leg? And when are you to be coming home?

(**MURDO** *rises and, walks restlessly about.*)

ANGUS

The Doctor says in a day or two.

MORAG

And isn't that the good news now, for I'm the lonely one yonder. But whatever has come over Murdo?

ANGUS

(*Smiling.*) Och, he's thinking of the time when he'll be manager at the new iron-mines.

MORAG

Whatever are you at, at all, at all?

MURDO

There's sense enough in all his talk. There are to be iron-mines on Ben Creach, and it's me that's glad of the chance there'll be to better myself.

MORAG

Oh, is that what the Captain is after up the Glen?

ANGUS

Indeed and it is just.—Chemistry and Science, as Murdo was saying.

MORAG

(*Angrily.*) And you'll be of the same mind, I'm seeing. Are you both crazed? (*Goes to window, then glances with contempt at both men, and turns to window again.*) There they go! And if there was a decent gun handy, I'd be making blackcocks of every one of them!

MURDO

Whatever are you saying, lass?

MORAG

They're for blasting the hillside, are they? Selling their souls for the dirty pieces of silver!

MURDO

Morag MacKinnon, is it out of your mind you are?

MORAG

Indeed, yes. (*Covering her face with her hands, she weeps.*) And who is it has driven me to it, think you? (**MURDO** *strives to soothe her, his arms around her.*)

MURDO

Wheesht now, wheesht!—What call have you to be bitter with me, lass, when I think of doing well for your own sake?

MORAG

(*Freeing herself from his embrace.*) Well? Is it well to be tearing Eilean Aros to bits?

MURDO

Och, it's the old quarrel, I suppose. You were ever the keen one for the old ways of the Highlands. It's always to be the deer-forest and the sheep-fank here, I suppose! The drovers' track for roads! The wool-comb and the spinning wheel forever! The hard life for poor folk!

MORAG

It's the clean life and the healthy—not the scum and the dirt of the cities.

ANGUS

Listen to that now.

MURDO

God! What would I not give for a year's schooling in those same cities, lass! Learning, Morag! Civilisation! That's the town, not the country!

MORAG

My pain and my longing—to hear you talk that way!

MURDO

(*Bitterly.*) Aye—it's just that way I'm talking. The good old Highland ways!—Three o'clock of a cold morning and up the hill to the lambing. Bringing the mails over Kellan cliffs when the snow's drifted yard deep. Driving the Doctor to Moy, thirty mile and back, when the North wind's skelping down the Sound. That's the good old ways for Murdo MacKay!

ANGUS

And that's a true word, lad.

MORAG

Yes, and it'll never be cold or wet at the mines? And the hours will not be long there? And the wild Irish and the foolish English will not be fighting and drinking when they're navvying on the hill?

MURDO

You'll craze me, lass, with your wild tongue!

MORAG

(*Fiercely.*) My tongue will never craze Murdo MacKay, for it's crazed he is already with his chemistry and his civilisation and the rest of it. (**SHE** *weeps afresh and sits down by the fire, her back to him.*)

ANGUS

Och, but you're bitter, Morag. And indeed and indeed, Murdo, there's truth in what the both of you are saying. And myself, I'm conseedering, and I'm seeing that Ben Creach will be strange when the heather and the mountain hare are off it forever. Look you, now. I'm not liking their mines at all, at all—or their water-power—or their water-dams either, now that I'm seeing Morag's way of it.

MURDO

(*Bitterly.*) You've soon changed your tune! Weren't you talking of the money that was in it, a minute ago?

ANGUS

(*Angrily.*) And who are you to be talking of changing tunes, my hero? You're not manager at the mines yet, Murdo MacKay, so you'll please not be talking to me that way!

MURDO

It's sorry I am, Angus. I should have minded my teeth were before my tongue. Aye, it's maybe only a kind of a dream, whatever!

ANGUS

(*Only half-mollified.*) Sorry! And well you might be! Talking to me of changing tunes! You and your mines! (*Main-door opens, after a knock, and* **CAPTAIN CHARLIE** *enters.*)

CAPTAIN

Ready now, Murdo. Will you please harness up?

(**MURDO** *goes out after glancing sadly at* **MORAG** *sitting by fire with face averted.*)

Still on the mines, I hear, Angus. Been "conseedering" that offer about the water power, eh?

ANGUS

(*Increasingly angry, and rising on his crutches.*) Conseedering, is it? Oh, yes!—Conseedering? The Captain will be having his little joke! But the Captain is forgetting the Crofters' Act. Give up my croft to you? Not for all the minerals that ever was! A water-dam at Coillemore, is it? Not for all the—the—not for all the mineral waters in the world!

(*Shakes his pipe triumphantly and stumps towards door of little room.*)

CURTAIN

ACT II

SCENE.—*The Farm-Kitchen at Ardsheilach. Six weeks later.*
MACPHEDRAN, *the village merchant, is sitting at kitchen table, with papers, pen and ink before him. He is a grey-headed man of sixty with short white beard, pale skin, and ferret eyes. His movements are furtive and yet business-like. He is dressed with white front and cuffs and black tie; his square topped felt hat lies on table. His suit of dark cloth is old-fashioned in cut.* MRS. MACALLISTER, *a crofter woman, stands beside him with pass-book in hand. She puts down some money on table; and* MACPHEDRAN *takes pass-book and marking it, signs, then returns it, and washes his hands in air, effusively, as he speaks. This washing of hands is almost a continuous gesture with him.*

MACPHEDRAN

The money, Mrs. MacAllister.—Fifteen shillings.— Well, well! and your cold is better, is it?—Well, well! Take care of yourself, now!—Good people are scarce, you know—good people are scarce.—Well, well!—I'll be seeing you through the field. (HE *rises.*)

MRS. MACALLISTER

Och, you need not bother, Mr. MacPhedran! A big man like you seeing me to the gate! No, no!

MACPHEDRAN

Oh, but yes, yes. It's not every day we're seeing people like Mrs. MacAllister. This way, missus, this way.— And do you tell me now that you—
(THEY *pass talking to main door, as* MRS. GALLETLY *enters brusquely by back door with* ANGUS, *now minus his crutches, but limping a trifle.* MACPHEDRAN *halts for a moment and says ingratiatingly.*)

MACPHEDRAN

Oh! Good-day to you, Mrs. Galletly.

MRS. GALLETLY

(*Curtly.*) Guid-day!
(MACPHEDRAN *affects to be hurt by her coldness and goes out with* MRS. MACALLISTER.
I declare to Guid, if the place isna like an inns this day.—Whit's MacPhedran wanting here?—Whit for did Jock gie him ma table for his trash?
(SHE *removes the paper, pens and ink to dresser, sets table aside, and then puts a white cloth on it, from dresser.*)
The cheek o' him!—First the Captain and Mr. Stockman—and could I gie them a gless o' milk aboot three?— And then MacPhedran. And then yersel'. It's like a feeing-day at Fenwick, I tell ye!

ANGUS

Look you, it's this way—

MRS. GALLETLY

And your powny in the stable, eating ma oats quite the thing!—And you sleeping in the hay-shed quite joco!— Whatever is the warl' coming to?

ANGUS

Look you, it's this way.—The Colonel's deer-fence above my croft is broken down, and the deer are coming through and eating my potatoes.

MRS. GALLETLY

Whit's that to dae wi' your powny eating my oats?

ANGUS

Well, look you. I had to put a stop on the deer.—First, I tried a storm lantern among the potatoes all night—

MRS. GALLETLY

And whit's that to dae wi' ma oats?

ANGUS

But after the first night, look you, the storm-lantern did nothing at all, at all, to stop them. They got used to it. Oh, he is a very wyce beast, is the deer. And then there was nothing for it but the gun.—And it's a fine stag of ten that same wee pony brought down the Glen to yourself this morning, at three o'clock of the dark, so that the keepers would not be seeing us.

MRS. GALLETLY

Guid sake! Ye havena brocht it here, wi' a' they folk aboot!

ANGUS

(*Slyly.*) Maybe you had no liking for the last venison I gave you?

MRS. GALLETLY

(*Mollified.*) Weel, I'm shair ye're rale kind, Angus. But it's dangerous, ye ken.

ANGUS

It's a nice stag of ten, look you; and just a present from Angus, for all your kindness to him when his leg was broken.

MRS. GALLETLY

Weel, I'm muckle obliged, Angus. But whaur did ye pit it?

ANGUS

In the little room. (**HE** *points.*) It's safer there, look you, with all these big people coming to-day.

MRS. GALLETLY

(Opening bedroom door and peering in.) Guid sake! Whit a mess!—A' the same, it's rale kind o' ye, Angus.

ANGUS

And you were wondering to see Mr. MacPhedran here, were you?

MRS. GALLETLY

I was wondering to see the cheek o' him—making an office o' ma kitchen.

ANGUS

Och, it's always here he comes to lift his accounts with the crofters round about.—He used to do that same with the people who were here before you—the MacArthurs. It's an old custom with him.

MRS. GALLETLY

Custom here, custom there! It's a custom that'll ha'e to be changed!

ANGUS

(Gravely.) Look you, do not you be quarrelling with Dugald MacPhedran, for he's the cunning one, is Dugald.—And he'll be having you in his debt before long, if he can manage it at all, at all—

MRS. GALLETLY

Us in his debt!—We could buy him up ony day, thank the Loard!

ANGUS

Maybe, maybe.—But he has nearly every crofter in the parish in his debt, has MacPhedran.—He can do what he likes with them, look you.

MRS. GALLETLY

D'ye tell me?

ANGUS

Aye.—You see, it's the votes he'll be wanting—for himself and his friends on the Parish Council and the School Board.—Aye, and the County Council.—He has a finger in every pie.

MRS. GALLETLY

And him an elder!—Whit a warld o' sin and deception, Angus!

ANGUS

Keep you away from yon one!—Look you, he's for bankrupting me, because I'm owing him money, and cannot pay him. He has had me papered twice already by the Sheriff Officer.

(Takes out yellow papers from pocket.)

MRS. GALLETLY

As bad as that, ye puir man!

ANGUS

Aye, as bad as that. *(With passion.)* And, look you, I know who's at the bottom of that same.—It's Captain Charlie, no less.—Oh, I've been hearing of him being often in MacPhedran's shop of late.—Oh, I've been hearing things!

MRS. GALLETLY

D'ye tell me?

ANGUS

Aye, they'll be making the crofter bankrupt, and then they'll can evict him.—That's the law, see you. The Crofters' Act allows them. And then their fine mines and their fine water-dams can be going on.

MRS. GALLETLY

Ye puir cratur! And ye're dune then?

ANGUS

Oh, I'm not so sure—I'm not so sure.—*(Then eagerly.)* Look you, if I was coming back to the farm-work here, maybe I could be making some money, so as to pay MacPhedran.

MRS. GALLETLY

(On her guard.) Mair likely you'd be paying something to the whisky-shops in Torlochan.

ANGUS

(Eagerly.) No—for I will not be drinking any more.— At least not till this trouble is over, look you.—I'll be signing the blue ribbon every day!

MRS. GALLETLY

Aye, oh, aye—every 'oor, nae doot.

ANGUS

(Despondent.) Och, ochan.[1] *(Eagerly.)* Look you, I could be doing a little at the farm here up to Martinmas, till my leg was strong. And if you could be paying me forehanded to-day for the first month, I would let MacPhedran have every penny you gave me this very day.

MRS. GALLETLY

Na, na.—I'm no' daft. *(Excitedly.)* But, aye, I will noo— I will—yes, I will! That is, if ye'll tell me something—?

ANGUS

(Surprised.) And what now?

MRS. GALLETLY

Whit was the guid advice your faither gi'ed ye on his death bed? Ye're aye havering aboot it, when ye're in your drams.

ANGUS
That! Och, it was just nothing at all!

MRS. GALLETLY
Aye, it was noo!—Well, ye'll no' get a penny oot o' me unless ye tell.—I've aye a hankering efter a daith word.—Whit wis't?

ANGUS
Ach, it was just foolishness.—But I'll tell you if you'll take no denial.—And you'll not be angry?

MRS. GALLETLY
Me angry!—No' wan bit!
(SHE *goes to dresser and, opening a drawer, takes out wallet, and counts out money.*) Come on, noo!

ANGUS
Well, he put his hand on my head, and he said, "Be you a good lad, Angus, and keep away from all bad people. And always you be putting salt in the well, and then you'll not need to be putting salt in the porridge".

MRS. GALLETLY
(*Disgusted.*) Ach! I might hae ken't it.—There! (SHE *pushes money over.*) And see ye work better for't than ye did last time!—Ach! The like o' that!—The auld heathen!
(SHE *returns bag to cupboard, locks it, and bustles angrily about her housework.* MACPHEDRAN *and* JOCK *enter by main door.* MACPHEDRAN *carries a heavy, elongated brown paper parcel.*)

JOCK
Come yer weys in, MacPhedran, and hae a dram.

MACPHEDRAN
Thenkee, thenkee!—A nice day, Mrs. Galletly!
(*But* MRS. GALLETLY *turns her back on him, and goes on with her housework.*)

MACPHEDRAN
Very kind of you, I'm sure, Mr. Galletly, to be giving me these fine pigs' heads. Where will I be laying them? (*As* GALLETLY *pours out whisky.*) Oh, just a taste now.— No, no! Stop! (*As* HE *lays parcel down on dresser.*) I'm very fond of a wee bit of tender pork now and then. (*Turns to* ANGUS.) Well, Angus, and there you are!

ANGUS
(*Producing pass-book.*) A fine day, Mr. MacPhedran.

MACPHEDRAN
Not bad, Angus, not bad.—And your leg is better? Take care of yourself, man. Good people are scarce, you know. Good people are scarce!—Man, but I'm sorry I had to put the Sheriff's Officer on your trail.—But business is business, you see.—The law, man, the law.—Aye, aye, the law. *(Drinks again.)*

ANGUS
(Producing money and handing pass-book to him.) Will you please to be taking two pounds ten off the account?

MACPHEDRAN
(Surprised.) Surely—surely! *(He makes up book, affixes stamp, signs, and takes money.)*

JOCK
Things are looking up, Angus, eh?

ANGUS
Och, well! A man must be doing what he can.

MACPHEDRAN
Well, well. *(Handing back pass-book.)* It was not my will at all to be pressing you, Angus, you'll understand.

ANGUS
Och, I'm understanding well enough.

MACPHEDRAN
But here's something, Angus, for you to conseeder.— I'm thinking of building a shop out there in Mr. Galletly's lea-field, to sell groceries to the navvies who will be coming to the new mines. It would be the very place for Morag.

ANGUS
(Smiling.) And is it a shop-girl, you'd be making of Morag? You'll see Morag behind your counter, Mr. MacPhedran, when the sea takes fire—not a minute earlier.

MACPHEDRAN
Tach!—Set you up!

JOCK
(To MACPHEDRAN.*)* Ne'er heed him.—Anither wee drap?

MACPHEDRAN
(His angry eye still on Angus)
No more—no more!

JOCK

Hae, man, juist a sup!

MRS. GALLETLY

(*Whipping up bottle and glasses and returning them to cupboard.*) Dinna be unmainnerly, Jock! Isn't the man telling ye he's had eneuch.—Come you awa' oot here, Mr. MacPhedran, and look at that new patent kirn ye sell't us twa months ago.—It's aye breaking doon.

JOCK

Talking aboot mainners!—Let the man ha'e his dram!

MRS. GALLETLY

He'll get it when I'm dune shewing him yon kirn!— He'll need it then.

(**SHE** *ushers* **MACPHEDRAN** *out by main-door.*)

JOCK

Eh, but she's the warrior!

ANGUS

She's all that.

JOCK

A fair warrior!—But whit kin' o' talk is yon ye gi'ed MacPhedran?— Ye're daft shairly no' to fa' in wi' this iron-ore business.—MacPhedran's nae fule.—And he says it's the best thing ever happened hereaboots.

ANGUS

Aye, for himself and his kind, no doubt.

JOCK

Aye, and for us folk.—A'll get a guid whack by way o' compensation for clearing this side o' the hill o' sheep.— But ye're shairly no' set on hauding oot again' the Captain for the sake o' a wee thackit hoose, and a wat field or twa?

ANGUS

You'll not be understanding, Mr. Galletly.

JOCK

A'm understandin' fine. It's juist Hielan' pride.

ANGUS

You'll not be understanding why we have the Crofters' Act in the Highlands, I'm thinking?

JOCK

Oh, damn the Crofters' Act! — We'll ride a cairridge and pair through the Crofters' Act! — Man, it wad pey ye to let the Captain buy ye oot, Angus.

ANGUS

But the Act will not let him buy me out. And the Act will not let me sell, even if I wanted to.

JOCK

Man, you Hielandmen are the great lawyers! — Fancy that! — And has the Captain nae mineral richts on your croft?

ANGUS

Oh, yes, he has mineral rights on the croft. But there are no minerals there that he'll be wanting. They're all in the hill.

JOCK

Aye, ye're richt eneuch — on the hill. But whit wis't he wantit at your bit place — a water-dam or something?

ANGUS

Just that! — But he'll never can be doing that without a lot of bother, look you. And maybe not even then.

JOCK

Whit wey that?

ANGUS

Because he could get water power from Glen Caol.

JOCK

But that's the ither side o' the hill, and the best ore's on your side. It wad cost a hantle sicht mair to bring water-power frae Glen Caol.

ANGUS

(*Smiling.*) Just that! — But it will cost him a great deal more still to put me out of my croft. — There were too many clearances from Coillemore in Glen Lean in the old days for him to be raising the memory of them by turning out Angus MacKinnon, the last of the crofters there! No, no! he'll not can do it.

JOCK

They're saying he could turn ye out, if he bankrupted ye.

ANGUS

And that's just what he is going to do.

JOCK

Whit? — It's a damned shame!

ANGUS

(*Calmly.*) It's all that.—Did not you hear MacPhedran talking about the Sheriff Officer?

JOCK

Oh, was that it?—MacPhedran's in it, is he?—A' the same, ye're a thrawn deil, Angus; and ye've fair raised them.—But it's hitting ablow the belt to bankrupt ye, so as to get your bit croft.

ANGUS

Och, well—we'll see—we'll see.

JOCK

Ye'll see, will ye?—Man, but ye're the game auld buckie.

ANGUS

I think I'll be taking a look at the pony now. (HE *rises.*)

JOCK

Weel, if ye're for the stable, tak' this. (HE *hands* ANGUS *the brown paper parcel.*) Pit it in MacPhedran's trap, will ye?—Some pigs heids he was mooching aff us. (*As they make for door at left back,* MRS. GALLETLY *enters hurriedly by main door.* ANGUS *goes off but* JOCK *remains.*)
Whit's a' the steer, guidwife?

MRS. GALLETLY

Whan am I gaun to get ma work dune this day? There's the Captain and Mr. Stockman juist aff the hill, and they're like famished teegurs. And I see the Colonel coming ower the low green wi' his gillies. Whit for can they no' tak' a' their meals on the hill, like the rest o' folk that gang deerstalking!

(GALLETLY *at once sets out bottle and glasses from cupboard.* MRS. GALLETLY
at once replaces them.)

Na, na, nae mair o' that! It's juist encouraging them to come aboot.—And clear ye oot o' this! There's been eneuch dramming here for a'e day!

(SHE *bustles* GALLETLY *out of doors by back as the* CAPTAIN *enters by main door, talking to* MACPHEDRAN. THE CAPTAIN *is in sporting kit, leather pads on shoulder, etc.* MRS. GALLETLY *sets table with plain fare: cheese, butter, scones, and milk.* THEY *sit down and make a meal.* MRS. GALLETLY *goes out by back door.*)

MACPHEDRAN

And the Captain is well, I hope? But be you taking care of yourself, sir. Good people are scarce, you know.

CAPTAIN

A tiring day, by Jove!—Stockman and I had a long walk and never a stag near us all the time.—A long tramp, I can tell you!—Well, and so you've got the Sheriff Officer on that chap's track at last, I suppose?

MACPHEDRAN
Aye, we've commenced on him. Och, it will be as easy as easy.

CAPTAIN
That's good!

MACPHEDRAN
Eighteen ten, he's owing me. He'll never pay—never.

CAPTAIN
What's the procedure?

MACPHEDRAN
See you now! He was served with a summons to Court at the Oban—registered post, of course. He never shewed face.

CAPTAIN
And then—?

MACPHEDRAN
And seven days after that, we got decree.—That was yesterday. And now he has only nine days to run.

CAPTAIN
That's jolly sharp work.

MACPHEDRAN
Oh, it's quick enough.—In nine days' time, there will be an expired charge against him. And then he's notour bankrupt, as the lawyers say. And that's enough for the Crofters' Act.

CAPTAIN
No chance of his paying up in time?

MACPHEDRAN
And who would lend money to a man so heavy on the drams as he is, think you?

CAPTAIN
Well, I hope there will be no hitch.—What was it you called it?—Notour—?

MACPHEDRAN
Notour bankrupt. *(Rolling the words on his tongue vindictively.)* Angus MacKinnon of Coillemore, notour bankrupt.

COLONEL
(Entering by main door.) Ah! There you are, Charlie.—Any luck?
*(*CAPTAIN *shakes his head.)* No?—Neither had we. Not a stag anywhere except in the Sanctuary. The beggars know how to chaw us, eh?— But what was that you said about Angus being bankrupt?

MACPHEDRAN

(*Gleefully.*) Och, we'll have him broken in nine days' time, Colonel; and then he'll have to go. It's the Crofters' Act he has been preaching and now he'll get his fill of it.

(The **CAPTAIN** *is meanwhile signing to* **MACPHEDRAN** *to hold his tongue.*)

COLONEL

(*Angrily.*) You're surely not taking that line, Charlie? —Ruining a man in order to get him evicted. It's not— hang it!—it's not cricket!

MACPHEDRAN

(*Now seeing* **CHARLIE**'s *signals.*) Och, we'd never ruin him, sir!—Och, no, no. It's his own doing, look you, with his drinking and carrying on.—We'll just be stepping in after he is gone.

COLONEL

But you're forcing this, Charlie.

MACPHEDRAN

Och, and it's just myself that's sorry for poor Angus!

CAPTAIN

Tuts! You are a twister, MacPhedran. Look here, father! Is it cricket?—Is it fair for this man to obstruct us in a work that will do good to the whole island?

COLONEL

Good to your own pocket, Charlie. Keep to facts.

CAPTAIN

Plain speech, Father?

COLONEL

It is.

CAPTAIN

And I'll be as plain. I have to break this man, in order to carry out the mine business.—He won't listen to reason. Very well—I'll break him.

COLONEL

By a mean conspiracy.

MACPHEDRAN

Och, not at all.

CAPTAIN

The law allows it.

COLONEL

Does your conscience?

CAPTAIN
I beg you to control yourself, father.

COLONEL
I will.—And I beg you to understand I object in every possible way to this breaking of a decent man.

CAPTAIN
You'll excuse me.—I want to see Stockman.

COLONEL
Charlie, Charlie! Think of what you are doing! What if Miss Mirlees heard of this?

CAPTAIN
Alice? What's this got to do with her? Please don't mix up my private affairs with business matters.

COLONEL
But, Charlie—!

CAPTAIN
I must really go now. Stockman is waiting for me.

COLONEL
You won't listen to me, you mean?

CAPTAIN
Still plain speech, dad?

COLONEL
Yes.

CAPTAIN
Then my answer is " No."
(**HE** *goes out by door on right and* **MACPHEDRAN** *sneaks out after him.*)

COLONEL
(*Going to door at back and calling with decision.*) Mrs. Galletly!

MRS. GALLETLY
(*Off.*) Aye!

COLONEL
Is Angus about, Mrs. Galletly?

MRS. GALLETLY
(*Off.*) Aye!

COLONEL
Please tell him I want to see him.

MRS. GALLETLY
(Off.) I wull!

ANGUS
(Entering at back.) The Colonel was asking for me.

COLONEL
Yes, yes.—Eh, how's the leg, Angus?

ANGUS
Oh, it is very well now, sir—And I hope the Colonel is well.

COLONEL
Eh, ah—oh—yes, thank you—ah—quite well.—I heard from—ah—MacPhedran, that you were in some little money difficulty, Angus.—I—ah—would—ah—be glad, y'know, if you'd allow me to offer a little—ah—help.

ANGUS
(Shyly.) Och, no. I'm not needing anything, at all, at all. But the Colonel is very kind—och, yes, very kind.— *(Then angrily.)* All the same, MacPhedran had no call to be talking of my affairs before people, look you.

COLONEL
(Soothingly.) Well, now, it's like this, Angus.—Is there any way I could get you some work, so that you could be making a little money in your odd time?

ANGUS
The Colonel is very kind—but I'm not wanting charity.

COLONEL
And who's talking of it? What about clearing some of my ground of rabbits, now—or some fencing? Yes, that's it—fencing—at the Gray Rocks above your croft yonder. The wire is broken there, isn't it?

ANGUS
It is that.

COLONEL
Well, get to work on it, man. The deer get through there rather badly, I'm afraid.

ANGUS
Indeed, yes—they do indeed.—And if the Colonel would be giving me the wire for it, I could be mending the fence very well.

COLONEL
Right!—I'll send up the wire. And let me have your account as soon as you're through, will you?

ANGUS

Thank you kindly, sir.

COLONEL

And, oh, by the way, I must give you a luckpenny, just to seal the bargain. *(Looks at pocket book.)* Hang it!— Thought I had a fiver here.

ANGUS

Och, no need at all for a luckpenny.

COLONEL

Oh, but yes.—And come to think of it, Angus, I really owe you something to compensate you for all the damage those deer must have done to your crops.

ANGUS

Och, no need for that, sir.—But they're the big thieves all the same, are the deer.

COLONEL

(Whispering.) Have a pot at a hind now and again, Angus. We'll never miss it.—But not too often. In reason, y'know—in reason. *(ANGUS smiles broadly.)* Aha! You rogue! You've been at them already, eh?

ANGUS

Well, you see, it's very hard.

COLONEL

I knew it—I knew it—you dog! *(Digs him playfully in the ribs.)* Hush! Here's the Captain back already. Mum's the word!

CAPTAIN

(At main door.) We're off, father. Coming?— Stockman's going back to Torlochan. Hotel trap's coming down for him. He has to go south tomorrow, you remember? *(Turns to go out.)*

COLONEL

Oh—ah—yes.—Just a moment, though, Charlie.— I have to see Mrs. Galletly first. Some things to settle, y'know. Have you by any chance a fiver on you?

CAPTAIN

One do? *(As he brings out pocket-book he drops a letter.)*

COLONEL

One will do.

(THE CAPTAIN gives Colonel the money and then stoops to pick up dropped letter. COLONEL waggles five-pound note behind his back, and signs to ANGUS to take it. COLONEL and CAPTAIN go out together by main door. ANGUS regards the note whimsically, puts it in his pocket, scratches his head

in puzzled fashion, and lights his pipe philosophically.)

MRS. GALLETLY

(Accompanied by MRS. DUNCAN, *a crofter woman, enters by back door on left.)* Come in, woman, come in.—I'll fin' MacPhedran for ye.

(MRS. GALLETLY *goes out by main door.)*

MRS. DUNCAN

A fine day, Angus.

ANGUS

It is all that, Mrs. Duncan.—Speaking for myself, I would say it is one of the very finest. *(Then scratching his head.)* You'll not now be wanting to make me the present of five pounds, Mrs. Duncan?

MRS. DUNCAN

(Amazed, but solemn.) Five pounds! Indeed and I am not, Angus.

ANGUS

No!—'Deed no!—I was just wondering.

(MACPHEDRAN *enters by main door,* MRS. DUNCAN *produces wallet and takes some money from it.* MACPHEDRAN *looks over her pass-book which she hands him.)*

MRS. DUNCAN

Twenty-three shillings, Mr. MacPhedran.

MACPHEDRAN

I expected thirty-three, Mrs. Duncan. You're slow— very slow, (HE *writes in book.)* And how is your brother up at Sunipol?

MRS. DUNCAN

Och, he's very much better now.

MACPHEDRAN

See you now.—Next time you meet him tell him I was asking after his health.

MRS. DUNCAN

I will surely; and thank you very much, Mr. MacPhedran.—You're the kind man.

MACPHEDRAN

Oh! And by the bye, say to him I was asking after the health of the last heifer I sold him, will ye?

MRS. DUNCAN

I will that, but why are you asking after an old cow's health, Mr. MacPhedran, and never even asking after mine?

MACPHEDRAN

I'm coming to that, Mrs. Duncan—just coming. But business first, Mrs. Duncan—business first. I was asking for the cow's health because she's never paid for yet. And I was wondering if she'd be well enough to walk back to me.

MRS. DUNCAN

(Blankly.) Oh, is that it?

MACPHEDRAN

Aye—that's just it. Be you telling him, will ye?— And now about yourself. You're well, I can see. But be you taking care of yourself, Mrs. Duncan. Good people are scarce, you know.—Good people are scarce.

MRS. DUNCAN

(Grinning affably.) Oh, Mr. MacPhedran! Good-day to you, sir! Good-day, Angus!

MACPHEDRAN—ANGUS

Good-day, Mrs. Duncan. (She *goes out by back door.*)

ANGUS

(Rising and handing over five-pound note and pass-book to **MACPHEDRAN**.*)* Will you be marking that off the book?

MACPHEDRAN

(Gasping.) Well, well!
 (**HE** *marks, stamps and signs book.* **ANGUS** *takes it, saunters back to fire unconcernedly, and, relighting pipe, sits down again.*)

STOCKMAN

(Entering by main door.) The Captain wants a word with you, MacPhedran, before he goes. He's gone to the yard. *(Points to door at back.)*
 (**MACPHEDRAN** *goes out by back door.*)

ANGUS

You're not for going back with them to the big house, Mr. Stockman?

STOCKMAN

No. The Torlochan trap's coming for me. My luggage went up this morning already.

ANGUS

Did Mr. Stockman have any luck on the hill to-day?

STOCKMAN

No. We never got near them. Never a shot from the Captain or myself the whole day.—By the bye, Angus, ever done any deer-stalking yourself?

ANGUS

(With a guilty start.) Och, yes, when I was younger. I did a lot of gillying at that time.

STOCKMAN

I wasn't asking about gillying, old bean. I was asking— ever done any slaying of the noble king of the forest yourself—eh?

ANGUS

(Pretending amazement.) Is it me?—Killing a deer?—Och, but Mr. Stockman knows that is only for the gentry!

STOCKMAN

(Tapping him on shoulder.) Well, you are an old submarine, I must say!—See here: it's this.—I'm due to go south to-morrow—and I've been fool enough to write home about the great deer-stalks I am having in the intervals of prospecting for the mine here. And—well—can't you see, old pippin? She'll be expecting to see me returning a mighty Nimrod—eh, what?

ANGUS

She?

STOCKMAN

My wife, sir—my trusty spouse!—Fact is, I can't see myself returning to her without a trophy of the chase, my aged friend.

ANGUS

I'm not understanding.

STOCKMAN

Of course! But you're not trying to, you elusive old bird. What I mean is—what price your helping me to camouflage a tiny bit? A stag's head to grace my ancestral halls is what I would be at, most potent signior.—See?

ANGUS

(Slowly.) Yes, yes. The Major will be wanting a stag's head?

STOCKMAN

At last you savvy! *(Produces card and writes.)* See here!—Get me a nice head, and send it on to this fellow.— That's the name of the man who stuffs birds and things in Oban. He'll prepare it and forward it to me. My address is on the front of this.

ANGUS

(Ruminating.) Sometimes we'll be finding a stag dead on the hill.

STOCKMAN

(*With conviction.*) I've no doubt on that point in the least, Angus. In fact, I believe they'll be *very* dead. (*Pulls out a wallet and counts out five Treasury Notes of £1 each.*) See here! Understand? A stag's head—a good one—if a royal, all the better.—Not from Captain Charlie's ground, of course. Wouldn't do. *Noblesse oblige* and all that, y' know.

ANGUS

Mr. Stockman was saying he was going by the morning steamer?

STOCKMAN

Such is my purpose, my worthy ancient!

ANGUS

Then, wait you!
(**HE** *opens door of little room and lifts out a sack shewing a few blood stains at its base. The antlers of a stag protrude, as he holds the sack open for* **STOCKMAN**'*s inspection.*)
A fine stag of ten, sir, that lay down before my own door last night and died on me right away.—Will that be suiting, Mr. Stockman? It could be going up in your trap to-night, if I wrapped it up well in two or three more sacks.—'You could be taking it to the man in the Oban yourself, sir.

STOCKMAN

(*Delighted.*) You are really the bally limit, old bean!— *Haec summa est,* as the poet sings!—Here!—(*Sweeps the notes into Angus' hand.*) Pack it well, and take it out to the trap as soon as it comes.—And so the foul deed is done! (**HE** *strikes a tragic attitude.*) It's a ripping fine head, that!

ANGUS

It is all that. There's more than iron on Ben Creach, let me tell you.—Does Mr. Stockman know a fine tune called "The Glen is Mine"?

STOCKMAN

Sir Oracle, I do not. But your remarks are astonishingly to the point. Pack the head well, my boy.
(**STOCKMAN** *goes to main door and* **ANGUS** *carries out sack past him.* **MRS. GALLETLY** *enters with* **MACPHEDRAN** *at door at back.*)

STOCKMAN

Oh, has my trap come yet, Mrs. Galletly?

MRS. GALLETLY

Juist this meenit come, sir.

STOCKMAN

Well good-bye, Mrs. Galletly! (*Then to* **MACPHEDRAN** *whose profile and tufted beard look the least bit reminiscent of a Pharaoh.*) Good-bye, Rameses! (*He goes out by main door.*)

MRS. GALLETLY

Guid-bye, sir.

(But **MACPHEDRAN** *can only gasp.)*

MACPHEDRAN

(Gathering up his papers on dresser at left.) Well, well! I must be getting home, too.

MRS. GALLETLY

And I'll be gled to see a toom hoose, I can tell ye.— Siccan a day as I've had wi' the lot o' ye.

ANGUS

(Entering hurriedly by main-door, hastily produces passbook and makes a bee-line for **MACPHEDRAN** *with it and* **STOCKMAN**'s *five pound notes in his hand.)* Will you be taking another five pounds off the account?

MACPHEDRAN

(Gasping, as he sets down his bag). Whatever are you doing, Angus MacKinnon, making fun of me all day; and wasting the good stamps on me?—Could you not be paying me all in one, and have done with it!

ANGUS

(Scratching his head.) Look you, it's not me that's doing it at all, at all.—I'm thinking it's Providence or— or—something queer, anyway.

MRS. GALLETLY

(Philosophically.) I wadna wonner.—Aye—a Higher Power—nae doot—nae doot.

MACPHEDRAN

(Affixing stamp wrathfully.) That's the third stamp this day on the same account! Are you for making a Post Office of me?

ANGUS

No, no, Mr. MacPhedran. There's nobody could be making anything of you but what you are making yourself.— And that's punishment enough for any man, I'm thinking.

MACPHEDRAN

(Angrily.) Tach! Talk!—See you now, Angus MacKinnon, I'll not be forgetting this. No, no. I'll not be forgetting it.

(Having collected his papers, he stamps out by back door full of wrath.)

MRS. GALLETLY

You're the queer man!

ANGUS

Queer, is it? My head is queer anyway—with the things that have been happening to me this day.

MRS. GALLETLY

Whatever are you havering at? There's naething oot o' the wey happened hereaboots, as far as I've noticed.

ANGUS

Is there not now? Well, then, go you out and see if there is not someone coming down the road with five pound notes in his hand, and him asking for Angus of Coillemore.

JOCK

(*Entering by back door.*) MacPhedran went aff withoot asking for his pork.

MRS. GALLETLY

Nae fear. Angus tied it up for him an 'oor ago. (**SHE** *is busy at housework again.*)

ANGUS

Yes, yes. I put the pork in his trap all right.

JOCK

(*Sitting down and taking his pipe.*) A thocht ye were for hame a while ago, Angus?

ANGUS

I was thinking so myself. — But the strange things have been happening to me this day, look you. And now I'm just waiting for more of them. — I've a feeling that I may be coming into a kind of a fortune.

JOCK

Dod, A'm feeling that wey mysel', wi' that big hill, fou' of money, so to speak, staunin' ower me a' day.

ANGUS

Och, that's no fortune at all, at all, if it will be spoiling Eilean Aros.

JOCK

Spiling?

ANGUS

Yes, spoiling. Man, did you ever see Glasgow?

JOCK

(*Enthusiastically.*) Aye, man! — it's the great place, yon!

ANGUS

Tach! (**HE** *spits contemptuously in the fire.*) That for Glasgow!

MRS. GALLETLY

Weel, ye'll see something yonder. And here ye'll see nathing but the mune.

ANGUS

Yes, yes.—But where in all the cities of the south will you find a bigger share of content than you'll get in Eilean Aros?

JOCK.

Och, aye.—They doze awa' fine hereaboots.

ANGUS

Doze, is it? It would do good to some of the black-faced men on the Clyde yonder, if they could be doing some dozing instead of catching trains all day.

JOCK

Aye, man, A wadna wunner!

ANGUS

And if we'd kept by the old Highland ways hereabouts it would be better for us too.—Sixty years ago, there was less money here and more people and more happiness. My father it was that told me!

MRS. GALLETLY

Aye, plenty o' folk and plenty o' poverty and plenty o' parish rates, nae doot

ANGUS

No—neither poverty nor rates.—There were corn and cattle and sheep here in plenty.—And never a shilling passing from hand to hand, for everything was paid in kind. A happy contented folk.

JOCK

Aweel, there's twa sides to every story.—But it's time we were seeing to the queys, wife.

(**THEY** *go out by main door.* **ANGUS** *walks about perplexedly, then lights his pipe slowly, takes out his passbook, and regards it benevolently.* **HE** *turns over its pages and reads.*)

ANGUS

Twenty-one.—Eighteen-ten.—Well, well!—Thirteen-ten.—Eight-ten.—Och, we're getting on!—Och, och, and yes!

(**HE** *again resumes his pipe, stretching himself in luxurious fashion in the arm-chair.*)

MRS. GALLETLY

(*Entering hurriedly by main door.*) Whitever's this ye're efter noo, ye sorrowfu' cratur?'

ANGUS

And what now, Mrs. Galletly?

MRS. GALLETLY

There's the Colonel and the Captain and MacPhedran a' back again, and siccan a tiravee as they're ha'eing wi' Jock oot there. Whit did ye dae wi' MacPhedran's pork?

ANGUS

And didn't the Colonel and the Captain go off by themselves? Whatever is MacPhedran doing in it at all?

MRS. GALLETLY

Och, didn't MacPhedran meet up on them wi' his trap, and gi'ed them a lift. And when the Captain stepped intae the trap, a deer's horn stuck oot o' a parcel ablow the seat and scartit his leg.—And MacPhedran's pork's no' there.— And they're accusing Jock o' poaching.

ANGUS

(Dismally.) Och, och! And did I put the stag's head in the wrong trap, then!—Wasn't the trap with the red wheels Mr. Stockman's?

MRS. GALLETLY

That was MacPhedran's, ye gomeral! Ye've been and pit the twa pigs' heids in Mr. Stockman's.—They were a present frae me to MacPhedran—no' for yon haw-haw buddy at a'.

ANGUS.

(Laughing uncontrollably.) Och! Och!

MRS. GALLETLY

Are ye daft?

ANGUS

No, no! But, look you, I'm thinking of the face of the bird-stuffer man in Oban when he opens yon parcel and sees the sows' heads!

MRS. GALLETLY

I dinna ken whit ye're blethering aboot. But ye'll lauch on the wrang side o' yer face, aince ye hear the Captain. He's roaring mad.

(**COLONEL, CAPTAIN** and **MACPHEDRAN** *enter by door on right, arguing volubly with* **JOCK**.)

CAPTAIN

Do you know anything of this, Mrs. Galletly?—this stag's head business? We must get to the bottom of it. Who put it in the trap?

ANGUS

(Stepping forward.) By your leave, sir, it was just me.

CAPTAIN

Aha!—Here we are at last!—Another nail in your coffin, my man!— And where did you get it, may I ask?

ANGUS

I found the beast dead on my own croft.

CAPTAIN

And you killed it, I'll swear, before you found it, eh?

ANGUS

I did that.

CAPTAIN

You hear, father?—You hear, MacPhedran?—He killed it!—You know what this means, father?

ANGUS

Och, the Colonel knows very well what it means. I have his permission to kill a deer now and then to save my crops as long as the fence at Coillemore is down.

COLONEL

But— (HE *can say no more, chuckling with supressed mirth, as he is.*)

CAPTAIN

(*Amazed.*) Father!—Is this true?

COLONEL

Well, yes—You see, I gave Angus permission to—

CAPTAIN

(*Angrily.*) Oh, when will this end?—I give one instruction.—You give the opposite.—Whatever was the good of transferring the estate to me, if you —?

COLONEL

Yes, yes, Charlie.—We'll talk of this later on, if you please.

CAPTAIN

Oh!—later on. Always the same old story! (COLONEL *and* JOCK *go out by main door.*)

MACPHEDRAN

But where is the pork?

CAPTAIN

Yes, that looks like another theft.

ANGUS

I'm saying nothing about the pork at all, at all, look you. But I'll say this. I got a good price for that stag's head in this room this very day, and because of that stag's head, there was five pounds taken off my account with you, Mr. MacPhedran. (*Producing passbook and handing it to* CAPTAIN.) And there, look you, is the receipt!

CAPTAIN

(*Looking at signature.*) MacPhedran!—Oh, let me get out of this, or I'll choke—MacPhedran!

> (**HE** *goes out hurriedly by main door, while* **MACPHEDRAN** *remains too dumbfoundered to say a word in his own defence.*)

ANGUS

(*Too absorbed in loving study of his pass-book to have observed the* **CAPTAIN**'*s exit.*) But you're not for understanding me, Captain, I'm not blaming Mr. MacPhedran at all, at all. I'm only saying—

> (*But the* **CAPTAIN** *is now out of ear-shot, and* **ANGUS** *looks up from his pass-book to find himself under the vengeful eyes of* **MACPHEDRAN**.)

MACPHEDRAN

(*Beside himself with rage.*) Angus MacKinnon!—you're bad!—You're bad!

ANGUS

(*With spirit.*) Bad, is it? I'm thinking then that there are two of us that is in it.—And as the man said at the boat-race, "If there's any difference between us, both of us is alike."

MACPHEDRAN

Look you, Angus MacKinnon, I'll be upsides with you for this—I'll be upsides with you for this. (*Raises a threatening fist, and goes towards main door.*)

ANGUS

Mr. MacPhedran!

MACPHEDRAN

(*Coming back.*) Well?

ANGUS

(*Washing his hands in air in imitation of the other's manner.*) Take care of yourself.—Good people are scarce.

CURTAIN

ACT III

Scene.—*The Living-Room of the Croft at Coillemore. A week later. Midway in rear wall is an open door, through which are seen the glen and the hills in full sunlight. Against the door are tilted several coils of fencing-wire. On each side of door, in same wall, there is a window with deep sill. On sill of that on left lies a set of bagpipes; under right window is a spinning-wheel. To left at back is a dresser with dishes on it. The right wall is bare save for a chromolithograph, unframed, and some pegs from which hang a shawl and some coats. A door opens off left wall at back; and, further forward in same wall is an open fire-place, with a girdle suspended over the peats. A peat-creel and two chairs are close to fire. In centre of floor is a plain table with baking-board, rolling-pin, flour, and dough on it. A chair is at each end of table.* MORAG *is busy at baking scones, passing to and fro from girdle to baking-board.* ANGUS *is sitting by fire examining pass-book.*

MORAG
What for are you looking at that book so often?

ANGUS
I thought I saw a man on the Torlochan side of the hill over there. He might be passing this place.

MORAG
And what then?

ANGUS
It's the way things are happening nowadays, look you!— He might be making me a present of a pound or two. And if no one comes as they used to be coming, I'll be a bankrupt man in three days' time.

MORAG
Och, you and your bankruptcy!—Be going down to the Colonel and he'll give you the money in advance for your work at the deer fence, and you can be paying MacPhedran on the way home.

ANGUS
Aye, I might be doing that.—But we'll see if some other queer thing will not happen to me first of all.—I'll be going up to the fence now, whatever. *(Takes up coil of wire.)* And if anyone comes this way, be sure you call me in.

MORAG
Is it call you in, whether they're king or beggar?

ANGUS
Whether they're king or beggar, be you calling me.

(HE *goes out turning to left.* MORAG *goes on with her baking, singing a Gaelic song.* MURDO MACKAY *appears at the window on right, comes to the door and looks in.*)

MORAG

Oh, and is it you that's in it? Did you come over the hill-road?

MURDO

I did that. It's Fast-day in Torlochan; and it's on holiday I am. — But what for are you asking about the hill-road? Did I ever come by any other?

MORAG

(*Airily.*) No. — But I thought maybe you'd be forgetting the way to this place now.

MURDO

(*Protesting.*) Now, Morag —

MORAG

Miss MacKinnon, if you please.

MURDO

And where's the sense in that?

MORAG

Sense enough for those that want to make a desert of Eilean Aros with their iron-mines and their blastings!

MURDO

Och! the iron-mines, the iron-mines! Is there nothing then at all under the blue sky but iron-mines?

MORAG

And have you found that out at last?

MURDO

Well, well! What word at all can I have for you, Morag, that you will not be angry with?

MORAG

It's not words I'm angry with. — It's with you and your like I'm angry, that are helping to bankrupt my father.

MURDO

Whatever are you saying? I'm helping no one to do that same.

MORAG

You're on the side of these iron-mine people, aren't you? And what else are they doing but bankrupting him, and in three days' time too, so that they can evict him under the Act.

MURDO
The dirty rogues! Is it that they're doing?

MORAG
There's your civilisation for you.

MURDO
And you can be thinking I'd stand by them in such a thing?

MORAG
Och, I'm not caring, Mr. MacKay, what you'd be standing by, or what you'd not be standing by, I'm sure!

MURDO
Och, you're sore on me, lass! — And I'm not bothering about these iron-mines any more, let me tell you. *(Producing letter.)* I've better news for you than iron-mines.

MORAG
And what now?

MURDO
(Opening letter.) It's this. My Uncle Duncan is dead in Lochcarron, look you. — And it's to myself the succession of his big croft is coming. — And there's a railway handy to it for Inverness where there's books and things in plenty. — And — and — oh, *mo chridhe!*
(**HE** *stretches arms appealingly.*)

MORAG
(Doleful.) Oh, Murdo! And will you be leaving Eilean Aros?

MURDO
Aye, I'll be going, but only if — (He *holds out his hands to her.*)

MORAG
(Going to him.) And you'll really be wanting me, lad?

MURDO
Aye, I'll be wanting you, my dear! (**HE** *kisses her.*) And it's now I'm thinking more of you than of all the big cities of the South and all the iron-mines that ever was. — Besides there's Inverness not so far away.

MORAG
Och, a snap of my thumb for Inverness. You'll have no time for that nonsense with a croft and a wife on your hands.

MURDO
Well, now, and couldn't I be getting the fine books yonder and couldn't I be reading at nights and studying, even if I was only a crofter in the daytime?

MORAG

(Mockingly.) I can see you'll be doing wonders.

MURDO

And I was hearing of a man in Ardnamurchan, in a wee blackhouse there with an earthen floor, and him working a typewriter, and making stuff to be printed in the papers.

MORAG

Och, good luck to the typewriter!—Lochcarron!—It's the fine country yon, and the crofts not bad at all, at all.— Well, we could be trying for our fortune, anyway, *laochain*.

MURDO

Trying, is it? I've all the fortune I'll ever want, if I've Morag MacKinnon.

MORAG

And a railway handy.

MURDO

Now, now, lass—

MORAG

To get away from her now and then.

MURDO

Och, will you wheesht! (**HE** *stifles her next words with a kiss.*)
(**ANGUS** *enters with a few ends of wire which he lays down.*)

ANGUS

And what's this of it?

MURDO

(Embarrassed as **MORAG** *goes back to her baking.)*—It's— it's a fine day, Angus.

ANGUS

(With gloomy regard.) Aye, it's a fine day when the fox turns preacher.

MORAG

Och, father, he's not against us, at all, at all,

MURDO

'Deed, no, Angus.—I'm not for their dirty iron-mines any more. The villains that they are!—trying to break you!—And I'm for starting a fine croft of my own.—And will you be letting Morag come to me now?

ANGUS

And what croft is there for a shifty lad like you, I wonder.

MURDO

The croft of my Uncle Duncan who died on us on Monday last.—It's straight back from the burying I am.— Faolinnvore it's called, in Lochcarron.

ANGUS

Lochcarron!—the ends of all the earth! (*HE sits down, overcome.*)

MORAG

Father!

ANGUS

And is it leaving me you are, Morag, and me in my old age?

MORAG

Och, it's but a day's journey, or maybe two in winter.

ANGUS

A hundred miles if it's a step!—Och, och! it's not enough that I'm to be losing my good name with the bankruptcy.— It's not enough to be losing the croft where I was born.— But the daughter of my heart must be leaving me too.

MORAG

Losing? Who's talking of losing?—You'll be coming with us to Lochcarron. Will he not, Murdo?

MURDO

What else would he be doing? And welcome!

ANGUS

Och, this day, this day!

MURDO

And as for the good name of you, Angus, I have some money laid by, and—

ANGUS

Aye, you're for bribing me now to let you be taking her away from me.—No, no! I want none of your money.

MORAG

Och, father, be you fair!

ANGUS

Will you listen to her?—Fair?—Is it fair for you to be leaving this house, and me in my trouble and shame?

MURDO

Now, Angus, have some reason in you.

ANGUS

(*Rising.*) Och, let me be going back to my work. It's all I have to think of now.—Reason?—Reason? (*Lifts a new coil of wire.*)—And the heart of me breaking!—And be you keeping your money; for I'll take a vow this very minute never to lift money from anyone but what I've earned with my own hands.

MURDO

But I'm not asking—

ANGUS

For I'm seeing that the money that is got for nothing has to be dearly paid for in the end of all.—So let me be going now to my work. And I'm seeing I'll be at the drams to-morrow; and there will not be enough drink in all Torlochan to drown this sorrow of mine!

MURDO

But I'm not—

ANGUS

Bribing me, is it?—Och, did I not say it was a fine day when the fox turns preacher?

(**HE** *goes out, and* **MURDO**, *downcast, sits by fire.* **MORAG** *goes on with her work, then comes behind him, her hand on his shoulder.*)

MORAG

And what need to be grieving, Murdo?—It's me that kens the ways of him. I'll be managing him, look you!

MURDO

He hits hard, and me meaning well.

MORAG

Och, but he's only a man. And there's nothing like the men for changeability.—Look at yourself! Iron-mines and civilisation one day; and a croft in Lochcarron the next! Trust you to Morag to put him right. (*Sound of voices outside.*) And what's this now?

(**COLONEL MURRAY** *and* **CAPTAIN CHARLIE** *enter.*)

COLONEL

A fine day, Morag.—Your father about?—How are you, Murdo?

MORAG

He's in the wood, fencing. I can be finding him in a minute.—Will you be coming, Murdo? (**THEY** *go out.*)

CAPTAIN

I think you'd best do the talking, father. He's as touchy as gunpowder with me.

COLONEL

Very well.—I'll say nothing about MacPhedran's refusal. I'll just pay him in advance for the fencing, and see that he gets enough to clear this debt.

CAPTAIN

I hope to goodness he'll snap at it—But you never can tell, with a sly old dog like Angus.—He may have heard something. News travels fast here. Ten to one he'll have heard some yarn about all the county people being down on me?

COLONEL

Some yarn! Well, are they not down on you?

CAPTAIN

(*Walking about restlessly.*) Good Lord! Not all the county!—It's only the Ellis-Maitlands and the Broughs that are at it.—It's always your profiteers that love to get their claws into our set. Makes the hair-restorer Johnny and the furniture-polish man feel big to point the finger of scorn at the old families.—I hope to heaven Alice won't hear anything of it!—Hang it all! You'd think a man was a criminal because he tried to start an iron-mine!

COLONEL

It's not the mine they profess to object to, Charlie. It's your method of clearing crofters, by breaking them.—I've always said you were wrong there.

CAPTAIN

Damn MacPhedran! Why wouldn't he let us settle this chap's account?

COLONEL

Well, we can get Angus to settle it himself.—Then there will be an end to this gossip.

CAPTAIN

Bad enough that Redfern should throw the iron-mine over, without this scandal.

COLONEL

Best thing Redfern ever did, dropping your mine.— Don't you worry.— There are surely other ways you can retrieve on those South African losses.

CAPTAIN

You think so?

COLONEL

Yes, what about the larchwood on the North there?— Time it was being thinned out.

CAPTAIN

So it is.

COLONEL

And then, what about the afforestation of the estate generally? If your engagement to Alice comes off—you could think of forestry.—A family man, eh?

CAPTAIN

Something in that.

COLONEL

Well, you think over it, boy. (**ANGUS** *enters wearily.*)

COLONEL

Ah! here he is! A fine day, Angus.

ANGUS

(*Quietly.*) A fine day, sir.

COLONEL

Quite well, Angus?—No?—You look a bit off colour.

ANGUS

(*Dismally.*) I'm as well as I'll ever be, I'm thinking.

COLONEL

Depressed a bit!—Oh, but we'll soon set that all right.— Well, we've come to tell you that this iron-mine business is off. The Company have got more suitable ground elsewhere than in Eilean Aros, it appears. So there's no question of your leaving Coillemore now, Angus.

ANGUS

(*Dejected still.*) Do you tell me?

COLONEL

Charlie and I think of doing some wood-cutting instead. The big larches, y' know.

ANGUS

Well, well!

COLONEL

So you could be having quite a busy time here, and might make some extra money when you had no work to do on the croft.

ANGUS

'Deed, aye.

COLONEL

And then, about this foolish bankruptcy business, Angus. —Well, it's like this—I'm going to advance you some money on your fence-repairing contract, so that you can be clear with MacPhedran before the next three days are gone.—It's three days, isn't it?

ANGUS

The Colonel is very kind.

COLONEL

Well, now, will twenty do? *(Takes out pocket-book.)*

ANGUS

(Blankly.) I want nothing at all.

COLONEL

Nonsense, Angus. Let's get this settled.

ANGUS

No, no! I've taken an oath this very day to lift no money I have not earned.

CAPTAIN

But hang it all, man, you must take it. You mustn't be bankrupted!—I'll be in a devil of a hole if you're bankrupted!

ANGUS

(Angrily.) But I want to be bankrupted!—And I want to be left alone!—And I just want to die and be done with it.—There's nobody cares for me at all, at all.—And I'm feenished, so I am.

COLONEL

Whatever's come over you?

ANGUS

Och, there's nothing I want now but to go up to Torlochan and get drunk till I'm senseless, I'm telling you!

CAPTAIN

You're senseless already, I think, to be talking that way. See here! We've been to MacPhedran to settle your account so as to keep you out of this bankruptcy business, and myself out of all this silly gossip about my bankrupting you. It's chiefly on my own account I'm taking all this trouble, I admit.—Understand?

ANGUS

I'm understanding.

CAPTAIN

But MacPhedran refuses all dealings except with the principal—that's you. He's got his knife in you evidently, and wants to break you.—Are you listening? Taking all this in?

ANGUS

Oh, I'm listening, right enough.

CAPTAIN

But MacPhedran can certainly not refuse the money from yourself. — So we are lending you the cash to pay him and spoil his little game. — It's some petty spite he has against you.

ANGUS

There was a man here —

CAPTAIN

Hang it! Will you take the money?

ANGUS

There was a man here to-day already, offering me money to do that same. But I found out that he wanted something from me by way of return for the obligement. — And I'm wondering now what is't you'll be wanting, if I'll be obliging you by going down and settling with MacPhedran.

CAPTAIN

Hang it all, man, we're wanting nothing! Obligement? Don't you see it's yourself you're obliging, by getting clear of bankruptcy.

ANGUS

Och! I might as well be bankrupt, and done with everything.

CAPTAIN

The man's mad!

ANGUS

And isn't it a strange thing now, that the Laird and his son come begging to a crofter almost on their bended knees, so that he will be taking money from them?

CAPTAIN

Clean daft!

COLONEL

You'd better leave us, Charlie. — You're too excitable.

CAPTAIN

(*Sulkily.*) Oh, very well! But I don't envy you your job!

(*He goes out.*)

COLONEL

(*Quietly.*) It's this way, Angus. — We're old friends, you and me — and I want you to help us out of a difficulty. There's a story got abroad that the Captain took an unfair advantage of you in trying to bankrupt you, so as to get you out of your holding and have the ground clear for his water-power scheme.

ANGUS

He's the foolish son to you, Colonel, that one; although it's to yourself I'm saying it.

COLONEL

Quite so; but *(smiling)* you see, he is my son.

ANGUS

He is that.

COLONEL

And now, quite privately and as between old friends, I may as well tell you that there's a lady now in this island, mixed up in this affair—a lady the Captain is specially interested in. He may marry her, in fact.—And if you are bankrupted—Charlie's—ah—prospects may be seriously interfered with.

ANGUS .

(Repeating incredulously.) If I am bankrupted, the Captain's prospects may be seriously interfered with!— It's surely not my Morag he is after?

COLONEL

No, no! That would be a bit—a bit strange, don't you think?

ANGUS

It would that.—But there's the strange things happening hereabouts nowadays, let me tell you.—And he would be the second man this day that was after her.

COLONEL

(Smiling.) No, no! it's an English lady.—She is on a visit here just now. And, you see, if she heard these exaggerated reports—these—ah — gossipy stories about Charlie—she might—not—well—she might not hit it off with Charlie.—Understand?

ANGUS

(Smiling radiantly and broadly for the first time in the conversation.)
Och! and is that it?—I thought by the way you went about it, you were wanting something from me?

COLONEL

And so we do. We are asking you to help us out of this —ah— difficulty—by refusing to let yourself be bankrupted.

ANGUS

'Deed so you are now! So you are!

CAPTAIN

(Entering.) Any forrader, father?

COLONEL
Hush!

ANGUS
So you are now! — Well, I'll be conseedering —

CAPTAIN
Good heavens! Is that all the length you've got?

COLONEL
Y' know, you've only three days left to do your considering in, Angus.

ANGUS
I'd like fine to be staying on in Coillemore, look you!

CAPTAIN
Man alive! And what's to hinder you?

ANGUS
I'll not can be doing that if Morag leaves me.

COLONEL
But I told you it wasn't Morag. — It's an English lady.

ANGUS
Oh, I'm understanding that bit of it fine. — But Morag is for marrying Murdo MacKay, and going away to Lochcarron on a croft there. And then I'll not want to be staying on at Coillemore any more.

CAPTAIN
But what's that to do with the bankruptcy?

ANGUS
Och, you'd wonder now — you'd wonder now! If the Captain — I'm speaking to the Captain, sir, for he's the Laird now, isn't he? — If the Captain — and this is how I'm seeing it — if the Captain was to give Murdo the old holding at Torr-na-Bhlar that is next to mine at Coillemore we could be repairing the old house — and Morag and he would not be leaving me to go to the ends of all the earth at Lochcarron.

CAPTAIN
Well! of all the old —! You're for driving a hard bargain, Angus?

ANGUS
Och, not so hard at all, at all. — I'm only saying that I will let myself be bankrupted, unless the Captain will be giving Murdo the holding at Torr-na-Bhlar.

CAPTAIN
Tuts, nonsense! *(Then reflecting.)* A bit thick, father, eh?

COLONEL
(Chuckling.) He has you tight, Charlie.—Allow Angus!

ANGUS
(With spirit.) I will not be having the Captain tight or anybody tight, if they'll be leaving me slack.—But the Captain was not slack with me when I was in his hands, and in MacPhedran's hands, because of him.

CAPTAIN
Oh, damn! Let's get home out of this!

COLONEL
No, no! Let's make an end of it. Promise Torr-na-Bhlar for Murdo. He'll be handy for the wood cutting, if we go on with it.

ANGUS
He will, indeed! He's the great scholar, is Murdo! Chemistry and civilisation and all that. He would make the fine manager for the cutting of the woods.

CAPTAIN
All right then—you old bloodsucker! Murdo is to have Torr-na-Bhlar—that's agreed! And you'll promise not to go bankrupt.

ANGUS
Yes, yes, I'll promise.

COLONEL
(Handing notes to CAPTAIN.*)* For heaven's sake, give him your hand on it, before he asks anything else.

(CAPTAIN *shakes hands with* ANGUS *hurriedly.*)

CAPTAIN
Now, you'll be sure to settle with MacPhedran.—How much do you need as an advance?

ANGUS
Eight pounds ten shillings. And I'll be taking it all off the fencing account.

CAPTAIN
(Counting out notes, which ANGUS *pockets.)* You'll see MacPhedran tonight, I hope, and clear off everything?

ANGUS
No, no.

CAPTAIN
What?

ANGUS

I'll see MacPhedran this very night, but it's only three pounds he'll get.—I'll be paying him in instalments.—It's what he's used to from me.

CAPTAIN

Instalments?

ANGUS

And I'll give him three pounds the next day; and two pounds ten on the day after, the last day of all for bankrupting me.—I like fine to see him sticking on the stamps, look you.

COLONEL

Well, you're the droll fish!—Good-day to you now. We've had a fine *ceilidh*.

CAPTAIN

Good-day!

ANGUS

Good-day, good-day!—Yes, yes, a fine *ceilidh* indeed!— It was all that!
(THEY *pass out.*) I must be telling Morag. *(Goes to door and waves.)*
(MURDO *and* MORAG *enter,* MORAG *with a letter in her hand.)*

MORAG

A letter for you, father. We went down to the stepping stones and met the post.

ANGUS

Och, wheesht till I tell you! *(Kisses her and shakes hands with* MURDO.*)* And haven't I the great news for you both from the big people! The Captain is to be giving Torr-na-Bhlar for a croft to Murdo, so that you'll not both be going away to Lochcarron and leaving me.

MORAG

Are you joking now?

ANGUS

Am I the man to be joking about such a thing?—I have the promise of Torr-na-Bhlar for Murdo from the two of them.—And they're for starting felling in the big wood of larches.—And I told them Murdo was the very man for manager.—And I am to be staying on in Coillemore.—And I'm to be paying MacPhedran with the good money they gave me, so that I'll not be bankrupted at all, at all!

MURDO

(Meditating.) It was the good croft in its time, was Torr-na-Bhlar, and might well be again.

MORAG

I'm scarcely for believing it yet! It's all so fine!—But you'll be missing the trains to Inverness, Murdo, and the book shops there.—However did you manage it, father?

ANGUS

I did no managing at all, at all.—It's one of the strange things that's always happening to me. It looks like what Mrs. Galletly would be calling a Higher Power—something that's working on you, so that your leg doesn't get broken, when you've had a taste too much, and the cart wheel goes over you.—You'll be staying on in Eilean Aros, lad, will you not?

MORAG

Of course, he'll be staying.

MURDO

Indeed and I will!—And my brother, Gillespie, can be having the succession to the croft in Lochcarron.—Forestry! Just fancy you!

ANGUS

Aye, science and civilisation, as you might say, at your very door. (*Looking at letter in* **MORAG**'s *hand.*) And is that not now another letter and it registered.

MORAG

Indeed and it is registered. I had to sign for it.

ANGUS

Och, och! More of the Sheriff Officer's papers about the bankruptcy! As if I cared for them now!—Be you opening it, lass, and reading it to me.

MORAG

(*Opening letter.*) There's a pound note in it!

ANGUS

(*Taking note.*) 'Deed, so there is. I can be reading that myself anyway. (**HE** *pockets note.*)

MORAG

And a letter from Mr. Stockman.

ANGUS

He'll be wanting some more pigs' heads maybe.

MORAG

What kind of talk is that?... Will you listen! (*Reading.*) "Dear Angus, The bird-stuffer man was angry when I opened out the parcel of pigs' heads and tootsie-wootsies. I know it's some bally mistake, as you're too decent an old bird to go playing practical jokes on me—"

ANGUS

Isn't he the fine man now!

MORAG

Will you wheesht! *(Reading.)* "So please send on the stag's head to Joliffe, Taxidermist, Oban, without delay, if it's not lost, or if you haven't already forwarded it to him—"

ANGUS

And didn't I send it to Mr. Joliffe a week ago?

MORAG

Wheesht now and listen.—*(Reading.)* "I made a present of the pork to Joliffe to soothe his wounded feelings, and beg now to enclose one pound in payment of the same. Hope to see you some time soon, if the iron-mine business goes on all right. Yours sincerely, W. Stockman."

ANGUS

He's the fine man!

MORAG

That money will be for MacPhedran, I'm thinking. Didn't you tell me he bought the pigs' heads from Mrs. Galletly? But a pound note will be paying for them ten times over.

ANGUS

Bought, is it? Catch MacPhedran paying anything for pigs' heads!— No, no, they were a present from Mrs. Galletly to MacPhedran.—There is no question of money in it at all, at all.

MORAG

Oh, was that the way of it!

ANGUS

And MacPhedran left the pigs' heads on my hands in exchange for the loan of a stag's head I was giving him. And so, look you, the pork was a present from me to Mr. Stockman. And this—*(Shewing pound note)*—is a present from Mr. Stockman to me by way of returning thanks, as the saying goes.

MORAG

My head is turning round on me, so it is, with all your talk!

ANGUS

(Producing note.) And now I'm for making a present of this to somebody else. (**HE** *hands the note to* **MORAG**) It's only the start of the wedding presents I'll be giving you my dear, but be you taking it now.—But there will be more coming to you as soon as the strange things start happening on me again. Just you wait!

MORAG

(Kissing him.) You're the droll man!

MURDO

'Deed, yes.

ANGUS

But what now is to hinder Mr. Joliffe sending me a present as well as Mr. Stockman, a pound or two maybe?— Are you quite sure now, lass, that there was only one registered letter this day?

MORAG

Och, you're the greedy one!

ANGUS

I am not, then.—But *(Putting on jacket and hat, he takes out his pass-book and looks at its pages.)* I have the greedy one to deal with, and that's MacPhedran.

(**HE** *takes the notes out of his pocket and arranges them on table.*)
One—two—three.—Be you giving me that to-morrow. *(Hands the three pounds to* **MORAG**.) One—two—and ten shillings.—*(Hands them also to her.)* And be you giving me that the day after. (**HE** *pockets the remaining three pounds.*) And now I'll be going off with the first of my instalments. It's a long tramp I'll be having down to him, every day of three days; but it will be doing me good—and him too, I'm hoping.— *Feasgair math,* Murdo! (**HE** *shakes hands with* **MURDO**, *but only slaps* **MORAG** *lightly on the shoulder, as* **HE** *makes for the door.*) But stop you! *(His eyes have fallen on the pipes.)* 'Tis a fine day that's in it—and I feel like the piping. *(Takes the pipes from window-sill.)* I'll just be playing for a spell, and me walking down to MacPhedran. Wait you till I'm over the stepping-stones, and I'll be giving you "The Glen is Mine."

(**HE** *waves his hand, swings the bag to his oxter, and passes out into the sunlight and the breeze.*)

MORAG

Good-luck, father!

MURDO

Good-luck, Angus!

(Presently the strains of the pipes in "The Glen is Mine " are heard. **MORAG** *and* **MURDO** *stand at door waving to* **ANGUS**.*)*

CURTAIN

The Treasure Ship

A Comedy in Four Acts

To Alec Wilson Yulll

ACT I
The Sitting-Room at Dr. Fraser's.
Monday Afternoon.

ACT II
The Sitting-Room at Dr. Fraser's.
Monday Evening.

ACT III
The Sitting-Room at Dr. Fraser's.
Tuesday Morning.

ACT IV
The North Pier.
Wednesday Morning.

THE TIME is present day. It is summer.
THE PLACE is the little town of Torlochan
in the West Highlands.

Persons

DR. FRASER	*The Doctor in Torlochan*
MRS. FRASER	*His Wife.*
IONA	*His Daughter.*
DR. MACDONALD	*His Assistant.*
MACLAREN	*A Grocer.*
MACIVER	*A Joiner.*
COONEY	*A Diver.*
MACPHERSON	*A Constable.*
MR. LAWRENCE)	
MRS. MANSON)	*Summer Visitors.*
MISS FALLONE (FANNY))	
KATIE	*A Servant.*

ACT I

SCENE.—*The sitting-room at* **DR. FRASER**'s, *Torlochan, West Highlands. Monday afternoon. It is an unusual kind of room, for while on the left of it* **MRS. FRASER** *is giving tea to some friends just now, on the right is a revolving chair of business type set before a large table crowded with heavy volumes, some sailing charts, numerous office files of the bent-hook variety, and a telescope surmounting all—and these, somehow, do not quite harmonise with chatter over tea. Even the fawn-coloured walls bear decorations that conflict, for several good modern water-colours and etchings alternate with material of purely antiquarian interest—an old map of Eilean Aros out of Blaeu's seventeenth-century atlas, an engraving of a Spanish galleon of Drake's time, a print of Torlochan by Darnell dated 1817, and a reproduction of a faded charter in scrawling script, with ribbon and red seal. Certainly an odd sort of room.*

In the back wall a large double-window, with heavy curtains on either side of it fully withdrawn, looks out over the little town's roof-tops to the sunlit waters of Torlochan Bay and the distant Highland hills encircling it. Below the window is a box-seat draped in cretonne, and on it lies a field-glass. Near the curtains on the right is a large cabinet without doors, but with a silken screen drawn aside to display the contents of its shelves. These are antiques, each with a fussy little white label affixed: swords, spurs, pistols, daggers, breastplates, morions, and a large salver—obviously a collection of some importance. But a twin cabinet to the left of the window is clearly its rival; for the sedateness of the old pewter it contains is enlivened by the flaring colours of the labels here: red, green and purple cards are fastened to chopins, chalices, tappit-hens, loving-cups and alms-dishes. Both cabinets are really intriguing, and the eye of the visitor wanders irresolute from left to right before he decides which first to inspect.

The other walls of the room have nothing of great interest to show: on the left there are a door at the back and a fireplace forward; and on the right only a bookcase at the front, and a curtained doorway in the rear.

Some ordinary chairs are set near the revolving one close to the large table; and on the other side of the room—the left—are several more; also a chesterfield, a tea table and a cake-stand, for here it is that **MRS. FRASER**, *the Doctor's wife, has just finished giving tea to her friends. She is a comely dame, about fifty-five, has a fresh happy face and is dressed in a slightly old-fashioned silk. She speaks with a faint hint of Lowland Scots; and, although you are in the Highlands, you must not be surprised at this, for Lowlanders sometimes marry Highlanders: it may not be advisable, but it does happen now and again. With her is* **IONA**, *her only child, a fair-haired girl of twenty, of the slim athletic type. And the guests are summer-visitors to Torlochan:* **MRS. MANSON**, *a stout lady of fifty, rather*

fashionably dressed for so quiet a place, and **FANNY FALLONE,** **MRS. MANSON**'s *niece, rather fashionably dressed for anywhere.*
FANNY *has just risen, and is crossing to look out of the window at the Bay.*

IONA

Wait, Fanny. Here's a chair. (*Taking a chair to window.*) That box-seat is ricketty. (**SHE** *presses her hand on it, testing it.*)

FANNY

Right-oh! I wasn't going to sit. (**SHE** *takes up field-glasses.*)

IONA

The joiner's coming up to mend it to-day. High time too.

FANNY

I only wanted a squint at the Bay. (*Looking out through glasses.*)

MRS. MANSON

No more, thank you, Mrs. Fraser. (**SHE** *sets down her cup.*) Such fine tea! Where do you get it, I wonder?

MRS. FRASER

At MacLaren's—the grocer's on the South Pier. He's Vice-Chairman o' the Syndicate, ye ken.

FANNY

Which Syndicate's that, Mrs. Fraser?

MRS. MANSON

The Moidores Syndicate, Fanny. The treasure-ship, you know.

FANNY

Oh! The sunken treasure? What a funny name! Moidores?

IONA

(*Bringing over some coins from cabinet.*) These are moidores—the gold ones. The silver ones are pieces of eight.

FANNY

How ripping! Fancy that pump out there sucking up pieces of eight all day long! Wouldn't Masefield just love this!

IONA

I'm afraid that pump's a fraud. These are all the coins we ever got.

FANNY

I've been watching for the diver going down, but there are no signs of him ... And don't you really get any treasure nowadays?

MRS. FRASER

No, we're daein' badly this year. We're only resting on our laurels in the cabinet there. (**SHE** *points to the right.*)

IONA

The green flag hasn't been up for five weeks now.

FANNY

The green flag?

IONA

Oh, didn't you know? They sound a siren and run up a green flag whenever the diver gets anything.

MRS. MANSON

I must have a real good look at your cabinet.
    (**SHE** *goes over to the cabinet on the right, and* **FANNY** *goes with her.*

FANNY

(*Taking up salver.*) I say! ... I should like to get a prize like this! Tell the Doctor—your father's Chairman, isn't he, Iona?—Well, tell him I'll take five pounds' worth of shares, will you?

IONA

(*With slight irony.*) Whole five? ... Yes, I'll ask father to have some application forms sent on to you at the Hotel.

MRS. MANSON

And some for me too, if you please, Iona. I take some every year, Fanny. Never make a penny. But I do think Armadas and that sort of thing should be encouraged! So exciting, don't you think?

FANNY

Aren't they just?

MRS. MANSON

Well, we must be going. By the by, Mrs. Fraser, I'm glad to see your husband has still the same nice assistant as he had last year... Dr.— eh —Dr.—?

MRS. FRASER

Dr. MacDonald —... Aye, he's a nice lad. And a guid doctor, they're saying.

FANNY

(*Enthusiastically.*) He's an A1 bikist at any rate Gave me a lift on his pillion yesterday. Some scorcher, he is!

MRS. MANSON

Well, we really must be going, Fanny. And I do hope the treasure-ship will be a great success this season, Mrs, Fraser. Good-bye ... Good-bye, Iona.
    (*Handshakes all round.* **MRS. FRASER** *goes out with the visitors.* **IONA** *goes to the window with field-glasses.*

MRS. FRASER

(Returning.) A kindly body, Mrs. Manson.

IONA

Yes, she's all right. But Miss Fallone! ... Oh! ... And I'm sure she was never invited to that pillion ride. She just insinuated herself, I'm certain.

MRS. FRASER

Weel, weel! What aboot it?

IONA

(Tragically.) It's her last ride.

MRS. FRASER

Iona! My dear!

IONA

I mean, on our bike.

MRS. FRASER

Whit harm's in that? Hae I no' seen ye often riding ahint Dr. MacDonald on that same bike yersel'?

IONA

I know how to. She doesn't.

MRS. FRASER

And wha tell't ye that?

IONA

I just know.
(**KATIE** *comes in to clear away the tea-table.* **IONA** *and* **MRS. FRASER** *fall silent at once.*

MRS. FRASER

(As maid goes.) Put the cakes in the tin, Katie.

(**KATIE** *goes out.*

MRS. FRASER

Weel, weel! ... But there's ae thing I will say—Ye're raither often on the bike wi' that lad. Ye couldna weel be oftener if ye were engaged.

IONA

Maybe we are.

MRS. FRASER

Iona!

IONA

I said, "Maybe".

MRS. FRASER

And are ye?

IONA

I don't know.

MRS. FRASER

Then ye can safely say ye are not. For if there's one thing a lassie kens or disna ken, it's that. *(Putting her hand on* IONA*'s head.)* Eh, woman, but ye're wild! And if I didna ken ye better, I could be angry wi' ye.

IONA

(Nestling to her.) Oh, mother!—I think—I think—I think I'm really in love.

MRS. FRASER

Aye? But ye thocht the same wi' the last twa assistants. Be carefu', dear, be carefu'.

IONA

(Brusquely.) Well, it kept them from running away from us. It was good for the practice.

MRS. FRASER

And maybe that's juist the reason Dr. MacDonald gied Miss Fallone a ride on his bike. Guid for the practice.

IONA

Aha! You rogue! *(*SHE *kisses her.)*
(A knock at the door on left. It opens, and MACIVER*, the Torlochan joiner, comes in.* HE *is a man of fifty, of fresh open countenance but with a roguish eye.* HE *is carrying some tools and a piece of wood; his accent is West Highland.*

MACIVER

I'll just be finishing the window-seat, if it's convenient, Mrs. Fraser.

MRS. FRASER

Quite convenient, MacIver. Gled tae see ye ... And ye mind me I've my ain wark to dae. I maun be seeing till't.
*(*SHE *goes off by door on left.*

IONA

(Taking up glasses again and looking out on the Bay.) Not much doing at the diving to-day, MacIver.

MACIVER

(Gruffly.) I'm sure I'm not sorry. Better if that same diving was stopped altogether.

IONA
Oh! Why? What have you against it?

MACIVER
I'll say no more. I'm knowing what I know.
(*Sounds of altercation are heard at the door on left which is opened, revealing* **KATIE**, *the servant, protesting against the entry of* **COONEY**, *a tall Irishman of forty, dressed in the rough blue serge of a seaman.* **HE** *carries a diver's head-piece in his arms.*

KATIE
You'll not be going in there with that dirty trash. You'll leave it in the kitchen.

COONEY
Trash? D'ye call this trash? And me loife dipinding on it!

IONA
It's all right, Katie. I know about it. The Doctor wanted it up here, so that it wouldn't come to any harm.

KATIE
And what harm, I wonder, could come to an old tin-kettle that should be in the ash-pit. (**SHE** *goes.*)

COONEY
Did ye iver hear a targe like her?

IONA
It's all right, Cooney. Sit down and never mind. I'll look for father.
(**SHE** *goes out.*

COONEY
Good-day to ye, MacIver. Did ye iver hear a tongue like that wan's.
(**HE** *lays down head-piece tenderly in a safe corner.*

MACIVER
(*Coming over to examine helmet.*) And what's happened to it now?

COONEY
A broken outlet-valve.

MACIVER
It's the spring that's gone, is it?

COONEY
Ye've said it. Nearly drowned me, it did. And the blood in me head fizzing like thim irritated waters.

MACIVER
Aye, it's the risky work you have.

COONEY
Risky? It's killing me, so it is. And the Doctor'll have to raise me screw, or divil another doive I'll do on his ould galloon.

MACIVER
'Deed then, it would be pleasing some of us very well, if the Doctor would stop that diving altogether and attend to his own proper business.

COONEY
Sure the Doctor's only wan out av many. He's not the whole Syndicate.

MACIVER
It would be well if the whole thing were put a stop to, I'm telling you. He's no time left for his own work.

COONEY
And doesn't he know all about where this Spanish ship was sunk and that Spanish ship was sunk? And which had the goulden dollars and which had noane.

MACIVER
Ach! let him come out of it.
(**HE** *starts planing vigorously, humming "Farewell to Fiumary" in a low voice.*)

COONEY
Dear-a-dear! Ye've a vice like a tin crocodile, MacIver! Stop for the love av Dublin! and come ye down to the Hotel Bar, and I'll ile its cogs for ye. The Doctor's late, and I'll stay for him no longer.

MACIVER
Wait you for five meenits till I finish this.

COONEY
I'll wait at the Hotel Bar then. For they've the good stuff yander. Hurry, boy!
(*As* **HE** *makes for door,* IONA *enters on left with* **MR. LAWRENCE**, *an English tourist, dressed in a loud knicker suit of tweed check.* **HE** *is a round-faced, pleasant man of thirty-five, and has a military bearing.*)

IONA
Going already, Cooney?

COONEY
I'm sorry, Miss, but the Doctor's late, and I've an appointment at the Hotel. And will ye plase say to the Doctor that unless he gets me a new tinned-copper helmet, wid a reduplicated safety valve, jewelled in ivry hole, I'll doive for him no more.

IONA

Right, Cooney! I'll tell him. And if you throw up your job, I'll apply for it. I'd love to go down among the mermaids.

COONEY

Sure, thin, ye'll never see wan lovelier than yerself— nor wan wid such a halloo av goulden hair, me dear. God save ye koindly!

(HE *goes out by door on left.*)

LAWRENCE

A jolly old bird.

IONA

(*Busy at ledgers.*) Yes. And can't he lay on the blarney? ... Take a seat, Mr. Lawrence. When did you say your sister's accident was? June?

LAWRENCE

June, yes—end of June.

IONA

I'm afraid our books are dreadfully behind. Father's so easy-going about accounts. Oh, here it is in the daybook. Not posted up yet. Yes— June and July.—Six guineas, Mr. Lawrence.

LAWRENCE

Right! I'll make out a cheque, if I may. (HE *takes out cheque book.*)

IONA

Certainly—and I'll receipt.
(*Having written the cheque,* LAWRENCE *saunters over to the cabinet of Spanish relics on right, while* IONA *writes a receipt.*)

LAWRENCE

(*Taking up the salver.*) Jolly old stuff this! " V. de G."? The Commander's initials? Name of Gomez, I think. What a lot of relics! ... Here too! (HE *moves to the cabinet on left.*)

IONA

No, no! That's different. Nothing to do with the Spanish treasure. That's father's collection of old pewter.

LAWRENCE

Oh! Pewter!... Don't know anything about that. (HE *comes back to the cabinet on right.*) Did you get much at the diving this year?

IONA

Hardly anything so far. Oh, I do wish we'd drop on something nice and hefty. You see, if we don't, you summer visitors fall off, and father gets grumpy.

LAWRENCE

Really?

IONA

Yes. The more finds, the more pictures in the papers. The more pictures, the more visitors. And, therefore, the more patients.

LAWRENCE

Well, you're frank enough, anyway. (**HE** *saunters over to the window and takes up the field-glasses.*) ... But, Good Lord! If that isn't Muriel out at the diving-hulk again!

IONA

(*Taking the glasses.*) So it is!

LAWRENCE

And on the very ladder where she sprained her ankle! Isn't she a young fool! Who's the youth with her?

IONA

(*Pettishly, as* **SHE** *lays down the glasses.*) Oh, another young fool!

LAWRENCE

But who?

IONA

Dr. MacDonald ... Father's assistant.

LAWRENCE

Well, anyway, I'll cut down and give Muriel a few thoughts straight from the shoulder. Also a few to your assistant.

IONA

He's not *my* assistant.

LAWRENCE

Oh! Then, Muriel's assistant. (**SHE** *winces visibly.*) Good-day, Miss Fraser.

IONA

Good-day, Mr. Lawrence.

(*As* **HE** *is going to the door on left,* **DR. FRASER** *enters there.* **HE** *is a man of about sixty with a shrewd face, clean-shaven, and has a professional manner of old-fashioned type.* **HE** *wears a pince-nez, through which he peers appealingly, and is clad in a suit of rough tweed, with Gladstone collar and stock.* **HE** *is heard saying "Good-bye" fussily to someone just before* **HE** *appears.*)

LAWRENCE

Hullo, Doctor! How are you? (**HE** *shakes hands.*) Just been settling your little bill for Muriel's ankle. Well, I'm off, for I see she's coming in from that old diving-hulk. Wonder which foot she's bust this time?

DR. FRASER
Oh! I trust she'll have no more of that.

LAWRENCE
Well, she's in good hands: your assistant sawbones is with her.

DR. FRASER
(At the window.) No? ... Yes, there he is! Rowing her in. I thought he was down country at Kellan! Well, well! Boys will be boys!—Oh, by the by, Iona, would you mind taking Mr. MacIver downstairs for some refreshment—some—er—milk, perhaps. You're tired, MacIver, I'm sure?

MACIVER
(Who had started for the door as soon as he hears the word "refreshment" halts, and asks anxiously.) Did you say refreshment, Doctor—or—or—milk?

DR. FRASER
I said both, MacIver—both. Meaning the same thing. Not quite a popular beverage, I know—but I said milk.

MACIVER
(Staggered by this truth, mutters.) My God!
(**HE** *goes out, followed by* IONA.

DR. FRASER
(Chirpily, as if relieved by MACIVER'S *disappearance.)* Seen my pewter, Lawrence?

LAWRENCE
Yes, yes. Not in my line though. But these other things are great. *(***HE** *turns to the cabinet on right.)*

DR. FRASER
Tuts! I wouldn't give a single bit of this pewter here, for the whole of that Spanish stuff.

LAWRENCE
Then why hide 'em with a curtain?

DR. FRASER
Oh, people come in here to look at the Spanish relics, and confuse the pewter with them, and paw around generally. So I shut off my beauties with this. *(Handling the curtain.)*

LAWRENCE
Some labels, eh? *(***HE** *approaches cabinet on left.)* What gorgeous colours?

DR. FRASER
Well, you see, I've just started collecting. And I have to make notes about the touches—the marks, you know, and all that, so as to get up the subject. Red is for Scottish stuff. Green for English. Purple for Flemish.

LAWRENCE

Oh! I understand.

DR. FRASER

(Taking up a red-labelled "tappit-hen") Now this, you see, tells me (HE *reads label and examines vessel for markings as he talks)* that it is of the first quality, since it is marked with a crowned hammer.

LAWRENCE

Really!

DR. FRASER

Yes. And also with the letters " W. H. " ... Now who was " W. H."? ... " W. H." was *(Reading label)* " William Hunter — Freeman Pewterer of the Edinburgh Hammermen's Incorporation 1749. His shop was in the East Bow Port."

LAWRENCE

I say! You have got it bad!

DR. FRASER

What?

LAWRENCE

This old pewter craze ... Well, well! these Armada things are my fancy.

DR. FRASER

Ah!... Now about our old treasure-ship, Mr. Lawrence. ... We are issuing some new shares presently ... Well, what about a little flutter in pieces of eight?

LAWRENCE

Can't, I'm afraid. Stony just now.

DR. FRASER

Nonsense! You know, the evidence is indubitable that here we have — not a mile from where we stand, sunk under the blue waters of this historic bay of Torlochan — a treasure that will outshine all the glories of Egypt, Tut-tut and Luxor, and all that.

LAWRENCE

But I'm on the rocks.

DR. FRASER

This venture, my dear boy, combines financial safety with high romance. You feel the pathos of the tragedy when the San Felipe sank with all its doughty men of arms on board, even while you add up your dividends. You know the lines:
" Full fathom five, thy father lies "?

LAWRENCE

(*Hurriedly.*) Yes, yes!

DR. FRASER

And then the wonderful close:
"A sea change
Into something rich and strange."

LAWRENCE

But, look here! How much have you fished up since I was here last summer? One sword, two collar studs, and something that looks like a damaged shoe-horn.

DR. FRASER

Collar studs! Shoe-horn! ... My dear sir, parts of a necklace of wonderful artistry! And at any moment we may hit on something inestimably valuable.

LAWRENCE

Hope it'll be soon then. Must be going, though. Bye-bye, Doctor. (**HE** *shakes hands.*)

DR. FRASER

Good-day, good-day! And think over what I've said ... Some day you'll be wanting shares in the Syndicate when we've none to sell.

LAWRENCE

I'll risk it, Doctor. Good-day to you!
(*As* **HE** *goes,* **MACIVER** *comes in, surly and impatient, puts on his coat and prepares to leave.*)

DR. FRASER

Finished, MacIver?

MACIVER

No, nor finished. I have an appointment, and I'm late for it already, with all your nonsense about refreshments.

DR. FRASER

But you promised to have the seat done for this afternoon?

MACIVER

I did that! But you're none too anxious yourself about your own jobs. So why should I be at mine?

DR. FRASER

What's that?

MACIVER

I'm saying, it's little the sick people that belong to this place see of you, until you've attended first of all to the big English visitors.

DR. FRASER
You're impertinent, MacIver!

MACIVER
Maybe I am. But there's need for that now and again hereabouts. (HE *makes to go.*)

DR. FRASER
One moment! Have I ever failed you, MacIver?

MACIVER
You have that. It was only a halflin assistant, just out of college, you sent my first wife in her last illness.

DR. FRASER
Even so, did she not get good medical attention?

MACIVER
And no account for that same, although it was eight years ago.

DR. FRASER
Tuts!

MACIVER
And me not knowing whether to spend or lay by, with that account hanging over my head.

DR. FRASER
(*Grimly.*) Well then, you shall have it now! (HE *goes to his ledger and begins to write.*)

MACIVER
But if any big Sassenach from the Hotel comes for his bill, it's: "Certainly, Mr. Lawrence"—"With pleasure, Mr. Lawrence"—"Your receipt, Mr. Lawrence"— "Much obliged, Mr. Lawrence." And off he goes, knowing what money he has left to him.

DR. FRASER
(*Busy writing.*) You shall have it! You shall have it! (HE *comes forward with the bill.*) There. (*Reading.*) To James MacIver. 1915. Wife No. 1, £2 10s.; 1918. Wife No. 2, £3 6s.; 1921. Wife No. 3, £1 10s. Total, £7 6s. (HE *hands over the bill as* IONA *comes in.*)

MACIVER
A thousand shames on you to be putting it like that. (HE *stamps to the door.*) You and your galloon, and your diving, and your nonsense that has the good life spoiled on the poor folk with your neglect of them!

(HE *goes out angrily.*)

IONA

My! Isn't he angry! What's it all about?

DR. FRASER

Oh, a bill! a bill!

IONA

Oh, that all! But, father, Cooney was here and left his helmet for you to see. He says a valve broke and nearly killed him yesterday.

DR. FRASER

(Savagely.) Pity it didn't! (**HE** *looks at the helmet.*)

IONA

Oh, father!

DR. FRASER

Well, what's the use of Cooney anyway? He brings in nothing nowadays. And if we can't stir up some interest in this diving business, the practice will go to the dogs!

IONA

Oh! Surely Cooney does his best?

DR. FRASER

But does he? I believe he goes down there and plays about on the sand at the sea-bottom—plays at skittles, or ninepins, or something. Where is he now?

IONA

At the Hotel.

DR. FRASER

(Bitterly.) He would be, of course! Well, send down for him, please! Something's got to be done, or we'll all be ruined!
(*The door on the left opens and* **DR. NEIL MACDONALD,** *the assistant, appears.* **IONA** *passes him, her head in air, and goes out.* **HE** *looks after her whimsically.* **HE** *is a young man of twenty-six, well set up, breezy and off-hand, but with the shades of the professional manner closing in on him already.*)

DR. FRASER

Well, sir? ... Thought you were off long ago to see those cases at Kellan. It's a long round, you know.

NEIL

Just going, Dr. Fraser.

DR. FRASER

Oh! Fancied you'd forgotten ... Here's the visiting list. (**HE** *gives him a slip of paper.*) Saw you out at the diving-hulk with Lawrence's sister. Any luck?

NEIL

No, sir. She didn't sprain anything this time.

DR. FRASER

(Severely.) I'm talking of the treasure-ship.

NEIL

Oh, that! No. Same old story! Plenty of good sea water pumping up. But never a single coin in the sieve.

DR. FRASER

Bad ... bad! Things are in a devil of a mess! I must look over my charts again. *(Turning to the table.)*

NEIL

I'd like a word with you first, sir.

DR. FRASER

Yes?

NEIL

(Taking a paper out of his pocket.) About this testimonial, sir. It's too good, y'know.

DR. FRASER

Nonsense, my boy, You're welcome to it.

NEIL

But I'll never have a look in for that appointment if I put in a letter of this kind to a Parish Council that's a nest of Socialists.

DR. FRASER

What's that got to do with it?

NEIL

All this about my being noble by nature as well as by birth, y'see. It will never do with that lot.

DR. FRASER

And what *will* do, then?

NEIL

Well, say I was born in the slums. Life and death struggle for daily bread. Something like that. Something decent.

DR. FRASER

Do you insinuate my testimonial is indecent?

NEIL

No. But I want something that makes me less of an angel. Something straight. There's no time to lose, for the appointment's to be made the day after to morrow.

DR. FRASER

There's no pleasing you, I'm afraid.

(HE *makes for the door of his room on the right.*

NEIL

(*Excitedly.*) I see what it is. You know your testimonial won't be any good with those Bolsheviks on the Parish Council. And then I won't get the post. And so you'll be able to keep me on here.

DR. FRASER

Oh, you want away? As soon as I've trained you — shown you all the practical work — you want away? Pshaw!

NEIL

But don't you see, sir—

DR. FRASER

Yes, yes! Off you go, you young fellows, one after the other, as soon's you learn the A. B. C. of the business.

NEIL

Really, sir—

DR. FRASER

Well, really? Is it fair to me? Is it fair to yourselves? Is it fair to the public?

NEIL

Oh! The public want new blood now and again! The public isn't quite fossilized!

DR. FRASER

Do you—do you suggest that I—that I—am a—a—fossil?

NEIL

I was talking of the public—not of you, Dr. Fraser. But, may I ask, do you insinuate that I am a greenhorn.

DR. FRASER

No, no! I don't say that. But, frankly, I think you've still much to learn—something more practical than all this about vitamines and lumbar punctures—all this newfangled stuff!

NEIL

Jolly useful stuff, sir, all the same. And let me tell you there are other things in medicine besides poultices and fly-blisters.

DR. FRASER

There are! And one of them is the knowledge of where and when to apply a blister or a poultice. That takes years, my boy, years!

NEIL

Some patients certainly have years of it.

DR. FRASER

What? Do you say I don't know my work?

NEIL

Oh, no, sir. You do know it. And I've learned a great deal from you! And now what about a fresh letter of recommendation for that old Parish Council?

DR. FRASER

So mine isn't fresh enough, is it?—Fossilized, maybe?— Well, there will be no fresh testimonial. (**HE** *dashes off to the curtained door on right.*)
(NEIL *follows, as* **DR. FRASER** *enters his room and shuts the door in his face.* **HE** *returns to the table irresolutely.* IONA *enters by the door on left, passes him without a word.* **SHE** *comes to chair at the fireplace, takes up newspaper and buries her head in it.*

NEIL

What's up now?

IONA

Oh, nothing.

NEIL

(*Bitterly.*) Glad to hear it. It's usually something I've done.
(A silence falls between them for some moments.

IONA

Miss Lawrence didn't sprain her other ankle to-day, I hope?

NEIL

Now, look here! She really did, last June—at least not the other, but the one.—I mean she really had a sprained ankle last June.

IONA

Did Miss Fallone have a sprained ankle when you carried her home on your pillion yesterday?

NEIL

Now, see here, Iona! Don't let's quarrel. I mayn't be here very long.

IONA

(*Suddenly interested.*) Oh?

NEIL

Yes ... There's a good appointment going vacant quite soon in Sandaig Parish. MacLachlan's leaving.

IONA

And you're applying?

NEIL

I want to. My application's in. My testimonials go in to-morrow. And I'm sure of it, if your father will give me a decent letter.

IONA

And won't father give you one?

NEIL

He's given me a rotten one.

IONA

Oh, what a shame! He's not going to help you then?

NEIL

Well, he gave me an old-fashioned kind of recommendation that's no use. I suggested changing it. He got angry. Then I said things I shouldn't have said. And now he's on his high horse, and declines to alter one word.

IONA

Oh, he'll come all right in two or three days! I know father.

NEIL

But I can't wait two or three days! The testimonials have to be in by Wednesday morning; and this is Monday ... Oh! I *did* rile him badly. And now his Highland pride has got him.

IONA

Couldn't I help?

NEIL

Would you? Oh!—Well—you see—(**HE** *glances apprehensively at the door of* **DR. FRASER**'s *room.*) But it's a long story; and I can't tell you now ... I—I—I say! Could you—could you come down to the garden to-night after I get back from Kellan?

IONA

Oh, I don't know. I—I—might.

NEIL

Ten-fifteen, eh? You could help awfully. Get him to write me something decent. You'll come?

IONA

I'll try.

NEIL

Right-oh! ... At the far hedge at ten-fifteen? Please! Say you will now!

IONA

Oh!—I—! Yes, all right! (**SHE** *nods.*)

NEIL

Bye-bye, then! I'm off to Kellan!
(**HE** *goes out by the door on left but presently pops his head in again.*)
I say! (*Bashfully.*) It's worth £500 a year that parish, with the private practice.

IONA

Oh?

NEIL

Great? Isn't it?
(*His head disappears, but is instantly popped in once more!*) And a free house!

IONA

How—how—interesting!... But—oh! Scoot! Here's father!
(**THEY** *both go off hurriedly at the left as* **DR. FRASER** *enters on the right accompanied by* **MACLAREN**, *a grocer in Torlochan. The latter is a man of sixty, with untidy white beard, and looks of profound wisdom. Indeed nobody could possibly be as wise as* **MACLAREN** *looks.* **HE** *is slow in movement and Highland in speech. Both carry charts in their hands.*

DR. FRASER

Let's compare them.
(**HE** *turns up a book on the table and* **THEY** *place the charts alongside a drawing in the book.*
Yes ... Just as I said ... Nine fathoms at ebb-tide.

MACLAREN

But all the same, I'm not so sure. Are you sure yourself it's the right place?

DR. FRASER

Mr. MacLaren, I'm sure of nothing in this world. But all the probabilities point to that spot.

MACLAREN

All the probabilities point to us having a very poor season with the visitors, if we'll get nothing but sand and stones at the diving, look you.

DR. FRASER

By the by, did you ever hear anything of a diving scheme organised long ago by old Ferguson, my wife's grandfather?

MACLAREN
Well, I may be old, Dr. Fraser; but I'm not so old as all that.

DR. FRASER
Tuts! You *are* touchy. I'm not asking if you knew old Ferguson. I'm asking: did you ever hear of his having been on a treasure-hunt, fifty years ago?

MACLAREN
No, I never heard. He dealt in coals, I understand.

DR. FRASER
Coals? MacLaren, you *do* put things in a very irritating way. What I'm after is old Ferguson's diving scheme, fifty years ago.

MACLAREN
And did he really do some diving? Well, well! And was it for the treasure ship, think you?

DR. FRASER
Man alive, what else would he dive for?

MACLAREN
For coals, maybe.

DR. FRASER
Good Heavens! Who ever *dived* for coals.

MACLAREN
Och, not a bad thing to be diving for, if there's plenty of them, and them sunk. I'm a business-man, you see.

DR. FRASER
Well, you want more than business methods here, MacLaren. Imagination! That's what's needed, if you're after Spanish gold, sir.

MACLAREN
Och, you could have too much imagination.

DR. FRASER
Tuts, man! See here! I've just come across some ancient papers of old Ferguson's among his account-books. You come up to-night after I've got them arranged and I believe I'll be able to shew you something. *(Mysteriously.)* You know, I think our location of the treasure-ship isn't quite right.

MACLAREN
And are you for shifting the diving-hulk?

DR. FRASER
(Nodding still more mysteriously.) You come up to-night. Then you'll see.

MACLAREN

But you'll surely not be for shifting the diving-hulk?

DR. FRASER

We'll go over those papers first of all. For the present I think we should stick where we are. It was at that spot we got this. (HE *takes up the big salver from the cabinet on right.*) And talking of that salver reminds me.—Look at all these precious things lying there unprotected! We should have a strong-room for them. Who knows but we might have a burglary here one of these days?

MACLAREN

And who now would commit a burglary here, with only one steamer calling each day? They'd never get off.

DR. FRASER

And yet, you know, a burglary wouldn't be a bad thing for us—if we got back the stuff. Plenty publicity, eh? "The Morning Post"! "The London Times"! Full of it!

MACLAREN

Aye, if we got the stuff back, it would do us good; all that advertising free, as you might say.

DR. FRASER

Tuts! But I'm nervous. There's no fear of a burglary. (*Taking up the salver again.*) A fine year for publicity when we got this. 1920 that was!

MACLAREN

Aye! We were crowded out with visitors that year. Man! I was cleared out of tinned fruit in three days that summer, once the tourists started coming!

DR. FRASER

Yes. It was the picture of this (*Takes up the salver admiringly*) in the London papers that did it. A great year for measles.

MACLAREN

And my Spanish wines went just wonderful! ... Sold out in a week! And then there was not enough Spanish wine left in the whole of Australia for those English people.

DR. FRASER

Yes, but look at us now!

MACLAREN

They're saying there are only twelve visitors at the Hotel this week.

DR. FRASER
And all so confoundedly healthy!

MACLAREN
Well, well! And what *can* we be doing?

DR. FRASER
(*Going over to the cabinet.*) Y'know, I can't get the idea of a strong-room for these things out of my head.

MACLAREN
Ach, you and your burglary! Sit you down, and let us be considering.

DR. FRASER
What is there to consider? The principal attraction here is a back number. There are bathing and golf; but what are they compared to a good-going treasure-hunt? And we want a fillip in the newspapers badly.

MACLAREN
Yes. But I'm seeing the difficulties are very, very great.

DR. FRASER
Couldn't we make some of this stuff do double duty? ... Find it all over again? (HE *waves to the Spanish cabinet.*)

MACLAREN
Is it take it down to the bottom of the sea and bring it up again? Och, no, no! That would not be right.

DR. FRASER
You're very conscientious of a sudden, aren't you?

MACLAREN
Och, that would not be right at all, at all! The people would be comparing the new photographs and the old. And we'd be found out, see you!

DR. FRASER
Quite good, MacLaren! Hadn't thought of that.

MACLAREN
(*Greatly flattered.*) But I have an idea of my own, look you, that is far better.

DR. FRASER
Oh?

MACLAREN
You were talking of strong-rooms and burglaries. Now why could we not be stealing the things ourselves? Then we could be having the fine horoyally in the newspapers. And after that we could be finding the things again.

DR. FRASER

I've got you! A sham burglary? A great idea! Splendid, MacLaren! Splendid!

MACLAREN

(*Preening himself.*) Oh, I have ideas now and then! ... Och, yes!

DR. FRASER

You have, sir! You have! Your plan's splendid! Only we'd better not do it ourselves. Better if we were somewhere else when it occurred, you see. An *alibi*, you understand?

MACLAREN

Yes, yes. We could be down at the Hotel. The very thing! ... But who now could we get to do the stealing?

DR. FRASER

I know! ... Cooney ... He's an accomplished poacher!

MACLAREN

No, no! He's too heavy on the drams.

DR. FRASER

(*Solemnly.*) MacLaren! I'd rather have Cooney with a dram than without a dram. He's always steadier at the diving when he's three sheets in the wind.

MACLAREN

Look you, I'm not caring for Cooney at all, at all.

DR. FRASER

Well, who else is there?

MACLAREN

'Deed, you may well ask. No one that I know of.

DR. FRASER

Cooney it is, then! (**HE** *rings.*) He's coming up presently to talk to me about his diving helmet. I'll see if he's arrived. (**KATIE** *appears.*) Oh, Katie! Has Cooney come yet?

KATIE

He has that, sir. Can you not hear him roaring in the kitchen?

(**DR. FRASER** *listens.*)

DR. FRASER

Oh, he's singing, is he?

KATIE

He thinks he is, sir.

DR. FRASER
Oh, send him up then, will you?

KATIE
I will that, and gladly! (**KATIE** *goes.*)

MACLAREN
What did I tell you? He's had a good drop already.

DR. FRASER
Not he. He's always singing.

COONEY'S VOICE
(*Humming outside.*)
"Cecilia was beautiful ...
Cecilia was fair." (**COONEY** *comes in, quite sober.*) Afternoon, gentlemen.

DR. FRASER
Oh, come in, come in, Cooney. I've seen that helmet. Bad ... very bad ... We'll have to get you a brand-new valve. But sit down. We've something to lay before you.

COONEY
(*Looking round.*) Not water, I hope.

DR. FRASER
(*Taking the hint.*) Oh, no. (**HE** *brings out a glass and a decanter of whisky and fills for him.*) Not water ... Now listen carefully, please. Mr. MacLaren here thinks the sunken treasure business needs a little waking-up. Newspaper articles and so on.

COONEY
Roight! What I've been saying mesilf, Doctor.

DR. FRASER
Have a peg, MacLaren?

MACLAREN
Just a wee drop.
(*The* Doctor *brings additional glasses, and* **THEY** *all imbibe.*

DR. FRASER
The question is—how to do it. Any ideas, Cooney?

COONEY
Nary a wan, Doctor. Unless, now—unless ye got a portrait of mesilf and that hilmet into the picture-papers. And big headlines, y'know: "Heroic Doiver Sticks to his Post", "Helmit Leaks, but he Recovers Treasure".

DR. FRASER

Fine, Cooney, fine!

MACLAREN

Very good, indeed, Cooney.

COONEY

(Continuing.) "Generous Directors Raise His Salary." *(A blank silence.)*

DR. FRASER

Ahem!—yes—quite good, Cooney. Have some more. (**HE** *fills* **COONEY**'s *glass.*)

COONEY

Funny thing, now! If I'd lost me loife this morning, it's the great advertoisement ye'd have had.

DR. FRASER

Cooney, Cooney! Don't let us talk of any possibilities so terrible.

MACLAREN

(Slyly.) There are more things than lives that might be lost.

COONEY

D'ye tell me now?

MACLAREN

Och, yes. Many things.—*(Again slyly.)* What do you think, Cooney? (**HE** *drinks.*)

COONEY

I'm past thinking, Mr. MacLaren. (**HE** *also drinks.*) I'm just living, if ye understand me.

DR. FRASER

Isn't he a wag, MacLaren? But, Cooney, what Mr. MacLaren means is that we might lose some of this treasure—see?

COONEY

Indade now, ye'd be safer pawning it.

DR. FRASER

Quite good, Cooney, quite good! But now let's see about this publicity business. (**HE** *points to the cabinet on right.*) Suppose we had some of this treasure stolen, Cooney? We couldn't do better than that, could we now? A great idea, MacLaren!

MACLAREN

Och, I have ideas now and then, Dr. Fraser. (**HE** *preens himself.*)

COONEY

Stolen, did ye say?

DR. FRASER

(*Hurriedly.*) Well, not exactly stolen, Cooney; but Mr. MacLaren had the brilliant idea that if these Spanish things were lifted away for a night or two, just as if they had been stolen—

MACLAREN

(*Regretting his claim for a monopoly of ideas.*) Now, don't be putting it all on my shoulders.

COONEY

Och, I mind ye now, Doctor!

DR. FRASER

Hush!

COONEY

I know! I know, Doctor! Sham burglary. Same as you spoke about yesterday.

MACLAREN

Well, well! And who'd have thought it of you, Dr. Fraser!

DR. FRASER

Tuts! Didn't *you* plan this yourself?

MACLAREN

I did that! But were you not leading me on to it, with your talk of strong-rooms and burglaries to be guarded against? Ach!

(**THEY** *glare at each other.*)

COONEY

Och, never mind! Sure, 'twas the same tailor made ye both ... Well, well! ... And ye'll want me to do the dirty work, av coorse?

DR. FRASER

If you'll kindly assist, Cooney.

COONEY

I'm game. Foive Jimmies, ye said yesterday.

DR. FRASER

(*Drawing out some notes.*) Yes, five.

COONEY

(*Taking the notes.*)
"Foive ye say, and foive it is,
   And then ye git another fizz."
(**HE** *has another drink.*) And it'll be foive for his nabs as well.

MACLAREN

Indeed then, and I'll not give you one penny.

COONEY

Then, sir, we cannot float this Honourable Burglary Syndicate.

DR. FRASER

Here, Cooney! (HE *pulls out other five pounds.*)—I'll pay meanwhile, and settle—at least I hope so—with Mr. MacLaren later ... Let's get down to business!

COONEY

Roight-oh, Doctor. Fire ahead.

DR. FRASER

The sooner the better, I suppose.

COONEY

To-noight's the noight. There's a full moon.

DR. FRASER

See here! I'll leave the front-door open—

MACLAREN

No, no. Be locking that. The window here would be far better.

COONEY

But we'll need a ladder for the window.

DR. FRASER

Right! The window be it. This one, eh? (HE *indicates the window on right.* COONEY *nods.*) I'll leave it open. Then I'll get the ladder from the tool-shed and hide it in the shrubbery.

COONEY

And what time now will the house be quiet, wud ye say?

DR. FRASER

Our people retire early—about ten. Say ten-fifteen?

COONEY

I'll be there on the very tick av it.

DR. FRASER

Ten-fifteen then, eh, MacLaren? (MACLAREN *nods.*) But we'd best get it exact. (HE *takes out his watch.*) Let's set our watches ... Or no! You wait in the road below the garden, Cooney, till you see the lights go out here. Give yourself five minutes more. Then get to work.

COONEY

Roight, sir, roight!

DR. FRASER

I'll leave the ladder among these bushes under the window here. (HE *goes to the window and points.*)

MACLAREN

(*Bitterly.*) And there will be a full moon for everybody to see Cooney on that same ladder! We'd forgotten that!

DR. FRASER

(*Angrily.*) Tuts, man! Who's likely to be on the roads after ten, round a quiet place like this house?

COONEY

No wan, av coorse, save a couple or two av swatehearts, maybe. And the Lord knows they'll see nothing in the woide wurrld but thimsilves!

MACLAREN

Well, well, have it your own way!

DR. FRASER

That's settled then. The lights out — then the ladder — then the window! And here's the stuff. (*Indicating the cabinet on right.*) A couple of sacks and some straw — and off you go.

MACLAREN

And where now is he to be taking it?

DR. FRASER

To his own house, of course. Where else?

MACLAREN

But they'll be searching —

DR. FRASER

Of course, of course! But Cooney will discover it in a peat-cutting or out on the hillside, don't you see, as soon as the police get busy, and before they ever get the length of searching his house.

MACLAREN

Och! Is that the way of it?

DR. FRASER

Yes. That's the way of it. You've no objections, Cooney? *Your* house, so far as I'm concerned, is as safe's the Bank. (HE *gives* COONEY *his hand.*)

COONEY

Thank ye koindly, sir.

MACLAREN

(*Warningly.*) And no drams, look you, Cooney!

COONEY

(In mock horror.) Drams? Mr. MacLaren! On a serious occasion such as this!

DR. FRASER

There, there, Cooney! Never heed him! (**HE** *claps* **COONEY** *on the back and appeases him.*) So that's settled. You'll take the things home. We can arrange about the finding of them later on.

COONEY

Very good, Doctor.

DR. FRASER

(Elated, and rubbing his hands.) And now, I think, we'll get some really good publicity out of this. Torlochan has been going to the dogs for want of publicity, and now we'll have loads of it ... All right, Cooney! Ten-fifteen—after the lights go out! (**HE** *gives* **COONEY** *his hand again.*)

COONEY

(Taking it, and MacLaren's also.) Roight, Doctor! ... Gintlemin! Proudest moment in me loife! ... The Torlochan Burglary Syndicate is now floated!

CURTAIN

ACT II

SCENE.—*The sitting-room at* DR. FRASER'S. *Monday evening. The heavy curtains of the window are open, and moonlight floods the room.* IONA, *rapt in contemplation of the beauty of the night, is kneeling on the window-seat and looking out over the roofs of the little town to the quiet waters of the Bay.* KATIE *comes in and lights the lamp.*

KATIE

Mrs. Fraser is coming up, Miss Iona.

IONA

All right, Katie.

(SHE *rises and goes to the table to get a book, while* KATIE *pulls the heavy curtains across and retires.* IONA *sits down to read.* MRS. FRASER *enters and, taking up her knitting, sits by the fire.*

MRS. FRASER

Ye havena tellt me yet whaur ye were after tea, Iona.

IONA

Oh, nowhere. Just out on the headland.

MRS. FRASER

A' by yer lanesome?

IONA

Yes. I have decided to commune with Nature more.

MRS. FRASER

Commune wi' Nature? Then it's serious this time!

IONA

Whatever do you mean, mother?

MRS. FRASER

And ye're really fond o' him, then?

IONA

I'm not talking of him, whoever him may be. I'm talking of Nature with a capital N.

MRS. FRASER

And I'm talking o' Him, wi' a capital H ... Aye, and ye'd be looking at the sinking sun and the wide sea, and sighing yer heart oot, eh?

IONA

(*Nestling to her.*) Mother! You're a witch!

MRS. FRASER

(*Kissing her.*) And he's said naething as yet, has he?

(IONA *shakes her head, a mist in her eyes.*

MRS. FRASER

Eh, but it's the holy, happy time for ye, lass. Waiting, waiting ... Sus-the-day! ... Puir women-folk ... Waiting.

IONA

Oh, mother! (SHE *snuggles to her again, her eyes now bright.*) I'm almost sure—almost! (*Then after a little while.*) Mother, do you know that Dr. MacDonald's leaving?

MRS. FRASER

Your father said something, but I didna fash. Assistants are ay talking o' leaving, ye ken.

IONA

Yes, but he—he's trying for Sandaig Parish, and I think he has a chance. And oh, mother, there's a—a—a free house. (SHE *buries her face in her mother's bosom.*)

MRS. FRASER

Oh, lassie, lassie! And has it come to this?

IONA

No—nothing's happened, mother—but I think I see signs.

MRS. FRASER

You wee rascal!

IONA

And the trouble is, the poor boy won't have a chance, unless father gives him a different kind of testimonial from the one he's given him.

MRS. FRASER

What's wrong wi't?

IONA

I don't know. But he—Dr. MacDonald—says father's Highland pride's got the upper hand, and he won't alter the letter.

MRS. FRASER

I ken, I ken. He's stubborn—aye!

IONA

And I thought—perhaps—you might—well—get father to soften a bit. You understand.

MRS. FRASER

Oh! What a wee plotter!

IONA

Come now! You can turn him round your little finger, I'm sure.

MRS. FRASER

Hech! I could at wan time, lassie. Nowadays it's a different story. But we could at least try.

IONA

(Joyfully embracing her.) Oh, mother!
(**DR. FRASER** *comes in hurriedly from his room on the right, a white paper of quarto size in his hand.*

DR. FRASER

Margaret, a discovery! You remember the stories of your grandfather's attempt at recovering the Spanish treasure? ... . Well, look at this! I found it among some old books of his, coal accounts and so on.

MRS. FRASER

Whit is't?

DR. FRASER

A chart of the water off the North Pier, I believe! You see the faint outline of a vessel's hull marked there? ... By Jove! I believe he was right, too!

MRS. FRASER

Right?

DR. FRASER

Yes. That hull is the San Felipe. It agrees with some of the old traditions of the place—the older accounts of the sinking, you know. Off the North Pier! ... We've been all wrong in our location.

MRS. FRASER

There was wan o' his coal boats sunk in the Bay in his time, I've heard.

DR. FRASER

Oh! You Lowlanders! Have you no imagination, Margaret?

MRS. FRASER

Weel? He *did* dale in coal, ye ken?

DR. FRASER

Margaret! Let's have a soul above commerce! Remember that your husband, at least, is Highland.

IONA

Now, father! Don't you go bullying mother!

DR. FRASER

Iona!

MRS. FRASER

Tuts, lass! Let him hae his fling!

DR. FRASER

Coals! ... Coals! ... And yet —
" Full fathom five thy father lies;
Of his bones are coral made " —
and you go talking of coals! Have you no poetry in you at all, you women-folk?

MRS. FRASER

Poetry? Plenty! We're communing wi' Nature every day ... Are we no', Iona?

DR. FRASER

(Testily.) Tuts! Look here, both of you ... See this? S-A-N for San, F — for Felipe: San Felipe ... And isn't that writing the same as on this? (HE *produces an old bill of lading.)* Your grandfather's writing on both? ... It's his idea of where the San Felipe lay.

MRS. FRASER

(Smiling broadly.) Weel, hae it yer ain way, John.

IONA

Mother! I'd not give in to him.

DR. FRASER

She can't do anything else with these before her eyes. (HE *flourishes the papers.)* San F ... The San Felipe without a doubt! ... We'll have a try at her. And then you'll see!

(HE *busies himself over the chart.* MRS. FRASER *makes some preparatory movements to the attack.*

MRS. FRASER

John.

DR. FRASER

Well?

MRS. FRASER

You were saying the other day that Dr. MacDonald was thinking of leaving.

DR. FRASER

I did.

MRS. FRASER

And where will he be going, I wonder?

DR. FRASER
Oh! the Lord knows!

MRS. FRASER
I'm sure *He* does. But do you know?

DR. FRASER
(Testily.) Well, he's trying for Sandaig Parish.

MRS. FRASER
Indeed. A guid place, I hear. And I hope he'll get it.

DR. FRASER
In other words, you hope I'll lose my assistant.

MRS. FRASER
Young folk will ay be steering, ye ken.

DR. FRASER
Well, he'd steer better if he'd mend his manners.

MRS. FRASER
He's ay been a staid, proper lad as far as I could ever see.

DR. FRASER
He practically called me an old fossil this morning ... An old fossil—huh!

IONA
I'm sure he didn't, father. He wouldn't say a thing like that.

DR. FRASER
Oh! And are you also on his side?

IONA
I'm on both your sides, father.

DR. FRASER
Indeed! Then perhaps you or your mother will make out a testimonial that will please this pretty boy. Mine won't.

MRS. FRASER
It maun hae been gey bad.

DR. FRASER
(Bouncing round.) What?

MRS. FRASER
The testimonial.

DR. FRASER
Now, look here. If you give a man a letter cracking him up no end, and he comes and says you've overdone it, what would you do? Tell him to go to blazes, wouldn't you?

MRS. FRASER

Never, John. I've a strong objection to such language, even in the mouth of a husband.

DR. FRASER

I'm not going to be dictated to by a whipper-snapper who thinks me an old fossil. Am I a fossil, Margaret?

MRS. FRASER

If ye gang on hardening your heart as ye're doing, there's nae saying what ye micht become.

IONA

Hear, hear, mother!

DR. FRASER

Now, understand this, you women—!

IONA

Your bed-time, mother. Come away. I won't have him browbeating you.

MRS. FRASER

Oh! let him be! He's ay up to some nonsense! He's Highland, ye ken.

IONA

But it's ten o'clock, mother!

MRS. FRASER

And wha's the bully noo, I wunner? Weel, weel, I'll be going. (SHE *picks up her knitting things.*)

KATIE

(Opening the door on left.) Mr. MacLaren, sir.

DR. FRASER

Yes, yes! Come in, MacLaren. Oh, Margaret! Mr. MacLaren and I have some business at the Hotel tonight.

(**MACLAREN** *enters and greets the* **LADIES**.

MRS. FRASER

We were just going, Mr. MacLaren. You'll excuse us.

DR. FRASER

(Hurriedly.) Yes, yes. We'll excuse you. I'll just show Mr. MacLaren this new discovery, and then we'll be at the Hotel till eleven, Margaret. And if there's anything urgent, just send for me there. Dr. MacDonald's down country, at Kellan, and won't be back till late, you understand?

MRS. FRASER

I understand fine, John. Good-night, Mr. MacLaren.

IONA

Good-night, Mr. MacLaren.

MACLAREN

Good-night. Good-night.

IONA

Good-night, father. (**SHE** *kisses him.*) Again! (**SHE** *kisses him once more.*)

DR. FRASER

(*Surprised at the second kiss.*) Aha! What's all this fuss about, eh?

IONA

Oh, father, I'm so happy!

DR. FRASER

Eh? Tut-tut! Wee Iona!

IONA

Oh, I'm not wee now, father. See! (**SHE** *stands back to back with him and then turns merrily.*) I'm growing up, y'know. Aha!

(**SHE** *kisses him again and goes out after her mother.*)

DR. FRASER

(*Pensively.*) Grown up? Yes. Wee Iona! I've been forgetting the growing up! (**MACLAREN** *coughs.*)

DR. FRASER

Ah, there you are, MacLaren! ... Well, I've something to show you. Something of importance.

MACLAREN

(*Sighing.*) No more burglaries, I'm hoping.

DR. FRASER

No, no. This burglary business is a mere flash in the pan. We want something of permanent interest ... And I've got it, sir!

MACLAREN

Indeed?

DR. FRASER

See here! (**HE** *fumbles among his papers.*)

MACLAREN

And what now, I wonder?

DR. FRASER

It's this! Are you really sure we're at the right spot for that treasure-ship?

MACLAREN

'Deed, Doctor, sometimes I'm not sure that there ever was any treasure-ship, at all, at all.

DR. FRASER

Nonsense! *(Triumphantly placing the newly-discovered drawing before him.)* What do you make of that?

MACLAREN

Well, I couldna say just right off.

DR. FRASER

That, I believe, represents the real position of the San Felipe. I found it among old Ferguson's papers, as I told you.

MACLAREN

Well, well! So you were saying ... This will be a pier here, I'm seeing?
(HE scrutinizes the drawing.

DR. FRASER

Yes. The North Pier. She lies about 1,000 yards West-South-West of it, I judge.

MACLAREN

Just that! But where are your points of the compass? And there's no plain shore-line marked to tell you where you are. Just a pier and a hull and some figures!

DR. FRASER

And what else could it be but the North Pier?

MACLAREN

The South Pier, of course. *(HE turns the paper round.)* And she'd be lying about 1,000 yards East-North-East from it.

DR. FRASER

But, observe—

MACLAREN

I'm observing! Och, yes, I'm observing! And that will be nice and handy to your chemist's shop, Dr. Fraser?

DR. FRASER

Mr. MacLaren!

MACLAREN

Och, yes, yes! And the ladies will be going down to the North Pier to watch the diver! And they'll be passing your window, full of the bottles of lavender water and the face-puffs, and what not!

DR. FRASER

Mr. MacLaren, you have a commercial mind!

MACLAREN

I have that—'deed, yes—I have that, if I have anything. And I'm thinking that galleon went down off the South Pier—look you! Close by my own shop-windows that have plenty of the bottles of good wines and spirits in them ... not to speak of the fine groceries generally.

DR. FRASER

MacLaren, this is not a joke!

MACLAREN

It is not, indeed! ... I'm seeing that well enough! There's money in it ... And let me tell you, the pickles and the chutney in my windows are as much in need of a sale as the face-powder and the scent-bottles in yours.

DR. FRASER

I say that all the evidence points to the man who made that drawing making it in the usual way, with the top of his paper to the North. That is the North Pier without a doubt!

MACLAREN

And I'm saying that galleon sank off the South Pier.

DR. FRASER

It was the North, sir!

MACLAREN

It was the South, I'm telling you!

DR. FRASER

The North!

MACLAREN

The South!

DR. FRASER

What a man! Let me read you what Froude says about the San Felipe.

MACLAREN

Read away as much as you like. I'm seeing fine it was the South Pier.

DR. FRASER

But let me shew you this passage—

MACLAREN

I'll look at no passage. We'll just be going on with what we're here for to-night.

DR. FRASER
But, man alive! can't you see—?

MACLAREN
I can see you're taking too big a hand in this business, Dr. Fraser. And at the next meeting of the Syndicate I'll have something to say.

DR. FRASER
Yes, say that the two Directors have planned a sham burglary to boost the diving-scheme! Tell them that, eh?

MACLAREN
Och, I'm not a fool.

DR. FRASER
No, MacLaren, you are not. Neither am I, I hope. And therefore, I think we should explore this business of that old hulk off the North Pier.

MACLAREN
I'm thinking that ship went down off the South Pier.

DR. FRASER
(*Shutting book with a bang.*) Well, we'll have to leave it at that. (HE *looks at his watch.*) Quarter-past ten. We're due at the Hotel now. And Cooney will be waiting for us to go.
    (HE *puts out the lamp, draws the heavy curtain from the windows, and instantly full bright moonlight floods the room. He raises the lower sash of the window.* MACLAREN *advances to it and listens. A whistle is heard.*)

MACLAREN
I thought I heard a whistle. (*The whistle is heard again.*)

DR. FRASER
Yes, there it is. He's signalling he's ready. Let us go.
    (*They go out by the door on the left. As they do so,* IONA *steals in on the right and listens. There are sounds of the closing of the main door downstairs, and of a heavy key turned in its lock.* IONA *looks disappointed, then goes to the open window and waves her handkerchief.*)

IONA
Neil! ... Hush! ... Wait!
    (SHE *listens again for the sounds of her father's departure, then speaks at the window.*) Oh, I say! How awkward! I can't get down. Father has locked up, and taken the key.

NEIL'S VOICE
(*Outside.*) All right. He's gone anyway. No one can hear us on this side of the house.

IONA

Oh, not so loud, please! Whatever are you doing in the bushes there?

NEIL'S VOICE

Great luck. I've found a ladder!

IONA

A ladder?

NEIL'S VOICE

Yes. I'll set it up. Then you'll see!
(*The top of ladder appears at the window, and immediately thereafter,* **NEIL** *puts a leg over the sill of window and sits there, half in, half out, his left foot resting on the window-seat.*

NEIL

How's that, umpire?

IONA

Not out anyway. But I'd rather you were.

NEIL

Nonsense! It's only me! ... And if your father will lock up at impossible hours, we can't help it, can we? ... Come and sit here.

IONA

(*Sitting on the window-seat, close to him.*) What a lovely night! Did you have a good run home?

NEIL

Ripping! My old 'bus just scorched up the coast like lightning. And the water like a dream! Silver and ebony, y'know. And only one wee sail on it, black against the moon.

IONA

Oh! I'd love to have been there!

NEIL

Isn't this gorgeous? Kind of a Shakespeare night. "Midsummer Night's Dream"—"Romeo and Juliet"— and all that, eh?
(**IONA** *slowly moves off to the table, turns over books aimlessly and picks up the chart.*) Oh, I say! You're not going, are you?

IONA

Oh, no—but—I—I—just wanted a look at this old chart. (**SHE** *moves towards the firelight.*)

NEIL

Oh, never mind the old chart!

IONA

But—it's a fresh discovery of father's—a new location for the treasure-ship.

NEIL

Oh, he's always making fresh discoveries!—But, I say, I can't talk if you keep wandering round.

(**SHE** *puts down the chart on the table and comes back to the window-seat.*

IONA

Will that do?

NEIL

(*Awkwardly.*) Yes, fine! ... But look here, Iona, I— I—Oh! I'll just have to say it by wireless. (**HE** *seizes her hand and kisses it.*) There!

(**IONA** *hides her face in her hands.*) What! You're not crying, are you? Juliet didn't cry, y'know.

IONA

(*Looking up happily.*) Oh, Neil!

NEIL

Iona! (**HE** *kisses her on the lips.*) It's all right, isn't it, about you and me? ... Love and all that, eh? I knew all along that it would come true!

IONA

Funny old Romeo! Say your speech now like a good boy.

NEIL

Haven't got any, dear. You and I. That's all! Oh, blow Romeo! Blow Juliet! What did they know about it!

IONA

And just think! It has happened to us! *I* never thought it could come true!

NEIL

My dear!

IONA

Of course, I knew it happened to people—people out in the world. I knew that all along. But I never dreamed it could come true for Iona Fraser.

NEIL

And I was always sure it must happen. For me, I mean. And I wanted it to happen, gloriously; better than for anybody anywhere at any time! And it has!

IONA
Ah!

NEIL
And I often wondered who it was to be. And you were passing me every day, and yet I never guessed!

IONA
Yes, yes. But, it's all so splendid in that waiting-time ... before you know.

NEIL
And now! (*HE kisses her again.*) Iona!

IONA
My dear one! But, Neil, don't let's eat it all up at once!

NEIL
Eat what, you wonder?

IONA
Our happiness. Let's keep some for again.

NEIL
Oh, come now!

IONA
Be sensible. What about business?

NEIL
Business?

IONA
Yes, the Sandaig business—the appointment. And— oh, Neil—the—the—the free house.

NEIL
Yes, and quite a good house too; although McLachlan has spoiled it with that hen-farm of his.

IONA
A hen-farm?

NEIL
Yes, just behind the garden.

IONA
Oh, I'd like that.

NEIL
Nonsense, Iona! We won't have time for it.

IONA

Yes, but I love hens, Neil ... And there will be loads of time ... What else should I have to do?

NEIL

Well, you know, there's always me to look after.

IONA

Oh, won't it be gorgeous!—looking after you! Just fancy!

NEIL

You dear!

IONA

But couldn't we have some chickens, Neil? They're just lovely, aren't they—chickens?

NEIL

But they'll grow up into scraggy old hens, and go cluck-clucking all round the place. I shouldn't be able to study, dear. Really.

IONA

Oh, very well! (SHE *becomes moody.*) We'll just have to do without, I suppose.

NEIL

Now, look here, Iona, I don't want to refuse you anything; but—

IONA

(*Tragically.*)—Yet all the same, you refuse the first thing I ask you, as part of our wedded life!

NEIL

No; by Jove! I can't do that! Have your chickens by all means.

IONA

But they're really not important.

NEIL

(*Decisively.*) You *shall* have those chickens, Iona.

IONA

What a determined fellow you are, Neil. I must just give in, I see.

NEIL

Thank you, dear. I think you'll find I'm right after all.

IONA

(*With a sigh of satisfaction.*) So that's that! And now, let's get down to real business—the testimonial.

NEIL

Wise little puss! ... But, I say! How wonderful your hair is in the moonlight!

IONA

Business first, please ... And moonlight afterwards.

NEIL

But Iona—!

IONA

No, no! Let's get down to hard tacks. What about that testimonial? We'll have to be sensible.

NEIL

(*Drawing out a paper from his pocket.*) Heigh-ho! Down with a bump! ... Here's the old thing.
 (**HE** *opens out the paper and, taking her arm, leads her to the fireplace.*

IONA

What does he say?

NEIL

He says a darned sight too much! He's going to ruin me, if he won't alter this.

IONA

Oh! I'm sure father wouldn't say a single syllable against you!

NEIL

No. The trouble is he says several thousand syllables too many for me ... Just read that!

IONA

Please, sir, Juliet can't read. Her eyes are wet.

NEIL

You rogue! I'll read it to you. (**HE** *reads.*)
" I have much pleasure in testifying to the high qualifications of Dr. Neil MacDonald.
For the past two summers he has acted as assistant to me in Torlochan, a district much frequented by tourists because of the sunken treasure-ship of the Great Armada, on which diving operations are still being prosecuted with increasing success." ...

IONA

Poor old dad! He never misses a chance, does he? Go on.

NEIL

Oh, well! (**HE** *reads again.*)

" I can heartily support Dr. MacDonald in his application. His name betokens his descent from the great House of Somerled; and from close association with him, I have every reason to believe that he is noble by nature as well as by birth."

IONA

Doesn't he lay it on!

NEIL

There are miles more of this. (**HE** *sighs resignedly and continues reading.*)
" He is a courteous colleague and a skilled doctor; and if he is successful in his application, while I shall rejoice in his good fortune, I shall deplore the loss of an assistant whom I have found it necessary to engage, consequent upon the unparalleled discoveries in connection with the Spanish treasure-galleon asleep beneath the blue waters of the historic bay of Torlochan.
John Fraser, M.D."
Did you ever?

IONA

Yes. But how splendid all that about you!

NEIL

Don't you know Sandaig? All the Members of that Council are red-hot Labour men—Bolsheviks!

IONA

Well?

NEIL

And so I must be set down as a 'lad o' pairts.' ... Deadly struggle in my youth, and all that ... You'll get your father to change this, won't you?

IONA

I'll try; but father's queer.—And then, you see, it's all quite true!

NEIL

Look here! You really love me?

IONA

Oh, Neil!

NEIL

Well then, prove it. Get him to write me something that will really help.

IONA

All right! That's that! (**SHE** *takes the testimonial from him and tucks it into his breast pocket.*) Let's put this out of sight now.

NEIL

And when we're settled down at Sandaig, we'll get your father to give up all this treasure-ship nonsense, eh?

IONA

Splendid! ... Oh, Neil! Just fancy. Sandaig and a free house!

NEIL

Isn't it wonderful? You and me!

IONA

Oh! I'll never understand—never! ... It's all so good.

(A murmur of voices outside.

NEIL

What's that noise? Somebody's in the bushes down there!

IONA

Who can it be? Come in here!

(THEY go behind the curtain on the right.

COONEY'S VOICE

(muffled tones.) "Cecilia was beautiful, Cecilia was fai—ai—air." Where's that blooming ladder that he said he'd lave? ... Och, here it is! And the window open too! Ahoy, MacIver! Hould the ladder stiddy, and up I goes.

(The head of COONEY appears above the window-sill.

COONEY

Hould it stiddy, MacIver! For I've no skill of climbing ladders if I'm not doiving ... no skill on dry land at all, at all, so I have nutt. Watther's me illimint ... except when I'm drinking, ye'll understand.

(HE enters the room; and MACIVER's face appears above the sill in turn. NEIL and IONA have disappeared behind the curtains on the right, but peep out now and again.)

MACIVER

Get you to your work now! Have you the sack?

COONEY

I have that! But do ye obsarve? ... The Doctor hasn't left me wan drop av drink. *(HE takes up an empty decanter from the table.)*

MACIVER

Hurry now!

COONEY

I'm hurrying all I know, without a taste of the crater ... "Cooney," says the Doctor, "this is a sham burglary." And to-morrow I'll till him it was well-named; for there wasn't wan drop of drink to it. Sham's the name for it, roight enough.

MACIVER
Hurry now! And I'll get down and watch the garden.

COONEY
And that ould scut, MacLaren, wasn't for paying me!

MACIVER
Hurry, man!
> (*His head disappears.* COONEY *comes forward unsteadily to the revolving chair, sits down in it, lights his pipe and looks round. The curtain on the cabinet on left being partially withdrawn, the moonlight falls on its contents.* HE *gets up heavily, goes to it and piles the pewter in a heap on the floor.* MACIVER's *head reappears above the window-sill.*

Will you make haste, now? Och, och! And will you look at that! You've got the wrong stuff. It's the stuff in the cabinet on your right, we're wanting.

COONEY
> (*Who is facing front, holds up his right hand in foolish fashion, as if to guide himself, says — "Roight!" — and going to the cabinet on right, piles the Spanish relics in a second heap on the floor.*

Me roight! Will, will, MacIver! Mistakes will happen in the best-regulated burglaries. Get ye down, boy, and watch.
> (MACIVER, *satisfied the other is at work on the proper stuff, disappears.* COONEY *sits down, and lights his pipe once more, singing "Cecilia" now and again between puffs. Soon* HE *discovers the properties of the revolving chair, and in childish fashion has several rides on it to his huge delight. Then suddenly coming to himself* HE *puts up his right hand again, and says —*

On me roight!
> (*But as the revolving chair has stopped with him facing the rear this time, his right hand indicates the heap of pewter as his proper spoil.* HE *stuffs it into the sack, staggers round for a bit and leaves the sack with pewter at the window. Then, coming back, he solemnly and in silence, carefully stows the Spanish relics into the cabinet on left — the wrong one — and draws the curtain over them.* HE *sits down in the chair again, and once more lights up.* MACIVER's *head reappears above the window-sill and* HE *comes in.*

MACIVER
Are you never coming at all, at all?
> (MACIVER *surveys the empty Spanish cabinet on the right, and satisfied that all is well, lifts the sack and subsides out of sight.*

COONEY
> (*Coming to the window, attempts to get on to the ladder, but fails.*) Funny things ladders, MacIver. I find them a dale aisier in the watther, ye'll understand. Can't balance on this at all, at all.

MACIVER

Come you down now, like a good man!

COONEY

(*His eye catching sight of the diver's helmet,* **HE** *has an inspiration.*) Bedad! I kin balance wid this on me head! (**HE** *assumes the helmet, and so accoutred, disappears, humming "Cecilia."*)
    (**NEIL** *and* **IONA** *emerge from behind the curtain on right, and look out of the window cautiously.*

NEIL

Did you hear? A sham burglary!

IONA

Yes. Isn't father the limit? Whatever shall we do?

NEIL

Do? We can do nothing! ... Oh! I'm sick of all this trickery!

IONA

He *is* a funny old father! But he's not half bad ... And anyway, he's Iona's father, isn't he?

NEIL

You dear! (*Then suddenly.*) Tell you what—! Yes, I'll do it!

IONA

Do what, Neil?

NEIL

I'll threaten to expose this faked burglary unless he gives me a decent testimonial.

IONA

Oh! But do you think that would be fair? Besides, he'll want to know—

NEIL

What I was doing here? Well, I'll tell him I've come to carry off Iona Fraser! ... And I'll write out a proper letter now, and get him to sign it.
    (**HE** *takes a pen and writes on a sheet of white paper of quarto size.*

IONA

Make it short.

NEIL

Right. Short and strong. That's the stuff! (**HE** *writes again.*) How will this do? "I have much pleasure in strongly recommending Dr. Neil MacDonald for the post of Medical Officer, now vacant, at Sandaig. He is a good doctor—knows his work—and does it." There! Now, he'll jolly well put his name to that or I'll know the reason why!

IONA

Poor old dad!

NEIL

Sorry, dear. But it has to be done, if we're to get that free house and those old hens. (HE *reads letter admiringly.*) Y'know, that's a jolly good letter of recommendation ... quite pat!

IONA

Oh, you've got that testimonial on the brain! And you'll mix it and me all up, I'm sure!

NEIL

You rascal! You know I won't ... And now you cut off to bed, while I wait up for father.

IONA

I'll wait too. I'm sure you'll make a mess of it, dear!

NEIL

But, look here, Iona—

IONA

There he is! ... The key in the lock!

NEIL

Now go, please.

IONA

(*Reluctantly.*) Well, I'll go. But I'll wait close by, in case you need me. I'll be listening.

NEIL

No! You mustn't.
(*But* SHE *has gone through the curtain.* NEIL *crosses to the fire and sits down with the testimonial in his hand.* DR. FRASER, *not perceiving him, enters meditatively, glances knowingly at the empty cabinet on the right and at the open window, then nods approvingly.*

NEIL

Good-evening, Dr. Fraser. (HE *holds the paper behind his back.*)

DR. FRASER

(*Starting in surprise.*) Good-evening! Where did you spring from? (HE *crosses to the open window, surveys the ladder, and turns to* NEIL.) Aha! So that's it ... You came in thus, eh? (HE *points to the window.*)

NEIL

I did; and I know everything.

DR. FRASER

(*Starting and turning to him.*) Ah!—indeed—? (HE *lights the lamp on the table, affecting to be quite at his ease.*)

NEIL

Yes, and I have come—

DR. FRASER

(*Interrupting him.*) You have. You have come, my boy. And at an opportune moment. At a time like this, one wants somebody in whom one can confide.

NEIL

Look here! I can't go on with this—

DR. FRASER

(*Surprised.*) Really! Then I will. As I said, this is just the time one feels the need of a confidant. Now look at this! (HE *waves his hand to the open window.*) And this! (HE *waves his hand to the empty cabinet on the right.*) Empty! You see?

NEIL

(*Hotly.*) You don't suggest that I am the thief?

DR. FRASER

Oh, no! I suggest nothing at all. I was just about to explain these—er—phenomena.

NEIL

I can't let you—

DR. FRASER

One moment. You see, we have arranged a little subterfuge here: a sham burglary, in fact; the desired end being not insurance, I may say, but simply a little press publicity.

NEIL

Yes, yes, but—

DR. FRASER

One moment! ... I have had assistants, Dr. MacDonald, to whom I could not have made such a confidence with impunity. But you are not one of those.

NEIL

Dr. Fraser, I protest—

DR. FRASER

One moment! ... Yes, I have known men who, on receipt of such a confession as I now make, would instantly have demanded an increase of salary. But you, sir, are of the race of Somerled—

NEIL

Oh, stow it, please!

DR. FRASER

Well, well! Let us leave it at that ... (HE *turns over the papers on the desk and picks up one.*) Oh, here now is something upon which I'd like your opinion. This is an old map of Torlochan Bay, with the outline of a ship's hull marked on it; also something that looks like a pier. Now would you not say this strongly resembles the North Pier?

NEIL

You'll excuse my not going into that, sir. And you're not going to bluff me with your confidences, and putting me on my honour. I'm not having any.

DR. FRASER

Not having any honour? Surely an unusual use of the Gaelic idiom, is it not?

NEIL

Look here! I've drafted a proper testimonial for myself. (HE *produces the paper.*) And you'll jolly well sign that here and now, or I'll split on your sham burglary, confidences or no confidences. I want it to-night; for the appointment's to be made on Wednesday morning.

IONA

(*Bursting in through the curtain.*) Well, I never! ... You're putting that old testimonial first after all! ... What about me?

NEIL

Sorry, dear! but he rushed me.... Dr. Fraser! I—I— I love Iona!

DR. FRASER

So do I, sir ... so do I. What about it?

NEIL

Well, can't you guess? It means, sir: May I marry your daughter?

IONA

(*Going to her father and patting him, with her arm round his neck.*) Poor old dad!

DR. FRASER

Iona! What does this mean?

IONA

It means, dad: May I marry your assistant?

DR. FRASER

Oh, preposterous! ... Where's your mother? ... Go to your room! ... Are you all mad?

IONA

Now, father, please be good!

DR. FRASER

(*Relenting a little.*) You little fool! Wee Iona! (*Tears are in his eyes now.*)

NEIL

I'm sorry, sir—

DR. FRASER

Then why the devil should you be sorry, with a girl like my Iona?

IONA

(*Gently.*) Hear, hear, father! ... Oh, poor old dad! ... But y'know, it had to come some day.

DR. FRASER

There, there! You've knocked me out, Iona! ... But cut off to bed now; and we'll talk this over in the morning. There now, there now! ... Time you were in bed!

(**IONA** *goes out through the curtain.*

DR. FRASER

Well, sir, I must bid you good-night. We'll talk of this in the morning.

NEIL

You're not turning me down then?

DR. FRASER

I've said we'll talk of this in the morning. The door's locked. I'll let you out. (**HE** *makes for the door on left.*)

NEIL

Thank you! And you'll think of altering that testimonial?

DR. FRASER

Oh, hang that testimonial!

NEIL

But it just comes to this—I'm dead sure of that appointment, if you'll give me a decent letter. And if I get it, I can marry at once.

DR. FRASER

(*Bitterly.*) Well, I'm not dying to see you married at once, am I?

NEIL

No. You're not. You want to keep me on, slaving for you. And you'd sacrifice your own daughter's happiness to gain your ends!

DR. FRASER
Put it whatever way you like, young man. But in any case, I'm not in a hurry to lose Iona.

NEIL
You *will* lose her, as you term it, if you don't consent.

DR. FRASER
I'm afraid I must ask you to go now.

NEIL
But, sir, if that testimonial were altered a little—

DR. FRASER
I'll alter nothing ... nothing. So now will you kindly go?

NEIL
(Hotly.) Not without a decent letter from you!

DR. FRASER
You won't go?

NEIL
No! ... I won't ... See here!—This letter is straight and simple. Says I know my work and do it. ... not much more ... Now you'll sign that at once, or I'll expose this sham burglary of yours; and you'll be in the felons' dock before long.

DR. FRASER
(Slowly and craftily.) Oh! You'd give me away! And then I'd be in the felons' dock! Your prospective father-in-law in the felons' dock, eh?

NEIL
(Staggered.) But—

DR. FRASER
Aha! Checkmate!

NEIL
But you can't—

DR. FRASER
Oh, can't I? You'd steal my daughter and my reputation as well? No, no! ... You can't do both!

NEIL
Steal?. . . Yes ... I'll tell you what I'll steal. Your signature ... That would be forgery, wouldn't it?

DR. FRASER
It would certainly be forgery.

NEIL

Well, here is a new testimonial. Now, you sit down and sign it; or else I'll forge your signature.

(HE *places the testimonial he has drawn up before* DR. FRASER.

DR. FRASER

You wouldn't dare?

NEIL

Yes, I'd dare! And if you give *me* away, you'll see your prospective son-in-law in the felons' dock...

(IONA *steals in furtively. The* DOCTOR *glances at her anxiously but does not say a word to her.*

DR. FRASER

You young devil!

NEIL

There! Sign, man, sign!

IONA

Father, please!

(*The* DOCTOR *sits down slowly, signs and rises wrathfully, his mind working furiously. He walks towards the fireplace brooding; the others watching him.* IONA *draws to the table and takes up the paper of quarto size her father has signed and reads it over.* DR. FRASER *paces back to the table, still brooding, hesitates a moment, dives at the sheet of quarto size he sees there — the wrong one — the chart of the location of the* SAN F., *tears it into four, and casts it on the floor.*

DR. FRASER

No, I'll be damned if I do!

(HE *dashes out by the curtained doorway.*

IONA

Why, he's torn up the wrong paper.

NEIL

What?

IONA

He's torn up the chart! (SHE *gives him the paper which* DR. FRASER *has signed and which was safe in her hands when* HE *tore up the wrong paper.*) Here's your old testimonial at last.

CURTAIN

ACT III

SCENE—*The sitting-room at* DR. FRASER'S. *Tuesday morning.* DR. FRASER *is busy writing at his table when* KATIE *ushers in* MACLAREN.

KATIE
Mr. MacLaren, sir. (SHE *goes out.*)
(DR. FRASER *points to the empty cabinet and winks at* MACLAREN.

MACLAREN
Yes, yes! I see, I see! But have you heard no news?

DR. FRASER
Man alive! what would I hear? I haven't been over the door-step this morning. You're as nervous as a cat!

MACLAREN
'Deed, yes; I'm not used to burglaries! ... But have you heard no news?

DR. FRASER
(*Testily.*) No. Have you?

MACLAREN
Well, I happened to pass the Police Station this morning early.

DR. FRASER
And what of that?

MACLAREN
There was a crowd of small children underneath one of yon cell-windows with the iron bars on them. And somebody was singing as if he had been taken in drink.

DR. FRASER
No new thing in Torlochan.

MACLAREN
Yes. But it was Cooney's voice—look you!—singing yon song about Cecilia.

DR. FRASER
Cooney! In jail!

MACLAREN
Och, yes, in jail, right enough.

DR. FRASER
But this is serious, MacLaren. He'll give us away! I wonder what has happened to that Spanish stuff?

MACLAREN
With the way he is this morning, he might well have made a bonfire of it last night.

DR. FRASER

Tuts, man! you always look on the black side of things. But it is certainly strange that Sergeant Campbell said nothing to me about Cooney this morning.

MACLAREN

Oh? And have you had the Sergeant here?

DR. FRASER

Yes, but he only made some notes. He's sending the Constable up later on. I've offered a reward, and the Sergeant is having bills printed about it.

MACLAREN

A reward?

DR. FRASER

Oh, you needn't be alarmed. It's a personal offer: twenty pounds. I'm sending this telegram about the burglary to the newspapers. (HE *lifts a telegraph form.*) And, of course, I mention the reward in it.

MACLAREN

Twenty pounds?

DR. FRASER

Yes ... And I fancy it's safe. Cooney would get the stuff properly hid, I imagine; then a celebration after it was all over, eh?

MACLAREN

'Deed, yes—if he did not celebrate before he began to hide it ... It's a big reward, look you.

DR. FRASER

All the more publicity, don't you see! But that Sergeant is a suspicious kind of chap. Fancy! He wouldn't do a thing about the bills until I put the money in his hand.

MACLAREN

I'm seeing he's a business man, and not strong on imagination ... Yes, yes, a wise man ... But what are we to be doing about Cooney?

DR. FRASER

Look here! I'm tired of Cooney. He's no use ... Now, you told me some days ago that MacCormack was still hanging around the town?

MACLAREN

He is that. And a better diver than Cooney, I always said.

DR. FRASER

Here's our chance then, with Cooney laid by the heels. Let's have MacCormack back at the diving instead of him.

MACLAREN

There's sense in that!

DR. FRASER

And why not try him at this new spot—off the North Pier? (HE *looks over his table*). Where's that sketch of old Ferguson's? (HE *goes over his papers.*)

MACLAREN

Off the South Pier, I am thinking.

DR. FRASER

Well, let's try both locations.

MACLAREN

We could well do that.

DR. FRASER

Then let's get to work, and stir things up, or we'll all be ruined! We'll try the North Pier first.

MACLAREN

Och, I'm not so sure of your North Pier.

DR. FRASER

Well, let's toss for it. (HE *spins a coin.*)

MACLAREN

Heads!

DR. FRASER

Tails! It's the North Pier then, first of all.

MACLAREN

(*Rising.*) Och, I'm sure the South would be far better!

DR. FRASER

Wait! Are you going? I'll just write a note to Inglis, and tell him to shift his moorings. I've indicated the spot to him already. (HE *writes a brief note.*) And would you mind sending off a boat to him with this?

MACLAREN

I will, surely. But I'm not so sure of your North Pier, look you.
(*he takes the note and passes reluctantly towards the door as* KATIE *opens it.* MACLAREN *goes out as* MRS. MANSON *and* MISS FALLONE *enter.*)

KATIE

Mrs. Manson, sir!

DR. FRASER

(Sotto voce.) Oh! hang Mrs. Manson. *(Then aloud.)* Ah! Good-morning, Mrs. Manson.... And Miss Fallone. An unexpected pleasure ... Won't you sit down?

MRS. MANSON

So early to disturb you, Doctor! (THEY *sit.*)

DR. FRASER

Not at all, not at all. The morning rush is over ... At least, I hope so!

MRS. MANSON

What a busy man! ... Well, I suppose you've heard? ... Poor Mr. Cooney!

DR. FRASER

What has he been up to next? ... Have you come about him?

MRS. MANSON

Well, not exactly about him. About something else in fact... But we met that nice Mr. Lawrence who is at our Hotel; and he asked me to tell you it was all right.

DR. FRASER

I confess I don't understand.

MRS. MANSON

Didn't you know Cooney was in the lock-up?

DR. FRASER

Yes, yes, I knew about that.

MRS. MANSON

Well, Mr. Lawrence has paid his fine, and got him out. We met them on our way here.

DR. FRASER

Oh! Very good of Lawrence, I'm sure.

MRS. MANSON

Of course, Cooney has been foolish.

FANNY

Oh, I hope you won't send Cooney away, Doctor! We've come to plead for him. And even if he was a little tipsy, it was only—What was it Cooney called it, Auntie?

MRS. MANSON

He said that *if* he had taken a drop, it was an act, not a habit!

DR. FRASER

What?

FANNY

An act, not a habit!

DR. FRASER

(Grimly.) Well, of course, Cooney ought to know.

FANNY

Oh, he's such a dear! And I do hope you'll forgive him. Please don't send him away.

MRS. MANSON

You see, we find him so interesting. And just yesterday he said Fanny might go down in his diving-suit, if she got your permission. That's what we've really come about!

DR. FRASER

Oh, Mrs. Manson! Impossible.

MRS. MANSON

Why, she's been up in an aeroplane. And down in a submarine. Done all kinds of things. Now be a good man, Doctor. She's set her heart on it.

DR. FRASER

I'm afraid it can't be done.

MRS. MANSON

Hasn't anyone but the diver ever been down?

DR. FRASER

(Brightening up.) Well, you see, only some of the larger shareholders.

MRS. MANSON

Oh, is that it? (**SHE** *takes out her cheque-book and fountain pen.*) Put me down for fifty pounds' worth more of shares, please!

DR. FRASER

Thanks! I'll just note it ... The papers will be sent on to you in due course. (**HE** *writes.*) "Fifty pounds, Mrs. Manson!" ... And I'll make you out an order. (**HE** *takes another sheet of paper.*) " One descent in diving-suit ... Miss Fallone." ... There! That's put it all right, I fancy!

MRS. MANSON

(Taking voucher.) Thank you!
   (**MRS. FRASER** *and* **IONA** *come in.* **MRS. FRASER** *has one arm affectionately around* **IONA**'s *waist; in her other hand is some knitting.*)

MRS. FRASER

Oh, I didna ken ye had patients, John!

MRS. MANSON

Oh! Good-morning, Mrs. Fraser! *(Greetings all round.)* No, thank goodness! Not patients, are we, Fanny? Just a little business; and that's finished.

IONA

Is the diary here, father? Dr. MacDonald wants to make up the visiting list for Kellan. He's waiting in the garden ... Oh! Here it is! (SHE *takes up a book from the table, and goes to the window.)* Hi! Catch! (SHE *tosses the book out and kisses her hand to* NEIL *below.)*

DR. FRASER

Iona! You tomboy!

FANNY

Such news, Iona! I'm going down in a diving-suit!

IONA

(Sweetly.) That's nothing, dear ... I'm getting married.

MRS. MANSON

Oh, how interesting.

DR. FRASER

Iona! You've no right to say that!

IONA

(Kissing him.) And are all the exciting things to be for the summer visitors only?

DR. FRASER

(Angrily.) Tuts!

MRS. FRASER

Now, Iona!

FANNY

Who is it, dear? Do I know him?

IONA

(Pettishly.) Oh, ask father. (DR. FRASER *turns away fuming.)*

MRS. MANSON

(Seeing a storm brewing.) I think—yes—I think, Fanny, we'll have to hurry off. We've so much to do.
(MISS FALLONE *and* SHE *take their leave with the usual fuss.*

MRS. FRASER

(Resuming her knitting as she sits down.) Iona tell't me last night, John.

DR. FRASER

Look here, Margaret, I've enough of worries, without any more. Here am I reduced to selling descents in diving dresses to summer visitors in order to make a little money! And all you women can think of is getting married.

MRS. FRASER

(Cheerily.) I'm not, John. Never again!

IONA

Now, mother! No hard hitting! (**SHE** *pets her father.*)

MRS. FRASER

Well, now! About Iona and Neil, John.

DR. FRASER

I'll hear nothing about that till times are better. We're going to the dogs, I tell you.

IONA

We are going to a free house!

DR. FRASER

(Unheeding her.) The chief attraction of this place has petered out. And the practice is petering out in consequence.

IONA

But, father—

DR. FRASER

And here you come, talking of marriage. The green flag hasn't been up on the hulk for weeks; and yet I'll wager you've been gossiping all morning about trousseaux and such nonsense!

IONA

Right, father ... you've guessed it ... And, I say, father ... you know something about hens, don't you?

DR. FRASER

Hens?

IONA

Yes. MacLachlan has hundreds at Sandaig. And the loveliest little fluffy chickens.

MRS. FRASER

Iona was thinking o' taking ower Dr. MacLachlan's hens, along with the hoose, John.

DR. FRASER

Now, look here, Margaret. You've got this all cut and dry, I can see. You'll be consulting me about food for the hens next, I suppose, eh?

IONA

Sure, father!

DR. FRASER

Oh, go on talking! Are you both mad? Can't you see we're on the verge of ruin?

MRS. FRASER

According to you, John, we've been for thirty years on that same verge. And it has nae terrors for me nooadays.

IONA

Look here, father! what are your objections to Dr. MacDonald? Straight, now. Out with them.

DR. FRASER

I'm not going to sit here and be catechised by a pack of women!—But if you want to know, I've every objection to Dr. MacDonald!

IONA

Well, I like that!

DR. FRASER

In the first place, he has not sufficient means of livelihood!

MRS. FRASER

But he might have, John, if he gets this new appointment at Sandaig.

DR. FRASER

How can he get it, if he won't send in a testimonial from me?

IONA

Well—but suppose he got it, anyhow.

DR. FRASER

Oh, suppose the moon fell out of the sky! He won't apply unless I give him a fresh testimonial. And he won't get that from me.

MRS. FRASER

Whit wey, John?

DR. FRASER

Because I won't be dictated to by every young whipper-snapper who thinks he knows better than myself what should be in a testimonial.

MRS. FRASER

Hielan' pride again!

DR. FRASER

The right kind of pride, I hope. Not a Lowlander's vanity anyway. Wedding dresses and fluffy chickens, and no money to pay for them! Huh!

MRS. FRASER

No money, John?

DR. FRASER

Well, very little, as long as things are doing so badly at the diving!

IONA

Oh, father! (SHE *goes to the window.*) That poor old hulk! ... Why, where has she got to?

DR. FRASER

(*Following her.*) Who?

IONA

The diving-hulk? She's not there! Oh, yes, she is. Why! they've shifted moorings! She's off the North Pier!

DR. FRASER

Yes, yes. We're trying a new location. (HE *looks over the papers on table.*) Where's that drawing of your grandfather's, Margaret?

IONA

Oh, that! Neil has it.

DR. FRASER

Neil?

IONA

Yes. Dr. MacDonald. We were looking at it this morning.

DR. FRASER

Dr. MacDonald! What's he doing with it? Is he still in the garden?

IONA

(*At the window.*) Yes.

DR. FRASER

Then call him up, please!

IONA

Neil, dear! You've got to come up! (SHE *blows him a kiss.*)

DR. FRASER

Stop those monkey tricks, will you?. . . You presume too much. ... The way you carry on nowadays!

IONA

Carry on? Oh, come now, father!

NEIL

(*At the door.*) You want me, sir?

DR. FRASER

I do. Come in, please. Now who, may I ask, gave you permission to remove any private paper of mine from this table?

IONA

It's the chart with " San F." on it, dear.

NEIL

Oh, that!

(**HE** *draws four pieces of paper out of an inside pocket.*

DR. FRASER

(Taking them.) Who tore this up?

NEIL

Yourself, sir.

DR. FRASER

Myself?

NEIL

Yes, last night. You tore it up and threw it away.

DR. FRASER

Nonsense. I tore up the testimonial you forced me to sign.

NEIL

Oh, no, sir. You tore up this instead.

DR. FRASER

Indeed? And where then is that testimonial? Give it to me.

NEIL

Sorry, sir; it's off.

DR. FRASER

Off?

NEIL

Yes. Posted last night. Had to be in time for tomorrow's meeting of the Parish Council.

DR. FRASER

Off?

NEIL

Yes, sir, off. So am I, sir.

(**HE** *hastens to the door, turns and kisses his hand to* **IONA**—*who returns the compliment.* **HE** *vanishes.*

MRS. FRASER

(*Laughing merrily.*) Oh, John, John, ye're nae match for the young yins. Ye may as weel gi'e in.

DR. FRASER

Give in? Never. I'll show that young scamp! I'll see my lawyer about this. He's practically stolen that testimonial.

IONA

Stolen. Oh, come now, father! You signed it!

DR. FRASER

I did. I signed it—but under duress. My hand was forced. The fact that I tried to tear it up proves that. He's a thief; and I'll expose him. Yes, duress! That's it!

IONA

Father, don't be foolish.

MRS. FRASER

Of coorse, ye could ay ca' Iona in as a witness, John. Make it a family matter, ye ken.

(*This flabbergasts the old fellow.* **IONA** *chuckles.*)

DR. FRASER

What are you sniggering at? Think I won't, eh? (**HE** *gets pen and paper.*) I'll write Thomson in Oban at once.

MRS. FRASER

(*Calmly.*) Get the young one then, John. He's a faur better lawyer than his father.

DR. FRASER

I'll get who I like. (**HE** *goes on writing.*)

MRS. FRASER

(*Smiling.*) Get them baith, John.

DR. FRASER

Oh! do please be quiet, and let me think!

MRS. FRASER

I'm gled you're gaun to do some thinking, John.

IONA

Oh, mother, stop! You're just irritating him.

MRS. FRASER

(*Sharply.*) You haud your tongue, lass. I ken whit's guid for him. Some plain talk frae a Lowlander's whit he's needing!

(*Silence; and* **DR. FRASER** *writes hurriedly. Then.*) When ye've said your say to Mr. Thomson, John, just put in a wee postscript from me to Mrs. Thomson, will ye?

DR. FRASER

Can't you write yourself?

MRS. FRASER

I could. But I thought we might save a stamp. We're on the verge o' ruin, ye ken.

DR. FRASER

(*Getting up.*) Tuts! I'll go to the study ... I'll get some peace there.

MRS. FRASER

Dinna forget the postscript, John.

DR. FRASER

Oh, hang the postscript!

(**HE** *makes for the curtained doorway.*

MRS. FRASER

Just say—(**DR. FRASER** *turns*)—Just say "A Happy New Year to all from all at Torlochan."

DR. FRASER

Are you mad? " A Happy New Year "!—And this is August!

MRS. FRASER

But it'll save a stamp at Christmas, John!

DR. FRASER

Oh, hang Christmas!

IONA

And, father—!

DR. FRASER

(*Turning once more.*) Well, what next?

IONA

Only another postscript from me. Say I am marrying a thief; and the honeymoon will take place in prison, will you?

DR. FRASER

(*Returning.*) Now, look here, you two! You think I'm not in earnest. But I am. Never was more serious in my life—

IONA

(*Interrupting.*) Your tie's all a-squint, father. Let me sort it. (**SHE** *starts fixing it.*)

DR. FRASER

(Struggling away from her.) Never mind the tie. The tie's all right. Now, I want you to understand, Margaret— Tach!

MRS. FRASER

(Rising.) You've nae ideas about ties, lassie. Ye maun loosen it and buckle it ahint. (SHE *takes the tie in hand.)* What was it ye were saying, John? ... I declare!—(SHE *tugs the tie apart)*—If I havena broken it! I maun get ye a new ane.

(SHE *leaves him with the two bits of tie in his hand, gazing helplessly after her,*
as SHE *goes out.*

DR. FRASER

Done on purpose, I do believe!

IONA

Father! How can you say such a thing! And mother helping you!

DR. FRASER

I don't want any tie.

(HE *makes for the curtained doorway again.*

IONA

But if a patient calls, father?

(HE *comes back helplessly and wanders around, his hands behind his back.* And I do think, father, you might meet mother half-way sometimes.

DR. FRASER

Sometimes! Do I ever have a chance of meeting her? I mean—it's she that meets me—yes, that's it, meets me and tramples over me. And you talk of half-way! Tach!

MRS. FRASER

(Entering with needle and thread in hand.) I declare, if ye havena run oot o' black ties! I'll just hae to sew it. (SHE *takes the remnants of tie from him and examines them.)* I wish you'd wear a sensible tie that ties, and no' this made-up trash. Sit doon!

DR. FRASER

(Protesting.) But, Margaret—

MRS. FRASER

Sit doon!

DR. FRASER

Tuts! I'll do without a tie.

IONA

But suppose a patient calls, father?

DR. FRASER
Oh, well! (**HE** *sinks in a chair and proceeds to sew the tie behind his neck.*)

MRS. FRASER
I maun get half-a-dozen new anes this afternoon. Sit still, John!

DR. FRASER
I do wish you'd hurry … I'll miss the post.

MRS. FRASER
And a guid thing, too! Ye'll be glad the morn that ye missed that post.

DR. FRASER
(*Grimly.*) I don't mean to miss it—whatever your desires in the matter may be.

MRS. FRASER
Sit still, John Hielandman! Sit still, man! There, the needle's broken! And be thankfu' it's no' in yer neck, wi' a' yer grumphing! Iona, run up to my room and bring me down my work-basket.

DR. FRASER
(*Ironically.*) Oh! bring the sewing machine when you're at it.
(**IONA** *goes out.*

MRS. FRASER
There's no call for such-like remarks, John, when I'm trying to help you.

DR. FRASER
The question is: Are you trying? But go on—go on! I'll stick it! And then you'll see! I'll get that post if I die for it.

MRS. FRASER
Weel, I'll see that you die in a dacent tie onyway.

DR. FRASER
Oh! I can't stand any more of this!
(**HE** *rises, just as* IONA *enters with a work-basket.*

IONA
Aha! Trying to escape! Come on, father. Get it over.
(*He sits down once more, and after some grunts, as his head is pushed this way and that, Mrs. Fraser knots and snaps her thread.*

MRS. FRASER
There! that's finished! And may you niver hae a patient that's a worse tholer than yersel'.
(**HE** *gets up and shakes himself.*

KATIE

(Opening the door.) Mr. MacIver, sir.
 (**MACIVER** *enters, with his plane and a bit of wood in his hands.*

DR. FRASER

Well? Anything I can do for you?

MACIVER

I was just looking in to finish yesterday's job.

DR. FRASER

Oh, no, MacIver! Oh, no, no! You are under a misapprehension. There is no job for you to finish.

MACIVER

Och, yes, but there is.
 (**HE** *goes coolly over to the window seat and lays down his tools.*

DR. FRASER

MacIver, you were insolent to me yesterday. There is nothing further required of you here.

MACIVER

Then I'll just be settling that bill of yours, if you'll be receipting it.

MRS. FRASER

I think we'll be going, Iona. Guid-day, Mr. MacIver.

MACIVER

Good-day to you, Mrs. Fraser.
(**IONA** *and* **MRS. FRASER** *go out, but the latter leaves her knitting behind her.*
MACIVER *hands over his bill to* **DR. FRASER**, *who gapes in astonishment, but takes the bill, receipts it, and hands it back.*

DR. FRASER

There! Seven pounds, six.

MACIVER

Well, I have a small contra-account here that will just balance it, I'm thinking. I'll be receipting it also.
 (**HE** *takes a pen coolly from the table, and writes across the stamp, then hands the account to the* **DOCTOR**.*)*

DR. FRASER

(Taking it.) What's this?

MACIVER

"To James MacIver, Joiner." That's what it is.

DR. FRASER

I can't read this scribble.

MACIVER

No more a scribble than your own hand of write. (HE *leans over* DR. FRASER's *shoulder and spells out the words to him.*) That's a T. T—O.... To—
"To Assistance at one Burglary, August 14th, Seven Guineas. Paid per contra account. Seven-Six. James MacIver."
(HE *adds a few words with his pen.*) "Balance due—one shilling."

DR. FRASER

(*Falling back in chair.*) MacIver! You—!

MACIVER

(*Cheerily returning to his work.*) No hurry! No hurry, whatever. A shilling's neither here nor there. I can be getting it again.

DR. FRASER

Good Heavens! Did Cooney bring *you* here?

MACIVER

He did that! And well for you he did, or he'd never have got that burglary finished. He was a wee bit overcome, you'll understand, and so was needing some help ... I can be going on with my work now, I suppose?

DR. FRASER

Yes, yes! ... But no, please, MacIver, no! There's a good fellow! Leave it for the present. The afternoon ... Yes, the afternoon.

MACIVER

And for why not now?

DR. FRASER

You see, I'm expecting the police ... an investigation this morning. The Sergeant's been up already. He's sending MacPherson.

MACIVER

Och, is that all?

DR. FRASER

Yes, yes. And you had better not be here ... But —er—MacIver, I suppose Cooney got the stuff off all right?

MACIVER

Och, yes, with my help, he got it off all right.

DR. FRASER

And where did he put it for safety, I wonder?

MACIVER

The Lord alone knows, for I was a wee bit overcome myself! But the last I saw of him, he had the sack of Spanish things on his back, and him asking me who could he get to be taking them to the pawnshop in Oban in the morning.

DR. FRASER

(*Clutching his head.*) Surely not, MacIver! ... Surely not!

MACIVER

Well, believe it or not, but that's the God's truth!

DR. FRASER

Good Heavens! Where can I find him?

MACIVER

Och! it will be all right. Indeed, it might have been worse if I had not been with him.

DR. FRASER

Worse?

MACIVER

Well, you see, he was for stealing the wrong stuff—these things in here.
(**HE** *draws the curtain of the cabinet on left, revealing the Spanish relics displayed there, then goes to the cabinet on right to make sure.*

DR. FRASER

Great Scott! My pewter's gone!

MACIVER

God shield us! ... And did he take the wrong stuff after all?

DR. FRASER

You dolts! ... You fools!

MACIVER

Well, now! that will be a lesson to Cooney to put water in it.

DR. FRASER

Bunglers!

MACIVER

Och, it's sorry I am. And in the circumstances, Doctor, I'll not be saying any more about that shilling.

DR. FRASER

Oh—!

MACIVER

No, no! ... No occasion for thanks at all, at all.

DR. FRASER

(Starting at a sound of voices below.) The police, MacIver! Quick, man! let us get this Spanish stuff concealed! I'll get something to bundle it ... I've reported it stolen! We must hide it ...

(**HE** *goes through the curtain and returns with a green table-cover.* You fellows *have* made a mess of this! My room! ... Quick!

MACIVER

Well, well! Two burglaries in one day!

(**MACIVER** *drags the table-cover over, and packs the salver and other relics into it, adding cushions and rugs as padding and including the half-knitted Shetland shawl and a ball of worsted in his haste.* **HE** *bundles all this up, and transports it to the* **DOCTOR**'s *room, but drops the salver, unnoticed by either, as he does so. Then* **HE** *returns quietly to his work at mending the window-seat. The* **DOCTOR** *sinks exhausted at his table, and his eye falls on the salver, as the sound of voices outside the door is heard.*

DR. FRASER

Quick, MacIver! That salver!

MACIVER

(Turning round.) Och, och! and did I miss it?

DR. FRASER

Hide it, man, hide it. Here's the police.
(MacIver grasps the salver and drops it into the box of window-seat.

KATIE

(Opening the door.) Constable MacPherson!

DR. FRASER

Come in, come in, Constable! Glad to see you. *(But his hand is shaking.)* Have you—er—have you got anyone yet?

CONSTABLE

(With airs of importance.) Do you mean apparahended, Doctor? If so, I have apparahended James Cooney this morning.

(*The* **CONSTABLE** *is a tall, dark man, with solemn features. He is overwhelmed by his uniform, and its official implications. He carries three pewter chopin measures in his hands.*

DR. FRASER

Cooney!

MACIVER

Well, well!

CONSTABLE

(Laying down the pewters on the table and producing a note-book and pencil.) Yes, I apparahended the accused at 7 a.m. this morning ... But not on the charge of burglary aforesaid.

DR. FRASER

(Sighing in relief.) Not burglary?

CONSTABLE

Not as yet, sir. Breach of the peace ... In connection with the latter charge, will it be pleasing to you, Doctor, to answer a few interirrigations?

DR. FRASER

Yes, go on; I'll answer anything. But where did you get these pewters? They're mine.

CONSTABLE

Then you recognise these vessels, Doctor?

DR. FRASER

I do. They are three of my finest specimens.

CONSTABLE

(Writing in his note-book.) Vessels identified.

DR. FRASER

May I ask where you got them?
   *(**MACIVER** examines the pewters with an air of exaggerated innocence.*

CONSTABLE

I recovered these measures of capacity arranged in a row along the front of the quay at seven o'clock this morning.

MACIVER

Well, well! See you that now. Isn't he clever?

DR. FRASER

How in all the earth did they get there?

CONSTABLE

Deponent cannot say. But each one of the vessels contained a small amount of a mixture of whisky, water and breadcrumbs, upon which the sea-gulls of the harbour were feeding with celeri—e—ty.

DR. FRASER

Celeri—e—ty?

CONSTABLE

Celeri—e—ty ... The accused, James Cooney, was dropping breadcrumbs into said vessels, and flourishing an empty whisky bottle, and singing in a loud voice.

MACIVER

Didn't I tell you he was a wee bit overcome?

CONSTABLE

The aforesaid sea-gulls exhibited signs of intoxication, as did also the accused, likewise.

MACIVER

And me sleeping sound and missing all this!

CONSTABLE

On inter-irrigation, the accused said that he did not know how the vessels came into his possession, but he thought they were Dr. Fraser's.

DR. FRASER

Yes, yes, of course ... Poor Cooney! ... Nothing to do with the burglary, I'm sure. It was that cabinet I complained of, Constable. *(He points to the right.)* You see?

CONSTABLE

I'm understanding that. But there's the queer thing now! Both cabinets emptied, and Cooney in possession of some of the contents of one, look you.

DR. FRASER

(Eagerly.) The burglars may have thrown away the pewter and Cooney picked it up, being overcome, as MacIver says.

MACIVER

Indeed, yes! Man, man! What a time the sea-gulls would be having!

DR. FRASER

Well, you've saved some of my pewter anyway, Constable — that's the great thing! You know nothing of the rest?

CONSTABLE

Nothing at all, sir.

DR. FRASER

All right! They'll turn up later on, I suppose.

(**HE** *places the three vessels on the shelf of cabinet on left.*

CONSTABLE

It was this other place that was robbed?

(**HE** *examines the cabinet on right.*

DR. FRASER

It was.

CONSTABLE

I see. (HE *looks slowly round room.*) Was the front door locked?

DR. FRASER

It was. I had the key in my pocket. I was at the Hotel from 10.20 last night till 11p.m. Then I returned home, unlocked the door, came up here, and—er—found the Spanish valuables gone.

CONSTABLE

Yes, yes! I have read the statement you made to the Sergeant. Now, I'm thinking I'd best be seeing all over the house.

MACIVER

(*Alarmed, opens the window-seat and takes out the salver.*) Well, well; will you look at this now? Fancy it so near us all the time!

CONSTABLE

Is this part of the stolen property, Doctor?

DR. FRASER

Yes, yes! ... Was it in the box-seat, MacIver?

MACIVER

It was that; and me working away here! Maybe there's more of it.
(*The* CONSTABLE *and* HE *rummage in the window-seat.*

CONSTABLE

Nothing more. But it's always something we have found. Well, I'll just be going downstairs and see over the ground floor and work up to here again.

DR. FRASER

Certainly, Constable, use your own discretion. (*The* CONSTABLE *goes out.*) ... MacIver! Whatever are we to do with that bundle?

MRS. FRASER

(*Entering hurriedly.*) Whit's the maitter noo, John? Guid day, Mr. MacIver.

DR. FRASER

Oh, nothing—nothing, my dear. Just an investigation by the police.

MRS. FRASER

(*Smiling.*) Oh! John, John, some mair of yer nonsense. Ye're the droll man! (SHE *passes from one chair to another, looking around.*) Whaur's ma knitting, I wonder?

DR. FRASER

Your knitting?

MRS. FRASER

Aye, I left it here, I think.

DR. FRASER

(*Shepherding her to the door.*) Well—er—never mind it just now, Margaret. I'll bring it to you later on. MacIver and I are busy. We think there may have been a small —a very small kind of a burglary here.

MRS. FRASER

Busy wi' a sma' kind of a burglary! (*Laughing.*) Oh, John, John!—But I maun git ma knitting—(**SHE** *rambles round the table.*)

(*The* **DOCTOR** *is distracted; and* **MACIVER** *amused.* **MRS. FRASER** *takes her time, smiling the while, and circles round the two men, peering here and there.*)

DR. FRASER

But, Margaret—Constable MacPherson's here ... An investigation, y'know.

MRS. FRASER

So you were saying, John. (*To* **MACIVER**.) You didna see a grey Shetland shawl and a wee ball of wool lying aboot, Mr. MacIver, did ye?

DR. FRASER

No, he didn't, Margaret. Now, please—please! do go!

MRS. FRASER

And whaur hae a' ma cushions got to?

DR. FRASER

Haven't I told you there has been a burglary here?

MRS. FRASER

A queer kind o' burglary—when they were stealing sofa-cushions. Noo, come on wi' ma knitting. Hand it ower, John! There's a guid man!

DR. FRASER

But really. I know nothing about it, Margaret. You're complicating things dreadfully.

MRS. FRASER

Complicating yer burglary, John, eh? Weel, tell me when yer nonsense is feenished, and I'll come doon and redd up efter ye ... Burglaries! ... Oh, John, John!

(**SHE** *goes out, smiling merrily.*)

MACIVER

Isn't she the cool one now?

DR. FRASER

(*Angrily.*) Now, if there's one thing I can't stand in a wife—

MACIVER

(*Cheerily.*) Och, that's nothing! Wait till ye've had three of them!

DR. FRASER

(*Turning to the door on the left, and listening there.*) Hush! MacPherson's coming back! Talking to Katie! ... He's going out of doors! ... Round the house! ... He's in the garden now! (**HE** *goes to the window.*) Yes, there he is! ... Whatever can we do with that bundle?

MACIVER

When he comes into the house again, I could be dropping it over that window in your room ... And when he comes up here, I could be slipping down and taking it to a safe place.

DR. FRASER

Drop it? You'd smash everything.

MACIVER

We'll have to risk it, whatever! But I could be packing them a bit better.

(**HE** *seizes some cushions and rushes into the Doctor's room.*

DR. FRASER

Hurry, man, hurry!

(**HE** *peers cautiously out of the window.*

MACIVER

(*Reappearing with the bundle.*) Och, och! And isn't that window stuck so fast that I cannot open it ... We'll have to be dropping it from this one!

(**HE** *balances the bundle on the sill and opens the window.*

DR. FRASER

My God! ... Take your time, MacIver! ... Wait till I give the word! ... (**HE** *listens at the door on the left.*) ... Yes, there he is at the foot of the stairs ... Steady now! I'll stamp my foot when he starts to come up ... then you let it go ... Now, he's moving! ... Get ready ... Go!

(**HE** *stamps his foot;* **MACIVER** *drops the bundle. A crash is heard out-of-doors.*

The **DOCTOR** *seizes two of the pewter pots and knocks them together as if testing them;* **MACIVER** *takes up his tools and sets to work at the window-seat.*

CONSTABLE

(*Entering.*) Was that a window broken? That noise?

DR. FRASER

(*Grinning feebly as he taps pewters together in foolish fashion.*) No. I—I—! It was just me! Testing these to see if they had got damaged.

CONSTABLE
You were extra powerful on them that time, surely.

DR. FRASER
Any signs downstairs?

CONSTABLE
No sign at all, at all.

MACIVER
I think I'll be going now, Doctor.

DR. FRASER
Oh, all right! And would you mind taking this telegram to the Post Office? It's for "The Northern Times", Constable. (HE *reads.*) "Daring burglary at the house of Dr. Fraser, Torlochan. Relics of the Armada stolen. Police Investigation begun. Twenty pounds reward."

CONSTABLE
Well, well!. . . Twenty pounds! ... And aren't you generous now!
(He braces himself importantly.

MACIVER
Indeed, and it's a big lot of money that! (HE *takes the telegram.)*

DR. FRASER
Oh, didn't the Sergeant tell you? ... I put it into his hands as a stake.

CONSTABLE
The dirty brock! He said never a word to me. But I'll show him!
(His movements, hitherto slow, become surprisingly alert; and HE *starts prowling round, tapping walls and looking under chairs as if for a clue.*

DR. FRASER
Will you kindly take this wire at once, MacIver? *(Bringing out a handful of money from a trouser-pocket and, spreading it on the table, he selects some coins and gives them to* **MACIVER**.*)* Five and three, it will cost. Hurry, please!

CONSTABLE
Stop you! ... You didn't say anything about us recovering that bit of silver plate. It's not often the police in Torlochan gets a chance in the papers. We could be adding a codicil or—or—something, couldn't we, Doctor.
*(*HE *takes the telegram from* **MACIVER** *and considers it.*

DR. FRASER
Tut, Tut! ... Never mind, Constable.

CONSTABLE

Och, but wait you, Doctor. Everything in order, you know. (*Biting his pencil and painfully spelling out his addition to the telegram, while* DR. FRASER *and* MACIVER *bend over him, fidgeting.*) V.i.g.g.i.l.l.a.n.s ... vigilance ... Stolen ... property ... Apparahended ... Clue? C.l. ... C.l.e.w ... Clue ... Listen to this now. How would this do, after your bit of the telegram? (HE *reads.*) "Later, owing to the vigilance of Constable MacPherson, assisted by Mr. MacIver, the local joiner, part of the stolen property was recovered by ten o'clock this morning. It is expected that the guilty party, or parties, will be apparahended before many hours are past, as Constable MacPherson is following a clue with his accustomed celeri—e—ty." Fifty-one words, Doctor. Four and thruppence more. (HE *counts out some silver from the heap on table.*) Nine and six in all.

(HE *hands the money and the amplified telegram to* MACIVER, *while* DR. FRASER *looks on helplessly.*)

MACIVER

Indeed, and it's the fine telegram now. I'll be seeing to it, Doctor.
(*He scuttles off hastily.*)

CONSTABLE

Big Campbell is the close one. Fancy him never saying a word to me about that reward!

DR. FRASER

Oh, he'd have forgotten for the moment!

CONSTABLE

Forgot, is it? ... Well, I'll not forget him ... You'll not be thinking now that Cooney had any hand in this, Doctor?

DR. FRASER

God bless my soul, no!

CONSTABLE

No! 'Deed, no! Maybe he'll just have found those vessels lying in the road, as you were saying.

DR. FRASER

Yes, yes, flung away by the thieves in their flight, you see?

CONSTABLE

(*Going to the cabinet on left.*) And this, you say, is where the pewter was kept?

DR. FRASER

Yes, just there.

CONSTABLE

Has your servant any followers? (*HE takes out his note-book.*)

DR. FRASER

Followers?—Sweethearts, you mean?

CONSTABLE

Yes. But the term used in the Coorts is "followers."

DR. FRASER

Well, there's young Chisholm—the baker. He comes Mondays and Thursdays. And MacPherson, the smith— his days are Tuesdays and Fridays.

CONSTABLE

(*Writing.*) "James Chisholm"... I know him—a soft lump of a lad. But are you sure that young Donald's here twice a week?

DR. FRASER

Donald?

CONSTABLE

Donald MacPherson—the smith. I'm a MacPherson myself, you see.

DR. FRASER

Ah! You can't imagine a MacPherson as a burglar, Constable? Quite good! Quite good!

CONSTABLE

Of course not. But I wasn't thinking of the burglary: I was thinking one of my own clan would be looking higher than a servant-lass.
(*HE draws himself up importantly and struts around.*

DR. FRASER

Quite, quite! No ... I'm sure both those lads are good lads, Constable. And this burglary is really so far a mystery—eh? A mystery—that's the word!

CONSTABLE

It's all that—But, fancy you!—big Campbell never saying a word to me about that reward!
(*A Siren sounds out in the bay. The* **DOCTOR** *and the* **CONSTABLE** *rush to the window.* **IONA** *and* **MRS. FRASER** *come in hurriedly.*

IONA

(*At the window.*) Hooray! The green flag's up at last, father! They've found something!

DR. FRASER

(*Also at the window, with glasses.*) Thank Heaven then! ... Yes! ... There! ... That's the new diver ... MacCormack!

CONSTABLE

Isn't that fine now?

MRS. FRASER

Oh, John, I'm glad.

DR. FRASER

And that's the despised "San F." on the old map for you! Didn't I tell you, Margaret? ... You and your old coal boat!

IONA

They're hauling up something heavy!

DR. FRASER

(*Excitedly.*) Here, take the glasses, Iona! ... My hands are trembling. What is it?

IONA

A big chunk of wood.

DR. FRASER

(*Taking the glasses from* **IONA**.) Spanish oak! One of the old galleon's timbers ... Aha! we'll soon have her plate-chest now!

MRS. FRASER

Oh, John! I'm gled I was wrang!

DR. FRASER

We're as rich as kings ... That treasure is ours—it's ours, I tell you!—ours, at last!

IONA

Hooray, father! Three cheers for the good old San Felipe! We're in luck, mother. (**SHE** *whirls her mother round in a wild waltz.*)

MRS. FRASER

Toots, lassie, ye're daft. But isn't this grand, John!

CONSTABLE

(*Shaking hands with each in turn.*) It's the great day, indeed ... Heartiest congratulations, Dr. Fraser! ... And Mrs. Fraser my best regards, mem! ... And Miss Iona ... many happy returns! ... You'll soon be having a fine motorbike of your own now, Miss Iona.

DR. FRASER

Motor-bike! ... My dear sir, there's enough treasure in that old hulk to buy a fleet of Rolls-Royces, let alone a motor-bike ...

CONSTABLE

'Deed, yes, sir ... I've no doubt you could buy up the whole of Torlochan now.

MRS. FRASER

Whit nonsense, Mr. MacPherson!

DR. FRASER

But he's right, Margaret! He's right! Can't you see? Our fortune's made! Buy anything! Get anything!

(**HE** *prances round, waving the field-glasses in air.*)

IONA

Hooray, father! We've found her at last!

DR. FRASER

Yes! ... We've found her! ... We've found her! ... We're saved! ... Get on with your trousseau now, Iona!

IONA

Oh, mother!

(*The* **WOMEN** *embrace. The Siren sounds loudly.*

MACIVER

(*Entering hurriedly with the bundle and depositing it on the floor so that it opens and reveals the Spanish relics, Mrs. Fraser's knitting, and the sofa-cushions.*)

Am not I the lucky one! ... Twenty pounds reward!

DR. FRASER

(*Flabbergasted.*) MacIver! ... You rascal!

MACIVER

And I take you to witness, Mr. MacPherson, that it was myself that found it.

MRS. FRASER

(*Discovering her missing work.*) I declare! ... If that's no' ma knitting!

CURTAIN

ACT IV

SCENE—*The North Pier, Torlochan. Wednesday afternoon. Full sunlight. In the rear is a low wall with a bench close to it. A little to the left, there is an opening in the wall, leading down some steps to a jetty. Boxes and barrels and ends of rope are strewn irregularly over the pier. Behind are the blue waters of the Bay, and beyond are the distant Highland hills.*

On each side is a decayed wooden building, known locally as a Shipping Box: that on the right bears the legend—"The Moidores Syndicate, Ltd."; that on the left—"Royal Mail Steamers". Access to the pier is by the back and front of the building on the left; but only by the back of the building on the right.

A bare-legged laddie is fishing over the pier-wall. CONSTABLE MACPHERSON, *sitting on a box in front of "The Moidores Syndicate" office, is reading a newspaper with great interest.*

A group of tourists and natives are standing at the seawall, looking out towards the right; some are using field-glasses. They begin to move off to the left, and as they go, there are heard such observations as "We'll see better from the Esplanade"; "Further round the shore, that's the thing"; "Oh, yes, there's treasure down there all right"; and so on. People cross and recross from time to time—sightseers and tourists.

MRS. MANSON *and* FANNY FALLONE *walk in from the right; each carries a field-glass. They halt at the bench, and look out to sea.*

MRS. MANSON
So glad I took those extra shares from the Doctor yesterday, Fanny ... Good afternoon, Constable.

CONSTABLE
Afternoon, ma'am. (HE *resumes his reading earnestly.*)

FANNY
Yes, those shares! Weren't you lucky! ... Oh, there's the diver! I can see his metal corselet glistening.

MRS. MANSON
So it is. Just fancy! Isn't he clever—finding all that old pirate's treasure!

FANNY
Oh, auntie, not pirate's!

MRS. MANSON
Well, it's treasure anyway. Yes, I can see him ... That's the new diver—MacCormack.

CONSTABLE
(*Rising with the paper in his hand.*) Did you see the fine notice they gave me for the burglary, ma'am?

MRS. MANSON

Yes. Does you credit, Constable—great credit, I'm sure! I saw the paper this morning.

CONSTABLE

Man, it's a great thing, literature!
                            (**HE** *sits down and resumes his reading.*

MRS. MANSON

(*With the glasses up.*) Well, I wish it had been Cooney found the treasure, Constable.

CONSTABLE

'Deed, yes—the dacent man! Him that worked for years at the same job.

FANNY

Oh, isn't it a shame!

CONSTABLE

It's all that! For no sooner does this new man get started when he hits on the treasure, first shot.

MRS. MANSON

Too bad. Poor old Cooney!

FANNY

Oh, auntie, look! ... What's happening? They're all running about.

MRS. MANSON

I can't see now. That boat's funnels are in the way. Let's go along the Esplanade.

FANNY

Yes, let's go along there. ... Oh, I say, what crowds! ... Come on!
    (**THEY** *go off as* **MACIVER** *comes in, smoking a rather large cigar with a brilliant scarlet band on it.* **HE** *takes the cigar from his mouth as he comes in, and regards it admiringly. The reward has evidently materialised already.*

CONSTABLE

Have you seen the paper, MacIver?

MACIVER

No. (*Taking paper.*)

CONSTABLE

Well, it's the fine notice they're after giving me for the burglary.

MACIVER

And is there anything about the reward they didn't give you for the burglary?

CONSTABLE

Och, you and your reward! — Well, it seems that Johnnie MacCormack's after finding that treasure at last.

MACIVER

(*Keenly.*) Aye! They're saying he saw a big heap of silver things — soup plates, and quaichs, and knives and forks. ... and a great crown with jewels all over it.

CONSTABLE

Well, well! And isn't that the good news.

MACIVER

Och, Torlochan will soon be famous. What with rewards for burglaries, and ships with treasures, we're doing none so badly.

CONSTABLE

Just fancy! A crown of yellow gold!

MACIVER

And now MacCormack's down again among yon jewellery and precious stones of all colours. Wait you! You'll soon hear the whistle going and see the green flag flying.

CONSTABLE

But I thought you were always against this diving, MacIver?

MACIVER

'Deed, so I was. But in those days they were getting no treasure at all, at all. And rewards were not very plentiful either, look you.
(*He holds up his cigar in rakish fashion, and regards it lovingly.* IONA *runs in, field-glasses in hand.*)

IONA

Morning, MacIver! Morning, Mr. MacPherson!

MACIVER

Morning, Miss.

CONSTABLE

Morning, Miss Iona.
(IONA *leaps on the bench, and, sitting on the wall, puts up her glasses and looks out to sea.*)

CONSTABLE

Is MacCormack still down, Miss Iona?

IONA

Yes. He's been down quite a long time.

MACIVER

He'll be making all that silver into a heap down below, I'm thinking.

LAWRENCE

(*Dashing in from left back.*) Oh, sorry to disturb you, Miss Fraser!—but have you see your father about?

IONA

Father? Yes, he's down that way. (**SHE** *points to the left.*) Anything wrong?

LAWRENCE

That old ankle of Muriel's. Sprained again.

IONA

(*Coldly.*) Oh, so sorry. Yes, you'll find father along there.

LAWRENCE

Thanks awfully!

(**HE** *goes off quickly, while* **IONA** *gets back to her glasses.*

MACIVER

(*To* **CONSTABLE**.) And aren't the English people the great ones for the sprained ankles?

CONSTABLE

Rub them with whusky—that's the thing ... But I'm hearing they have no good whusky down in England.

MACIVER

So they're saying ... And to think of all the poor lads from this place that are in the London polis ... Terrible!

CONSTABLE

Aye, terrible!

MACIVER

Man, isn't it warm! I think there will be a better view up at the Hotel!

(**HE** *drifts off just as* **DR. MACDONALD** *appears.*

NEIL

Hallo, MacIver. Great day, isn't it?

MACIVER

Aye, and very warm.

(**HE** *makes for the direction of the Hotel Bar.*

NEIL

(**HE** *nods to* **CONSTABLE** *and crosses to* **IONA**.) Oh, there you are! (**HE** *kisses her, while* **CONSTABLE** *bends over his paper, his back turned to him.*)

IONA

Oh, Neil! Do be careful!

NEIL

Well, great times these! Your father ought to be braced no end by that silver goblet, eh?

IONA

Yes.—But, oh, I'd quite forgotten. See here.
(**SHE** *takes a handkerchief out of his breast pocket, makes a sling of it, and putting it round his neck, pulls his left forearm into it.*

NEIL

What's up?

IONA

You've sprained your wrist.

NEIL

Oh, have I?

IONA

Yes. Muriel Lawrence has sprained her ankle.

CONSTABLE

(*Who has turned to look at them, smiles and says*) Rub it with whusky, Doctor!

NEIL

(*Smiling.*) Now, now, Constable! Keep to your own job.

CONSTABLE

Right you are, Doctor. (**HE** *rises and drifts towards the same direction as* **MACIVER**.) Man, but it's warm! I wonder where MacIver can be at all, at all!
(**HE** *goes off.*

IONA

Never mind him, Neil—listen to me ... You—have— sprained—your wrist ... See?

NEIL

Really, I don't understand, Iona.

IONA

Muriel Lawrence has sprained her ankle again.

NEIL

But what's that got to do with me?

IONA

Well, you can't bandage her ankle if your wrist is sprained, can you?

NEIL

But, look here—

IONA

Oh, it's getting a bit thick, this sprained ankle business.

NEIL

Oh, come now, Iona!

IONA

Well, I'm not going to have you messing about that girl's ankles every other day.

NEIL

I say, dear, this isn't a bit like you.

IONA

No, but it's like Muriel.

NEIL

Iona!

IONA

I don't believe it's sprained.

NEIL

But if it is?

IONA

Then send father.

NEIL

Look here, Iona. I've never yet played possum when a patient wanted me.

IONA

But I don't believe she's hurt.

NEIL

You don't know, dear.

IONA

I'm certain she isn't.

NEIL

She may be ... You're absurdly jealous and without cause.

IONA

Please don't take that tone with me.

NEIL

Hush! There may be a bone broken ... Your father may not be available ... Where is she? ... I'd best go. (HE *moves off.*)

IONA
You're going although I ask you to look for father first?

NEIL
But the girl may be in agony — Yes. I'm going.

IONA
(*Walking away in the opposite direction.*) Oh, very well then — go!
(*Taking off his sling,* NEIL *goes off.* IONA *halts, then runs after him calling:*

NEIL!
(HE *comes back.*) Oh, Neil! I've been foolish and bad ... I don't know what has come over me. (HE *kisses her.*)

NEIL
It's this ghastly atmosphere of excitement and fashion and insincerity.

IONA
I wish that old treasure-ship had never sunk here ... And I wish dad could see things as you do, and stick to his own work.

NEIL
Oh, he'll come right in the end.

IONA
I'm sick of all this. It's gambling, nothing else.

NEIL
Worse. It's sacrilege. Here we are with a sky and a sea like these; and all that beastly crowd can think of is raking about for silver among dead men's bones ... But I'd best be off, dear. (HE *takes her hand.*) Friends again, eh?

IONA
Yes. And I'd like to come with you — just for penance, you know; but I have to wait here for mother.

NEIL
(*Kissing her.*) All right! I'll cut off to Muriel. Cheerio!

IONA
Cheerio!
(HE *goes off.* SHE *takes up the glasses and looks out to sea, as* DR. *and* MRS. FRASER *come in by the right back.* DR. FRASER's *dress includes a white yachting cap, and grey flannel trousers.* HE *has a flower in his buttonhole, and altogether is quite the gay dog.*

MRS. FRASER
Oh, here she is!

DR. FRASER

Anything to be seen?

IONA

No. The men on the hulk are all running about so much, I can't make out what they're doing. But they're still working the air-pump, so MacCormack's not up yet.

DR. FRASER

(*Dreamily.*) " Full fathom five! " ... Wonderful fellow, Shakespeare ..."A sea change into something rich and strange!"... Aha, Margaret! ... Romance—eh?... This is life to me!

(**HE** *expands his chest importantly and struts around.*

MRS. FRASER

Oh, John, John! I'm feart it's naething but an auld coal boat.

IONA

Really, mother!

DR. FRASER

Oh, let her talk. She's been at it all morning. What do you think, Iona? She says that the San Felipe—San F., you know, on that map—is an old coal boat called the Sam Ferguson—Sam F.

IONA

Oh, mother!

DR. FRASER

Samuel Ferguson, her grandfather's name. A coal boat, it seems, was named after him.

MRS. FRASER

I'm shair I'm richt.—Sam F., Samuel Ferguson. Whit else could it be?

DR. FRASER

Tuts! ... the Lowlander again!

MRS. FRASER

And I want him to stop this nonsense before we're a' black affrontit.

DR. FRASER

Margaret, Margaret!

MRS. FRASER

Weel, I've tellt ye!

DR. FRASER

Told me what?

MRS. FRASER

I tellt ye on Monday nicht that there was an auld coal boat sunk oot there langsyne. And ma grandfaither had the maist shares in her.

DR. FRASER

I know all that.

MRS. FRASER

And that coal boat was ca'd efter ma grandfather. Sam F. Samuel Ferguson. That's whit it is.

DR. FRASER

And when, pray, did coaling schooners carry silver plate? You've heard MacCormack's story! When he was down yesterday he saw a huge heap of silver.

MRS. FRASER

I'll believe it when I see it ... And onywey, Sam is for Samuel, and F. is for Ferguson.

> *(The Siren sounds a loud blast suddenly.*

IONA

(With the glasses.) Oh, there goes the green flag! They've got something ... They're hauling in a line.

DR. FRASER

Is MacCormack up yet?

IONA

Not yet. . . It's just a line they're pulling. Oh!— Oh!—Hooray! ... Silver! ... I can see it shining . Ugh! they're crowding round it now, and I can't see.

DR. FRASER

(Taking the glasses.) Lemme—lemme look.

MRS. FRASER

(Hesitatingly.) Maybe the Spanish ship gaed doon in the same place as the coal boat.

DR. FRASER

Nonsense!

MRS. FRASER

Oh, John, I hope it's true ... And I hope I'm wrang.

DR. FRASER

(With a deep sigh of satisfaction.) Yes, I see it—a great bowl of silver. Well, Margaret, didn't I tell you?

IONA

It's such a big one. It *does* look splendid. Won't Neil be pleased!

DR. FRASER.

Neil?

MRS. FRASER

Dr. MacDonald, John.

DR. FRASER

And where does he come in, may I ask?

MRS. FRASER

Did ye no' tell Iona yesterday to get on wi' her trousseau, John?

DR. FRASER

Oh, that! ... Merely figurative language, Margaret ... merely figurative language.

IONA

Oh, father! Nonsense!

DR. FRASER

My dear girl, I was excited and not quite myself, yesterday.

MRS. FRASER

Tuts! They were the only sensible words ye ever said, yesterday.

DR. FRASER

My dear Margaret, things are considerably changed in the last twenty-four hours ... What did that diving-hulk signify twenty-four hours ago?... A possibility only ... To-day it signifies untold wealth.

IONA

Whatever do you mean, father?

MRS. FRASER

He means he'll be able to buy Neil a fine practice in London, lassie.

DR. FRASER

Egad! We could buy *all* London now!

IONA

I don't think Neil would like London.

DR. FRASER

It's no concern of mine what Neil likes, Iona ... What do you say if you and mother and I took a little cruise round the world, hey?

IONA

Oh, thank you! A cruise to Sandaig Parish is more to my mind.

DR. FRASER

Fudge!

MRS. FRASER

Ne'er heed him, Iona.

IONA

(Coolly looking out to sea.) Sandaig Parish is all Neil wants.

DR. FRASER

(Snappily.) How do you know he'll get it?

IONA

Oh, I just know.

DR. FRASER

Well, there's a better man in for it.

MRS. FRASER

And wha's that?

DR. FRASER

Dr. Bosomworth.

MRS. FRASER

Yon long-haired assistant ye had fower years ago.

DR. FRASER

The same. And I have given him a testimonial.

IONA

One of your own composition, father?

DR. FRASER

Of course.

IONA

All serene, mother. (**SHE** *looks composedly through her glasses.*)

DR. FRASER

Tuts! You young people nowadays! (**HE** *is speechless for a moment. — Then.*) I'm not going to stay here and be jibbed at ... Coming, Margaret?
(**HE** *walks off in high dudgeon; and with a knowing smile to* **IONA**, **MRS. FRASER** *follows.*

IONA

Cheerio, mother!
(As **DR.** *and* **MRS. FRASER** *go, the* **CONSTABLE** *and* **MACIVER** *come in. Salutes are exchanged.*

DR. FRASER

Oh, there you are, MacIver. I want a word with you ... *(Then, to his wife.)* I'll follow you in a moment, my dear.

(**SHE** *trots off; and* **DR. FRASER***'s stare at the* **CONSTABLE** *indicating that he is not wanted, the latter retreats towards* **IONA**.

IONA

Have a squint, Mr. MacPherson. (**HE** *takes the glasses.*)

CONSTABLE

Thank you kindly, Miss.

(**THEY** *exchange the glasses from time to time and look out to sea as the* **DOCTOR** *takes* **MACIVER** *aside.*

DR. FRASER

I saw Cooney along the West shore there, (**HE** *points to the right*) five minutes ago—a bit overcome, as you would say.

MACIVER

Dear-a-dear!

DR. FRASER

Get a hold of him and keep him quiet, will you? See he doesn't let anything slip about that burglary affair.

MACIVER

Och, yes, I'll see that he gives no trouble.

DR. FRASER

Couldn't you coax him home?

MACIVER

Aye, or to the Hotel, maybe?

DR. FRASER

Good Lord, no. If he got to drinking there, he'd be sure to blab.

MACIVER

'Deed, yes, so he might ... Man, isn't it warm to-day! (**DR. FRASER**, *taking the hint, slips him a Treasury note.*) Oh, thank you, sir.

DR. FRASER

Well, then, I rely on you, remember. Get him home if you can. If you can't, keep him quiet.

MACIVER

I'll keep him as quiet as a wee burglar, so I will.

DR. FRASER

Hush—h—h! ... But I must be going ... Quiet's the word.

(HE *hastens off after his wife.* MACIVER *signals to the* CONSTABLE, *who comes towards him.* MACIVER *looks off towards the right, and points.*

MACIVER
Och, now, will you look at that!

CONSTABLE
It's Cooney, is it? Man, man! he has no legs on him at all, at all!
(*He hastens off to the right.*

IONA
(*Looking out through her glasses.*) What's the trouble now, MacIver?

MACIVER
Och, it's just poor Cooney, and him a bit overcome.

IONA
(*Looking to the right.*) Oh!—poor Cooney! I'd best be off.
(SHE *gets down from the wall.*

MACIVER
Och, it's nothing, Miss Iona. Just a touch of sunstroke, or—or something.

IONA
(*A little alarmed at what she sees.*) Yes, but I think all the same I'll go along to the South Pier ... Poor Cooney!
(SHE *goes off, as* COONEY, *quite tipsy, is brought on by the* CONSTABLE, *who seats him on a pile of boxes.*

COONEY
MacCormack's a dirty swine! ... Stealing me job whin me back was turned.

CONSTABLE
Wheesht you! There are many people about.

COONEY
Johnny MacCormack can doive noane, I tell ye.

CONSTABLE
I have no wish to apparahend you again, Cooney, so be you quiet like a good man ... And I'll show you the paper here with a fine bit about myself, and how I'm tracking down them desperate burglars that were up at Dr. Fraser's.

COONEY
(*Attempting to rise.*) Are burglars about? Thin this is no place for me.

CONSTABLE

Sit you down now. You've no legs on you, at all, at all.

COONEY

I'll twist MacCormack's neck, so I will!

CONSTABLE

Well, he's the good diver anyway. He got up one of the Spanish ship's timbers last night.

COONEY

Ach! ... If it's firewood ye want, MacCormack's your man. (COONEY *smiles, for even if half-seas over he enjoys his own daft talk, although not quite fully aware of its appositeness at times.*) Hullo, MacIver! Did you hear the news? They ran up the green flag yesterday, bekase Johnny MacCormack fished up some firewood — (HE *drowses off again*) — some fire — firewood.

CONSTABLE

Wheesht you, Cooney!

COONEY

(Sleepily.) MacCormack can't doive for nuts.

MACIVER

No, but if all they're saying is true he can dive for the gold and the silver.

COONEY

Begob! If I lay me hands on him he'll soon have a crown av goold and a harp av silver.

(He drowses off, chuckling.)

MACIVER

(Shaking him.) Will you not be coming home, Cooney?

CONSTABLE

(Interposing.) Here, here. This is my job, MacIver!

MACIVER

But the Doctor told me to take him home.

CONSTABLE

Home is it? Man, did you ever see Mrs. Cooney?

MACIVER

I know, I know. But the Doctor said I was to take him home. *(Shaking* COONEY.*)* Will you be coming home, Cooney?

COONEY

(*Rousing.*) Annything in raison, MacIver; but home I will nutt go.

MACIVER

(*Virtuously.*) Well, I've done my duty, anyway!

COONEY

Jiver hear what Johnny MacCormack did in the Great War, MacPherson?

CONSTABLE

'Deed, I never heard.

COONEY

No? ... Nayther did I—nayther did annywan ... But I think mesilf he'd be in his doiving-suit the most av the toime, waiting underwather until it was all over.

CONSTABLE

Och, Cooney—Cooney!

COONEY

MacCormack's longest doive—1914 to 1918.
(*He subsides out of sight behind the boxes into slumber once more, as* **DR. FRASER** *and* **MACLAREN** *come in—* **MACLAREN** *a little excited, the* **DOCTOR** *posing as quite at his ease.*)

DR. FRASER

Well, a great day—a great day for Torlochan, MacLaren. (**BOTH** *look out to sea with their glasses.*)

MACLAREN

'Deed, yes.

DR. FRASER

(*Strutting about.*) MacCormack's a jewel—a gem—a—. Hallo! Cooney here?. . . Can't you get him home, MacIver?

MACIVER

I've done all I can, Doctor.

CONSTABLE

Och, he'll just be sleeping all the time. Never you fear, sir.

DR. FRASER

(*Dubiously.*) Well, I hope so—I hope so. (**HE** *retreats to the rear and looks out through his glasses again.*) Aha! MacCormack's coming up—yes, there's his helmet. He's aboard now. Shall we get a boat and go out to them?

MACLAREN

No, no. There might be accidents in a small boat ... And has MacCormack anything with him?

DR. FRASER

Wait. His helmet's off ... He's talking ... He's evidently giving them good news ... They're shaking hands with him ... Well, MacLaren, what did I tell you?... It was the North Pier.

MACLAREN

Yes. But it's not so long since that you were doubting if there was ever any treasure in the Bay at all, at all.

DR. FRASER

No, no; I never lost faith. It was you were the unbeliever.

MACLAREN

Did you not say something on Monday night last about probabilities?

DR. FRASER

I may have. But my first concern was for the Syndicate ... not for my chutney and my pickles.

MACLAREN

Your first concern, I'm thinking, was for your sponges and your tooth-pastes.

DR. FRASER

MacLaren, you have a commercial mind.

MACLAREN

Dr. Fraser, you have no mind at all.

COONEY

(*Uprising.*) Firewood—firewood! Best Spanish oak! —MacCormack's finest firewood, sixpence a bag!

CONSTABLE

Wheesht, Cooney!

(**DR. FRASER** *and* **MACLAREN** *gaze apprehensively at* **COONEY**. *But* **HE** *subsides almost at once.*

DR. FRASER

What a man! Can't you keep him quiet, Constable?

CONSTABLE

Och, he'll be all right where he is.

(**LAWRENCE** *comes in quickly.*)

LAWRENCE

Oh, there you are, Doctor! Will you please come to Muriel? I'm afraid she's sprained that old ankle again.

DR. FRASER

Oh, sorry to hear that. Would you mind getting Dr. MacDonald? I'm very busy.

LAWRENCE

But the Constable told me Dr. MacDonald is no use, as he has just sprained his wrist.

COONEY

(Who has again sat up.) And I'll sprain MacCormack's neck.

CONSTABLE

Wheesht, Cooney, wheesht!

DR. FRASER

(Irritably.) Oh, well, I'll come. *(To* MACIVER.*)* Mind you keep that fellow quiet.

(As HE *and* LAWRENCE *go off left front, and* MACLAREN *follows them in bad humour,* MRS. FRASER *and* IONA *appear.*

MRS. FRASER

Are ye playing hide-and-seek wi' me, John, I wonder?

DR. FRASER

(Irritably.) Lowlands again! Do try to show some dignity, Margaret!

MRS. FRASER

(Laughing.) Oh, John Hielandman! John Hielandman!
(He bounces off after LAWRENCE.

MACIVER

(Touching his cap.) It's glad I am to hear the good news, Mrs. Fraser.

MRS. FRASER

Oh, thank you, Mr. MacIver.

MACIVER

(To the CONSTABLE.*)* Maybe there will be more rewards going, Mr. MacPherson, before this is all finished.

CONSTABLE

It's more than likely; and the Hotel will be getting the most of them, I well believe.

MACIVER
Och, but you're cross now!
> *(He goes aside and sits down on a box, looking dreamily out to sea.*

IONA
(Turning at the sound of voices.) Oh! there is Mrs. Manson, mother!
> *(MRS. MANSON and MISS FALLONE enter. Greetings all round.*

MRS. MANSON
Well, here we all are. Quite exciting, isn't it? Fancy getting Prince Charlie's treasure after all these years!

FANNY
Oh, auntie! Not Prince Charlie's!

MRS. MANSON
Of course not! Mary Queen of Scots, wasn't it?

MRS. FRASER
Weel, it was a long time ago, onywey ... Before the coal boats started running frae Glesca.

IONA
Mother!

COONEY
(Sitting up.) Firewood—firewood! This way for MacCormack's firewood!

FANNY
What a terrible man!
> *(COONEY only chuckles in reply, and subsides gracefully. The Siren sounds loudly.*

IONA
(Putting up glasses.) Oh! there goes the green flag once more. MacCormack's doing wonderfully ... Silver again ... A kind of chalice ... Look!

MRS. MANSON
(Taking the glasses.) So it is. How splendid! They're holding it up for us to see.

FANNY
(Taking the glasses.) Isn't it lovely!

MRS. FRASER
(Declining the glasses.) Na, na, I'm nervous. *(The Siren sounds loudly once more.)*

DR. FRASER

(*Entering hurriedly with* MACLAREN.) Where are the glasses?
(HE *takes them from* MACLAREN, *looks through them anxiously for a moment,
then sits down on a box, the picture of dismay.*
My God! This will never do!

IONA

Father!

MRS. FRASER

John, John! Whit language!

DR. FRASER

Oh, for Heaven's sake, leave me alone, Margaret.

MRS. FRASER

I certainly wull. You never used such words in all your life before! We'll be going down the Esplanade, Mrs. Manson.
(*The* LADIES *go off left back.*

DR. FRASER

MacLaren, this will never do! MacCormack's bringing up the whole Armada, damn him!

MACLAREN

And how will it never do?

DR. FRASER

We must spread that treasure out, man—spread it out! ... Keep it going for weeks, for months, for years ... But this chap's bringing up something every half hour ... We must stop him, or we'll all go to the dogs.

MACLAREN

Well, well! ... When we are getting nothing we are all going to the dogs ... And when we are getting the stuff we are all going to the dogs.

DR. FRASER

But don't you see he's bringing up too much at once? We'll all be ruined ... Send out and stop him ... He's too—too enthusiastic, this MacCormack—that's what he is—too enthusiastic! Think of my practice!—think of your shop—your chutney—your pickles!

MACLAREN

'Deed, yes! MacCormack's far too smart on it altogether. Cooney would have been more reasonable.

DR. FRASER

Whatever shall we do? ... Oh, yes! There's MacIver! ... MacIver!! Get a boat, please. *(The Siren sounds again.)* Great Scott! Will you listen to that! There's more of it! (**HE** *buries his face in his hands.*) This is barefaced robbery! ... He's gutting that ship! ... Oh, for Heaven's sake, MacIver! Get a boat and stop MacCormack from going down any more to-day ... And here! (**HE** *tears a leaf out of his pocket-book and scribbles a hasty note.*) Take this out to Captain Inglis.

MACIVER

Very good, Doctor. But it will not be easy stopping MacCormack ... They're saying he's real keen on the diving this trip.

DR. FRASER

Yes, yes; but say I am anxious about his safety ... Haul him up!—feet first, if you like—but haul him up, the big ass!

MACIVER

All right, sir. I'll tell him what you say.

DR. FRASER

And say—say—oh, say anything. But get off now, and row for all you're worth.

(**MACIVER** *takes the note and hurries off by the steps to jetty. The Siren sounds once more.* **DR. FRASER**, *just risen from his seat, sinks back on it overwhelmed.*

DR. FRASER

Again! ... Good Lord!

MACLAREN

Och, Cooney was the wise lad ... Cooney was far safer.

DR. FRASER

(Groaning.) Yes, by gum! ... Cooney was a gem. He'd be playing dominoes down at the sea-bottom by now, instead of wasting the mercies like that fool.

MACLAREN

(Leaning over the wall.) Och, there is MacIver off now ... He'll soon put a stop on this nonsense.

DR. FRASER

Fancy Inglis allowing MacCormack to play that silly game!

MACLAREN

'Deed, yes; they might have had more sense, and seen that a wee bit at a time is what we want. We could have been spreading it out over all the season.

DR. FRASER

The season! ... My dear sir, we could have spread the amount of stuff MacCormack's getting to-day over *all* the seasons for the rest of our lives. *(The Siren sounds again.)* More of it! ... Good Heavens! Will they never stop?

MACLAREN

(Looking through his glasses.) Yes, they're hauling up again ... Man, man! What a heap they have of it already!

(**COONEY** *sits up sleepily and rubs his eyes.*

DR. FRASER

Here, I'll go out myself! ... There's a boat at the other slip ... The dolts!—the fools!—the blackguards!

(**HE** *goes off, followed by* **MACLAREN**.

COONEY

What's all the whistling? ... Is there a round av habby-horses in this place?

CONSTABLE

Och, no. It's just MacCormack finding things you never found, my man.

COONEY

I know ... More firewood. Well, ye'll not want for kindling this winter, annyway.

(**HE** *subsides, chuckling.* **MRS. FRASER** *and* **IONA** *come in.*

IONA

(With the glasses.) That was MacIver went out to the hulk ... Oh, they're loading the silver into his boat! ... What a pile! ... Hooray! ... Look, mother, look!

MRS. FRASER

'(Declining.) Na; I'm owre flustered, Iona ... Just tell me whit's happening.

IONA

Oh! MacIver's dropped a big silver tray into the water! ... But he's got it again ... No? ... Yes, he has ... Now he's covering up the pile of silver with sacking ... And now he's pulling in like billyo ... Isn't it thrilling?

(**NEIL** *dashes in, waving a telegram wildly.*

NEIL

I've got it! I've got it!

IONA

What, dear? ... Sandaig?

173

NEIL

Yes. Sandaig Parish.

IONA

Oh! Neil! (SHE *takes both his hands and kisses him impulsively.*)

MRS. FRASER

Oh, Neil! ... Hoo nice! (SHE *also kisses him.*)

COONEY

(*Who has been sitting up for a moment and looking on.*) How noice, O'Neill... A good Oirish name ... Come over here and let me kiss ye, boy.

MRS. FRASER

Puir auld Cooney!

IONA

And so we've really got it?

NEIL

Yes. Five hundred a year. And a free house.

COONEY

And free firewood, me lad! Ye can't miss it.
(*In the midst of the congratulations, DR. FRASER comes in.*

DR. FRASER

Hello, hello! What's all this?

IONA

Oh, it's just Neil, father ... He's got Sandaig Parish.

DR. FRASER

What? Did Bosomworth not apply?

NEIL

Yes, sir; but they liked the testimonial you gave me better than the one you gave him.

DR. FRASER

Tuts! a pack of ninnies! ... Where's MacIver? (HE *looks over the wall.*) Oh! here he is! (HE *descends the jetty steps hurriedly.*)

IONA

Oh, Neil, fancy!—Sandaig and a free house!

MRS. FRASER

Here's MacIver at last.

NEIL

Good man, MacIver! ... Hooray!

(*There is a sound of distant cheering. It draws nearer. A* CROWD *of summer visitors come on, watching* MACIVER *draw in-shore. Some crofters join the mob; and* MRS. MANSON *and* FANNY FALLONE *are also there. They all move to the sea-wall and look down, waving to* MACIVER, *and cheering him and the* DOCTOR. MACIVER *comes up the jetty-steps bearing a sack full of the treasure, while* DR. FRASER *hurries after him.* MACLAREN *hastens in. A semi-circle is formed round* MACIVER *kneeling over the sack, as he opens it, and pulls out an assortment of white metal vessels, each one of which bears a large coloured label, somewhat the worse for its immersion in sea-water. At sight of these,* DR. FRASER *staggers, his hand to his head.*)

DR. FRASER
My God! The pewter!

MRS. FRASER
Whit nonsense! ... It's silver, John—only damaged a wee bit wi' the sea-water.

DR. FRASER
(*Bewildered.*) But, Margaret —

MRS. FRASER
Silver, aye! ... And maybe gold as weel ... Salt water blackens everything, ye ken. (*To* MACIVER.) Pack them up again, Mr. MacIver, and very carefully, if you please. They're valuable.

MACIVER
(*Doing as he is bid.*) I'll be a specialist before long, look you, at the packing of treasures.

MRS. FRASER
Tak' them up to the Doctor's room. Careful, man, careful!
(MACIVER *bundles the sack on his back and goes off left. The Siren sounds several blasts. The* CROWD *turns seawards instantly, and from it voices are heard: "It's the diver coming off"; "Yes, there he is"; "Let's go along and see him land." The* CROWD *moves off quickly.*)

MRS. FRASER
Whit's up noo, Iona?

IONA
(*With the glasses.*) It's MacCormack coming off from the diving-hulk. They're landing him at the South Pier.

MRS. FRASER
Aff wi' ye then, and hear a' the news.

IONA

Right-oh, mother! Come on, Neil!

(**IONA** *and* **NEIL** *run off. The Siren sounds several toots.*

MACLAREN

(*Bitterly.*) MacCormack! They're for making a hero of him, are they? I'll soon put a stop on that! (**HE** *also departs.*)

COONEY

(*Rising.*) Be all that's crazy! That man MacCormack'll be a timber merchant before he's done.

CONSTABLE

Sit ye down, Cooney. Sit ye down.

COONEY

I'll sit down on wan spot and wan spot only, Mr. MacPherson, and that's Johnnie MacCormack's face.

(**HE** *staggers off after the others.*

CONSTABLE

Cooney, Cooney, wait you, and I'll show you the paper with the fine notice.

(**HE** *goes off after* **COONEY**.

DR. FRASER

(*Mopping his brow and sinking on to the seat.*) What a nightmare! ... Good Lord! ... My own pewter!

MRS. FRASER

Nae pewter aboot it, John. It's your treasure at last.

DR. FRASER

Margaret! Are you mad? Can't you see?

MRS. FRASER

I can see fine that yon's nae pewter. It's treasure— treasure— treasure! ... At least, that's whit it is for these folk; sae treasure let it be.

DR. FRASER

But there will be all kind of experts up here from London to-morrow. They'll see at once that it's only pewter.

MRS. FRASER

Na, na! They'll never get the chance.

DR. FRASER

Whatever do you mean, Margaret? (**HE** *gets to his feet.*)

MRS. FRASER

I mean anither wee burglary, John ... this very nicht. But on this occasion, it will be personally conducted by your wife, and not by you.

DR. FRASER

But—Margaret!—

MRS. FRASER

I'm rale sorry for thae experts, John ... Coming a' the wey frae London juist to report anither hoose-breaking job ... But it canna be helpit. (SHE *takes his arm.*)

DR. FRASER

(Protesting violently.) Margaret, I'll not hear of this!

MRS. FRASER

Ye needna hear anither word aboot it, John. It's ma burglary this time.

DR. FRASER

(As SHE *leads him away.)* But—but—!

MRS. FRASER

Aye, aye, John. Come awa' noo!
(And her smile is provokingly happy and full of assurance. The Siren sounds once more.

CURTAIN

The Lifting
A Play in three Acts

ACT I
The Change-House at Croggan.
Night in September, 1752.

ACT II
The Larach at Garmonyreoch.
Next Morning.

ACT III
The Change-House at Croggan.
Evening of Next Day.

Donnacha MacLean	*Keeper of the Change-House.*
Alasdair	*His Gillie.*
Iain MacLean	*Master of the Brig, Margaret*
Flora MacLeod	*Crofter Girl from Innis Fada*
Seonaid MacLeod	*Her Cousin.*
Callum MacLean	*Tacksman in Eilean Aros.*
Corporal Swanson	)
Private Copping	) *Soldiers from the Duart Garrison.*
An Officer	)
Crofters and **soldiers**.	

The first act of *The Lifting* has already appeared as a one-act Play : "The Change-House" in Messrs. Gowans and Gray's Repertory Series and the author gratefully acknowledges the courtesy of these Publishers in permitting him to use that act in this lengthened version of the play.

The Lifting was first produced by The Scottish National Theatre Society, at the Athenaeum Theatre, Glasgow, on 3rd February, 1925, under the direction of Frank D. Clewlow, with the following cast :

Donnacha MacLean	Archibald Buchanan
Alasdair	John Rae
Iain MacLean	R. B. Wharrie
Flora macleod	Nan R. Scott
Seonaid macleod	Meg B. Buchanan
Callum maclean	Charles R. M. Brookes
Swanson	James A. Gibson
Copping	Moultrie R. Kelsall
An Officer	George F. Yuill
Other Soldiers and Crofters	

For the play J. Seymour Halley composed a prelude to each of the three acts, making a suite entitled "Dule in Aros."

ACT I

SCENE.—*The Change-House at Croggan, Eilean Aros, late on a September night in 1752. a large, mean, dimly-lit room—half kitchen, half drinking-chamber. In the back wall is the main door, flanked by a window on right, and a cupboard on left. The door is secured by a wooden bar. The moonlit window is half-draped by a ragged curtain which flaps eerily as occasional squalls break over the building. Below the window lie a spade, some rakes and a fishing net; and several oars stand upright in corner to right. In wall to left is a rude hollow, serving as a fire-place. Peats are aglow in this, and on either side of it is a rude chair. From the dusty mantelshelf hang two crusies alight. Further back in same wall is a door to rear of house. Midway in wall to right is a door leading to the sleeping-chambers. Further back, against same wall is a table with drinking vessels, and a wooden bowl containing water for cleansing them; some cloths for wiping and drying lie handy. In the centre of the floor is another table with a rude bench and chairs ranged around, and many wooden cuachs and tappit-hens of pewter disposed on it.*
DONNACHA MACLEAN, *the inn-keeper, a big strong man of sixty, dressed in peasant costume of hodden grey, is making some pretence of clearing the centre table and setting the room in order. But it is clear from his aimless air that something else than the business in hand is first in his mind.* ALASDAIR, *his gillie, a somewhat vacant-faced lad of eighteen, is really working hard at the same task at the other table. Yet at times he goes to the moonlit window and peers out at the driving clouds.*

DONNACHA
Will you be leaving that window, and getting on wi' your work?
(ALASDAIR *resumes cleaning the drinking vessels; but is evidently amused and perplexed at being ordered about by one who is idling.*)

ALASDAIR
It's well the people crossed before the storm began. The wind's rising. The Loch's white wi' scud.

DONNACHA
(*Bitterly.*) Aye! The Croggan folk were aye keen on a hanging. A night in the wet heather's nothing to them, if they'll can see a pretty man at the end o' a tow in the morning.

ALASDAIR
Poor Callum! What time will they do't, think you?

DONNACHA
About ten, I'm hearing.
(ALASDAIR *is drawn to window again.*)

ALASDAIR
The moon's coming out—

DONNACHA
Will you get on wi' your work, *amadan*.

ALASDAIR
(*Coming back from window.*) Save us, the moon's broke through! I can see the gibbet, now—plain on the hill-top it is!

DONNACHA
Wheesht you wi' your gibbets! My heart's sore enough for Callum already, without your harping on't. Get you to your work, *illle*.

ALASDAIR
(*Resuming tidying, but still amused at the contrast between his own industry and the other's idleness.*) Rob More was saying he was on Maol Ban this evening, and he was seeing Iain Dubh's brig in the Lynn o' Lome.

DONNACHA
Iain Dubh back! Are ye sure, lad?

ALASDAIR
Rob's no' likely to mistake. He was in her crew at one time.

DONNACHA
Iain Dubh back! And his own cousin to die a dule-tree death the morn at Gualachaolish! I had rather than fifty pund Iain didna land for a week to come!

ALASDAIR
He'll never can land if the storm gets worse.

DONNACHA
Will he no'? Ye dinna ken Iain, I'm thinking. (*Then, horror-struck.*) My sorrow! What will be the end o' this? Iain back!

ALASDAIR
(*At window again.*) The tide's high the night. We'll need to be pulling up the boats.

DONNACHA
Will you be keeping to your work? All the same, I'd best be taking a look at the boats. It will indeed be the high tide this night wi' that wind.

(**HE** *goes out by back door, and* **ALASDAIR** *sets to dusting tables clumsily. A knock is heard at main door, and a voice singing "The Sea-Reivers." Door opens and* **IAIN MACLEAN** *enters, still singing. He finishes his verse with a swaggering roll of his body, claps* **ALASDAIR** *on the shoulder, and shakes hands with him.* **IAIN** *is a man of thirty-five, with quick dark eyes and dark hair. His* *manner is restrained in order to conceal a nature impulsive and candid. His dress is of rough seafaring type.)*

Well, Alasdair, there ye are, busy wi' the ale-stoups as usual. Be getting me some of the good stuff, *ille*.

ALASDAIR

(Filling a cuach and handing it to him.) It's you after all, Captain. Rob More saw the brig from Maol Ban the day, but the master wasna for believing it could be you.

IAIN

And what for no'? It's four months since I left, and time I was home to this good ale, lad. Nothing like it in Holland, I'll assure you. *Slainte mhath!* **(HE** *drinks.)* And what now, will you tell me, are all the watch-fires doing across the Sound at Gualachaolish?

ALASDAIR

The people crossed to-night, fearing the storm would keep them from crossing in the morning.

IAIN

They'd good cause for their fears, I'm thinking. If the wind gets to the north 'twill be the big storm. But what's ado over there? A wedding at the marriage-tree at Killean?

ALASDAIR

A wedding! Have ye no' heard? *(Goes to window.)* Aye—there's the moon again. Look!

IAIN

What is't, *ille?*

ALASDAIR

Yon—on the hill.

IAIN

Mary Mother! A gibbet! What's afoot, lad? Who is't?

ALASDAIR

Callum o' Strathcaol.

IAIN

Callum?

ALASDAIR

Aye. Ye've been four months away. Ye wadna hear o't.

IAIN

(Breathlessly.) What was it?

ALASDAIR

He shot a sodger in Glenlussa, and the sodger died on them.

IAIN

God above!

(DONNACHA *enters at back.* IAIN *grasps his hand warmly.*)

Is this true, Donnacha? Did the red-coat die after the ploy in the Glen? And is Callum to swing for't?

DONNACHA

(*To* ALASDAIR.) Be getting Rob More to help you pull up the boats.

(ALASDAIR *goes out.*)

(*To* IAIN, *gravely.*) I see you have it, Iain. It's owre true.

IAIN

Donnacha, Donnacha! Here is the black day! It was my hand fired yon shot.

DONNACHA

(*Gently.*) It's what I was aye thinking, Iain.

IAIN

(*Distractedly.*) Callum was wi' me in the wood; but he had no hand in it, I tell you! I but meant to wing the fellow for his insolence. My sorrow! I kent the man was ill, but he showed no sign o' dying when I sailed.

DONNACHA

He died a week after.

IAIN

Donnacha, Donnacha! Callum maunna die that gate. How many red-coats are there in the garrison?

DONNACHA

Sixty or thereby. That'll mean forty at the gibbet. We'll can do't! God! that it may rain in torrents the morn!

DONNACHA

For why?

IAIN

To soak their powder-horns well,*ille*.

DONNACHA

You'll never be thinking of a lifting, Iain?

IAIN

What else, man? Ay, from the gibbet-foot itself, if need be.

DONNACHA
Iain, Iain, bethink you!

IAIN
I've twenty men on the brig; and the Croggan lads will surely no' be backward to help. We can count on fifty in all. You've some arms here?

DONNACHA
You'll never do't. It's too desperate a stroke.

IAIN
Maybe. But it's Callum we're fighting for. We'll get them near the water's edge. I'll have the boats handy; and we'll have him on the brig like the hawk, and it swooping, man!

DONNACHA
The hawk leaves blood on the heather at times, Iain.

IAIN
And what though? Anything rather than Callum dying the halter-death.

DONNACHA
And that's true. But—the brig—?

IAIN
The brig's standing off and on for me all night.

DONNACHA
It's the rough sea. And if the wind goes full north—

IAIN
Man, you daunt me there! But we've the rough lads for the rough sea. We've seen Corrievrecken afore now. All the same, you're right, Donnacha. *(Biting his fingernails.)* If it comes full north, she'll have to run for Kerrera and shelter there. And then where are we?

DONNACHA
We're by wi't then, I'm fearing.

IAIN
No, nor by wi't. We maun lippen on Croggan lads at that rate. Are there any here who havena crossed?

DONNACHA
Kenandroma and Portmore.

I'll make sure o' them, brig or no brig. (**HE** *goes swiftly to back door.*) Be you looking to your arms, Donnacha.

(**HE** *goes out.* **DONNACHA** *going to aumry, takes out some arms parcelled in cloths, and, unwrapping them, lays them on table.* **HE** *is examining these, when a knock comes to main door. He wraps up arms again hurriedly, and* *replaces them.* **FLORA** *and* **SEONAID MACLEOD** *enter.* **FLORA** *is a fair-haired girl; her mien gentle and drooping. The other—her second cousin—* **SEONAID,** *is a bright-eyed dark-haired lass, with something of brusquerie, and more of confidence, in her bearing,. Both are travel-stained and weary.* **THEY** *remove their plaids as they come in, and drop the portion of their arisaids which they are wearing as hoods.*

FLORA

A stormy night, goodman of the house. Is this the Inns?

DONNACHA

By your leave, my lass, not much of an Inns, only a poor kind of a change-house. We've little comfort for folk wanting to rest overnight. Is it far you'll have come?

FLORA

From Innis Fada.

DONNACHA

Shield us! What a journey! And would you not now be trying the Widow MacKinnon's?—the first house—

SEONAID

Goodman, is it Gael you are? We are ill with the great weariness. Can we no' be stopping here?

(**FLORA,** *almost fainting, has sat down suddenly, her head in her hands.*)

DONNACHA

(*Regarding* **FLORA.**) Well, well, your will to you. It is indeed a long journey. My chamber is none of the best, look you. (*To* **SEONAID**). Take you the crusie, and I'll help this weary one.

(**HE** *assists* **FLORA** *to rise, and they go out by door on right.* **DONNACHA** *comes back, and speaking over his shoulder, says:*)

I'll be getting you a bite and a sup o' kail.

(**HE** *busies himself at fire and at cupboard with dishes.* **SEONAID** *returns, and sits down by fire, watching* **DONNACHA** *keenly as he stirs the kail-pot.*)

SEONAID

It's cold I am. She's lying down for a bit.

DONNACHA

Aye, a long journey that. And where now did you land, I wonder?

SEONAID

At Carsaig. We're for Duart. But there was a thick mist at Kinlochspelvie, and we missed our way.

DONNACHA

You'll have friends at Duart?

SEONAID

Aye, a brother o' this one.

DONNACHA

Well, well! "Bare is shoulder without brother," as the saying is.
        (**SEONAID** *makes a startled movement, and catches her breath.*)
And she'll be kin to you, the lass ben?

SEONAID

A second cousin, goodman.

DONNACHA

So? It'll be a long time now since you left Innis Fada?

SEONAID

A day and a night in the boat, and a day tramping the heather here.

DONNACHA

A long time that. I wonder now, will I be kennin' the lad you're seeking?

SEONAID

(*Bitterly.*) You'll ken his name at least well enough. He was Seoras MacLeod, the sodger killed by the man that's to hang the morn.

DONNACHA

My pain and my longing! Is this the lad's sister?

SEONAID

(*Listlessly.*) Aye, but she ken's nothing o' his death as yet. She thinks him only deadly ill.

DONNACHA

Och, ochan![1]

SEONAID

Myself, I heard the truth but an hour back. A waif word from an auld wife by the roadside set me speirin'.

DONNACHA

And you've said nocht to the lass?

SEONAID

I hadna the heart.

DONNACHA

This night, this night!

SEONAID

Was he long ill of his wound?

DONNACHA

Six days.

SEONAID

We only got his message, a poor shaky scrape it was, and no date on't, four days ago.

DONNACHA

It's taken months to reach you, has it?

SEONAID

Aye. It's a long road to Innis Fada when there's writing to do. It maun have miscarried, gone round by Kintail and Skye, I'm thinking.

DONNACHA

Poor lass!

SEONAID

Ochanoch! It will kill her when she hears.

DONNACHA

Poor lass! (**HE** *moves restlessly about, and at last goes to window.*) The moon's clear again. You maun keep her from seeing yon. It will set her to the asking of questions.

SEONAID

(*Joining him at window.*) The gallows! I didna ken it was to be here!

DONNACHA

Aye, just here. Poor Callum!

SEONAID

Callum?

DONNACHA

The lad that's to die the morn. Alas.

SEONAID

And you can be pitying him? Myself, I'm glad to see that gibbet, glad, glad!

DONNACHA

I'm no' so sure 'twas Callum's hand that fired the shot, look you. The trial at Inneraora was none too fair.

SEONAID

Of course, of course! You'll be of the same tartan as Callum, I'm thinking?

DONNACHA

Aye, and not 'shamed o't either.

SEONAID

And not 'shamed! I was thinking that would be the way o't. MacLeans! Unfriends to the King and a' that's kindly.

DONNACHA

And where's your King?

SEONAID

(Evasively, as she controls her anger.) Will I be taking up a sup to the lass?

DONNACHA

(Muttering.) MacLeods! MacLeods! *(Then in his usual tone.)* Indeed, yes. *(He fills a bowl with broth.)* But you'll no' be telling her this night?

SEONAID

She'll hear nothing from me till we're close on Duart the morn. His grave will be there?

DONNACHA

Aye, nearby the Castle. Had ye no other friends in the Isle?

SEONAID

Only an acquaintance. A shipmaster. He came from hereabouts, and sailed our way sometimes. A MacLean he was—Iain Dubh by name.

DONNACHA

God shield us! *(HE drops a bowl.)*

SEONAID

What's amiss, goodman? You ken him?

DONNACHA

Aye, I ken him. But he's from home, look you. Sailing the high seas he is. Yes. That's what he's at. Yes; sailing the deep seas. Yes, yes. He's from home is Iain.

SEONAID

You're the strange man.

DONNACHA

I am that. And these are the strange times, let me tell you.

SEONAID

Wheesht! I hear Flora stirring. She may be coming down. You'll let nothing slip your tongue about Seoras' death.

DONNACHA

Is it me? No, no. I'll be going, for I was ever the poor hand at hiding my own mind. Be saying to her that I've gone down to draw up the boats, will you?

(HE goes out; and after a little, FLORA enters and sits down by the fire.)

FLORA

I'm shivering. It's fine to see a fire. Where's the goodman? Did he have any word of Seoras?

SEONAID

What word would he have? The folks hereabouts are no' like our own people; they've no dealings wi' the soldiers.

FLORA

Poor Seoras! Was there no word of a plague in the countryside? I'm wondering if it was the plague that was in it with Seoras?

SEONAID

(Filling bowls with soup from pot, and bringing scones from cupboard.)
Let your mind be at ease; for it's tomorrow we'll be at Duart. Say your grace, now, and take a sup and bite, for it's long fasting you are.
(**THEY** *bend their heads in silent prayer, and then make a simple meal. The wind moans around the house. A step is heard on the gravel.)*

FLORA

There's the goodman's foot. I maun try him about Seoras. Maybe he'll be more open wi' me. *(Knock at door, and* **IAIN** *enters.)*

IAIN

Your pardon. Is himself at home? What! And is it Flora of Valtos, and Seonaid too? It's a far cry to Erisort! *(To* **FLORA**.*)* Whatever are you making of it here, lass?
(Both girls have risen in surprise. **FLORA** *is blushing.* **SHE** *goes to* **IAIN** *and weeps on his breast.)*

FLORA

Och, Iain, but it's me that's glad to see you!

IAIN

You're ill, lass?

FLORA

Tired, tired. We've been long journeying.

IAIN

Sit you down now, for you're trembling, and as white's the *canach*. And what brings you to my calf-country? *(***FLORA** *weeps silently.)*

SEONAID

She'll no' can tell you. We had word from her brother, Seoras, the first word since he ran away from home three years ago. We were to come to Duart. He was a sodger, and lay deadly ill there.

FLORA

Is there plague in the garrison, Iain? Oh, I hope it will no' be plague.

IAIN

Plague! It might well be in a stack o' black stones like yon barracks. But I ken naught o' the countryside's news as yet. I'm but half an hour landed. You must ask the goodman.

FLORA

You've been sailing the wide world, Iain, I'm thinking, for it's little we've heard of you in Erisort this year and more.

IAIN

(*With meaning.*) I ken what you're thinking, lass. Aye. Dunkerque, Havre, and the Baltic, many trips, and four months on this last. But it's sorry I am to hear of the poor lad, Flora. And yet—

FLORA

Yes?

IAIN

And yet a sodger like him'll be better in his bed the morn than out o't.

FLORA

For why?

IAIN

There's trouble in the country-side these days.

FLORA

What is't, this trouble?

IAIN

Don't ask me, lass. (**HE** *sinks his face to his hands, then looks up, smiling.*) Och, but let us no' be thinking o't! It's yourself that's here, and that's the great matter.

FLORA

Iain, Iain! You've the great sorrow on you!

IAIN

It'll be gone before the sun sets again, lass. I'll win through't. Never fear!

FLORA

And you'll can take me to Duart the morn?

IAIN

No' for a day or two, Flora. You maunna move out o' this till the trouble's over.

FLORA

My sorrow! To be so near Seoras, and to wait and wait!

SEONAID

(Hurriedly.) Wheesht you, lass! Iain kens best.

IAIN

Where's the goodman?

SEONAID

Down beaching the skiffs.

FLORA

Maybe you'll be getting more out o' him than incomers like Seonaid and myself, about Seoras, I mean. We'll wait up for him now you're here.

SEONAID

(Alarmed lest the truth come out.) Indeed then, and I think you're no' wise, Flora, and you dead tired. Myself, I'm worn out, and it's lying down I'll be. *Oidche mhath,* Iain.

IAIN

Oidhche mhath, Seonaid.

(**SEONAID** *shakes hands with him and goes out.*) Come now, Flora, you'll no' be mourning for Seoras. If it's plague that's in it, he'll be up and about in two weeks' time or less.

FLORA

Aye, if he comes through.

IAIN

He'll be no brother o' yours if he doesna. Healthy as the deer, he should be, a Valtos man.

FLORA

I'm fearing.

IAIN

And some fine day soon we'll cross to Gualachaolish, and take through the hill to Duart. 'Tis there is the fine country, Flora, when the sun's out and shining bravely. You'll think yourself in Innis Fada again.

FLORA

You're sure you've the good hope of him?

IAIN

I'm sure, lass. And we'll be putting the mountain-moor under our feet: and we'll be together again. Think you o' that!

FLORA

Oh, Iain!

IAIN

And round us the lambs bleating, and the happy folk at the *cas-chrom* or the peats.

FLORA

Like Innis Fada!

IAIN

Finer than Erisort itself is that same country! *(Then softly.)* But I'll be taking that back, for Erisort will ever be the dearest o' memories to me. The shieling above Keose, lass, eh?

FLORA

(Smiling.) I mind it well, Iain.

IAIN

White love! And can I be forgetting?

FLORA

(Disengaging the hand which he has taken.) But I mind too that you went off without the good-bye to me or any o' mine, Iain MacLean. I'm fearing you're the light-hearted one.

IAIN

Be you fair now, Flora! I had a hunted man to run to France. It was life or death, up anchor and go, never a moment to spare.

FLORA

You might well have sent some wee word at least to Flora MacLeod.

IAIN

I could send no word with safety, lass. Tearlach Og's is a hard service, you ken. But often I was for Erisort since then, yet aye failed till this run. Once I had cleared my business here, I was straight for Innis Fada.

FLORA

(Mockingly.) You tell me!

IAIN

It's fifteen months since I've seen you, my dear, and have not I been wearying sore?

FLORA

You ay had the soft tongue, Iain.

IAIN

Mo chridhe, it's truth I'm giving you.

FLORA

(Suddenly reminiscent.) Oh, Iain! Do you mind when we first met? The wee lamb in the blackboyd bush, and me slashing away to set it free?

IAIN

And me, not knowing you were there, slashing away from the other side, and meeting you in the heart o' the thicket? 'Twas the droll ploy!

FLORA

'Twas the bonnie lamb, yon!

IAIN

Mary Mother! and did i not get there the start? seeing the finest face in all the world and it bleeding among the thorns.

FLORA

Scartit face or no', 'twas me was the first to get to the lamb.

IAIN

Indeed and you didn't then, Flora, for 'twas myself that put him in your arms.

FLORA

(Irritably.) Och! Maybe I was not there at all then!
(Then smiling radiantly.) But, oh! wasn't he the wee darling?

IAIN

And wasn't he the ungrateful one, all the same? Never a *baa* by way of a thank-ye, but off to the old ewe in a scamper.

FLORA

Indeed and you're wrong now. For I thought he said something to me when I kissed his nose in the bush yonder.

IAIN

You only thought he did. I wouldna have so failed you, had you been as kindly to me.

FLORA

Now, aren't you the brazen one, Iain MacLean?

IAIN

The wooden one more like, that I hadna the sense to profit by that bush o' brambles, and you fast held in it.

FLORA

What a man to rave!

IAIN

If only I'd been gleg enough!

FLORA

(*Rising.*) I think I'll be going.

IAIN

No, nor going. (*His arm steals round her.*) Listen, white love! Fifteen months is a long time, and here at last is the day I've been wearying for. You'll no' be going, will you?

FLORA

Iain Dubh, but you've the sweet tongue (**THEY** *kiss.*) Wheesht! There's the goodman! I'd best be going. *Oidhche mhath, mo chridhe!*

IAIN

Oidhche mhath! Sweet sleep to you, my dear one!
(**FLORA** *goes out by door on right.* **IAIN** *paces up and down distraught.* **DONNACHA** *enters by back door.*)
I made nothing o' Kenandroma or Portmore,

DONNACHA.

They're the white-livered lot. They'll no' move the morn unless the men from the brig are in the fight.
(**DONNACHA** *marches up and down the room in gloomy meditation, unheeding.*)

IAIN.

What's come to you, Donnacha?

DONNACHA

The last curse, I'm thinking. (**HE** *crosses to the door of the girls' chamber and listens there.*) His sister's here.

IAIN

Whose sister?

DONNACHA

The sister of Seoras MacLeod, the red-coat that was shot in Glenlussa.

IAIN

Mo thruaighe! (**HE** *rises, bewildered as the truth dawns on him.*) Oh, Flora, *mo chridhe!*
(**HE** *stumbles towards the main door, and rushes out into the dark.*)
(*At the outcry,* **FLORA** *and* **SEONAID** *appear at the door of their room.*)

FLORA

Someone called, goodman.

DONNACHA

(*Distracted, shaking his fist savagely.*) MacLeods! MacLeods! Get you gone from under my roof! (**HE** *goes out hastily after* **IAIN.**)

FLORA
I'm sure I heard my name cried out.

SEONAID
I wonder now.

FLORA
(*Looking from window.*) Oh, see, Seonaid! See! The moon's out, and there's a gallows-tree on the hill over. It's the wild country this!
(**SEONAID** *buries her face in her hands.*) What is't, Seonaid? You're hiding something from me, woman! I've felt it all night. What is't! Oh, it canna be! It canna be!

SEONAID
Wheesht, Flora, wheesht!

FLORA
It's no' for Seoras—yon? It wasna because o' yon he sent us word?

SEONAID
No, no, be thankit! But, my grief! my grief! It's killed he is, and yon's the gibbet for his slayer!

FLORA
(*Weeping.*) Ochonarie!

SEONAID
Wheesht, you, lass! Wheesht! Here's this wild landlord back again.
(**DONNACHA** *appears, leading* **IAIN** *dazed and dishevelled,* **IAIN** *signs by a finger on his lips that* **DONNACHA** *is to keep silence.* **FLORA** *flies to* **IAIN**, *and sinks weeping on his breast.*)

IAIN
Be leaving us, Donnacha! Seonaid!
(**SEONAID** *goes out by door on right;* **DONNACHA** *by back door.*)

FLORA
Oh, Iain, you've heard? Seoras is killed on us.

IAIN
(*Brokenly.*) Aye, lass. I've heard. I never dreamt—

FLORA
Ochonarie!

IAIN
(*Comforting her.*) My dear!

FLORA

And now it's you are for some wild ploy the morn! And who kens, who kens, but you'll be lost on us too. You'll no' be going, Iain; you'll no' be going.

IAIN

I maun go.

FLORA

For why?

IAIN

To save a man that's innocent o' your brother's death, Flora.

FLORA

(*Going to window, and shrinking back from what she sees on the hill-top.*) Oh! Is't that?

IAIN

My poor lass!

FLORA

Oh! the black day. And what's to come to Flora MacLeod, wi' brother gone and lover gone? You'll no' do't.

IAIN

I canna let Callum die that gate.

FLORA

You'll never come back, I'm fearing. And then it's alone I'll be, alone!

IAIN

My lass!

FLORA

Oh! it's home I'd be in Erisort.

IAIN

Aye, and it's the morn you'll sail too. The brig's no' slow; and it's soon you'll be home again. Poor Seoras! I'd give my right hand—

FLORA

Aye, aye! but the morn, the ploy the morn!

IAIN

Tach! It's but a little thing that! I'll win through, lass, I tell you.

FLORA

He didna' do't, you say, this Callum?

IAIN

No.

FLORA

And who then? *(Now fierily.)* Can you no' be laying your hands on the right man, and be done wi' t without bloodshed? It's killed you'll be.

IAIN

I think I ken the right man.

FLORA

(Joyfully.) And you're for seizing him the morn? Oh! gang to your ploy then, and a blessing wi' you! Bring him to the halter, and save your friend.

IAIN

My dear, my dear! Oh! what is't you're saying now! The man who slew your brother had no mind to do that same. He'd no desire of his death.

FLORA

And what now? Oh, Seoras! Seoras! Is it to this it's come? You'd few friends in life, lad, and none in death. You're slain, and all I get is words and words and words. Your blood cries out, and there's none will answer.

IAIN

(In anguish.) Flora!

FLORA

Take not my name on your lips, Iain MacLean, if it's thus you're to fail me. There are men in Erisort still, be thankit! And some o' them'll be in Duart before long, once I tell them my story.

IAIN

Flora, lass! *(He sinks to a chair, his head in his hands.)*

FLORA

What is't I'm saying? You've the great sorrow. My words are wild, and I'm not for seeing my way clear. I'm not for understanding this at all, at all.

IAIN

You're hard, lass, you're hard!

FLORA

Mo thruaighe! I've hurt you sore. Have pity on poor Flora. Her mind's not her own. Oh! to be back in Erisort wi' you, and forgetting all this blackness.

IAIN

My grief! It's the strange world! Still-and-on, let us be keeping the stout hearts. This life's indeed the steep hill, but the day's long, and we'll be at the top yet.

FLORA

I'll be going now. I'm but grieving you.

IAIN

No, no!—But go if you will, my dear. You're worn out.

FLORA

Oidhche mhath, Iain. *(She kisses him.)*

IAIN

Oidhche mhath, mo chridhe!
  (SHE goes out wearily; and HE sits down by fire to brood, gnawing at his finger-nails. HE goes to window and looks out anxiously at sky. The wind is heard rising a little. DONNACHA enters with ALASDAIR.

DONNACHA

I've been up on Maol Ban—

IAIN

The brig?

DONNACHA

The wind's full north—a gale. She's heading for Kerrera.

IAIN

(With a despairing toss of his hands.) Here's the end o' the rescue then.

DONNACHA

Aye, ye've lost the help o' twenty stout men wi' that wind, lad. Be thinking better o't.

IAIN

These cowards at Kenandroma and Portmore! The rest over there will be o' the same mind! We're done, Donnacha!

DONNACHA

Aye, we're done, Iain.

IAIN

(After a moment's gloomy meditation.) I'll put a stop on this, though. I'm for Duart. Out wi' a boat, Alasdair!

DONNACHA

Man, man! What is't you're for doing?

IAIN

I'm for the Major at Duart, I tell ye! If any's to hang it maunna be poor Callum!

DONNACHA
Bethink you, lad! They'll hang ye both. Aye, and so wad they every MacLean in the Isle, if they dared.

IAIN
Out, Alasdair, out! I'm for crossing the Loch.

DONNACHA
You'll launch the skiff yourself then, and that you'll never do in a storm like this! Man! the squalls are coming off Craigaven like whooping devils; the loch's foaming like a witch's pot.

IAIN
It's round by the head o' the Loch I'll be going then, Donnacha, even if I've to crawl on hand and knees. I'm for Duart this very night.

DONNACHA
You're flinging away your life, Iain MacLean; for Callum's doomed, whatever.

IAIN
Stop you! Rob More has a garron. I'll do't riding! (HE *dashes out into the night.*)

DONNACHA
Cry up Portmore, Alasdair! Cry up Kenandroma! Haste ye! Tell them your story. Say that Iain Dubh's flinging away his life! I'll up to Rob's after him.
  (ALASDAIR *stumbles out noisily. The clamour brings* FLORA *and* SEONAID *on the scene.* THEY *are in a state of alarm and disarray.*)

FLORA
What's all the outcry for, goodman?

DONNACHA
MacLeods! MacLeods! Spawn o' traitors!
(HE *rummages in the aumry, seizes a rope and runs out into the wind and rain.*)

FLORA
Whatever has come over him at all, at all?

SEONAID
I wonder what will it be?

FLORA
Wheesht you! I hear Iain's voice out there, Oh! *mo thruaighe!*
(*She goes to open door and peers out into the dark.*)

SEONAID
He's coming. I hear them. Yonder!

DONNACHA

(*Entering.*) Bring him in here till I bind up his head.

(THE GIRLS *draw back as a posse of men enter with* IAIN *in their midst. Two* CROFTERS *hold him; and his arms are bound to his side by a rope.* DONNACHA *and* ALASDAIR *are in front but* FLORA *brushes them aside, as she goes to* IAIN, *who has a wound on his brow.* DONNACHA *takes a white cloth from aumry and binds up* IAIN'S *head.*)

IAIN

It's the good-bye, lass. You and I maun part.—I tell't ye they had the wrong man for the gibbet.—And that's true.—'Twas my hand held the black gun o' misfortune; and it's me should be in Callum's shoes the morn.

FLORA

Iain! lad!—And was it you?

SEONAID

(*Taking a knife from her waist-belt, and dashing at* IAIN.) Scum of the pit!

(FLORA *grasps her hand, disarms her and tosses knife aside.* SEONAID *crouches away from her in remorse.*)

FLORA

(*To* SEONAID.) Isn't there pain and sorrow enough in the world? (*To* DONNACHA.) Why have you bound his hands?

DONNACHA

To save him from himself. He was for giving himself up, so as to save Callum. But if he had, the red-coats would have hanged them both, look you.

FLORA

My pain and my longing!

DONNACHA

And so we are taking him away to a safe place in the hills till it's all over to-morrow at the gallows on Gualachaolish.

FLORA

Yes, yes, goodman, be taking him away to a safe place. What for should two men die the morn instead of one?

IAIN

(*Bitterly.*) Aye! Be taking me from this. For it's not one roof should be covering her head and mine any more. Oh, *mo chridhe! mo chridhe!*

(THE MEN *pass out into the night with their prisoner.*)

FLORA

Fare you well, my love, and for ever!

(*Then, turning to* SEONAID, *she falls weeping on her breast.*)

Oh! Seonaid, Seonaid!

CURTAIN

ACT II

SCENE.—*The Larach at Garmonyreoch. Next morning. A ruined building with walls of turf, earthen floor, and roof blackened by peat-smoke. There are gaps in the walls and in the roof, through which the sunlight streams. In rear wall is a door of wicker-work standing open, and through it is seen a Highland moorland stretching up and away into the distance; a clear blue sky above it. On each side of the door are small windows without panes. There is a cupboard in left corner. In left wall at back is a door opening into a shed. Near it are several milking cogies. In right wall is a great gap, capable of allowing exit or entry to anyone stooping. Two rough wooden seats are near centre of earthen floor, where is a broad circle of iron within which smoulders a peat fire. The smoke from this ascends to a hole in the thatched roof.*
To left of fire is a rough bed of heather and bracken laid on the floor, and on it DONNACHA *lies asleep. Close to bed is a craggan, or churn made of pottery.* ALASDAIR *is standing by open door at back, looking out to the right under his upraised hand.*

ALASDAIR

Donnacha! Donnacha!

DONNACHA

What is't, *ille*?

ALASDAIR

The hanging's over. The people are coming back.

DONNACHA

Ochanoch! Poor Callum!

ALASDAIR

And the red-coats are crossing the loch as well.—There's something in it that is not right.

DONNACHA

(*Springing up and coming to door.*) Och! is there anything in this world at all, at all, that is right these days! Aye, there they go, the red-breasted ones, the cold-hearted ones!—Och, Callum, Callum! and a sore death they gave you!

ALASDAIR

(*Looking out to left.*) Save us! Yonder are more o' them.—On this side too!—All over the low ground!

DONNACHA

(*Looking to left also.*) Aye! Dots o' red in the heather. What else can they be but sodgers?—They're well round us.

ALASDAIR

Maybe its Iain Dubh they're seeking.

DONNACHA

Ye'd best be wakening him anyway.

ALASDAIR

(Going to door on left.) Will I be loosening his bonds?

DONNACHA

Aye, be loosening them.
(**ALASDAIR** *goes into shed, and brings in* **IAIN**, *his bonds cut, their ends dangling from his wrists. His head is now without the bandage.* **HE** *loosens the remaining strands of rope from his wrists, and tosses them away listlessly; then sits down without a word, close to fire.* **DONNACHA** *puts a kindly hand on his shoulder, but* **IAIN** *flings it off sullenly.)*
Man, man, will you still be foolish! We did it for the best. They'd have hanged you as well as Callum, I tell you, had I not kept you from giving yourself up.

IAIN

(Covering his face with his hands.) I ken, I ken! Poor Callum! Is it finished?

DONNACHA

Aye, it's finished—And now the red-coats are all round this place and coming up on us fast—You'd best be stepping, lad, or they'll have you trapped. It's a search they're making.

IAIN

(Dully.) What matter now!—Och, Callum, Callum!

DONNACHA

Come! Be stirring. Alasdair will guide you to a new hiding in the corrie.

IAIN

Callum! Callum! Like brothers we were, in the good days of youth.

DONNACHA

Come now! for you've still work afore you.

IAIN

Work?

DONNACHA

The lasses. You maun land them safe in Erisort. You have the brig. Be rousing.

IAIN

(*Starting up.*) Flora! Aye, the brig! They maunna take me yet.

DONNACHA

Good lad! Bring him to the Laigh Corrie, Alasdair, and wait for my signal. I'll bide here for the red fellows, and find out what's afoot.

(**ALASDAIR** *and* **IAIN** *slip out cautiously by door at back.* **DONNACHA** *watches them for a little, then goes to gap in right wall and scans the country keenly in that direction. As he does so his back is to the main door, and he does not perceive the advent there of the uncouth figure of a red-haired man in the soiled uniform of a soldier. The* **NEWCOMER** *starts at sight of* **DONNACHA,** *inspects the place hurriedly in a glance, then, as the sound of approaching voices is heard, steals off furtively to left. A moment later,* **DONNACHA** *cries out in alarm as he looks through the gap.*)

DONNACHA

God shield us!

(**HE** *retreats in amazement into the middle of the shieling, gazing at* **FLORA** *and* **SEONAID** *who enter through.*

What want you here?—Did you come by way of the wood?

SEONAID

We did that.

DONNACHA

Then the sodgers will not have seen ye.—What want you, I'm saying? There's danger in this place. *Ochanoch!* Can I never be rid o' you MacLeods?

FLORA

Be kind, goodman! We're here but to warn you.
The soldiers came to the change-house late last night, searching.

DONNACHA

(*Turning to* **SEONAID** *fiercely.*) And I'll warrant *you* told them Iain Dubh was here? And now you're repenting, eh?

FLORA

No. She told nothing. But some o' the cowards from Portmore let slip a word o' this place.

DONNACHA

Well, let the sodgers come; for Iain's where they'll never find him.—Still-and-on, there's danger for yourselves. They're the rough fellows, the red-coats.

SEONAID

(*Fingering the knife in her waist-belt.*) And did we no' learn that well last night, goodman?—But I've still a knife.

DONNACHA

You're the stout one.—But wait you!

(**HE** *goes to door in rear wall, looks out to left and turns hurriedly.*)

Aye, here they come—the red fellows.—But see, now! (**HE** *lifts two milking cogies and gives them to the girls.*) Slip you out by the hole in the wall there, and get down where the goats are tethered, and be milking them—I'll be at the churning. (**HE** *sits down by the churn of pottery and starts rocking it.*) We maun pretend we're the busy folk and you belonging to this place.

(**THE GIRLS** *slip out by the gap; and he goes on with his churning. Voices are heard out of doors, and presently* **TWO SOLDIERS** *enter by door in rear wall.*)

DONNACHA

(*Rocking churn vigorously.*) Good-day to you! A fine ling that!

1ST SOLDIER

What's that you're doing?

DONNACHA

Just churning some goat's milk.

1ST SOLDIER

Is this Garmonyreoch?

DONNACHA

It is that.

1ST SOLDIER

Are you Donnacha MacLean?

DONNACHA

At your service.

1ST SOLDIER

We've orders to search this place. Go on, Copping, (**2ND SOLDIER** *goes into shed.*)

DONNACHA

It's easy searching. There's nothing here but four walls and them broken. What's the trouble? Whom are you seeking?

SOLDIER

Oh, a MacLean, of course.

COPPING

(*Returning.*)—Nothing there. (**HE** *goes to gap in right wall and looks out.*) Hallo!—Women!—Come here, Swanson.

(**SWANSON** *joins him at gap.*)

SWANSON
A picture, hey? — Milking goats!

COPPING
That fair-haired rascal's a beauty. By Gad, I'll have her!

SWANSON
Steady! There's been trouble enough about that sort of thing.

COPPING
You're a dull one! Old Sobersides!

SWANSON
Let's get to business, and quiz this fellow.

DONNACHA
Maybe I'll be knowing the man you're wanting.

SWANSON
I'll swear you do. A tow-headed fellow in a blue coat and drab breeches. Callum MacLean of Strathcaol by name.

DONNACHA
Callum! — And was he not hanged this morning?

SWANSON
As if he didn't know! They're the wily birds, eh, Copping?

COPPING
Allow those fellows!

DONNACHA
And is Callum really out of it?

SWANSON
(Regarding him keenly.) Aye, he's out of it.

DONNACHA
Well, well! And there was no hanging?

COPPING
Tuts! It's plain this is news to him. He knows nowt. *(Goes to gap again.)* I'm for a jaw with the girls.

SWANSON
Let 'em alone, I tell ye. You'll get a scratched face if you go down there. We'll cut on to the change-house. It's only four mile from this.

COPPING
What's four mile if you have a thirst like mine, bully boy? — Let's stump it. (**THEY** *go towards door.*)

SWANSON

Through the wood's the shortest way.

(THEY *disappear.* DONNACHA *goes cautiously to gap, and then waves excitedly. The girls come in.*)

DONNACHA

Here's the good news, now!—Callum's escaped, and me thinking him on the sod of truth. There was no hanging at all, at all. And now they're searching for him.

SEONAID

(*Bitterly.*) And you're thinking that the good news?

DONNACHA

Are not you the bitter woman! And you kennin' well it was not Callum that fired the shot.

FLORA

Then it's not Iain they're seeking? We thought it was Iain they sought at the change-house last night.

DONNACHA

It's not Iain they're after.

FLORA

Then he's safe?

DONNACHA

I'm not sure. Who knows what those Portmore lads have been saying.

FLORA

Oh! Pity me! (SHE *sits down, overcome.*)

SEONAID

Have you no pride, Flora MacLeod?—Weeping for a man that slew your brother!

DONNACHA

(*To* FLORA.) Wheesht you, lass! Iain's safe. He's but half-a-mile away; and I can bring him here with a small kind of a whistle.

FLORA

(*Shrinking in dismay.*) Here?

DONNACHA

See you! Now that this place has been searched, it will be safer for Iain here.

SEONAID .

Let us be going then. She maun never look on his face any more.

DONNACHA

But he's for taking the both of you home on his brig — safe back to Erisort.

SEONAID

(Bitterly.) Safe? It's not me will set foot on a ship of Iain Dubh's, let me tell you.

FLORA

Oh, wheesht, Seonaid, wheesht! — Yes, yes, goodman! We'd best go back to Erisort. And *(to* **SEONAID**) even if we're aboard his ship, we need never pass words wi' him.

DONNACHA

That is right, and very right, lass. And now, I'll signal Iain. (*HE goes to door in rear wall, but draws back in consternation.*) Save us! Here's another red-coat. A new man. Whatever is he doing marching up and down? Yonder! Only fifty yards off! (**THE GIRLS** *look out.*)

SEONAID

A sentry! We're watched. Look! He's turning this way — coming nearer.

DONNACHA

Then out by the breach you go, and to your milking again. That's the safest plan.

(*The* **GIRLS** *go out by the gap once more. The* **SOLDIER** *is seen to cross the opening of the door several times, shouldering his musket as if on guard-duty.* **DONNACHA** *regards him keenly from behind the door, then stoops, and lifting a heavy billet of wood, seems to contemplate an assault on the* **SOLDIER**. *The* **RED-COAT** *halts in his evolutions, and* **DONNACHA** *instantly retreats into shed. The* **SOLDIER** *after a momentary hesitation enters. and peers round cautiously.* **HE** *is now seen to be the same uncouth tow-headed fellow who had looked into the shieling earlier in the day. Finding the place apparently empty,* **HE** *goes to gap on right and looks out eagerly for a space, then heaves a sigh, lays down his musket, loosens his belt and sits down by fire, whereat* **HE** *lights his pipe.*
DONNACHA *looks in from door of shed, and comes behind the* **SOLDIER** *balancing the billet of wood in his hand. The* **SOLDIER** *puffs contentedly and then says:*

SOLDIER

I hear ye breathing deep, Donnacha. — Draw you into the fire, like a good man, and be giving us your crack.

DONNACHA

(Dropping billet in amazement.) Father of the flood! And is it Callum?

CALLUM
Just Callum! And have you now, I wonder, such a thing as a cupful of milk and a scone in this place? (**HE** *draws closer to the fire.*)—Man! I'm as cold as the beadle's mother.

DONNACHA
(*With tears in his eyes, as* **HE** *grasps* **CALLUM**'s *hand.*) Och, ille, ille! And you got clear, lad! (**HE** *brings out milk and bread from cupboard.*) And none the worse of all your troubles, as far as I can see.

CALLUM
Well, well! A friend's eye is a good looking-glass. But stop you! (**HE** *goes to door at back, looks out left and right, and returning, sets to eating ravenously.*) See you! A man can live on little, but not on nothing. (*Goes on eating greedily.*)

DONNACHA
Och, and isn't it me that's glad to see you!

CALLUM
Well, it's glad I am to see myself.—But weren't they the big fools, putting me to all this bother?

DONNACHA
Fools? And who now?

CALLUM
Och! the lawyers and all the big ones down at Inneraora yonder. Trying to hang the wrong man for shooting the wrong sodger.

DONNACHA
The wrong sodger? Was it not then Seoras MacLeod that died?

CALLUM
It was that. And not the big Campbell fellow Iain aimed at. More's the pity!

DONNACHA
But you said never a word o' this at the trial.

CALLUM
Is it me? Telling on Iain to save my own neck! No, no!—Besides, wouldn't Iain have been the angry one, with me miscalling him for a poor kind of a shot.—But wait you!
  (**HE** *picks up his musket; goes to the door, performs two or three evolutions outside, as if* **HE** *were on sentry-go; then re-entering, looks out for a little at gap, comes back to fire, and goes coolly on with his smoking.*)

DONNACHA
Well, well! And how now, I wonder, did you manage clear of them?

CALLUM

Och! you see, the sodger that was gaoler to me at nights, had a mother that was a MacLean.

DONNACHA

See you that now!

CALLUM

And didn't it turn out that his mother's cousin was married on a granduncle of mine over in Tiree.

DONNACHA

Well, well! And so he let you go, did he?

CALLUM

Aye, he did that.—But not till I'd half-throttled him. And that was middling easy, for he was coming into my cell alone every night, bringing me my supper of brose, you see.— Och, yes, he was a good lad; and he could easily have made a better fight for it—but him being connected through this granduncle o' mine, he didna just do all he might have done. So he said never a word when I took the keys off him. And he couldna tell his shoe from his stocking when I took my hands off his throat.

DONNACHA

Wasn't that fine now!

CALLUM

And I took his pipe and tobacco pouch as well.—*Och, ochan!* Didn't he plead hard for that pipe! But I just told him that, once I got clear, I'd leave enough pipes with his mother's cousin over in Tiree to last him all his life.

DONNACHA

Real decent he was, that one! And I hope now, nothing will happen to the poor man.

CALLUM

Och, he'll be as safe's a weasel in the bracken. The mark of my fingers on his thrapple would be enough to clear his whole clan—let alone him.

DONNACHA

But where got you the fine uniform?

CALLUM

These things? Tach! Plenty of them in a store next my cell.—And so there was I; the night dark; and me coming out through the guard at Castle Duart, just like one of themselves, after I'd locked up the fellow that was a kind of second cousin to me.—Och, it was no trouble, no trouble at all!—But stop you!

(HE *goes out of doors again, shoulders his musket, does several turns at sentry-go and comes back.*) Well, well, it's good to be smoking by a peat-fire once more.

DONNACHA

(*Rising.*) And now I'll be taking a turn out to the Laigh Corrie to see a friend of yours, and give him the good news that you're still in life.

CALLUM

It's no' Iain Dubh surely?

DONNACHA

Who else?

CALLUM

Iain! Is it here he is? Man, man! tell him to be going out of this country at once! It's not safe here, at all, at all. A man cannot lay down his head these days where he'll find it in the morning.

DONNACHA

(*Laughing.*) You're the queer one! Your own neck barely out o' the halter, and yet you're sweating over the safety of others.

CALLUM

(*Excitedly.*) But it's Iain! Tell him to be fleeing, will you. Man, man! if they should hear that he had a hand in the killing of Seoras MacLeod.

DONNACHA

(*Still laughing.*) You're indeed the strange man, Callum!

CALLUM

(*With growing excitement.*) Be going now! Be going, Donnacha! Iain hasna my skill o' dodging the red-coats. He's too straight-forward, see you!—Be going! I'd die rather than harm come his way. For more than brother to me has been Iain Dubh.

DONNACHA

Well, well! I can ay be telling him what you're saying.

(HE *goes out hurriedly by door in rear.* CALLUM *shoulders musket, makes two or three evolutions in front of door, sets down his musket and is returning to fire, when* SEONAID *comes in by the gap with her milking cogie.* SHE *halts at sight of him, sets down her cogie quickly, takes up* CALLUM's *musket from where it stands by wall and points it at him.* HE *laughs quietly, and sitting down, rakes the peat ash.*)

CALLUM

Have no fear, lass. I'm as harmless as a powderless musket.

SEONAID
(Lowering the weapon and examining it.) Oh! is that it? And you've a Highland tongue?

CALLUM
(Roguishly.) Aye, and lips as well.

SEONAID
(Handling her knife.) Your lips will taste my knife then, if their words are not good.

CALLUM
All my words are good when a Highland lass is by.

SEONAID
Then you're better than some other sodgers that I ken. What seek you here?

CALLUM
Little and much! (HE *regards her admiringly.*)

SEONAID
So?

CALLUM
Little it would be for you to let me be sitting on here.

SEONAID
And much?

CALLUM
Much would it be for me to be listening to your scolding, and my eyes taking in all the splendour of you, O woman of the Isles.

SEONAID
Of the Isles?

CALLUM
Aye. Your tongue tells me that. Where else but from the machairs of Innis Fada would be coming a face and a step like yours?

SEONAID
And where but in Eilean Aros could be found a man with words so many or so foolish?

CALLUM
There are not in the four quarters of the earth—let alone in Eilean Aros—words many enough for me to be praising your spirit or your beauty, my treasure.

SEONAID

Did I not tell you I had a knife?

CALLUM

And what now? Is it the colour of my coat that is not pleasing to you?

SEONAID

(*Bitterly.*) I liked well that same colour—for am I not a MacLeod?—until last night, when I met those red hounds at Croggan.

CALLUM

(*Springing up.*) And did they lightly you? Tell me their names, my dear, and I'll strew their flesh to the ravens.

SEONAID

Och, you're the great hero, I can see! Did I not tell you I had a knife? If one laid hand on me, do you think he'd long be breathing?

CALLUM

Here's for the last breath then o' Callum o' Strathcaol.
 (**HE** *seizes her knife-hand, and kisses her before she can defend herself.*)

SEONAID

(*Gasping and drawing off.*) Callum o' Strathcaol!

CALLUM

My soul before God, lass! I lightly you not.—Strike, if you will.—But I'm seeing clear, there's no hope for me in life, if you'll not be the woman of my love.

SEONAID

Callum o' Strathcaol!—The man from the gallows! (**SHE** *flings away the knife, turns off shuddering, and covers her face with her hands.*)

CALLUM

Och, the gallows? Just three beams o' wood and a bit o' string. Hard words never hurt Callum. (**HE** *puts his hand on her shoulder.*) But tell me now your name.— It should be the soft one and the sweet to match the eyes of you; and them hidden as God never meant them to be. Speak you now; for it's meat and drink to me to hear your voice, my dear!

SEONAID

It's the great haste you make at the wooing, O man o' Aros.

CALLUM

Aye. But this has been a morning of haste with me, you'll understand.

SEONAID

It's surely that, when you come courting the cousin of Seoras MacLeod.

CALLUM

Shield me, God! Is it you that's in it? *(Turns away in despair.)*

SEONAID

(Softly.) Och, be not grieving, lad. I know well it was not you sent Seoras to his death.

CALLUM

Be praised, you ken the truth o' that! And now be telling me your name, treasure of all women of the world.

SEONAID

And aren't you the bold one, to be bringing words like those to a lass you have never seen before.

CALLUM

And who told you that? Have not I been watching over you from the wood, and you at the milking of the goats down there?

SEONAID

Spying, was it?

CALLUM

No, nor spying. But there was a sodger or two around this place and I thought it safer to keep nearby.

SEONAID

Oh! So that was the way of it.

CALLUM

That was the way of it. And then when the sodgers had gone, I came closer in the wood, and saw the wonder of your face, *mo chridhe!*

SEONAID

And what of that?

CALLUM

(With passion.) Splendour of heaven! Your face and the sun shining there, and you ask what of it? —'Twas the face of my dreams, my lass.

SEONAID

Och, wheesht you with your dreams. You're a piper of only one tune, I'm fearing.

CALLUM

(Solemnly.) Wonderful are the ways of God! for I never saw you till that moment, my dear. And yet I knew you instantly for the woman fashioned for Callum MacLean since the beginning of time.

SEONAID

And is it bard you are now; and you at the making of songs?

CALLUM

You may well ask; for it's singing my heart is, now that it kens the ways of love. Sudden and sharp and bitter they may be, yet still they're the heart's desire, even though they slay.

SEONAID

Think shame to be talking so wild. Who's talking of slaying?

CALLUM

(*With deep emotion.*) Aye, I talk wild; and yet with reason; for it's death to my soul if ye'll no' look kindly on me.

SEONAID

Och! the bard still at his songs.

CALLUM

Look you! I'm a broken man and poor—only Callum o' Strathcaol—a hunted one. But I'm Gael, and I'm bringing you all my love. Be saying you winna cast me utterly aside. Give me the wee word of comfort, lass. Tell me—tell me your name, my dear! (**VOICES** *outside.*)

SEONAID

I maun be going. There's someone coming

CALLUM

Stay you now! It's but Donnacha and his friends.— Give me your name to be speaking it over to myself when I'm far from you, lass.

SEONAID

Did I not tell you I was of Clan MacLeod?

CALLUM

A good name. But you've a finer one in front of it, I'm thinking.

SEONAID

(*Shyly.*) Seonaid.—I'd best be going now.

CALLUM

(*Lifting knife and handing it to her.*) Take this wi' you then—and this— (**HE** *kisses her, despite her resistance.*) It's the hasty wooing. But never was I surer of myself than now, my love.
(**SHE** *picks up the cogie and goes out by the gap, as* **DONNACHA** *and* **IAIN** *come in by door in rear.*)

IAIN

(*Grasping* **CALLUM**'s *hand.*) Oh, lad, lad! And it's safe you are!

CALLUM

What else but safe?—Did you think that a wheen stones called Castle Duart could hold Callum? It's not easy to put trews on a cat, let me tell you.

IAIN

We maun have you aboard the brig this very night.

CALLUM

And that's the good news! Where is she now?

IAIN

And there's my trouble. Still sheltering behind Kerrera she is, waiting for a shift of wind.

CALLUM

Well, well! We maun just be hoping for that before morning. But isn't it the good fortune to be seeing you again, my hero!

IAIN

Oh lad, lad. Many a turn the world takes, but this is the happy turn! *(They grasp hands again.)*

CALLUM

The fortune of Fingal to us both, Iain!—But tell me now, for I've been wondering—where were you thinking of lifting me this morning?

IAIN

Lifting?

CALLUM

Aye. Lifting from the sodgers.

IAIN

(In distress, and hanging his head.) Och, Callum, Callum!

DONNACHA

(To CALLUM.*)* Be quiet now with all your questions. You're safe; and what more could you be wanting?

CALLUM

Aye, I'm safe. But still I'm for the questions. *(To* IAIN.*)* Brother of my soul, were you for leaving me to the halter, and you not putting out a hand to help? Had you no plans?

IAIN

Be sparing me, Callum!

CALLUM

And is this Iain Dubh? Friend of my youth—ever beside my shoulder in time of trouble—

DONNACHA

Be stopping, Callum, before you say the foolish word. No shame to Iain that no lifting was tried. Well-planned was that same, but the men of Portmore were cold of heart and failed us.

CALLUM

Portmore! The shaky ones! Of course, of course!

DONNACHA

But was not Iain for giving himself up in your place to the red fellows at Duart? And had I not put the withies on his wrists and held him prisoner up here, he'd have done that same.

CALLUM

Iain! Iain! And me doubting you!

IAIN

Tuts, man! The great thing is that now you're safe.

CALLUM

I'm grateful, *laochain*[1] (HE *wrings* IAIN's *hand.*) But let's see if you'd any skill of a lifting in what you planned. Where now did you think of trying? Was it at the hazel-wood of Auchnacraig, I wonder?

IAIN

No, no! We'd planned for further on. At the water's edge, close to the Stone of the Big Step.

CALLUM

(Warmly.) And what sense was in that?

IAIN

(Also warmly.) Sense?

CALLUM

Aye, sense. The hazel-wood would have been the place. The ground boggy, and the sodgers' footing unsure.

IAIN

But at the Big Step, we could have driven them into the sea at the first fire; and we'd have had the boat handy for you.

CALLUM

At six o'clock? Man, man! And you a sailor! The tide, man! The tide! At six it was on the ebb, and no boat could have come near enough at the Big Step. A foolish plan that!

IAIN

Foolish! That's a fine word for a friend, Callum MacLean.

CALLUM
The hazel-wood was the place, I'm telling you.

IAIN
And I'm saying that at the Big Step it would have been far better than this botched business you're drawing out.

CALLUM
(Angrily.) Is it botching you're talking of?

DONNACHA
(Intervening.) What nonsense to be bickering about a lifting that was never needed. Will you wheesht, the both of you.

IAIN
Foolish, says he!

CALLUM
Tach! You and your botching.

DONNACHA
Tuts! There's no sense in either of you.—A pair of bairns!

IAIN
Och, let yourself be keeping a knot on your tongue, my man! What right had you to be strapping me up like a sheep and carrying me off against my will?

CALLUM
(Taking DONNACHA's *part with vigour.)* And what else could the honest man be doing? I'm thinking you were not in when sense was being shared.

IAIN
My quarrel just now is with this fellow—not with you.— What right had he, I'm saying—?

DONNACHA
The right of the stronger man, if you're asking.

IAIN
Stronger?

CALLUM
Aye. And a good right, that same—a good right.

IAIN
A good right?

CALLUM
Aye. A good right.—And now will the two of you be quiet—fools, and big fools that you are! For it's myself that has the chief cause for complaint that neither of you had brains enough to see I'd manage clear without any nonsense of help from either of you!

IAIN
(Raising his voice.) Will you listen to him? Nonsense!

DONNACHA
(Also raising his voice.) Is it nonsense you're saying? *(HE lifts his fist.)* I'll make you so as you can't drink milk from a spoon!

CALLUM
(Suddenly remembering the proximity of SEONAID.) Wheesht, with your shouting! *(HE goes to gap in right wall and looks out apprehensively.)* The lass will be frightened! The noise of you would scare the deer out of a wilderness.— Save us! Are there two of them?

IAIN
(Joining him at gap, and looking out.) Flora!

CALLUM
You ken them!

IAIN
Donnacha, Donnacha. What's this of it? Why is she here? My grief! my grief!

DONNACHA
She came here but to warn us that the red-coats were searching Croggan last night. She thought it might be yourself they were seeking.

IAIN
(In agony.) My lass, my lass! And mine no more. But there's danger for her. The red-coats are all around.

DONNACHA
Never fear! I'll keep her safe till you get her on the brig for Erisort.

IAIN
(Dazed.) Erisort! The place of memories!—But I canna face her, Donnacha—I canna face her.

ALASDAIR
(Coming in hastily.) There are more red fellows swarming up the brae. We'd best be making for the Corrie again.

IAIN
Again? There's danger for her in this place, I tell you, Donnacha!

DONNACHA

No, no. I'll see to that.—Be you going with Alasdair.— Lie close to this house and watch owre her if you like. But be you going now!

(IAIN *takes a last look through the gap at* FLORA, *and then goes hastily with* ALASDAIR.)

IAIN

(As he goes.) Come you, Callum.

DONNACHA

Aye. You would be wise to be following them.

CALLUM

'Deed yes. But there's more than Iain Dubh has a lass on his mind, let me tell you.—See you yon one with the raven hair and the face of Saint Bridget, Donnacha?

DONNACHA

The sharp-tongued one?

CALLUM

Sharp-tongued to yourself, you big stot!—She has as sweet a mouth as there is in all Albainn, let me tell you.

DONNACHA

Och, and is that how things are? You've heard the saying, surely: "Hasty the wooing; quick the hate"?

CALLUM

Aye! And keen's your insult; but keen's my knife. Be taking back that word of yours about the lass's tongue!

DONNACHA

Och, I'll say she has the finest tongue in all the Isles, if you'll but be going. Be stepping now; or it's that same lass will be the sad one, and her crying over her lover's corp, for the red fellows are coming up fast.

CALLUM

(*Unheeding this warning.*) I tell you, Donnacha, she's the wonder of women, that one, and the splendour of all the Isles. Let you be watching over her as the goat its kid; for it's she has the heart of Callum MacLean. And if evil befall her, evil befall you; and all the curses—

DONNACHA

Yes, yes. I'll guard her well. But now be you taking to the heather, lad.

CALLUM

Sorrow is on me that I maun leave her, and me only seeing her for the little moment.

DONNACHA
Och, be going now.

CALLUM
For the little moment! Och, only a turn of her head and the eyes of her on me; and there was Callum MacLean asking nothing better for his share of Paradise than love from that woman.

DONNACHA
Will you be going now? Or it's soon you'll be seeing Paradise at the end of a red-coat's musket, and it smoking, my hero!

CALLUM
I'd best be shedding this trash, first of all. (HE *takes off the red-coat, unbuttons his leggings and reveals himself in a short blue coat and drab breeches.*) And isn't Iain the daft one? Him thinking the Big Step was better than the hazel-wood at Auchnacraig for a lifting?

DONNACHA
Will you be going now? Or is it putting you out I must be?

CALLUM
Ochanoch! And so it's the heather for Callum once more! But—just fancy you, Donnacha. A lifting at the Big Step!—Tach!
(HE *goes out crouching.* DONNACHA *stands at the door, watching the fugitives, and then turns to look out to left at the advancing soldiery in the distance. As* HE *comes back, sighing, to fire,* FLORA *and* SEONAID *enter by gap, carrying their milking cogies.* FLORA *glancing through the open door, catches sight of the hunted men departing over the moor.* SHE *crosses to door and looks out.*)

FLORA
What's this of it?—What company of men is that on the hill, goodman? Crouching as if it's in hiding they were?

DONNACHA
'Deed yes. It's just a hiding the poor lads are seeking.

SEONAID
Look! They've halted. Are they going to fight with one another?

DONNACHA
No, no. They had a bit of an argument here, and they're just going on wi't up yonder—fools that they are! Callum would quarrel with his own shinbones, look you!

FLORA
They're the angry ones, I can see.

DONNACHA

Well, well, and aren't they bitter now, thumping their fists and kicking badgers out of their heels. Yes, yes, it will be the old story of the lifting—a thing that never happened. Just like bairns they are!

SEONAID

The lifting? What was that?

DONNACHA

Och, just some nonsense of their own that doesna concern you or me. Tuts! aren't they indeed like bairns, arguing away on the open hillside; and the sodgers so near!

FLORA

Oh, Seonaid, look! Is not yon Iain Dubh?—My love, my love! And have you been here, and had never a word for me?

SEONAID

What word would you have from him, when there's blood spilt atween you?

DONNACHA

Oh, wheesht you, with your bitterness! If the truth were known you'd say less on that score.

FLORA

(Eagerly.) What's that you say, goodman?

DONNACHA

I'm saying that it was but a chance shot killed your brother. Iain Dubh aimed at a Campbell man, and missed him. It was Callum o' Strathcaol that saw it, and Callum himself that told me this very day.

FLORA

(Dully.) So?—Still-and-on, there's Seoras' blood atween us—Oh, my love, my love!

SEONAID

And where now is the pride of you gone, to be crying after the like of him?

FLORA

(Controlling herself.) Aye! That's a' by and done wi'. *(To* DONNACHA *pleadingly.)* You see, it was but to give him a friendly warning we came here, goodman. Only a friendly warning, you'll understand. Nothing more.

DONNACHA

(Looking at her sorrowfully.) I'm understanding fine, lass.

SEONAID

Aye. Nothing more. It's not for the women of the MacLeods to go craving love among men.

FLORA

(*Pained.*) And who's thinking anything so foolish. (**SHE** *goes to the door and looks out.*) He's looking round— (**SHE** *calls.*) Iain! Iain! O, he's seen me! He's making the old sign, goodman, we used to have at trysts in Erisort, and him coming from far away, over the moor to me! (**SHE** *raises her arms above her head and clasps her hands there.*) The old sign. His hands are clasped. My love!

SEONAID

Aye, his hands are clasped. But does that hide the red stain on them?

FLORA

My sorrow and my pain! (**SHE** *sinks on chair, her head on table.*)

DONNACHA

(*At door.*) They're on the run now! The red-coats maun have sighted them.—Aye, yonder are the sodgers on the ridge—ready for firing.—There!—

(*A distant volley is heard.*) Callum's down!—No!—A trick! He's up and off like the mountain roe! They're clear!—Good lads!—They'll never take them now!

FLORA

(*Moaning at table.*) Mo thruaighe, mo thruaighe!— The old sign in Erisort! (**SHE** *clasps her extended hands above her bent head, and rocks her body in grief.* **SEONAID** *moved at last, leans over her, tenderly smoothing her hair.*) The old sign!

CURTAIN

ACT III

Scene.—*The Change-House at Croggan. Evening of next day.* SEONAID *sits brooding by the fire.* DONNACHA *is pacing up and down restlessly.*

SEONAID

Oh, why will they no' be coming?

DONNACHA

They'll come, they'll come! But they're safe in the Corrie for a wee while yet.

SEONAID

The Corrie?

DONNACHA

Aye, the Laigh Corrie, the place they were making for yesterday when the red-coats fired on them.

SEONAID

But they're on Maol Ban now. They've left the Corrie.

DONNACHA

And who tellt ye that, I wonder?

SEONAID

(Evasively.) They're in hiding on Maol Ban now, whatever.

DONNACHA

That's strange, and no word to myself. You're surely not keeping from me what I should know, my lass?

SEONAID

(Turning away her head.) It was Callum who told me. He slipped down here in the gloaming when you were at Portmore.

DONNACHA

So-ho!—And that's how the wind blows! It would take many sodgers to keep Callum from a lass, I'm thinking. Words of love 'twixt you and him, I'll warrant— enough and to spare. But had he no word for me?

SEONAID

He asked if you'd seen aught of the brig—that was all. *(A wind shakes the house.)* Oh, why will they no' be coming?

DONNACHA

Woman's patience!—till you count up to three.

SEONAID

They're late—late—long past their hour. They were to have been here by ten.

DONNACHA

Aye, if the brig came in, ten was the hour. But not unless the brig came in. They're safer in the heather till she anchors in the loch, I tell ye.

SEONAID

Ochonarie!

DONNACHA

(Savagely.) Save us from women and them in love! What call had Callum to choose a time like this for his courting, I wonder?

SEONAID

They're long, long. Why will they no' be coming, goodman?

DONNACHA

Because they're wise men and not fools!—There are too many redcoats between this place and the hill where they hide for them to move before the brig comes in.

SEONAID

Mo thruaighe! but it's the long waiting!

DONNACHA

It's the wise waiting. Soon you and your man will be safe on the brig, and sailing for Innis Fada. But you must have patience, and win clear of these red sodgers. *(Suddenly he stops to listen.).*—Did ye hear that?

SEONAID

No, nothing but the wild wind.

DONNACHA

(Picking up a storm lantern and lighting it.) The wind? That was the rattle of a cable in a hawse pipe. I'll swear the brig and her anchoring. *(HE listens. A bosun's call is heard in three sharp notes.)* That's the signal. I maun shew a light. (**HE** *goes out hurriedly by door at left.*)

SEONAID

(Weeping quietly.) My pain and my longing!

DONNACHA

(Returning and extinguishing lamp.) Aye, it's the brig right enough. And now if the lads would only come. *(He goes to door in back wall and peers out into the blackness for a moment, then closes door and walks restlessly to and fro.)*

SEONAID

I'm fearing—I'm fearing! Oh, why will they no' be coming? They're late—late.

DONNACHA

The sodgers are watching this place. That's why. But wait you! Our folk will be coming. It's as black's the pit outside, but Alasdair will guide them safely. And Iain kens the heather well hereabouts.

SEONAID

(Bitterly.) You've no word of a better man than either.

DONNACHA

Of Callum, is it? Never you fear! Iain will see to him. He talks o' naught but getting Callum clear. He watches owre him like the hind its fawn.

SEONAID

Maybe they've had to part company.

DONNACHA

Och, trust you Callum to get across a dark moor, if there's a lass at the journey's end.

SEONAID

A lass?—Callum?—Whatever are you saying?—Is Callum then the light one wi' the lasses?

DONNACHA

Och, that was but a manner of speaking. No, no! I was only of yourself I was thinking.

SEONAID

(Rising eagerly towards him.) Is it truth now you're telling? Goodman, goodman, if I thought he but played wi' me. *(Her hand steals to the knife at her belt.)* Ochanee, ochanee! it's what I feared. (**SHE** *turns off weeping silently.*)

DONNACHA

Keep me! but you take it sore, lass. Have you now, I wonder, been at the drinking of a love-charm?

SEONAID

(Rocking her body.) My grief! my grief!

DONNACHA

Aye, aye, and is that the way o't. You that were always so dour wi' poor Flora, because of her love for her man. Aye! You'll ken now, I'm thinking, what love is, and its bitterness.

SEONAID

(Brokenly, as **SHE** *looks apprehensively at door on right.)* Wheesht, wheesht.—She'll hear you!

DONNACHA
Little fear. She's worn out and sleeping sound. Well, well! And has it come to yourself at last?

SEONAID
Mo thruaighe! Why isna Callum here?

DONNACHA
Wait you! Callum will be here. He'll be here, whatever. But bethink you now!—If it's sore you are, parted but an hour from your love, what must it be for Iter parted from her love for ever?—Bethink you! You that are setting trouble atween them without ceasing.

SEONAID
And was the trouble my doing? It's her brother's blood that's atween them.

DONNACHA
Aye. But who is it is ever quick at the opening of that sore? Harsh words and bitter tongue! Little else from you for either, woman of the hemless lips!

SEONAID
Ochonarie!

DONNACHA
And here am I would be shewing that the thing was but an accident. One man aimed at, and another hit—the wrong one. Only a wounding intended; no killing thought of, at all, at all. And a wee bit wound it was, yet it festered and poisoned the lad so that he died. A string o' mishaps— naught else.—And still-and-on you'd harp and harp eternally about blood-guiltiness.

SEONAID
Flora! Poor lass!

DONNACHA
Aye, poor lass! But no pity for Iain Dubh? Oh, no! The heart of him rending; for he kens he'll never see her more, once he's landed both of you safe in Erisort.—Oh, no! No pity for Iain Dubh. And you'll never say a word o' pleading for him to Flora. Oh, no.

SEONAID
Och, Callum, Callum! Why will you no' be coming? Where are you at all, this night of blackness?

DONNACHA
Aye, aye. You have your own griefs, lass! (HE *comes to her tenderly and bends over her.*) But let that same sorrow open your eyes and your heart. Be you speaking the kind words to Flora, now that you have understanding of what love is. (HE *strokes her hair in fatherly fashion.*)

SEONAID

Poor Flora! Poor lass! — Yes, yes, I'll be trying —

DONNACHA

(*Eagerly.*) Aye. Be trying! You'll can be shewing her that Iain Dubh never meant harm to her brother. He'd no grudge against the lad —

(**CALLUM** *enters suddenly by main door.*)

SEONAID

Callum!

(**THEY** *embrace.*)

DONNACHA

Whatever is this? Have you no care for your life? Where now are Iain and Alasdair?

CALLUM

In the finest place in all the world on a wet night. Stretched they are on a bed of heather and pine in the cave of Maol Ban.

DONNACHA

And it's stretched you'll be in the clods, my hero, if you're not wise. Look you! get you back to Maol Ban and its cave, till the whistle sounds its second blast.

CALLUM

Och, a blessing on the whistle! Am not I just coming down to ask about that same whistle, and why it's so long o' sounding?

DONNACHA

Aye, it's long they are, indeed!

CALLUM

Could you not be going out with a lanthorn and signalling them that you're ready? And I'll be waiting here with Seonaid, and guarding this fine place till you're back.

(**HE** *gives a significant look at* **DONNACHA** *and signs to him to go out.*)

DONNACHA

Well, well! Was there ever a courting so wild as yours, Callum MacLean!

(**HE** *lights a lanthorn and goes out by back door.*)

SEONAID

(*Taking* **CALLUM** *by hand and leading him to door.*) Oh, can we not be going now if the brig is here?

CALLUM

Canny now. The brig's here. But so are the redcoats.

SEONAID
Then there's danger to be waiting.

CALLUM
Aye, and danger to be hastening.

SEONAID
But I heard three blasts on the pipe.

CALLUM
That was only the first signal. We maun wait for twice three. It's then the boat will be at the beach.

SEONAID
And we're safe when the boat comes in?

CALLUM
You're in the great haste surely, lass. You'll be safe only when the anchor's atrip and we're abroad and sailing for Erisort. Three times three that wee whistle will sound then. And will not that be the fine music, *mo chridhe?* (**THEY** *embrace again.*)

SEONAID
But could we not be going to the beach, even now?

CALLUM
No, no, we maun wait for the second signal and gang warily at that. The red fellows are all round this place. I'd trouble enough to get through their sentries. (**HE** *sets about obscuring the window better by means of the covering of sacking; then turns and takes her in his arms.* **THEY** *sit down by the fire together.*) O, woman of my love!

SEONAID
(*After a moment or two of silent ecstasy.*) It would be dark, and you coming over the mountain moor?

CALLUM
It was that. And only a wee spot o' light from this place to guide me.—But was not I the happy one yonder, even in the dark and the rain, and me knowing that light was coming from a star wi' the name of Seonaid to it?

SEONAID
Och! What a tongue! But I'll wager now, it's no' the first time you'll have come over the hill in the dark to a speck o' light in a wee house.

CALLUM
'Deed no'; I've had my own share of night-wandering. Not the first time for Callum, this.

SEONAID

But ay there would be a light to guide you? A peat-fire and a lass beside it? Not the first time for Callum?

CALLUM

(Sentimentally abstracted.) 'Deed no.

(**SEONAID** *starts apart from him angrily; and* **HE** *gets up in confusion, following her appealingly.*) What foolishness have I been saying now?— Och, no! no! It's not that way I was meaning at all, at all. I was not considering what my rattle of a tongue was saying. Och, no! Never a peat fire and never a lass for poor Callum.

SEONAID

Never a fire, O man of many tales? And where now, would that speck of light be coming from?

CALLUM

Now, now, be you not taking me up wrong, lass.—Sit you down and let us be talking kindly.

SEONAID

Talking!—it's talking has bewitched me, I'm thinking; and you deceiving me! Oh, Callum, Callum! (**SHE** *comes back to him, pleading.*) Tell me it's no' true.

CALLUM

(Drawing her to him.) And isn't that just what I'm telling you! And still-and-on, you're not for believing me. Am I not telling you there was never a lass by the fire except yourself, and me night-journeying through the hill to her?

SEONAID

I'm thinking that's no' true.

CALLUM

Och! And aren't you women the hard ones! Never yet did I get woman to believe that story!

SEONAID

(Gasping.) Never?—Then it's a tale you've often been telling?

CALLUM

(Seeing the game is up.) Indeed, then, I have just! Isn't it what I'm saying to you? And the lasses were right—very right, not to be believing me.

SEONAID

My sorrow and my shame!

CALLUM

Be you not grieving, my dear. It's not from you I'd be hiding truth.—Och, yes, many's the lass I've dallied wi' in my time.—But here's one (**HE** *fondles her hair*) has my whole heart. And glad am I that she's angry wi' me, wasting my youth running after this *caileag* and that, when a woman like Seonaid MacLeod was in the world. And indeed now, it's angry I could be wi' myself, were I not at this moment too happy for such nonsense.

SEONAID

(*Conquered.*) Mo chridhe!

CALLUM

Treasure o' mine!
(**DONNACHA** *comes to door at back.*)

DONNACHA

Out, Callum, out! The red-coats are moving this way. They'll be searching this place. Ye maun hide in the hill till they're gone.

CALLUM

Ochanoch! The heather again!
(**FLORA** *comes in by door on right, languid and distraught, as* **CALLUM** *and* **SEONAID** *embrace.* **HE** *goes out with* **DONNACHA**. **SEONAID** *sinks by fire despondent.*)

FLORA

You're sorrowing sore, Seonaid. What is it now?

SEONAID

Ochanee! Will we ever see Erisort at all, at all? The soldiers are close by once more, and the lads are still in the heather. Callum was here, and he's off again.

FLORA

Poor Seonaid! Was Iain here?

SEONAID

No! Why are you asking?

FLORA

(*Sadly.*) Mo thruaighe!

SEONAID

Oh, lass, lass. Think kindly of Iain. He had no thought to kill poor Seoras.

FLORA

My sorrow! Still-and-on, he killed him.

SEONAID

I ken—I ken. It's the dark world.—But, oh! have pity on yourself, lass. This thing is breaking you.

FLORA

My grief, my grief!—You'll not be understanding, Seonaid.

SEONAID

(Fierily.) And why will I not be understanding? Is not my own man out there, and he as wet and cold and hungered as Iain Dubh? And both watching owre us from the heather like the moorcock its children?

FLORA

And is this Seonaid MacLeod that is speaking?

SEONAID

Aye; and the heart of her changed, since she found the. man of her love in the same clan as Iain Dubh?

FLORA

(In glad surprise.) Seonaid! (THEY *embrace.*)

SEONAID

You love him, lass?

FLORA

Indeed, yes!—O, what am I saying!—I canna tell! I canna tell!

DONNACHA

(Entering.) Callum's off to the cave again. But not for long I'm hoping, for the sodgers are now taking a cast south from Portmore. Be you listening for the next pipe?; for it's then the boat will be ready. Look you—like this. (HE whistles *three sharp notes, and repeats them a second time.*) When you hear that, out of this with you to the rocks of the shore, like the wild geese, and them homing.

SEONAID

Oh, it's glad I'd be to hear the last o' the calls on that same pipe.

DONNACHA

Ah, but it's only myself will be listening for that one. It will be your good-bye to Donnacha. Three blasts three times, and then Croggan no more for you, my dears. And when you hear that whistle, and you heading for the open sea, be thinking kindly o' Donnacha—old and lonely and comfortless—sitting here by this poor fire and wishing you well.-—Your heart's desire to your hearts, my dears. (*He lays his hand on* FLORA's *shoulder.*) .

FLORA
And Iain?
Will he come at the second call?

DONNACHA
They'll come, will Iain and Callum, be you sure o' that! Look for them at the Big Rock.

SEONAID
And you, goodman?

DONNACHA
No, no! I'll bide the brunt here. (**HE** *takes up a gun, and examining its priming, sets it down again.*) Maybe I'll can set the sodgers on another scent, ye see.

FLORA
But there will be danger for you.

DONNACHA
None in the wide world. The sodgers can have nothing against me, when this place is clear of you all, for then I'll be but a plain change-house keeper once more.

FLORA
You're the good friend. (**SHE** *takes his hand.*) You're sure Iain and Callum ken the signal?

DONNACHA
Aye, they ken. And glad I'll be to have ye all safe, and me hearing the third pipe.

FLORA
The third pipe! I wonder, will it ever sound?

SEONAID
Oh! Wheesht you with your wondering! You're tired out and so am I. Let us be going in now and resting.

DONNACHA
Yes, yes, be you lying down and resting. I'll be at the watching and rouse you when the time comes.

FLORA
It will be the easy rousing then, for there will be little sleep I'm thinking. (**THEY** *rise to go out by door on right. A shot is heard, a little distance off.*)

SEONAID
That was a shot. This night, this night! —My pain and my longing. Callum! Callum!

DONNACHA

Och, it will be only some nonsense of the soldiers at Portmore. (HE *peers out.*) They get scared at times, and let off a shot if a bush tosses in the storm, look you!

FLORA

Can you see anything?

DONNACHA

Only the light in the Captain's window. (HE *listens.*) And not a sound but the wind and the rain.

FLORA

You're sure that shot didna come from Maol Ban?

DONNACHA

No, no! It was from Portmore. Sometimes the sodgers will be quarrelling there, you see. (HE *closes door.*)

Get you to your rest, you weary ones. It's nothing but some nonsense, I'm telling you.

SEONAID

You're sure?

DONNACHA

My life on't. I can trust my own ears, I tell you. It came from Portmore, yon shot. — Get you to rest now! '

SEONAID

Mo thruaighe! I'm fearing!

(FLORA *and* SHE *go out by door on right looking back apprehensively at* DONNACHA. HE *sits down by fire, then rises and paces restlessly to and fro, halting at times to listen at the outer doors. Suddenly* HE *runs to door at back and opens.* IAIN *and* ALASDAIR *enter supporting* CALLUM, *whose face is pale as chalk, and his right arm in a sling.* DONNACHA *puts his finger to lip to enjoin speaking in low tone's, and nods his head to the women's quarters.*)

DONNACHA

Callum, lad!

(HE *helps* CALLUM *to a seat by fire.* DONNACHA *gets some brandy and gives it to* CALLUM, *who revives a little.*)

IAIN

A bullet! The shoulder! He ran into a sentry near the cave.

CALLUM

(*Smiling wanly.*) I'm saying, Iain, — this — this is the kind o' thing would have happened if you'd tried a lifting at the Big Step.

IAIN

Wheesht you! Wheesht wi' your nonsense!

CALLUM

I'm telling you the woods at Auchnacraig would have been the place. (HE *faints.* THEY *busy themselves with brandy for him, and improvise a rude bandage for his shoulder.*)

DONNACHA

Whistle or no' whistle, we'd best get him down to the beach.

IAIN

Wait you! Let him rest for a bit. Be giving him a sup, Alasdair. (HE *takes a pistol from his belt and looks to the priming.*

DONNACHA

What is't you're planing, lad?

IAIN

(*Looking at pistol*) I could be sending them sniffing on a cold track, while the rest of you run down to the boat. (*He goes to door and peers out to right.*)

DONNACHA

Is it decoying them you'd be? Oh!—lad, lad!

IAIN

And what for no'? There's the boat for the rest o' ye.— I can surely swim as far's the brig. (HE *peers out again.*) Lights moving at Portmore, Donnacha.

DONNACHA

Aye, so I saw.

IAIN

They maun have heard the shot.

DONNACHA

Is he dead—the sentry?

IAIN

No, no! We've had enough o' killing.

CALLUM

(*Chiming in.*) Aye, but it was not in his mother's lap he was, when I got hold of him!

IAIN

He's gagged and bound in the cave. (HE *peers out.*) Well, the hunt is up. We'd best be stepping.

DONNACHA

I'll be rousing the lasses.

IAIN

Aye, for they'll need time. That shore's knee-deep wi' weed. And it's" dark, dark! Man, man I was as blind as an ox in a mist, when we came out from yon cave.
(The whistle sounds three times twice over.)

CALLUM

(Sitting up feebly.) And isn't that now the fine music?

DONNACHA

(Knocking at door on right.) Flora! Seonaid! *(The girls come in distractedly.* SEONAID *goes to* CALLUM, *wailing.)*

SEONAID.

Ochonarie! Callum! What's this has come to you?

CALLUM

(Smiling.) Wheesht you, lass! It's only a new fashion in liftings that Iain and myself were after trying.

DONNACHA

Come now, come now! We maun be going!
(donnacha and alasdair help callum to his feet, their arms around his waist. they go out by door on left. seonaid follows. flora, who has drawn to one side as they go, looks back at iain, still peering out of main door, and grasping his pistol.)

FLORA

Will you no' be coming?'

IAIN

(Absorbed, starts.) Be you going down to the boat, lass There's danger here.

FLORA

And if there's danger, where should I be but with the man of my heart?

IAIN

(Starting in amazement.) Oh lass, lass! Whatever is it that you're saying?

FLORA

Iain, Iain! Here's one would be giving you all her love.

IAIN

It canna be.—Go you, Flora.—There's Seoras' death atween us.

FLORA

I ken.—I ken! But I was seeing that all wrong up till now.

IAIN

No, no! His blood's atween us! Aye, and so too will be Callum's if I canna save him.

FLORA

My grief!

IAIN

Be going down to the boat, lass. It's begging you I am!

FLORA

"The Lord do so to me and more also, if aught but death part thee and me."

IAIN

(Greatly moved.) There's danger here.

FLORA

(Very simply.) I'll no' be leaving you.

IAIN

(Exalted.) My dear love! *(He takes her in his arms.)*

FLORA

Mo chridhe!

IAIN

And me thinking this my dark hour and the last!—But dark never no more, for here is the happy one! And you can still be giving me all your love?

FLORA

I have no words. Am I not here?

IAIN

God send we may cheat the red fellows yet! (**HE** *again looks out.*) The sodgers are long o' stirring. Callum may still win clear.—Oh, if we could but hear that third pipe!

FLORA

Can we no' be going?

IAIN

No, no! I maun see Callum safe. We maun wait the third pipe. And then—

FLORA

And then we'll soon be back in Erisort!

IAIN

Erisort? I wonder will it ever be?

FLORA

Think you on Erisort, ma man, for it's there we were happy. But you've the great trouble on you! Oh! your eyes so wild!

IAIN

I'm seeing it—I'm seeing it.

FLORA

(Terrified and clinging to him.) Is it the sight is on you, Iain?

IAIN

(Coming to himself as if from a trance.) I dinna ken; but it was naught evil. 'Twas the old shieling above Keose, lass. *(His face becomes serene again.)* Aye, we'll be going there when this dark day's but a memory that's faded. It will be moonlight there. And your face will be like the white moss, shining and shining in the night, my love, and your words lovelier than the wee burns tinkling in the dark.

FLORA

Iain, Iain!

IAIN

And the snipe and the curlew will cry about us in the hill yonder. And down by the shore Keose will shew a lit window or maybe two; and there will be a wee murmur o' talk floating up from the fishers at Cromore. But Flora MacLeod will be high on the hill above them all, her cheek on the bell-heather; yet she'll no' be minding the roughness o' that pillow, for Iain Dubh, her lover, will be sharing it with her.

FLORA

(Yielding herself to his passionate embrace.) Mo chridhe!

IAIN

My true love! *(**THEY** embrace for a brief moment. Then **HE** suddenly looks out.)* The red-coats! They're on the march! Oh, if that wee whistle would but sound!—But whistle or no whistle, come you, Flora! You maun get to the beach.

FLORA

And you, Iain?

IAIN

I'm with you, lass. I think I see my way now.—Come you!

*(**HE** leads her quickly out by door at back. For a few moments the chamber is empty. Then there is the sound of men running, and of voices. The main door is opened rudely and an **OFFICER** and **FOUR SOLDIERS** enter. Confused orders are given.)*

Officer

The door on the right, Swanson!—Quickly, men! Try the passage on the left!—Now, get to it—get to it!—Quickly men!

(A hurried search is made.)

Copping

(From door on left.) They're on the beach, sir! There's a boat!

Officer

Get to the beach, men. Seize that boat!

(**SOLDIERS** *stream out by door at back. The room is empty for a space. A noise of shouting out-of-doors is heard, then a shot; and* **IAIN**, *still with pistol in hand; races in by door at back, panting.* **HE** *crosses to the open main door at back, then shouts.)*

IAIN

To me! dogs of the Sassenach!

(**HE** *flies out, and the* **OFFICER** *and Two* **SOLDIERS** *follow in pursuit.* **COPPING** *and* **SWANSON** *enter after them, panting.* **COPPING** *goes to main door and looks out.* **SWANSON**, *exhausted, sinks on a chair.)*

SWANSON

My wind's gone, Copping.—Getting too old for this game.—Where are they?

Copping

(Looking out.) On the hill.—They're shouting.—Wonder if they've got him.

SWANSON

Clever dodge that.—The boat's got off by now, I'll wager.—A decoy, Copping—as neat a decoy as ever I saw!

Copping

Aye. The Captain'll get it over the fingers for this night's job. He's messed it. *(A shot is heard.)* Hello.—Let's clear.—They're firing at this place.

(**THEY** *scramble out hastily by door at back, closing it behind them, just as* **IAIN** *rushes in by main door.* **HE** *is panting and bedraggled.* **HE** *shuts door hurriedly, then, crossing to fire, hangs a plaid over two chairs in front of it so as to darken room.* **HE** *blows out the crusies. He opens the door fully next of all, and, standing to the side, looks out to right. The sound of voices and running of feet is heard.* **IAIN** *presents his pistol at the open door.)*

IAIN

Halt! On your life, halt!

VOICE

In the King's name, surrender.

IAIN

Whom do you seek?

VOICE

Callum MacLean of Strathcaol. Lay down your arms!

IAIN

He is not here.

VOICE

In the King's name, lay down your arms.
(*A movement of feet and a clicking of flint-locks is heard.*)

IAIN

Halt, I tell you! Halt!

OFFICER

In the King's name—
(*Two muskets ring out.* IAIN *sinks wounded.* THE OFFICER *and* TWO SOLDIERS *enter and examine* IAIN *briefly.*)

OFFICER

This isn't Callum—curse him! Out again, lads.
(*As the two* SOLDIERS *go out by main door* FLORA *enters by door on left, and runs to* IAIN. SHE *supports his head.* THE OFFICER *halts irresolutely at sight of* FLORA, *but finally follows his men hurriedly.* DONNACHA *comes in by door on left and kneels beside* IAIN.)

IAIN

(*Weakly*). Callum! Callum!
(*The third call of the bosun's pipe is heard—three blasts thrice over.*)

DONNACHA

(*Brokenly as* HE *bends over* IAIN.) The third call! The boat's off!

IAIN

Callum—Safe?

DONNACHA

Aye, he's safe. The brig's sailing.

IAIN

(*With a chuckle.*) I'm saying, Flora, I tellt Callum— I'd shew him what a lifting was.—Him and his nonsense— about—about—the wood at Auchnacraig.

FLORA

Iain! Iain!

IAIN

(Still chuckling.) He'll see now that I ken something about a lift—lift—lifting! Eh, Flora? (**HE** *swoons, but recovers.*)

DONNACHA

Oh, lad, lad! I'm fearing.

IAIN

Tuts man! I'm as strong's a Uist pony. It's but a scart.—See this! (**HE** *raises himself with an effort.*) There!

DONNACHA

Oh, lad, lad!

IAIN

Flora!—lass!

FLORA

(Kneeling by him.) Mo chridhe!

IAIN

My dear love!—If aught but death—
(**HE** *sinks back in* **FLORA**'s *arm and dies as another call of the bosun's pipe is heard, but now further off—three shrill notes thrice over.*)

FLORA

(Keening in a low voice.) Mo thruaighe! Mo thruaighe! Mo thruaighe!

CURTAIN

The Inn of Adventure

A Comedy in Three Acts

TO
THE MEMORY OF
James Salmon
AND
Joseph Seymour Halley

The scene throughout is the common room of the Inn of Aros, in the West Highlands. The period is October 1829.

ACT I   Wednesday Evening
ACT II Thursday Morning
ACT III Friday Evening

Persons

CAPTAIN MACCOLL	RETIRED, LATE 61ST FOOT.
BELLE MACDONALD)	Landladies of the Inn of Aros
BETA MACDONALD)	
MAIRI MACDONALD	their Niece, a girl of sixteen
PHILIP LINNELL	Lieutenant in H.M. Navy, on Special Revenue Duty
ISHBEL MACLEAN	Daughter of a Highland Laird
CARSAIG)	Young Highland Lairds
ARDOW)	
ANNA MACDOUGALL	Housekeeper to Ardow
TOSTARY)	
OOLAVA)	Old Highland Lairds
MOY)	
SILIS	Servant Lass
DONALD GORM	Highland Tinker

THE INN OF ADVENTURE was first produced by The Scottish National Theatre Society, at the Athenaeum Theatre, Glasgow, on 13th October, 1925, under the direction of Frank D. Clewlow, with the following cast:

Mairi MacDonald	MAISIE GREENLEES
Belle MacDonald	NELL BALLANTYNE
Captain MacColl	JAMES ANDERSON
Philip Linnell	MOULTRIE R. KELSALL
Tostary	W. CRUIKSHANK
Moy	GEORGE F. YUILL
Beta MacDonald	MEG B. BUCHANAN
Ishbel MacLean	CATHERINE FLETCHER
Anna MacDougall	ELLIOT C. MASON
Carsaig	ANDREW STEWART
Ardow	JOHN J. NAPIER
Silis	DORA BIRD
Oolava	JAMES A. GIBSON

BELLE, BETA, SILIS and DONALD GORM speak with a Highland accent. All the other Persons of the Play talk straight English.

ACT I

SCENE.—*The common room of the Inn of Aros, late on a night in October, in the year 1829. On the plastered walls, once white but now stained and cracked, are several sombre portraits in oils, two or three faded samplers, a pair of crossed swords, and a gun of ancient type.*

Along the right wall a plain wooden staircase ascends to a low gallery running along the back wall; below the middle of the gallery is a bow window, with bull's-eye panes and a low sill. Some pots of homely flowers are set on this sill—tansy, sweet william, southernwood and wallflower. At the back, under the staircase, a door leads to the landladies' quarters; to the left of the window is a Queen Anne sideboard, with some plate and crockery on it.

In the left wall, near the front, is a door leading downstairs; and further back a wide fireplace with a peat fire. Two lit candles are set on the mantelpiece, and beside them are two small books in brown leather binding. A Jacobean settle and some chairs are placed in front of the fire; and between the settle and the sideboard are a small writing-table and a chair.

To the right of the room's centre is a large table, with several lit candles on it, and some chairs close to it.

The general air of the place is one of simple comfort.

MAIRI MACDONALD, *a girl of sixteen, is reclining on the settle beside the fire, reading a book of verse. Her dress is cherry-coloured, loose-skirted, high-waisted, with full sleeves caught in at the wrist by ribbons; her slippers tied with dark ribbon crossed over the ankle.*

A sound of a distant HIGHLAND CHORUS *sung tipsily comes up from below. It breaks off in a cackle of laughter, and a* BELL *jangles noisily,* MAIRI *sits up in alarm, and listens. A strident* VOICE *is heard declaiming angrily, and there is a crash of chairs overturned. The* BELL *rings again.*

The door at the back opens, and BELLE MACDONALD, *one of the Inn's landladies, appears and crosses quickly to the door on the left. She is a well-preserved woman of fifty-five, dressed in plain black bombazine. She opens the door and listens, as the noise below increases.*

MAIRI

Oh, Auntie, what is it?

BELLE

Just Donald Gorm, lass, in another of his tantrums. But *(rolling up her sleeves)* he's quite the gentleman. He never strikes a woman.

(She goes out, and another long peal is heard. Instantly BETA, BELLE's *sister, appears at the door under the staircase. She is three years* BELLE's *junior, but her visage and manner are sharper. Her dress is similar to that of* BELLE, *but brown.*

BETA

What's this now?

MAIRI

Auntie says it's Donald Gorm.

BETA

The drunken wastrel! I'll Gorm him!

(She also rolls up her sleeves and makes for the door on the left. But before she reaches it **BELLE** *runs in, pursued by* **DONALD GORM**, *a boozy Highland tinker. He is of middle age; his clothes tattered, face and hands unclean, and hair tousled. A string of tin-ware—mugs and platters—hangs from one shoulder, and a heavy haversack from the other.* **BETA** *at once confronts him, while* **BELLE** *retreats behind her.*

BETA

What's this, ye dirty tinker?

DONALD

She spilled the good dram on me, so she did! Knocked it out of my hand, when I was just beginning to commence on it. And who now is to pay for it?

BELLE

What else could I do, and you after striking the serving-lass!

DONALD

Well then, let her keep her long tongue to herself, saying I was drunk. Me drunk! Me! As if three glasses of yon stuff could put Donald Gorm drunk!

BETA

Striking Silis, was he! I'll show him striking!
(She cuffs his cheek soundly and bundles him to the door.

DONALD

Och, Miss Beta, Miss Beta! and you'd lift your hand to poor Donald!

BETA

I would that. Out of this now, or it's more you'll get.
(She thrusts him forcibly down the stair, and follows after.

MAIRI

(excitedly to **BELLE***).* Oh, Auntie, wasn't that fine—the way she gave him yon!

BELLE

Mairi! What a thing to say! *(She listens at the door on the left for a little, then closes it with a sigh.)* Aye, she's at him again. I hope she'll not hurt him too sore, poor man.

MAIRI

Who is he, Auntie?

BELLE

Och, just a drunken tinker, come for the horse-fair on Friday. But what with the drink that's in him, and the handling Beta will be giving him, I'm fearing it's little of that fair he'll see. Likely as not, he'll just be sleeping for a couple of days under some old peat-stack till it's all over ... Wheesht! Here's Beta.

(*She goes out by the door at the back, and* **BETA** *enters, imperturbably letting down her sleeves. Business-like, she crosses to the door at the back without a word.*)

MAIRI

(*eagerly*). Oh, Auntie, did you hit him again?

BETA

(*briefly, as she goes out at the back*). Did I not!

(**MAIRI** *crosses to the open door on the left, listens there for a little, then sighs as if in disappointment, and settles down to her reading once more. (The sound of a* GAELIC CHORUS *is heard, however, and she rises alertly to listen at the door again. But it dies in the distance, and, plainly disappointed, she returns to her book. After reading for some moments, her lips move in a whisper as she repeats the words she sees. She becomes excited, sits up, reads aloud quite clearly; then jumps to her feet, and declaims:*)

MAIRI

"Charge, Chester, charge! On, Stanley, on!" were the last words of Marmion!"

(**BELLE**, *who has come in quietly at the door at the back, looks on amazed.*)

BELLE

Keep me. Mairi! Did I not get there the start!

MAIRI

Oh, Auntie, what did Auntie Beta do to Donald down below.

BELLE

Just cuffed his lugs well once more, and put him on the road. Oh, he's quite the gentleman when he sees Beta, is Donald ... But what is this you're ranting? Is it bard you are, as soon's you set foot in the Highlands?

MAIRI

No, no. It's not mine ... it's Sir Walter's. I'm reading such a wonderful poem ..."Marmion." ... And I got quite carried away!

BELLE

Aye, I'm hearing Sir Walter's the great man!

MAIRI

And—just fancy! I saw him only a week ago, walking down Princes Street just like any ordinary person ... At least, not quite like ... He limps, you know.

BELLE
The poor man! With all his grandeur, and him halting.

MAIRI
Oh! and sailing up the Sound this morning I saw the Castle of Ardtornish ... Ardtornish, where Edith of Lorn dwelt, you remember? It was all so romantick!

BELLE
Aye, I'm glad you enjoyed the sail, lass.

MAIRI
Strange fine things happening in those old times. Not like these dull days of ours.

BELLE
Well, speaking for myself, Mairi, I find the times hereabouts none so dull, especially near a horse-fair, with people like Donald Gorm coming about.

MAIRI
Yes, yes! And wasn't Auntie Beta fine!

BELLE
Och, wheesht you, with your Auntie Beta ... Aye, an Inn in the Highlands need not be long dull with drovers on the roads, or a laird maybe dropping in, or a packman on his rounds.

MAIRI
But no lords and ladies ... Sir Walter's the great hand at the lords and ladies, you know.

BELLE
The world's ay the world, lass, whether there are lords and ladies, or only dusty millers on the high-road.

MAIRI
Ah! but you never have a minstrel with his harp on his shoulder, or a knight in glittering mail tossing off the red wine and riding out into the dark and the rain.

BELLE
Dearie-me! no. The red wine's not so plentiful hereabouts. But we could ay promise you plenty rain.

MAIRI
Now you're laughing at me.

BELLE

Not a bit, lass. I'm only saying we have our own ways. That's all. And I'll wager if it's adventures you're wanting, just you set up as a landlady at a Highland Inn. I've seen this room that busy with travellers, and them quarrelling, you'd be afraid of your life. And all because there weren't enough eggs to go round.

MAIRI

Eggs?

BELLE

Aye, just eggs. You'll get plenty of adventures, let me tell you, when a pack of drovers tumbles in, and the hens not laying.

MAIRI

(*laughing*). Oh, Auntie, that would indeed be romantick! The Inn of Adventure—for you never know when the hens will stop laying!

BELLE

Laugh away, lass. But I'd like to see your great Sir Walter waiting for his breakfast when the hens were off duty.

(**CAPTAIN MACCOLL** *enters hurriedly by the door on the left. He is a man of about sixty, with a martial air, clean-shaven and grey-haired. He wears a fawn-coloured surtout and a black stock, and carries a dark soft hat in his hand.*

BELLE

(*eagerly*). Have you found him?

CAPTAIN

Hush! ... So you've company, I see?

BELLE

And is Mairi only company? ... Dear-a-dear! I clean forgot to tell you she was coming by the packet-boat this morning.

CAPTAIN

Not Mairi, surely—the wonderful niece, all the way from Edinburgh!

BELLE

And who else would it be? ... Stretch yourself, lass, and let the Captain see the length of you for a woman of sixteen ... Aye, and she's all our own for a holiday of a full month, let me tell you. She's big, but she's a MacDonald, of course ... This is Captain MacColl, Mairi ... You've heard tell of him often in our letters.

MAIRI

(*curtsying shyly, while the Captain bows*). Oh, and were you the friend of the great Duke? (*She is all eyes now.*)

BELLE

Lord Wellington's her great hero, Captain ... one of her heroes at any rate, when Sir Walter's not about ... Aye, the Captain's been all over the world with the Duke ... Spain and Portugal, and all the rest of it.

CAPTAIN

Tuts! never heed Spain, Miss Mairi. Tell us what you think of the Highlands, a much finer country ... This is your first visit, isn't it?

MAIRI

Yes, my very first. And, oh, they're wonderful, the Highlands! ... Just as Sir Walter portrays them ... so poetick, so romantick! ... And were you and the Duke in all the great battles!

BELLE

Aye, were they. And where now would the Duke have been without the Captain? Many a helping hand the Captain gave him ... But time you were in your bed, Mairi ... You'll hear plenty about the Duke later, for the Captain's ay at his battles.

CAPTAIN

Oh, Miss Belle, Miss Belle! Come now!

BELLE

Aye, but you are, just. Those wee history books are never out of your hands; and you rampaging because they're not telling the truth.

CAPTAIN

Oh, come now, Miss Belle!

BELLE (*to* **MAIRI**)

Say good-night now, and off with you.

CAPTAIN

There's no escaping her, Mairi. She orders me about just the same. (**MAIRI** *curtsies and says good-night; then goes out at the door at the back. But she leaves her book on the settle.*

BELLE

(*eagerly*). Mr. Linnell? ... Have you found him?

CAPTAIN

Yes. Striding about on Kellan shore, and switching the sedges to bits, like a man possessed.

BELLE

Poor man! And where is he now?

CAPTAIN

I brought him home. But Tostary and Moy got hold of him below-stairs, and they're still there, I fancy.

BELLE

And what business have they with him? It's not about Miss Ishbel, I hope?

CAPTAIN

No, no. It's some affair about the Revenue.

BELLE

But—Miss Ishbel? Is there no news of her?

CAPTAIN

Hush! here's Linnell. And they're with him.

(*The door on the left opens, and* **LINNELL** *enters, in talk with* **TOSTARY** *and* **MOY**. **LINNELL** *is a young man of twenty-four, dark-complexioned and plain-featured; his expression is grave. His dress is that of a Revenue officer.* **TOSTARY** *is a stout man of sixty; he wears a kilt and a long cape.* **MOY** *is fifty-five, a thin hard-bitten man. He wears a bottle-green coat, dark breeches and top-boots.*)

LINNELL

Good-evening, Miss Belle

BELLE

Good-evening, Mr. Linnell

(**TOSTARY** *and* **MOY** *bow to* **MISS BELLE** *and the* **CAPTAIN**, *who return their salutes somewhat stiffly.*)

LINNELL

I have the report in my room. Will you please come up and we can examine it?

(**TOSTARY** *and* **MOY** *accompany him upstairs: all three go out by the door on the right of the gallery.*)

BELLE

(*looking after* **LINNELL**). Aye, he's sore hit, poor lad! ... But what news of Ishbel?

CAPTAIN

She's the fickle one. Little wonder he's downcast. She ran off with Carsaig last night. Her father's mad with rage. The story's all over the countryside.

BELLE

Run off with Carsaig ... that windlestrae! After all her philandering with that fine lad! ... Does he know the way of it?

CAPTAIN
I'll wager he does ... It's countryside clash, I tell you.

BELLE
(contemptuously). Countryside clash! What will they not clash about, and little of it true!

CAPTAIN
Well, it's not the first time for either, as you and I know well, although it's not likely Mr. Linnell has ever heard of that ... Besides, they were seen riding the north road fast and late last night ... And it's certain their horses are in Ardow's stables this morning.

BELLE
Ardow? She's spent the night at Ardow, has she? Aye, that's just where Carsaig would take her ... He and Ardow are thick as thieves ... Poor Ishbel!

CAPTAIN
You may well say! ... Aye, Carsaig and Ardow! As wild a pair of roebucks as e'er the Highlands reared.
    (BETA *enters, unperceived by them, from the door at the back.*

CAPTAIN
Oh, tongues will be wagging, I can assure you.

BELLE
(now observing BETA*'s presence).* Wheesht!

CAPTAIN
(his back to BETA*).* Eh?

BETA
It was " Wheesht " she said, Captain MacColl.

CAPTAIN
(wheeling round). Oh, it's you, Miss Beta

BETA
Yes, only Miss Beta ... And she's to hear nothing, it appears ... The landlady has secrets with a guest that her own sister may not share. Is that the way of it?

CAPTAIN
Guest? Is it me? ... Well, well. In an official sense I've been your guest for many years; but I'm the oldest friend of you both hereabouts, and you'll ay find me where you leave me ... Tuts, Beta, woman! We've nothing to hide ... Tell her, Belle.

BELLE

Tell her yourself. I'm for none of her snash.
> *(She goes out in a flutter at the door at the back.*

CAPTAIN

And what's a poor man-body to do with women so wild!

BETA

Wild, is it? There's folk here would drive a saint wild!

CAPTAIN

I believe you, Beta. We soldiers are clumsy people. Tramping behind a drawn sword's bad for the manners, you know ... You see, it's Mr. Linnell we're concerned about.

BETA

And why?

CAPTAIN

You must have noticed that he's been hanging around the skirts of Ishbel MacLean for some months back ... a love-sick man, if ever there was one.

BETA

Then it's some months lost to him. Ishbel had her eye set on another quarter.

CAPTAIN

On Carsaig?

BETA

Where else?

CAPTAIN

Aye, I knew Carsaig and she had been warm about a year back. But I thought that was all done and by with since Mr. Linnell came about her.

BETA

Just what a man would think.

CAPTAIN

Aye, the men are poor creatures for discerning things like these ... Aye, aye, I can see it now. Very like she was but using Mr. Linnell as a screen for an attack elsewhere, eh?

BETA

Oh, keep on guessing and you'll keep on learning.

CAPTAIN

Och, women, women! They've ay strategy.

BETA

Havers! They've sense: that's all.

CAPTAIN

Agreed, Beta, agreed. More than their share of it, maybe ... But here's our present trouble ... Ishbel made a runaway match with Carsaig last night.

BETA

She did well to run off. Her father could never abide Carsaig.

CAPTAIN

Maybe, maybe. But the story has got to the ears of Mr. Linnell, and now he's like a man demented.

BETA

He's been long that ... And he was double demented ever to have thought of Ishbel MacLean. She was but coquetting him.

CAPTAIN

I tell you he's in a dangerous mood.

BETA

Then let him keep to his work, and stop dawdling after the lasses. Wherever in all the world is his cutter nowadays?

CAPTAIN

Refitting at Greenock, I hear.

BETA

And they're long about it — while my gentleman has the easy time. It's work he wants, I tell you.

CAPTAIN

(irritably). I'll not hear a word against him on that score. He's Charlie Linnell's son, and he'll do his duty just as his father would ... Isn't he busy on the cliffs every day with his spy-glass, on the look-out for the *Hearty Kate*, and the other Irish smugglers? And he has papers enough to look after like other Government folk.

BETA

Tuts! the man's bone-lazy: nothing else.

(**BELLE** *re-enters, still angry.*

BELLE *(to* **BETA***).*

And now are you satisfied?

CAPTAIN

Yes, yes, she's satisfied. And now will you stop your bickering before he comes in on us!

BELLE

Wheesht! They're on the move, up above.
(The women make a pretence of being busy at the sideboard; and the **CAPTAIN** *takes up the little book from the mantel, as* **LINNELL** *comes downstairs with Moy and Tostary.*

LINNELL

I'll see to the matter instantly. I'll go down to Duncan Ban even now, and tell him to warn me at once if he sees any sail the least like that Irish schooner.

TOSTARY

Och, what hurry! A glass of wine with you, Mr. Linnell. Some claret, Belle.

LINNELL

Thank you, but no. I must get my other message off to Loch Scridain at once.

MOY

There's discipline for you! The regular Navy!

TOSTARY

Well, you'll pardon me not accompanying you, sir. I'm tired and must rest a bit. And I want a word with Captain MacColl, if he'll oblige me. *(He turns to the* **CAPTAIN***, and bows are exchanged.)*

LINNELL

I'll say good-night then.

TOSTARY.

Good-night! And much thanks, sir.

MOY.

Good-night, good-night!

*(***LINNELL** *goes out on the left.*

TOSTARY

(taking a decanter and a glass from **BELLE***).* You'll taste, Captain MacColl?

CAPTAIN

Thankee, no. I never wine so late.

TOSTARY

Then you'll excuse Moy and myself. We've had a long drive, and the wind was chilly.

BELLE

You'll ring if you want me, Tostary

TOSTARY.

Thank you, Belle. I shall.

(BELLE *and* BETA *go out at the back.*)

MOY.

A likely lad, this Mr. Linnell

TOSTARY.

Aye, a good fellow. Eh, Captain?

CAPTAIN

(*sharply*). Oh, come to the point, Tostary ... You know who he is?

MOY

Gently, Captain MacColl, gently.

TOSTARY.

It's all right, Moy. He's told me all I wanted to know. So he *is* Charlie Linnell's son, eh? I guessed as much when I heard you were so intimate with him.

CAPTAIN

Yes, he is Charlie Linnell's son. But why should that interest you, of all men?

MOY

Quietly, now, quietly, the both of you.

TOSTARY

Oh, a natural curiosity, first of all. And next, a natural desire to avoid trouble with him.

CAPTAIN

And your curiosity is now satisfied. He is the man you took him to be ... As for the avoidance of trouble, I am afraid I can't help you there.

MOY

It's surely not at your invitation he's here?

CAPTAIN

I had nothing whatever to do with his coming to this place. Indeed, I should have done all I could to prevent his coming, had I but known in time ... But now that he is here, I'll not hold my peace if he should ever ask me who in all the old Regiment were his father's bitterest enemies.

MOY

Och, what need for hard words! Enemies? No, no ... But we had to have some thought as to where the blame lay in the matter of yon dicing at Alverca.

CAPTAIN

Aye, and I know what you and Tostary not only thought but said about that same dicing ... Branded his father as a cheat ... A lie, now twenty years old, but still a lie!

TOSTARY

Well, we could only judge as best we might from the facts before us.

CAPTAIN

And was Charlie Linnell's character not a fact? And the other man's want of character not a fact?

MOY

Och, what need to rage? It's all an old story.

TOSTARY

We did not come here to quarrel, Captain MacColl.

CAPTAIN

Oh, no. Only a sudden interest in the Revenue, I suppose?

TOSTARY

I'll admit that was but an excuse to get a sight of the lad, and a word with yourself regarding him.

CAPTAIN

Well?

TOSTARY

Well, it's unfortunate that he has been posted to Revenue duty up here of all places, where so many of his father's—well—of his father's brother-officers are to be found. The main point is—you don't think, do you, that he's come expressly for the purpose of inquiring into that old affair?

CAPTAIN

Expressly? Godsake, no! I never dreamt of that!

MOY

Well, we trust you'll do nothing to inflame the lad.

CAPTAIN

And if I did, would I not have just cause? Was not his father my closest friend?

MOY

Easy, now, easy.

TOSTARY

But suppose his father did do what the Regiment thought he'd done —

CAPTAIN

Dammit, I'll suppose nothing so foul! ... Suppose I gave you a mouthful of broken teeth. (HE *advances in a rage on* **TOSTARY**.)

MOY

Now, now, Captain MacColl! Tostary has said nothing amiss. He was but putting a case, as you might say.

TOSTARY

I'm only trying to explain that it would be folly for this youth to act as if we blamed him for his father's misfortune.

CAPTAIN

God give me patience! Hark till him, Moy! Heard you ever such blethers ... The honour of the father attacked, and yet the son is not to feel the sting.

MOY

Yes, yes, the lad will have his feelings.

TOSTARY

But, devil take it! We're not living in the times of our grandfathers, a hundred years back, to make such a fuss about family honour. We're men of the world, and to-day's another story.

CAPTAIN

Another story, is it? ... And what if I called you the son of a ... (HE *pauses.*)

TOSTARY

(*Advancing on him*). By God, sir ...!

CAPTAIN

There, you see. Family honour will out, even in Tostary ... What I would have said was ... (*a pause*) son of a gun ... And yet it drew you.

MOY

Spiked, Tostary, spiked! Gad, he had you there! ... But come now, good friends all of us, yes, yes, all of us.

CAPTAIN

Friends be damned! (HE *turns his back on them.*)

MOY

Easy now. Eeasy's the word.

CAPTAIN

You've flung mud at this lad's father for twenty years, and yet you'd forbid me to help him clear his father's name!

TOSTARY

Tuts! ... Well, Moy, it's the road for us now, I suppose. It's getting late.

MOY

Aye, it's late ... I'm sorry, Captain MacColl ... We meant no harm, you'll understand ... Goodnight.

CAPTAIN

(curtly). Oh, good-night.
(They go out on the left. The **CAPTAIN** *instantly crosses to the door at the back.*

CAPTAIN

Belle!

BELLE

(coming in with **BETA***).* And are they gone at last?

CAPTAIN

Yes, yes, they're gone ... But quick now ... Mr. Linnell will be back soon: he's only gone off as far as Duncan Ban's. Set out the cartes, Beta. And when he returns, we maybe can coax him to a game that'll lift him out of this black humour.
*(***BETA** *brings the cards from the sideboard, and lays them on the large table,*
BELLE *draws in the chairs.*

BETA

Just that, something that would lift his mind off the lasses.

CAPTAIN

Och, Beta, but you're bitter ... Now here's something I'd like to know, Belle ... Does this lad ever ask about the lairds hereabouts—which of them were in the old Regiment with his father, and so on, eh?

BELLE

Aye, now and again, he'll ask, Was this one or that in the Sixty-First?

CAPTAIN

My God!

BETA

Whatever's this now?

CAPTAIN

Nothing, nothing. But, all the same, for any sake, keep him off that talk, if he begins again.

BETA

Here's a pickle! As if we hadn't trouble enough about his love affairs, without this father of his tumbling in on us!

CAPTAIN

(severely). Miss Beta, his father's dead and gone, but he was my very dear friend.

BELLE

That wild tongue o' yours, Beta!

BETA

And how was I to know whose father was whose friend?

CAPTAIN

(meditatively). Aye, I'll wager that's it! ... I'll wager that's what he's after. To ferret out all that old quarrel!

BELLE

A quarrel? What's this you're saying, Captain?

CAPTAIN

Lordsake! Did I speak aloud? Then you must keep a quiet sough on anything I've said. I'm just guessing in any case. I may be all wrong.

BETA

Of course you're all wrong. You're ay after some mare's-nest.

BELLE

(shocked). Beta MacDonald!

CAPTAIN

Well, I trust I'm wrong, Beta. But we'll see, we'll see.

BELLE

(briskly). And now let us be going on with the game. (**THEY** seat themselves.) I'll take **DUMMY**.

BETA

And am I to be punished again, with the Captain for partner? It's not fair at all, at all. It's your turn, Belle I had him last night. (**SHE** rises)

BELLE

Sit where you are, woman. It's the Captain will have all the punishment, with you for partner.

(*The* **CAPTAIN** *deals;* **BELLE** *lays out* **DUMMY**; **BELLE** *leads; the* **CAPTAIN** *takes the trick, and leads.*

CAPTAIN

I've a mind to go after that Linnell lad even now, and have it out with him.

(**BELLE** *plays.*

BETA

(to the Captain as she slaps down a card).

Tuts! keep your mind on the game,
   (BELLE *plays from* DUMMY, *and the* CAPTAIN *starts to take the trick, when* BETA *speaks again.*)

That was a trump she played.
   (BELLE *gathers the trick and leads, as* LINNELL *enters from the door on the left. All stop playing.*

CAPTAIN

Ah, there you are, Philip! And in the nick of time. We'll start afresh, and you can partner Miss Belle.

LINNELL

(*picking up the little book from the mantelpiece*). I'm afraid I've no mind for whist to-night. I'd just make a mess of it. Pray excuse me, Miss Belle. May I take a look at your book on the war, Captain?

CAPTAIN

By all means. But they're silly stuff those history books. The men that wrote them knew little of Spain and less of war, to my way of thinking.
   (BETA *plays on* BELLE's *lead, followed by* DUMMY *and the* CAPTAIN. BELLE *takes the trick and leads. The* CAPTAIN *takes the next trick, and* BETA *the next, displaying her triumph openly. Then* BETA *leads as* LINNELL *speaks.*

LINNELL

(*reading*). "MacMurdo"?... "MacKenzie"? ... Strange there were so many Highlanders in the Sixty-First, sir?

CAPTAIN

Aye, it's a far cry from the Highlands to Gloster. But we weren't Scots for nothing, you'll understand.
   (BELLE *plays from* DUMMY, BETA *is impatient with the* CAPTAIN *to go on playing, but he is giving all his attention to* LINNELL *for the moment.*

LINNELL

I hardly follow.

CAPTAIN

Well, we were keen on promotion. And for a Scot in those days that was to be ay seeking south. One man from hereabouts joined the Glosters; then another got a helping hand from him to come down there; and so on and on, you see.

LINNELL

So that in the end nearly all the lairds from this island were in the Sixty-First?

CAPTAIN
(eying him cautiously). That was the way of it. It became a kind of tradition hereabouts.
(BETA *attracts the* CAPTAIN's *attention by snapping her fingers at him, and he plays carelessly.* BELLE *takes the trick to* BETA's *obvious disgust.* BELLE *leads. The* CAPTAIN *takes the next trick and leads.*

LINNELL
(reading again from the book). "Badajos"? Yes, that's what I wanted. I noted the name last night, when I took a glance at the volume in passing; and I made up my mind to come back to it and ask you about it, sir ... I never knew the Sixty-First were at Badajos. My father never spoke of it.

CAPTAIN
Oh, yes, we were there, lad. But that was in the year 'nine, three years before the great Assault. The place wasn't famous then.
(*During this speech,* BELLE *plays, then* DUMMY, *and* BETA *takes the trick,* BELLE *takes the next two tricks in rapid succession.*

LINNELL
I see. I wonder why he never mentioned it.

BELLE
(leading). Are you quite sure you'd not like a hand, Mr. Linnell?

LINNELL
(absorbed). Thank you, no, Miss Belle
(BETA *plays, and* BELLE *plays from* DUMMY. *The* CAPTAIN *is now evidently perturbed by* LINNELL's *questioning, and hesitates over his cards.* BETA, *impatient, glares at him.*

LINNELL
(reading). "Alverca"? It's strange I never heard him speak of Alverca.

CAPTAIN
(about to select one of his cards, drops all in confusion). And why should you, Philip? Alverca was but a halt in the by-going, as it were.

LINNELL
But this writer says they were there for three weeks?

CAPTAIN
That writer's a fool then. Nothing of the kind. Three weeks! Nonsense! And it was merely a rest, I tell you. No action of any consequence, and yet he must drag it into a campaign like yon!
(*The* CAPTAIN *retrieves his cards, and plays at last. But to* BETA's *dismay* BELLE *takes the trick.* BELLE *leads,* DUMMY *and the* CAPTAIN *play; and* BETA *takes the trick and leads. The* CAPTAIN *throws down his last card at once, as do the others, and* BETA *again takes the trick.*

LINNELL

How long was the Regiment really at Alverca?

CAPTAIN

Oh, I don't know—some days, I suppose.

LINNELL

(rising, and pacing up and down in some agitation). How many days, sir?

CAPTAIN

(agitated in turn, and picking up some cards aimlessly). Really, Philip, you must not catechise me. These things are long past, and my memory's not what it used to be.

(**MAIRI** *enters suddenly by the door at the back. Her hair is loose, and she wears a wrapper. She does not perceive* **LINNELL**, *and crosses to* **MISS BELLE**

MAIRI

Oh, Auntie, my book ... I forgot it.
(She picks up the volume of Scott from the settle.

BELLE

(rising in dismay). Lassie, lassie! you must not come into the common room of an Inn unless you're bidden. You must learn the ways of this place. We have only one common room here for everybody, you must understand.

MAIRI

(looking round and catching sight of Linnell). Oh, Auntie!

LINNELL

I didn't know you had a visitor, Miss Belle. Don't let me disturb you, pray. I'll go.

BELLE

No, no. It's just my niece from Edinburgh— my brother's child, Mairi MacDonald ... Mairi, this is Mr. Linnell of the Navy, who stays here, *(Linnell bows and Mairi curtsies.)* Mairi is on holiday with us.

LINNELL

Really! For long? *(His melancholy has lightened considerably.)*

BELLE

A whole month. But it's her first visit, and she doesn't know the ways of this queer old house as yet.

LINNELL

But I trust she won't regard me as a stickler for the formalities ... Ah! *(he glances at her book)* a reader of Sir Walter, I see.

BELLE

Aye, she's the great reader. And I'll warrant she thinks she can have her bed-candle here, just as she has in Edinburgh. But, no, no, Mairi! I'll take no risks. You'll have the place on fire if you read in bed.

MAIRI

Oh, Auntie, just for a few minutes!

LINNELL

Is it "Waverley"?

MAIRI

(handing him the volume). No, "The Lord of the Isles" and "Marmion".

LINNELL

Ah! for a Highland holiday, what could be better!

MAIRI

Yes, isn't it fine poetry!

BELLE

(cutting in). No doubt it's all that, Mairi. But trot off now, or you'll be taking cold. Sir Walter can wait till the morning. *(She takes the book and lays it on the mantelpiece.)*

MAIRI

(protesting). Oh, but Auntie ...

BELLE

Come, and I'll go with you. Our game is finished anyway. Goodnight, Captain. Good-night, Mr. Linnell. You'll excuse the lassie running in on us.

(**MAIRI** *curtsies,* **BETA** *rises, and both go out with* **BELLE** *at the back.*

LINNELL

(turning to the Captain impulsively). This Alverca affair ... I'm sorry, sir. I should not have spoken as I did.

CAPTAIN

(gently). Well, I'm glad you have spoken. But what need to quiz me, your father's oldest friend? Why not have come to me openly about what you're seeking?

LINNELL

Seeking!

CAPTAIN

Aye, seeking. You've been quizzing Miss Belle and the Lord knows who—everybody but myself, it seems. It's some wild-goose chase: your father's connection with the Sixty-First at the bottom of it all, eh?

LINNELL

Then you understand, sir?

CAPTAIN

(gently). Understand what, lad?

LINNELL

Why I have come to this place.

CAPTAIN

No, but I can guess. Yet why should I have to guess?—I who owe my life to your father—who loved him like a very brother. You must have seen how close we were down in Devon.

LINNELL

I did, sir. But I also saw how powerless you were to lift the gloom that overcame him at times when you visited us. I could see too that it had something to do with some men in his old Regiment, with men, in short, who came from this part of the country ... A name would be named, and brightness would fall from him for hours thereafter.

CAPTAIN

So that's what brought you here?

LINNELL

What else? Oh, I must clear his memory from that old stain.

CAPTAIN

Stain?

LINNELL

Yes, stain. Was there ever a man of them from hereabouts came about us down in Devon except yourself? And I know of three at least who came year after year to the hunt within ten miles of us, yet never looked near.

CAPTAIN

Lad, lad!

LINNELL

Oh, you tell me nothing! What was at the root of it all?

CAPTAIN

A moment. I think I can show you something that will help you to understand.
  (*He goes upstairs quickly and turns through the door on the right.* **LINNELL** *paces up and down restlessly until the* **CAPTAIN** *returns to him.*)

CAPTAIN

See here! (*He tosses some small objects on the table.*)

LINNELL

Dice! And green with age?

CAPTAIN

Never mind the colour, lad ... Try them.

LINNELL

(tossing them several times). Cinque and cinque, every throw ... They're loaded!

CAPTAIN

Aye, loaded.

LINNELL.

Not my father's, I'll swear.

CAPTAIN

Godsake! no ... The other man's ... But they got swept to the floor with the glasses and all the rest when the row began ... The other fellow swore they were your father's ... And there was no proof one way or the other.

LINNELL

When was this?

CAPTAIN

Twenty years ago and more. In Spain—at the very place you hit upon in your reading to-night— Alverca ... The Regiment was quartered in the old convent there—just as the little book said—for three weeks.

LINNELL

Yes, yes, but what followed the dicing?

CAPTAIN

Oh, a duel of course. The other man was wounded. The rest was talk.

LINNELL

And the affair was never cleared up?

CAPTAIN

Never. But does that leave you or me in any doubt as to the real owner of these dice I picked up that night in Alverca?

LINNELL

No, no ... But who was the other? Is he in this countryside?

CAPTAIN

His grave is.

LINNELL

Ah!

(A knocking is heard below-stairs. Both start.

CAPTAIN

(listening). Drovers, most likely.

BELLE

(entering hurriedly from the back). Somebody late abroad surely.

CAPTAIN

Aye, close on eleven.

BELLE

(as she goes out on the left). And the servant lass bedded!

CAPTAIN

And so, Philip, you've taken all this roundabout to discover something you might have had straightaway from myself for the asking.

LINNELL

Ah! it's easy to be wise after the event! But I was working in the dark—dreading the light even— confused—dubious as to the next step. All I saw was that I must come up here.

CAPTAIN

Aye, and I'll wager you even went the length of asking for a transfer from the Navy to gain your end?

LINNELL

I did. The speediest way was to transfer to the Revenue. I'd heard this post was vacant ... I tell you, as soon as I'd heard that, it was laid upon me to come up here. The very men who had slighted him—my father, I mean—slighted him down in Devon are here.

CAPTAIN

They are, damn them! Sorrow on me that I should have to speak so of any man of the Sixty-First; but there it is. Good soldiers, mind you, in their time; but dull wits in anything outside soldiering. God! How I hate the lot!

LINNELL

And then you were here. And time and again I meant to seek your confidence sooner than this.

CAPTAIN

Oh, lad, if you only had!

LINNELL

But there were other matters that troubled me ... Well, there were ... oh, how shall I explain ...?

CAPTAIN

I know, Philip ... Another burden for you ... Ishbel?

LINNELL

You've heard the story ... They say she's off with Carsaig. But I'll not believe it. She's staunch, I tell you ... It's said they were at the house of Ardow last night ... I've never met this Ardow. Is he young?

CAPTAIN

Yes, and one of Carsaig's own kidney—a roving blade.

LINNELL

There's some devilry in this. Ishbel was as good as promised to me.

CAPTAIN

Women are strange.

LINNELL

But not Ishbel. She'll not alter.

CAPTAIN

Carsaig has known her longer, lad.

LINNELL

But in these things time does not count ... Oh, I've a mind to ride to Ardow at once, and learn the truth.

CAPTAIN

Do not bring Ardow into this ... also.

LINNELL

Also? ... What do you mean, sir?

CAPTAIN

I mean that his father once fought a duel at Alverca.

LINNELL

My God! Then his father was the cheat? ... And he's dead.

CAPTAIN

Aye, but living again in young Ardow—as bad and bitter as the old fellow. And I'd have you keep clear of him, Philip. Sorrow enough that your fathers fought, without the sons doing that same.

LINNELL

Tush! I'd no thought of a vendetta.

CAPTAIN

Good. But young Ardow's as hot-headed as yourself. And he's both fool and knave. Keep clear of him, I say.

(**BELLE**, *unperceived by* **LINNELL**, *whose back is turned to her, comes to the door on the left, and beckons excitedly to the* **CAPTAIN**, *signalling to him to get* **LINNELL** *out of the room. She then retreats downstairs again.*

CAPTAIN

I hear these new-comers moving below, Philip. They'll be coming up here; and you're in no fit state to meet strangers at present, with all this trouble so heavy on you. So let us go up to my room till Belle sees these folk settled for the night. There are some old letters of your father's I'd like to show you. They bear on this business of that dicing at Alverca ... Shall we go?

LINNELL

Gladly. Ah, I should have come to you first of all. I see that plainly now.

(They go upstairs and through the gallery door on the right. As they go, **BELLE** *opens the door on the left cautiously and watches them till they disappear, then ushers in two women, somewhat travel-stained —* **ISHBEL MACLEAN** *and* **ANNA MACDOUGALL**. **ISHBEL** *is about twenty-six, dark-haired, and dressed in a dark riding habit; she wears a hat known as a Joseph.* **ANNA** *is about sixty, heavy in build but active in all her movements; her dress and cloak are of rusty black. She carries two travelling packs.)*

BELLE

(crossing diagonally to the stairs). This way, Miss Ishbel.

(All go upstairs and along the gallery to the left door there. As they disappear through this, the **CAPTAIN** *comes out from his room, and looks after them; then, descending the stair, he looks again at the door on the left of the gallery, his finger to his lip as if pondering the situation.* **BELLE** *comes out on the gallery, sees him, and, making a sign for silence, descends to him.)*

CAPTAIN

That's Ishbel! What in all the world has brought her here?

BELLE

The worst wind of fortune ... with Mr. Linnell in this house.

CAPTAIN

But what's ado?

BELLE

Just woman's perversity.

CAPTAIN

But isn't Carsaig with her?

BELLE

Och, ochan! Hasn't she broken with Carsaig already!

CAPTAIN

And for why?

BELLE

The Lord alone knows! Horses at midnight, and a marriage planned for this morning, says Anna. And now it's no marriage will there ever be, I'm seeing. Poor Ishbel! Her name a by-word from now on!

(ANNA *comes downstairs very quietly,* BELLE *starts.*) Shield us! who is this now?

ANNA

Only Anna MacDougall ... She's lying down. And time too, for she's worn out, poor lass ... Och, this night, this night! Whatever will be the end of this! ... Has her father been here yet?

CAPTAIN

Not he. He'll not stir a foot to help her. Swears he disowns her, they're saying.

BELLE

Aye, and they're saying too that if you poured cold water on his old bald head it would be boiling. She must bide her time till he cools.

ANNA

Stubborn old stot!

CAPTAIN

Well, well, Anna, it's no easy task you have— housekeeping at Ardow.

ANNA

Housekeeping at Ardow, is it? I'm done with that. I'm by with young Ardow, the black rascal!

CAPTAIN

He's all that ... But whatever made you bring Ishbel this gate? If she's cast off Carsaig, here's another cast-off of hers to reckon with, behind that door even now.

ANNA

And who's that?

BELLE

Mr. Linnell, the new Revenue officer, poor man!

ANNA

Och, that flyaway! But he's surely never in earnest?

CAPTAIN

Well, he thinks he is.

ANNA

(*seating herself easily on the settle*). Then he'll do a lot of thinking before he's finished with Ishbel. She's a weathercock, if ever there was one.

BELLE

(*taking a seat beside* ANNA). And what now has come over Carsaig?

ANNA

Oh, ask the drink and the dice at Ardow. Carsaig and yon black one are still busy at them since last night, I'll warrant.

CAPTAIN

Carsaig! Last night! His wedding eve, and he at the dicing! ... God! what a slight to the woman!

ANNA

Oh, it wasn't Carsaig's fault. His nerves were on the raw with the runaway ploy. Ardow's was all the blame, to be leading him on.

BELLE

The young lairds, the young lairds! They're all the same; and what's to come of this countryside! Oh, but they're foolish, foolish!

ANNA

It was dice and drink night-long. The house was shaking with the storm, but you could hear the noise of yon two's quarrelling through every blast.

BELLE

Mo thruaighe! As bad as all that!

ANNA

And at last we could bear it no longer; and down we came to listen at their chamber door, fearing they'd be at each other's thrapples.

BELLE

This night, this night!

ANNA

And what, think you, they were after? What, but gambling away the good lands their fathers gave them!

BELLE

Och, ochan!

ANNA

Aye, Highland hilltop against Highland hilltop: Ben Iolaire against Ben Creagach, Ben Creagach against Ben Add; and the fine straths between. And not an acre of Carsaig's, I'll wager, will be left to him when they finish, with yon dark one across the table.

BELLE

That ever the like should be in Eilean Aros!

CAPTAIN

It was dicing they were. You're sure it was the dice?

ANNA

Sure? Aye ... I know the clink of dice in yon house too well, from his father's time right on.

BELLE

And Carsaig's a landless man!

ANNA

On they went shouting and roaring at each other. We rapped their door well, and called on them to open; and they but jeered at us, and never the opening. The end of it was that we could bide there no longer: we were indeed in fear for our lives ... Drink and dice, drink and dice! ... So, in the grey of the morning, we rode off for the Inns at Kilbride.

BELLE

A dirty hole.

ANNA

Aye, a day there was enough for us. And so we came on here ... But, save us! Here am I havering, and clean forgetting what was my message ... A sup and a bite, Belle, for we're starving after the fare at Kilbride.

BELLE

I'll make a posset. Come you in with me, Anna.

CAPTAIN

(*speaking, just as they reach the door at the back*). You're sure it was dicing, Anna?

ANNA

What a man for the questions! Yes, yes, I know the clink of the dice too well—the green rattlers, his father called them.

CAPTAIN

So the dice were really his father's, Anna ... and green?

ANNA

Isn't that what I'm saying. His own father's, and green with age. They might well have been his great-grandfather's by the colour of them.

CAPTAIN

Then, wait you a moment, Anna. I want Mr. Linnell to hear that bit of the story. (*He dashes to the foot of the stairs, and cries out excitedly:*) Philip! Come down! We have them, lad!

ANNA

Och, I've not time for Mr. Linnell, or your questions, Captain, I've that posset to see to. Come you, Belle.

(She goes out with BELLE *at the door at the back, leaving the* CAPTAIN *perturbed by her abruptness.* ISHBEL *comes out of the gallery door on the left, sees him, and comes downstairs hurriedly.*

ISHBEL

Is Anna here? ... Someone called. *(*LINNELL *has now come out from his room, and he and* ISHBEL *stand gazing at each other. He comes down to her, his hands outstretched, but she moves away from him, then turns to the* CAPTAIN, *saying)* Please! *(Without a word the* CAPTAIN *goes quickly upstairs and so into his room,* ISHBEL *turns to* LINNELL*)* Why are you here?

LINNELL

I have rooms at this Inn.

ISHBEL

You've left Callachly?

LINNELL

A week ago.

ISHBEL

About myself—you've heard?

LINNELL

Yes ... gone away ... I did not know ... you'd returned.

ISHBEL

I've broken with him ... Oh, what a world!

LINNELL

Broken already! Aye, what a world!

ISHBEL

You're bitter.

LINNELL

Haven't I cause?

ISHBEL

I never gave you cause.

LINNELL

Never? Then, the woods of Draolinn, that night on the beach of Drumlang? Were they only a make-believe?

ISHBEL

Well, here's your revenge. For, have I not also been lightlied?

LINNELL

Heavens! Has Carsaig—?

ISHBEL

No, no. It was I that broke with him. And with good reason.

LINNELL

Better reason than when you broke with me?

ISHBEL

(*breaking down*). Oh, where's to be the end of this! (*A* KNOCKING *is heard below*). I'd best be going ... . Oh, Philip, be you still the good friend.

(*Much moved, he kisses her hand, and she disappears upstairs,* ANNA *and* BELLE *come in at the back with* BETA *following,* ANNA *has a tray with the posset-cup and other dishes on it; she goes upstairs,* BETA *crosses to the door on the left and listens. The knocking is repeated*

BELLE

Will we ever get to sleep this night at all, at all? I hope it will not be Donald Gorm again.

BETA

No, no; Donald has had enough hard knocks for one day. It'll be the Glasgow horse-coupers more likely. They're ay early at every fair.

BELLE

Go you down then, and tell them we're bedded out.

BETA

I'll tell them no lies. I wonder at you, Belle MacDonald.

BELLE

We've had enough ado this night. Be sending them on to the Inns at Callachly. (BETA *goes out by the door on the left*) You're tired, Mr. Linnell A glass of wine?

LINNELL

No, thank you, Miss Belle.

BELLE

(*persistent, and setting out a glass and the claret jug*). A wee drop?

LINNELL

Well, yes. You're very kind.

(*He is drinking, and looking again at some pages of the little history book, when* CARSAIG *and* ARDOW *are ushered in by* BETA, CARSAIG *is a man of thirty, with high colour and fair hair. Despite his confident bearing, he is very restless.* ARDOW *is about the same age, has a blasé air and a trick of holding his chin high; he is pale-featured and dark-haired. Both wear riding cloaks and Hessian boots.*

CARSAIG

Good-evening, Belle. My regrets for a late call. Beta tells me Miss Ishbel's here.

BELLE

(bridling). She is, Carsaig.

ARDOW

And Anna MacDougall?

BELLE

She is, Ardow.

CARSAIG

Have they retired?

BELLE

I'll see, sir.
 (She moves towards the stairs, but halts as **CARSAIG** *speaks again.*

CARSAIG

Ah, Mr. Linnell, I did not perceive you. *(He bows: then in a matter-of-fact tone, as he turns to* **ARDOW***)* We'll stop here overnight, eh, Colin?

ARDOW

Of course. I'm horse-sick, I can tell you. No more riding this night, by your leave.

BELLE

I'm sorry, Carsaig, but we've no rooms free.

BETA

What nonsense, Belle! We've plenty odd corners we could make a bed in. And I think the gentlemen of our own countryside have ay first call on us.
 (She glances meaningly at **LINNELL***, and* **BELLE***, frowning, goes off upstairs.*

CARSAIG

Hear, hear, Beta! ... Ah, yes *(turning to* **LINNELL***).* I thought you lodged at Callachly, Mr. Linnell?

LINNELL

(precisely). I did till a week ago.

ARDOW

(cavalierly). So this is Mr. Linnell?

LINNELL

It is, sir. And who the devil are you?

ARDOW

Colin MacCalman of Ardow, at your service.

LINNELL

(on his feet at once). Indeed! *(The two men regard one another keenly.)*

ARDOW

Ah, a uniform? I'm sorry, sir. I did not take you. You are the new Revenue officer?

LINNELL

(bowing). Sir, I am obliged. I have heard of you.

ARDOW

(bowing in turn). My misfortune that we haven't met before.

(BELLE comes downstairs, followed by ISHBEL.)

ISHBEL

What are your wants, Carsaig?

CARSAIG

Only a word in private.

ISHBEL

All here are my friends. I include Mr. Linnell You may say your word before them.

(BELLE and BETA steal off by the door at the back.)

ARDOW

Mr. Linnell, may I beg the favour of your company below-stairs?

LINNELL

By all means. I've no wish to intrude.

ARDOW

(as they make for the door). Oh, it's not the intrusion I'm considering. 'Tis your health, sir. After you. *(He bows at the head of the stair.)*

LINNELL

What do you hint? ... *(He halts.)* There's a lady here.

ARDOW

There is. And her fingers are crisping already. It's really safer downstairs for us both.

CARSAIG

(angrily). Enough, Ardow.

LINNELL

Are you in your senses, sir! *(then, to ISHBEL)* Your pardon. *(He bows, and turns to find ARDOW has gone out. He follows him hastily.)*

CARSAIG

Ishbel, lass, I'm sorry that fellow has so loose a tongue. But he'll hear from me further about this ... For myself, what shall I say? ... Yesterday I was daft.

ISHBEL

Indeed, yes.

CARSAIG

That wild gallop with you along the shore! There was magic—yes, magic in the air last night.

ISHBEL

In the wine-flagon, rather. And black the magic there.

CARSAIG

I know, I know. That wine was madness.

ISHBEL

And gambling on your wedding-eve?

CARSAIG

My curses on that dicing-cogie!

ISHBEL

Your wedding-eve! Oh, I've heard little worse, save a story of my father's of horses stabled in a church in Spain, while the nuns knelt at the high altar.

CARSAIG

Forgive me, lass! I was crazy with delight at having you with me at last. I could have hung my hat on the horns of the moon. And then, the wine and the wine, my grief!

ISHBEL

And your birthright gamed away! Neither stick nor stone left to you!

CARSAIG

Tuts! I'll win it back, all of it. And I've not lost all if I've you...

ISHBEL

No, Alan, I've had my lesson. We must make an end ... Oh, what kind of friend is Ardow to be robbing you!

CARSAIG

Robbing? It was fair play, and a debt of honour. And indeed he offered to return half his winnings. But how in common decency could I have taken them back? Wait you, I'll have better luck next time.

ISHBEL
Next time! You're indeed daft ... No, no, Alan, I'm by with you.

CARSAIG
But, Ishbel ...!

ISHBEL
No. There's a door shut in my mind, and I can't see past it. This is the end.
(Without a word further, SHE passes him, goes upstairs, and so to her room, while he stands as if dazed. BELLE comes in from the back, bringing in bed-candles, which she sets down on the sideboard.

BELLE
Are you still in the mind to be stopping here to-night, Carsaig?

CARSAIG
No, I'll be going ... Yes, I'll be going.
(HE goes out hurriedly on the left just as LINNELL enters there. THEY scowl at each other. LINNELL moves restlessly about the room. BELLE is placidly concocting a negus at the sideboard.

BELLE
A glass of negus, sir?

LINNELL
Nothing, Miss Belle. I'm for nothing.

BELLE
(crossing to the foot of the stairs and calling). Your negus, Captain!
(The CAPTAIN appears at his door and comes down. He offers a glass of negus to LINNELL

CAPTAIN
Good stuff, Philip.

LINNELL
No, thankee ... Carsaig's been here.

CAPTAIN
Indeed?

LINNELL
And that sneering puppy, Ardow.

CAPTAIN
Well, well, so you've met? ... And Miss Ishbel? Is she still here?

LINNELL
Yes, thank God!

CAPTAIN
Aye, and you've met young Ardow already?

LINNELL
Yes, and he's just as you said—both fool and knave. I've had warm words with him down below.

CAPTAIN
(eagerly). Heavens above! He didn't connect you with your father, did he?

LINNELL
I shouldn't have cared if he had, the hound! No, no, I'd other grounds for quarrel ... Pah! how he jested about this elopement!

CAPTAIN
Body o' me! I'll rip the guts out o' him!

LINNELL
Ugh! His talk was too vile even for a taproom. I'd gladly meet him at forty paces any day!

CAPTAIN
Tuts! Here am I inflaming you when we need all our wits about us. Forty paces? No, no. Would that clear your father's name?
(**LINNELL** *starts and looks eagerly at him. Something in the* **CAPTAIN***'s tone has roused him.*

LINNELL
What do you mean, sir?

CAPTAIN
(grimly). I think we have them—your father's old messmates in this countryside—old Ardow's cronies ... Black Judases! *(He takes out the dice and tosses them.)* Cinque, cinque! ... God! but we'll roast them with these wee dice, and clear your father's memory.

LINNELL
(excited). Only show me. You think we can?

CAPTAIN
Yes. For Carsaig lost every rood of his land to young Ardow last night ... at the dice.

LINNELL
The dice?

CAPTAIN
Aye, the very neighbours of these—his father's dice; the bone not very good, and green with age, even as these are.

LINNELL

And loaded?

CAPTAIN

Some of them, I'll warrant.

LINNELL

Like father, like son.

CAPTAIN

Just that. I'll wager the son has plenty more, the match of these fellows. *(He tosses the dice on to the table once more.)* Cinque, cinque ... Aye, the bone not good, and green with age. Anna MacDougall will bear me out in that, if need be.

LINNELL

Ah!

CAPTAIN

Gad! We'll make Tostary and Moy and Oolava eat dirt before the week's out! Yes, we'll have them on Horse Fair night.

LINNELL

On Friday?

CAPTAIN

Aye. Every man-jack of them is sure to be here at the Horse Fair.

LINNELL

And you see a way?

CAPTAIN

I see a way, if you'll help me.

LINNELL

Captain!
(They grasp hands warmly. The lock of the door at the back suddenly clicks, and the **CAPTAIN** *turns swiftly.*

CAPTAIN

What was that?
(The door under the stairs opens slowly on a corridor now dark save for the light of a candle carried by **MAIRI**, *who steals in. Her hair is loose, and she is swathed in her wrapper.*

MAIRI

Hush! ... Sir Walter!
(She tiptoes to the mantelpiece, picks up her book, places her finger on her lips to enjoin secrecy, and vanishes by the way she came. **LINNELL**, *as if fascinated, gazes at the closed door; and at sight of him thus transfigured the* **CAPTAIN**

crosses to the sideboard to take up his bed-candle. He lights this at one of the candles on the mantelpiece, and turns to find LINNELL *still at gaze on that magic door.*

CAPTAIN

Well what about turning in, Philip?

LINNELL

(beginning to pace up and down, as if again the old restlessness had returned). Yes, yes, presently.

CAPTAIN

(quizzically). Well, well!
(He goes upstairs, looking back now and again with a smile at LINNELL, *who has taken up his bed-candle and is lighting it at a mantelpiece candle. This done,* LINNELL *makes for the stair, but, half-way across the room, he halts and looks again expectantly at the door at the back.*

CAPTAIN

There's an extinguisher on the mantelpiece, Philip.

LINNELL

Pardon?

CAPTAIN

Oh, put out the lights, man.

LINNELL

(blowing out his own bed-candle at once, and speaking in a whisper). What's to do?

CAPTAIN

No, no, not that one ... Look at the mantelpiece.

LINNELL

Ah, of course ...!
(He retraces his path, lights his bed-candle again, extinguishes the lights on the mantelpiece, and tiptoes across the room once more to the stairs. But his eyes are fixed on the door at the back, and he stumbles at the first of the stairs' steps, then assuming a business-like air he follows the CAPTAIN —*who has been surveying the performance from the gallery*—*through the little door of their room.*

CURTAIN

ACT II

Scene.—The same. Next morning. The curtains are pulled aside and the window is open. It is full sunlight out-of-doors, and great free spaces of hill and glen and loch are seen. There is a slight darkening of the sky from time to time as if rain were threatening. The CAPTAIN *sits by the fire, horn specs on nose, reading one of the little war books,* LINNELL *sits at the large table, busy with his Revenue papers.*

CAPTAIN

(laughing suddenly). Ha!

LINNELL

Well?

CAPTAIN

Not to interrupt your ship's accounts, Philip—but just listen to this fellow on the battle at Salamanca. He's got everything jumbled up.

LINNELL

He wasn't there, of course?

CAPTAIN

No, sir, he most certainly was not. Listen. *(He reads)* "Clinton's division, reaching the hill, at once charged with the bayonet, and the enemy abandoned the position in confusion." ... Heard you ever such nonsense! And they call that history! ... Might do for a dispatch ... But history ...? Well, I like my history with a wee bit more detail.

LINNELL

A trifle casual, sir.

CAPTAIN

A trifle! A trifle, say you? I'd like to have a trifle of his gizzard in my hands! ... What about the rye-grass, three feet high, that the Regiment was in the thick of, eh? It's a detail, of course, but that ryegrass was on fire.

LINNELL

And three feet high!

CAPTAIN

What about the French skirmishers in front of us, and what about their cavalry on our right?

LINNELL

Oh, he'd skip all that, I suppose?

CAPTAIN

He does, sir, he does, damn him! ... And isn't he glib about yon hill! The very hill where your father cut down a Frenchman and saved my life! ... It's just "the hill," if you please ... My God! on that night it was a burning mountain tipped with shining steel ... Tuts! *(He flings the book aside.)*

LINNELL

The man's a fool; that's plain.

CAPTAIN

And the rest's in keeping with that kind of muck ... However, he does admit the Sixty-First were at Salamanca; and he hints we were of some use at Talavera. But not a word of us at Busaco—or Fuentes d'Onor, Ciudad Rodrigo, or the Pyrenees; not a syllable about the Nivelle battle, or the Nive—or Orthez—or Toulouse. May I be shot if I don't think I'm dreaming, Philip! Maybe there never was any Sixty-First, after all! Ha!

*(**SILIS**, the serving-lass, now enters with difficulty on the left. She is carrying a light chair.*

CAPTAIN

Well, well, and what's this?

LINNELL

(holding the door for her) Is that better?

SILIS

Oh, thank you, sir.

*(Panting, she passes to the stair, and so to the door on the gallery's left, **BELLE** and **BETA** enter, carrying wraps and cushions. They also make for the stair.*

BELLE

(halting). You must excuse us. We're redding up the room for Miss Ishbel.

(The men bow, but do not answer.

BETA

Oh, come your ways, Belle. A hint's ay lost on some folk.

BELLE

I'm hinting none, Beta. I was only thinking aloud, so to speak—wondering if the gentlemen would prefer to be in their own rooms, while the ladies came down here to let us get on with the redding.

LINNELL

By all means, let the ladies come down. We can move elsewhere; we mustn't intrude.

BETA

I've heard tell the Inns at Callachly are very comfortable, Mr. Linnell.

BELLE

(*protesting*). Beta MacDonald!

LINNELL

(*bridling*). Exceedingly comfortable, Miss Beta. And yet I've no thought, I assure you, of returning there at once.

BELLE

Of course not, sir. Stay you on as long as you've a mind to.

(BETA *goes upstairs to* ISHBEL's *room, with a toss of her head, passing* SILIS *coming down, who crosses the room and goes out on the left.*

LINNELL

Thank you, Miss Belle. All the same, I shall probably have to leave here, once the Horse Fair's over.

BELLE

The Horse Fair?

LINNELL

Yes, to-morrow, isn't it? ... It's awkward, of course, my being here just now. (*He glances up at the door of* ISHBEL's *room.*)

BELLE

Yes, sir. And it's just as awkward for Miss Ishbel.

CAPTAIN

(*irritably*). We're not discussing the lady.

BELLE

(*easily*). I hear you, Captain (*Then, to* LINNELL) You see, she cannot go home as yet, for her father's the wild old man. She's as keen as yourself to be off out o' this.

LINNELL

(*perturbed*). Yes, yes, I understand.

BELLE

Her father will have none of her just now.

And so, you see, we plan to cool him down by keeping her quiet here for a bit.

LINNELL

However, Miss Ishbel's home affairs are really no concern of ours, are they?

CAPTAIN

Didn't I tell you, Belle?

BELLE

But I'm only explaining. *(Then to* LINNELL*)* Och, yes, it's her father's the trouble. We must give him time to simmer down. The last time she ran off with Carsaig, it was three weeks before the old man got off the boil.

LINNELL

(horrified). The last time?

BELLE

Aye, a year ago come Michaelmas. Oh, we know her father's ways by now, you may be sure ... We'll just let him simmer down, you understand.

(She goes off upstairs, nodding knowingly to LINNELL*)*

LINNELL

Captain! Did you hear? ... "Last time!" Is this true?

CAPTAIN

Well, Philip, I cannot quite remember all the pranks of the young folks hereabouts. There's been a good deal of that kind of thing among them of late.

LINNELL

Come now, you're jesting?

CAPTAIN

Indeed, I'm not! The young people are ill to bind ever since those fellows, Byron and Scott, began their heady poetry stuff.

LINNELL

Of course, you're only chaffing me!

CAPTAIN

Nothing of the kind. Poetry's as catching as measles, these days. And runaway matches have been quite common these two years back. Young Lochinvars are as busy as can be all over the country, aye, even in England, I believe. The English have discovered the advantages of a Scots marriage; and I hear there's a place down on the borders—Gretna Green by name— where they ...

LINNELL

Nonsense, sir. Ishbel's not that kind of woman.

CAPTAIN

Nonsense yourself! Every woman's that kind of woman ... And they're worse than ever since this fellow Byron got such a hold ... You read him yourself, I judge.

LINNELL
You're pleased to be sarcastic, sir.

CAPTAIN
And you, Philip, to be indiscreet.

LINNELL
Indeed?

CAPTAIN
Yes. What the devil do you mean by talking about the Horse Fair keeping you at this Inn? You'll give away all our plans if you are not careful.

LINNELL
I'm sorry. I got confused with Beta's nagging.

CAPTAIN
Be wary, lad'. It's a big stake—your father's good name, no less.

LINNELL
I'll not forget.

CAPTAIN
If you should run across young Ardow again for God's sake keep a grip of your tongue.

LINNELL
Oh, never fear.

CAPTAIN
Keep friends with him for any sake! — until the very moment you prove him cheat.

LINNELL
Have an easy mind, sir. I'll take good care to see nothing of him till to-morrow night.

CAPTAIN
I trust not ... And now, stir your stumps; and let us get out-of-doors before the ladies come down. *(He goes to the window. The sky is darkening.)* Sure enough, it's going to be a downpour. We'd best take our cloaks.

LINNELL
Hang these old Inns! Only one withdrawing-room!

CAPTAIN
Aye, they'd queer ideas about disposal of rooms in the old days. *(They move towards the door on the left, as* **ANNA** *comes out of her room and looks over the gallery. She wears a simple indoor dress.)* We're going, Anna, we're going. You'll have the place to yourselves now.

(ANNA *is joined by* ISHBEL, *who now wears a dress of Empire gown fashion. The* CAPTAIN *and* LINNELL *go out as the women come downstairs.* ISHBEL *sits near the fireside, with some crochet work.* ANNA *goes over to the window. The* CAPTAIN'*s voice is heard out-of-doors.*

ISHBEL
(still crocheting, looks round). Where are you, Anna? What's happening? Is that the Captain I hear out there?

ANNA
(with a guilty start). Aye, it's the Captain I was just looking if he had sense enough to take his cloak, and it raining.

ISHBEL
(getting up as ANNA *returns to the fireside).* And the poor man must fly out amid the showers, so we may have the room! ... Oh, what a life! *(She sighs and wanders around aimlessly.)*

ANNA
Och, sit you down and give over grieving.

ISHBEL
It's easy saying " give over", Anna ... I've a mind to go back to my father, after all. I'd rather have him baiting me than be shut up in this queer place any longer.

ANNA
And are you for changing your mind again?

ISHBEL
My mind's my own to change, if I choose, surely? And I'll go back to Draolinn if I want to.

ANNA
(rising). Then let us be going.

ISHBEL
(sitting down). If my father were only kindlier, Anna!

ANNA
(still on her feet). Are you going then, or are you not going?

ISHBEL
What use in going? Father will not change. No, we'll not go.

ANNA
(sitting down). You're just like a windblown straw, lass ... turning this way and that. I don't know what to make of you.

ISHBEL

(her face in her hands). Oh, if it were only my father!

ANNA

And who else is there?

ISHBEL

There's Carsaig. I wonder what's come to him! Poor Alan!

ANNA

(amazed). And are you grieving for him next! Poor Alan, did you say? ... Did you not send him to the rightabout yesterday?

ISHBEL

(distracted). Aye, and now I wonder did I do well?

ANNA

Tuts! you're for home, and then you're not for home. You're for off with Carsaig, and then you're for on with him.

ISHBEL

Poor Alan! All his lands gone to the dicing-cogie!

ANNA

Wasn't it his own doing?

ISHBEL

Oh, you're heartless, Anna! *(She weeps.)*

ANNA

There, there! Hush now! Things will take a turn. His lands will come back to him.

ISHBEL

It's not the loss of his lands that weighs on me: it's the want of heart that led to their loss.

ANNA

Well, well, all the same I'd like fine to see those lands back where they rightfully belong.

ISHBEL

Oh, it's easy seen you little know the ways of a trouble like mine, Anna MacDougall!

ANNA

Say you so now!

ISHBEL

Aye, you wouldn't talk so light, had you ever known what love is.

ANNA

(sighing). Ah, well, in love or not, it was just myself had as fine a lover as Carsaig, once upon a time.

ISHBEL

(amazed). Anna!

ANNA

Aye, lass, that had I.

ISHBEL

(coming to her, and patting her cheek). And who now was that, I wonder!

ANNA

Och, never you mind. It's an old story. Aye, at Laggan long ago ... an old story.

ISHBEL

Anna! Truly!

ANNA

Aye, truly. And many a lingering day he spent, that lad, hanging around me, hither and yont, at Laggan, when I was a young lass.

ISHBEL

Poor Anna! And now ... he's ...?

ANNA

No, nor dead. It wasn't that. It was just ... well, it just seemed that it wasn't to be.

ISHBEL

(sadly). Aye, that's often the way!

ANNA

(her face lighting up merrily). But ... I'll tell you a secret!

ISHBEL

(eagerly). Yes?

ANNA

He kissed me once.

ISHBEL

Ah! ... Just once?

ANNA

Aye, my dear. And I'm ashamed to say I liked it.

ISHBEL

Now, aren't you the darling! *(She hugs* **ANNA**.*)*

ANNA

And that's all there is to tell.

ISHBEL

What a wonderful Anna!

ANNA

Aye, that was all ... It's the way of the world. You see, love-making's often only a diversion for a man, like fishing, or hunting, or the cartes, or the dice, and so on.

ISHBEL

(starting away from her). The dice!

ANNA

I'm sorry, my dear! It just slipped out.

ISHBEL

(weeping anew). Oh, Alan, Alan!

ANNA

Tush, look around you, lass. The men-folk are not all weaklings.

ISHBEL

Weakling or no', he's Alan. I can't put him out of my life.

ANNA

Have sense, woman! Hush you now!

(**MAIRI** *enters at the back, carrying her precious volume of Sir Walter and a scroll of paper.*

MAIRI

Oh, I beg pardon. I was looking for Auntie.

ANNA

Come away, lassie. You'll be Mairi, the niece from Edinburgh? I'll find your aunt for you. (**SHE** *rises.*)

MAIRI

Oh, don't trouble, please. I'll just go away. I only wanted to write.

ISHBEL

Nonsense, Mairi. You mustn't bother about us. I'm Ishbel MacLean, you see; and this is Anna MacDougall.

MAIRI

Miss Ishbel! Really?

ISHBEL

(amused). Yes, really.

MAIRI

(with eager eyes). Oh!

ANNA

But will you not sit down, and go on with your writing? *(Anna herself resumes her seat.)*

ISHBEL

Yes, do ... What is it, may I ask? Letters home?

MAIRI

No, letters home are for to-morrow. This is a kind of a ... a kind of composition.

ISHBEL

Ah, yes, you're at school in Edinburgh, of course. At which, I wonder?

MAIRI

Miss Simpson's Seminary. But this isn't for school. It's only something of my own.

ISHBEL

A private diary, I'll be bound ... I used to keep one myself when at school in Edinburgh. But, go on with your task, Mairi ... just as if we weren't here. We'll not disturb you.

MAIRI

(arranging her papers on the little table). Oh, thank you very much. *(She sits down and fidgets over her writing. There is silence for a little. Then the* **CAPTAIN** *comes in briskly by the door on the left.*

CAPTAIN

Ah, good-morning, ladies. Well, well, here you all sit round the fire, although the rain's off and the sun shining, and it now a day of days! It's out o' doors you should be while it's still fine.

ISHBEL

(glancing at the window). And how long will it remain fine, Captain? ... But it looks tempting. Shall we go, Anna? *(She rises, and so does* **ANNA**.*)* Do you accompany us, sir?

CAPTAIN

Ah, an invitation! I was indeed fishing for it. 'Twas for just that I returned. Thank you, I'll come, and gladly. Haste you, Anna!

ANNA

Keep your orders for your housekeepers, Captain MacColl. I haven't taken service with you yet.

CAPTAIN
(rallying her). Not yet, Anna. But set your hopes high. A time may come.

ISHBEL
(laughing). Well, Captain, if you're not gallant, at least you're brave.

CAPTAIN
I'm trying to be both, Miss Ishbel.

ANNA
Keep on at the trying then, for you're sorely in need of practice.

CAPTAIN
A hit to you, Anna. *(He bows, and* **ISHBEL** *and* **ANNA** *go upstairs to their room.)* And what about you, Mairi? Are you not coming?

MAIRI
(counting on her fingers, and then scribbling industriously). No, thank you. I'm occupied.

CAPTAIN
(There is a silence, and the Captain faces the room, bored by the waiting.) What a time women take to dress. How long do you need to put on a hat, Mairi?

MAIRI
Oh, hush, please! I'm writing.
(Another silence while the **CAPTAIN** *walks about, irritably. But at last* **ANNA** *and* **ISHBEL** *appear, dressed for out-of-doors. As the group go out by the door on the left,* **LINNELL** *enters there, and bows are exchanged. He looks round the room, and discovers* **MAIRI**

LINNELL
Good-morning, Miss Mairi

MAIRI
Good-morning, Mr. Linnell

LINNELL
You're busy?

MAIRI
Yes.

LINNELL
Well, I'll keep you company.

MAIRI
Oh, but you mustn't. I have to do this all by myself.

LINNELL

But I mean I've writing of my own to do. Ship's accounts ... I'll take the other table. *(Without a reply,* MAIRI *scribbles on industriously.* LINNELL *goes upstairs to his own room, and returns with some bundles of papers. He sits down at the large table, and gets to work at once. After a time he says:)* Hard work yours, Mairi?

MAIRI

Yes. *(She is writing carefully and does not look up.)*

LINNELL

Ever seen ships' estimates?

MAIRI

(still engrossed in her work). No.

LINNELL

They're for my cutter, you see.

MAIRI

Yes.

LINNELL

She's refitting at Greenock.

MAIRI

Yes.

LINNELL

That's a long way off, isn't it?

MAIRI

Oh, please!

LINNELL

Pardon! I'm sorry.

MAIRI

Hush! It's a composition.

LINNELL

What! A real authoress?

MAIRI

Oh, do be quiet, pray! *(She heaves a long sigh.)*

LINNELL

Oh, very well—But I sometimes make up things myself.

MAIRI

Really?

LINNELL

Never mind. I shouldn't have spoken.

MAIRI

It's very difficult this ... It's poetry, you see ... Perhaps I'll show it you later on.

LINNELL

Thank you. I hope you will.
(There is another silence. Then **MAIRI** *puts down her pen and rubs a troubled brow. She shifts about and is evidently thinking hard. She turns over some pages of Sir Walter.* **LINNELL** *steals furtive glances at her, and coughs.)*

MAIRI

(suddenly). I'm stuck. "Maiden" ... "maiden." ... Can you conceive a rhyme for "maiden", Mr. Linnell?

LINNELL

Let me see. Yes, "laden".

MAIRI

Oh, thank you ... That's it now ... "laden" ... "sorrow-laden". The very word.

LINNELL

Pleased to be of service.

MAIRI

(writing). Are you a poet, Mr. Linnell?

LINNELL

Well, no. It's too hard work. But I'm fond of poetry ... old ballads and so on.

MAIRI

This isn't a ballad ... Ah, but there's another rhyme I want. One for "tresses."

LINNELL

(instantly). "Caresses."

MAIRI

(primly). Oh, no.

LINNELL

But yes. "Tresses ... caresses." What's wrong there?

MAIRI

Well, I want to show this to Auntie Belle, once it's finished. It's all about a story I heard her speak of to Auntie Beta. And I don't think she'd like that word.

LINNELL

Nonsense. "Caresses" is quite a good word in poetry. Look at Sir Walter. He tosses caresses about, I can tell you.

MAIRI

Does he indeed?

LINNELL

Assuredly.

MAIRI

Well, I'll think about it. *(She goes back to her writing.)*

LINNELL

You must be very fond of Sir Walter, when you take his book for a bed-book.

MAIRI

Oh, yes! Isn't he fine! ... You know that passage in "The Lord of the Isles", don't you, about the old Highland castles?
"Each on its own dark cape reclined,
And listening to its own wild wind."

LINNELL

Wonderful!

MAIRI

Isn't it? I've put Donaldina in just such a Highland keep. She's the heroine in my poem.

LINNELL

Donaldina? Sir Walter had better look to his laurels! May I see how you progress? *(He comes over to her.)*

MAIRI

(hiding her scroll). Oh, no, you mustn't! Not yet ... They're my own real thoughts, you see ... And they look so strange when they're written down in black and white.

LINNELL

(catching sight of some words). What a romantick title ... 'The Deserted Bride".

MAIRI

(hiding the papers). Oh, please, don't look.

LINNELL

The Bride? That's Donaldina, I suppose?

MAIRI

(her reserve giving way at last). Yes, But it's really all about Miss Ishbel. I heard my aunts talking of her trouble last night. And I couldn't put in her real name, could I? So I thought of Donaldina.

LINNELL

Ah, Miss Ishbel ... Yes, yes. Carsaig did desert her, I suppose?

MAIRI

Of course he did ... Wasn't it horrible? And when I heard my aunts discuss her sad case, I just had to write. It was all so beautiful ... so tragick!

LINNELL

Tragick is the very word.

MAIRI

Now you wouldn't think it, but I'm making Carsaig the hero. Of course, I don't call him Carsaig.

LINNELL

No?

MAIRI

No. I call him Fitzgeorge.

LINNELL

Good.

MAIRI

And then there's Carsaig's rival ... the other man.

LINNELL

(with an involuntary start). And who can that be?

MAIRI

I don't know as yet. My aunts just spoke of "the other man".

LINNELL

I see.

MAIRI

And then I've made Miss Ishbel fair-haired, so's she won't be recognised.

LINNELL

Very far-seeing, that!

MAIRI

And Carsaig's hair's to be the other way about —dark, you know. Otherwise he is just as he is in real life, tall and elegant ... And I make him well-meaning, although everybody thinks him wicked.

LINNELL

Ah! Misunderstood, of course.

MAIRI

Yes, and then there's the other man, his rival. I haven't got to him yet, however. But I think I'll make him fat and really a vile creature. His name is to be Oswald.

LINNELL

A very proper name for a villain.

MAIRI

Well, Fitzgeorge—that's Carsaig—runs off with Donaldina—and you know who she is, Ishbel. And then there's a wayside inn where they halt for the night; and Fitzgeorge gambles with the landlord of the inn and loses all his money first of all, and then his lands. Of course, I don't say "lands"; I say "heritage". It's more poetick.

LINNELL

And then?

MAIRI

And then Donaldina—that's Ishbel—gets exceedingly angry with Fitzgeorge—that's Carsaig, you remember?

LINNELL

But what about Oswald—the villain?

MAIRI

Oh, yes, I must work him in somewhere. I think it would be a good plan—don't you?—to make Oswald a confederate of the landlord, and ... and ... drug Fitzgeorge's wine, or something like that.

LINNELL

Well?

MAIRI

Yes, now I remember how I planned—yes, that was it. But Oswald drinks some of the poisoned wine himself, and dies. And before he dies he confesses that he had drugged Fitzgeorge's wine, so that Fitzgeorge —that's Carsaig—played badly, and lost his heritage.

LINNELL

But if the wine killed Oswald, why didn't it kill Fitzgeorge?

MAIRI

(brightly). Oh, that's an easy one! Because Oswald drank too much. He would, the beast!

LINNELL

Yes, I'm glad he's dead.

MAIRI

And then Donaldina—that's Ishbel—gets to know of Oswald's treachery, and so she forgives Fitzgeorge —that's Carsaig.

LINNELL

Ah!

MAIRI

Yes, for she sees that Carsaig—I mean Fitzgeorge, has been tricked. And she is sorry for him, and marries him in the end.

LINNELL

(absently repeating some of her words as if to himself). "She sees Carsaig has been tricked ... and marries him in the end." *(Then in a tense voice.)* Good God! whatever are you saying, Mairi!

MAIRI

Oh, what's wrong? Are you ill?

LINNELL

No, no. But make sure Miss Ishbel doesn't see your poem ... She might be hurt, you know.

MAIRI

Oh, I'll take care she doesn't see it. And even if she did, she'd never make it out. Why, it's all changed into poetry, and I've made the colour of her hair quite different!

LINNELL

Excellent! I'd forgotten you'd changed her hair.
(A tapping comes to the door on the left; it opens, and **ARDOW** *enters quietly.*

ARDOW

Pardon! I knocked below, but there was no answer.

MAIRI

I'll get Auntie. She's upstairs. *(She rises)*

ARDOW

No need, my dear. It was Mr. Linnell I sought. I only wanted a word with him in private.

MAIRI

Oh! And you're both so glum ... You're not going to quarrel, are you?

LINNELL

No, no, Mairi. I fancy it's a business matter. And people are always serious about business.

MAIRI

I'll be going then. But I'll come back, Mr. Linnell, when you've finished, and then you'll help me more with this. *(She flourishes her scroll.)*

LINNELL

Surely.

(She goes off by the door at the back.)

ARDOW

Lieutenant Linnell, I have a message to you from my friend, Mr. Alan MacKinnon of Carsaig.

LINNELL

Yes?

ARDOW

I am to say that in view of the residence at present here of Miss Ishbel MacLean of Clachaig, he regrets your continued stay at this Inn. And he suggests that, for the work of a Revenue Officer, the Inn at Callachly offers accommodation quite as suitable.

LINNELL

And so begs me to leave?

ARDOW

You take his meaning admirably, sir. And, speaking as a man of the world, I think his request very reasonable ... You are his rival in a certain quarter; and your continuance of your lodging here puts him at a disadvantage.

LINNELL

I see. Solicitude for his chances in his suit to Miss Ishbel ... Quite a compliment to me.

ARDOW

I'm afraid Carsaig isn't concerned in the least about compliments in this matter ... I have given you his message. He regrets your continued stay here.

LINNELL

Then will you please convey to Caisaig how much I deplore my inability to relieve him of his regrets?

ARDOW

I warn you the matter's serious. It's best we avoid haste.

LINNELL

Then convey my answer at your leisure.

ARDOW

Sir!

LINNELL

Sir to you!

ARDOW

Oh, very well! ... And now I shall be vastly obliged if you will mention the name of a friend who will act for you.

LINNELL

With pleasure! Captain MacColl.
(They are glaring at each other when **MAIRI** *comes in, her scroll still in her hand.*

MAIRI

Finished? ... Ah! ... Just as I thought ... You've quarrelled after all! ... Fie ... It's well I came back so soon.

LINNELL

(turning his back on her in irritation) Tush, child!

ARDOW

You're not slow in the uptake, Miss Mairi.

MAIRI

(stamping her foot). I'll not have it! You're like children in the huff. I'll get Auntie Belle *(***SHE*** makes for the stairs.)*

LINNELL

Come, come! It's no concern of Miss Belle's.

MAIRI

Quarrelling? Keep me! And your fathers such friends.

ARDOW

What's this?

LINNELL

Tuts, Mairi! Run off now ... You've no business here, and neither has your aunt.

MAIRI

(pertly). Oh, yes, but I have business here, or wherever there's a quarrel. I was the great peacemaker at my school in Edinburgh ... Miss Simpson's.

ARDOW

What's this about my father?

MAIRI

Did not Auntie Belle say last night both your fathers were in the same regiment!

ARDOW

(*transported with rage*). Linnell! My God! the very name! ... So you're the spawn of that toad! Then Carsaig's quarrel can wait, my buck. And I claim the privilege of a first meeting.

    (*He slaps* LINNELL *on the face with his glove.* LINNELL *makes a movement toward him in retaliation; but* MAIRI *comes between them.*

MAIRI

(*running towards the stairs*). Auntie Belle! Auntie Belle!

LINNELL

(*restraining himself*). By Heaven! your claim is granted.

BELLE

(*coming downstairs*). Have done, gentlemen, have done!

LINNELL

Captain MacColl will act for me in this also.

ARDOW

Then he must make sure you don't fire like your father ... before the signal.

LINNELL

(*advancing on him, despite* BELLE'*s hands on his shoulders*). You hound!

BELLE

Be wise now, the both of you!

MAIRI

(*at the window, which she has opened*). Captain! Captain!

ARDOW

Keep off, you fox. This is not Spain. We fight fair in Scotland.

LINNELL

(*struggling to free himself from* BELLE'*s clutches*). Take that back!

BETA

(*coming downstairs*). What's this, what's this! Give over now, give over!

    (LINNELL *has seized* ARDOW, *but at the sound of* BETA'*s voice he desists.*

LINNELL

Tuts! too many women!

ARDOW

But not Miss Ishbel as yet!

LINNELL

My God! Keep her name out of this.

CAPTAIN

(*suddenly appearing at the door on the left*). What's to do ... what's to do ... A quarrel, eh?

(**HE** *comes between the men. The women fall back.*

ARDOW

Captain MacColl, I came here with a message for Mr. Linnell from Carsaig. He asked me to convey his regrets ...

CAPTAIN

Stop, stop! I think I know what's coming ... Perhaps the ladies ... (**HE** *looks meaningly at* **BELLE**)
(**BELLE** *leads the way, and the women file out at the back, rather reluctantly, as the* **CAPTAIN** *holds the door for them. He closes the door and comes forward.*

CAPTAIN

Well, well, Ardow, I never heard the like precision, but it meant only one thing. Pistols at forty-paces, eh?

ARDOW

Yes.

CAPTAIN

And isn't that awkward at a time like this? ... So many people about for the Horse Fair, you see.
(*He emphasises his last words, and looks with meaning at* **LINNELL** *Then he manoeuvres for a position somewhat behind* **ARDOW**, *who is facing* **LINNELL**. *He shakes his fist at the latter.* **ARDOW** *cannot see this or succeeding signals without turning away from* **LINNELL**; *but the quarrel is too recent for him to do anything but face his enemy.*

LINNELL

Carsaig asks me to leave this Inn, Captain, because of the presence of Miss Ishbel here.

CAPTAIN

Indeed! And who is he to order you about? Of course, you accepted his challenge? (*All the same, he shakes his head and lifts a clenched fist at* **LINNELL**; *his signals quite negativing his words.*)

LINNELL

Yes, sir, I did. *(Again the Captain shakes his head vigorously).* I also named you as my second ... But ... but on further consideration, I see the reasonableness of Carsaig's request, and now beg Ardow to convey to Carsaig that I have decided to do as he asks.

(The **CAPTAIN** *nods approval with delight.*

ARDOW

(amazed). What! You'll go?

LINNELL

Yes.

CAPTAIN

(in mock reproach). Tut, tut, Philip! Where's your spirit?

LINNELL

(to the Captain). I think I am the best judge, sir, if you'll allow me.

CAPTAIN

Well, well! settle as you please. But who'd have thought it? Not I, Philip ... not I. *(But he is manifestly well content.)*

LINNELL

But here, sir, is another matter. I have also an offer of a meeting with Ardow.

CAPTAIN

(dismayed). What! Are you all mad!

LINNELL

You may well ask, sir. For I fear I was not quite myself when my quarrel with this gentleman arose.

ARDOW

Godsake! ... And are you for sneaking out of this also?

CAPTAIN

Keep your head, Ardow ... Go on, Philip.

LINNELL

I need not detail the grounds of that quarrel. The upshot is that I now offer Ardow my apology for any affront I put upon him this morning.

ARDOW

The devil you do! Stap me if you're going to escape me with a few fine words!

CAPTAIN

What, what! young man! Do you forget I'm here? And you'd force a quarrel in the face of an apology, would you? What would your club in Edinburgh say to that sort of thing, eh?

ARDOW

To hell with clubs and all Edinburgh! I'll have him on grass before the week is out, and it's already Thursday.

CAPTAIN

Softly, now, Ardow. I've seen more duels than you've fingers on you. And I think I know something of their punctilio. I'll gladly act for Mr. Linnell in this second affair if he approves.

LINNELL

By all means, sir.

CAPTAIN

Good. And now, Ardow, it is my duty to tell you that, in my judgment, here is an affair of honour where ample apology has been offered ... So take care! ... Name your second now ... name him, sir. And I trust he'll know more of the rules of the game than yourself.

ARDOW

Pshaw! I'll not trouble you with my second. Fine words will have their way, I can see; and he'll go skin-whole in the end of all.

CAPTAIN

Softly, sir, softly! I'm warning you!

ARDOW

But, by God! the whole countryside shall know him for the white-livered Sassenach he really is. I'll take care of that.
(**LINNELL** *makes an impulsive movement towards* **ARDOW**, *but the* **CAPTAIN** *steps between them.*

CAPTAIN

(*angrily*). Any more of this, Ardow, and I'll have you before your club, I warn you!

ARDOW

Oh, hell take you and the clubs! (*Then to* **LINNELL**) And you too! ... The best thing for you, my rabbit, is to show a clean pair of heels, if you value your peace of mind!
(**LINNELL** *makes to throw himself on* **ARDOW**, *but the* **CAPTAIN**'s *arm is powerful, and he is swept aside.* **ARDOW** *smiles superciliously and swaggers out on the left.*

LINNELL

God give me patience till to-morrow!

CAPTAIN

Aye, those were bitter pills to swallow. But you did well, lad.

LINNELL

Oh, I could have throttled him time and again but for your signals!

CAPTAIN

Yes, but we'll hook him to-morrow, never fear—thanks to that fine apology.

LINNELL

Be damned to the apology: it blistered my lips.

CAPTAIN

But the cause, lad, the cause! And we'll have him to-morrow night, or may I be shot.

MAIRI

(entering with two cloaks on her arm). Auntie Belle says will you please take these cloaks out to the ladies, Captain? It's coming on to rain again.

CAPTAIN

(taking the wraps). And am I to do nothing in my old age but fetch and carry for the ladies! Where are they, pray?

MAIRI

(looking out of the window). Not far from where you left them. See: they're sheltering under the big oak at the turn of the road.

CAPTAIN

(going to the window). Godsake! I'd clean forgotten them! ... Ah, but thanks be! It's off already, that rain. So there's no hurry for the cloaks ... But it was ay an excuse for your coming in here to see how we were progressing, Mairi, eh? *(He lays down the wraps and shakes a reproving finger at her.)* I'm fearing you're just a wee spy!

MAIRI

So Ardow is gone. I don't like him. But I trust you made it up with him, Mr. Linnell, as I told you to?

LINNELL

Oh, more or less.

MAIRI

Ah, didn't I tell you I was the great peacemaker! It was more rather than less, wasn't it?

LINNELL

(smiling). Well, I'll answer a poetess with poetry. Listen. *(And he recites slowly:)*

" My grandfather's man and me cast out,
How will we bring the matter about?
We'll bring it about as well as we can,
And a' for the sake of my grandfather's man."

There! That's a fine old song, if only I could sing it to you. And that's the kind of poetry you should write, Mairi. Something with a swing in it.

MAIRI

Oh, hush! You mustn't tell!

LINNELL

(mischievously). Pardon! I forgot. The Captain mustn't know you write poetry, of course.

CAPTAIN

Hallo! A conspiracy? Have you been versifying me, you rascal?

MAIRI

(pertly). Not as yet, Captain

CAPTAIN

Aha, you rogue! *(He makes as if to catch her, and she flies to the door at the hack, but does not go out)*

LINNELL

No, it isn't you, Captain It's a "love-lorn maiden, sorrow-laden" affair.

MAIRI

(stamping her foot). Tell-tale.

LINNELL

The hero loses his heritage ... And the lady throws him over because he's too fond of the dicing ...but she takes him back because she finds he's been cheated ... I'm not really telling anybody but a friend, Mairi, am I?

MAIRI

Tell-tale again! I'll never show you another thing. So there! *(She flounces out by the door at the back)*

CAPTAIN

Then it's Carsaig and Ishbel she's versifying? The wee scamp!

LINNELL

Yes. And there's a home-truth for me in her way of the story.

CAPTAIN

And what's that?

LINNELL

Don't you see?

CAPTAIN

No.

LINNELL

Well, to-morrow night I must prove Ardow plays loaded dice, mustn't I?

CAPTAIN

Assuredly, if you're to clear your father's name.

LINNELL

Aye. But don't you see that if I do, I clear Carsaig's name as well? ... Man alive, I am throwing her into Carsaig's arms.

CAPTAIN

Surely Ishbel won't take it that way, lad?

LINNELL

Why shouldn't she? She'll behold her poor Carsaig as grossly deceived—cheated—trapped— decoyed—his lands stolen by loaded dice. Can't you see how she'll melt to him!

CAPTAIN

Tuts! you have it all mapped out like a novelle.

LINNELL

By God, I have ... And myself playing Providence to Carsaig.

CAPTAIN

Aye, I see where you are ... Aye, women, women! they're the strange ones! ... It's hard on you, lad. But if you don't expose Ardow, what's to come of your chances of clearing that old stain?

LINNELL

Old, yes, old. Twenty years old.

CAPTAIN

But, Philip, you can't renege! I hold you to your promise. And I know you'll do what's right.

LINNELL

And, in Heaven's name, what is right?

CAPTAIN

To clear that stain.

LINNELL

Tush! an old wives' tale.

CAPTAIN

It wasn't an old wives' tale for you last night.

LINNELL

I tell you, if I expose Ardow, I help Carsaig to win her.

CAPTAIN

Now, now, have sense, lad. Think, man, think.

LINNELL

Aye, think ... But give me time to think. I must see a clear path in this.

(The door on the left opens, and **ISHBEL** *and* **ANNA** *enter. The men fall instantly into an awkward silence.* **ISHBEL**'s *manner is cold: she does not bow to them, but passes without a word and goes upstairs.* **ANNA** *is about to follow, but the* **CAPTAIN** *beckons her, and she comes back as* **ISHBEL** *enters her room.)*

CAPTAIN

What's this, Anna? She went past us as if we'd been stones.

ANNA

The Good Being alone knows! ... We met Ardow soon after you left us ... On the shore-road, it was ... She would not look his way. But he said something in passing, and she called him back.

CAPTAIN

Yes, yes.

ANNA

It was only two words or three he gave her. What they were I didn't hear, for I'd gone on ... I had no wish to speak to him after our last night at his house ... the brock! And it's long and long it will be, let me tell you, before I darken his door again. Him with his cocked-up chin!

CAPTAIN

Yes, yes. But what happened when Ardow spoke to her?

ANNA

She went like ice; turned and walked off from him; and never a word from her since.

ISHBEL

(looking out from the door of her room, and calling). Anna, will you please come?

*(***ANNA***, in confusion at having been caught gossiping, goes off upstairs, entering her room as* **ISHBEL** *comes out fully onto the gallery.*

ISHBEL

Good-bye, Mr. Linnell I hear you are leaving this Inn.

LINNELL

(aghast). Yes, I ... I have so decided.

ISHBEL

(turning away). Then it's true! *(She enters her room)*

LINNELL

There, you see! ... She thinks me coward!

CAPTAIN

Nonsense, man ... She's just bewildered.

LINNELL

No, no, she thinks me coward ... She can believe that of me! Ardow has told her.

CAPTAIN

The scum!

LINNELL

Oh, never mind him ... But she! ... She could think that ... She could say that!

CAPTAIN

Keep a grip of yourself, man.

LINNELL

(hysterically). By God then, I shall unmask Ardow! ... She's forced my hand, and I'll prove him swindler like his father before him! ... Then she'll see! ... Then she'll see! ... Captain, I'm with you now. *(They grasp hands.)*

CAPTAIN

I knew you'd do the right thing.

LINNELL

Damn the right thing! ... I'll show her who's the coward ... Herself, by Heaven! ... herself!

CAPTAIN

Come, come, lad! Be wise.

LINNELL

Faithless! And a shrew to boot!

*(**ANNA** comes downstairs. She has a salver with a glass on it, and she is passing to the door at the back, when **LINNELL** turns a wild eye on her.*

LINNELL

Oh, there you are, Anna. Well then, tell Miss Ishbel I'm packing in haste, will you? Say I'm quaking and shaking and shivering in deadly fear, but that I'm packing, packing, packing ... oh, so quickly! That's it. Tell her that, will you? *(He dashes upstairs and so to his room on the right)*

ANNA

Keep me! Always the ranter, that one! What's wrong with him now?

CAPTAIN

An overdose of youth, Anna ... And, I fear, he must pay for the folly of youth just as others have done before him.

ANNA

There you go! At the old story again ... But I'm busy. My lady has a headache, and I'm making a brew for her.

CAPTAIN

I'll not detain you then. But I've often my thoughts on other times, look you, when I see the young folk repeating the errors of my own early days.

ANNA

The old story! And I've no time for it, I tell you. *(She moves away not too hastily, and as if she still would hear.)*

CAPTAIN

And is it a crime to be remembering?

ANNA

Rank sentiment as usual ... But I'll say this, Duncan. You were never so daft in your youth as this Linnell

CAPTAIN

Aye, as daft every bit, only in a different way, lass. He's over-hasty, while I was over-cautious, waiting and waiting.

ANNA

Tuts! It's little use blowing cold coals.

CAPTAIN

Och, the wars, the wars! And the years I sailed foreign! And the senseless waiting!

ANNA

Aye, you were blate.

CAPTAIN

Och, lass, if I'd been wise!

ANNA

Well, we're no longer young, either of us. So what use to be sighing over it? We're as best we may be, and the King himself is not as he would wish.

CAPTAIN

My luck was never in it. I'm thinking I was born when the tide was ebbing. I should have spoken you long before I saw Spain.

ANNA

Och, there you go once more! ... But I must be stirring or she'll be after me ... A blessing on you, Duncan!

CAPTAIN

And a blessing on you, lass!

ANNA

Lass! Do you know what you're saying ... *(a pause)* ... lad?
(Smiling happily, she goes out by the door at the back. As she goes the **CAPTAIN** *stands gazing at her intently, his face transfigured by old memories.* **LINNELL** *appears, distraught, at the door of his room, dragging a heavy valise to the top of the stair. Looking down, the young man sees the old folk gazing at each other and all unconsciously repeating the very attitudes of himself and* **MAIRI** *in the same surroundings on the night before, even to the extent of the* **CAPTAIN** *continuing to gaze at the door through which* **ANNA** *has just disappeared. Despite his own desperate case,* **LINNELL** *senses the resemblance of the two scenes, scratches his head in amazement, and then laughs aloud.*

LINNELL

Ho-ho!

CAPTAIN

Philip, are you going out o' your mind! This is rank hysteria! A tragic hero one minute, and laughing at yourself the next!

LINNELL

(dragging his valise down the stair, and then halting to confront the **CAPTAIN***)*. And why shouldn't I laugh at myself! Why shouldn't I, when I remember how I stood last night even where you stand just now, and looked at that door closing even as you did just now. Closing on what, eh? Ho-ho! On Helen of Troy, Fair Rosamond, Cleopatra and the Queen of Sheba, sir. Ho-ho!.. . Oh, women, women, women! ... Ratsbane, hemlock, deadly nightshade! Take one, take all. They're not a patch on women! ... Ho-ho, Captain! *(He makes for the door, dragging his valise awkwardly, and quite distraught.)*

CAPTAIN

(restraining him). Philip, you can't go like this. You're clean daft, man, clean daft.

LINNELL

I know, I know! But it's this house. Let me out of it, and I'll show you sense ... Faithless and a shrew! ... God! Heard you ever the like! ... Yes, I'm for Callachly, Captain ... I'm going, for I'll choke if I stay a moment longer.

CAPTAIN

Stop you. Are you for driving there?

LINNELL

Yes, yes. Away from this place. The women have put a spell on it, I tell you. Out we go, you and I. It's not safe.

CAPTAIN

(firmly). Then it's myself will do all the driving. *(He lends a hand with the valise.)* Off we go then.
(They go out by the door on the left, and as they go, ANNA comes in by the door at the back, with her salver and glass, and, unperceived by them, watches them depart. She moves to the window to watch them pass below. A few moments elapse as she stands, craning her neck in the eagerness of her survey. Then ISHBEL *comes out of her room, and coming downstairs, discovers* ANNA *at the window.*

ISHBEL

You take a long time about a little task, Anna. This headache is terrible. Give me the glass. *(She takes the potion and drinks it off.)* Who's out there?

ANNA

Oh, just some people going to the stables.
(She comes away from the window in some confusion. ISHBEL *takes up* ANNA's *position at the window, and looks out)*

ISHBEL

Why, it's the Captain, just at the stable door, and he's kissing his hand to me. Whatever does he mean? *(ANNA moves off in increasing confusion. ISHBEL leaves the window and comes over to her.)* Anna MacDougall, look me fairly in the eyes, *(ANNA looks at her for a moment, and then turns her head away.)* Oh, Anna! The Captain! It was the Captain ... the lad at Laggan long ago?

ANNA

(with bent head). Aye, lass ... at Laggan ... long ago.

CURTAIN

ACT III

Scene.—The same. Evening of the next day. MAIRI *is writing at one end of the large table, midmost of which a branched candlestick is set; and the* CAPTAIN *is seated near the light, reading a somewhat larger volume of war history than his last.*
From time to time the faint sounds of the pipes are heard out-of-doors, and an occasional outburst of a hearty Gaelic chorus from below-stairs.

CAPTAIN
Tuts!

MAIRI
What's wrong, Captain?

CAPTAIN
It's these writing fellows. Another man on the war. Ugh! *(He tosses the book aside.)* I wish Philip were here.

MAIRI
Philip?

CAPTAIN
Mr. Linnell

MAIRI
Oh, so do I.

CAPTAIN
Indeed! And why?

MAIRI
Oh, just because. *(She scribbles industriously.)*

CAPTAIN
A woman's reason.

MAIRI
Why do you wish him here?

CAPTAIN
(rising to his feet). So that I could tell him my heartfelt opinion regarding the scoundrels who write books about battles they never saw.

MAIRI
Wouldn't it help if you told it to me?

CAPTAIN
(starting). What! ... No, my dear. The things I want to say need someone strong enough to receive them.

MAIRI

Has he got the wrong names for places?

CAPTAIN

Yes, and for everything else. This man has no sense at all. He should be confined to barracks ... or ... or ... somewhere, for his natural life.

MAIRI

Then why go on reading his book every now and again?

CAPTAIN

You have me there, Mairi! ... I suppose it's just for the pleasure of condemning him ... Now consider, my dear. This man never even mentions my old regiment—the Sixty-First ... It was bad enough to read another of them yesterday who allowed we had been present at two of the battles in the Peninsula, and said nothing of the dozen other stricken fields we'd known ... But this ... this ... this insect! ... this insignificant midge! never lifts our name. Just keeps on dancing in the air all the time and nip-nipping in a way to drive a soldier mad.

MAIRI

How stupid!

CAPTAIN

(*fiercely*). And where, will you tell me, would Lord Wellington have been at Salamanca without the Sixty-First?

MAIRI

(*alarmed*). I ... I ... I don't know, Captain.

CAPTAIN

Neither do I? Neither could anybody!... The thing will not bear thinking on! ... Tuts! I'll write a book about the war myself; and see if I don't scalp this fellow!

MAIRI

Splendid!

CAPTAIN

And I'll do the old regiment handsome, let me tell you. Mind you, I'll be fair; but if any other regiment expects to find themselves cracked up in it, they'll be a bit disappointed. They can write their own histories of the war, and be ... well ... yes ... be hanged to them.

MAIRI

Perhaps Mr. Linnell could help you?

CAPTAIN

By gum! There's an idea!

MAIRI

He's so kind and helpful.

CAPTAIN

And clever as well. Best man of his year in the Navy. And what a fool he was to exchange for this Revenue business! ... The very man for me when I start that history, Mairi. A brain like Nelson himself, I verily believe. A genius. These writing men will certainly have to take notice of us.

MAIRI

Oh, dear!

CAPTAIN

What's wrong?

MAIRI

I didn't want him to be a genius ... I shouldn't like anybody so dreadfully clever ... I'd want a normal man for a husband.

CAPTAIN

Good Heavens! you're not thinking of marrying him, are you?

MAIRI

(all at once occupied, with her writing). Oh, no.

CAPTAIN

And what then?

MAIRI

Well, you see, it's my new poem.

CAPTAIN

Lassie, lassie, another poem! And you made one no later than yesterday. This is forced marching, and I'm not fond of it.

MAIRI

But my first one isn't finished. It's just that I've got an inspiration for this one.

CAPTAIN

I see. And his name is Linnell, eh?

MAIRI

Oh, no. He's only one of the characters in the poem: he's only a bit of the inspiration.

CAPTAIN

And what's this about a husband?

MAIRI

Well, I'm putting Philip—Mr. Linnell—into it under another name ... I call him Filippo.

CAPTAIN

Humph! That's a deuce of a difference.

MAIRI

And then there's Aurelia—that's a good name, isn't it?—And Aurelia is to marry Philip ... Oh, I mean Filippo.

CAPTAIN

Well?

MAIRI

Well, Aurelia's quite a nice girl; and I'm sure she'd want somebody really human for a husband.

CAPTAIN

Good Lord, Mairi! The things you say!

MAIRI

I call my poem "The Inn of Adventure." It's about everybody here.

CAPTAIN

Keep me out of it, or there will be trouble, I warn you.

(A loud shouting from below.

MAIRI

(in alarm). What's that?

CAPTAIN

That's the beginning of Horse Fair night ... It's often like Bedlam.

(**BELLE** *and* **BETA** *enter hastily from the back.*

BETA

Heard you ever the like! I'll go down to them. It gets worse every Horse Fair. *(She makes for the door on the left.)*

CAPTAIN

Beta! *(She comes back to him, while* **BELLE** *crosses to the sideboard and prepares a bowl of punch.)* Just take a look around while you're below, and observe if any of the lairds have arrived. And take special note if Ardow is there.

BETA

Oh, they're all there half-an-hour ago; and Ardow's with them. Busy in the drink-room with the horse-coupers and drovers. Beating up prices they are.

CAPTAIN

Then I'll go with you. *(He rises and turns to* BELLE.*)* Miss Belle, if Mr. Linnell comes up, please ask him to step into my room and wait for me.

BELLE

But you'll see him yourself, if you're below.

CAPTAIN

I'm not so sure. I fancy he'll not come near the drink-room; and it's there I'm going now.

BELLE

I'll tell him, Captain.

(He goes out after BETA, *just as a door slams loudly and a fresh* NOISE *of roistering is heard from out-of-doors.* MAIRI *pulls the curtains, opens the window, and looks out.)*

BELLE

(working away unconcernedly at the sideboard). What is it now?

MAIRI

Oh, Auntie! There's a man down there wanting to fight. The door's open now, and you can see him quite plain ... Oh, that was Ardow! ... He came out and struck the man with his riding-switch!

BELLE

(looking out as the shouting is renewed) Och, it's only Donald Gorm! Wanting to fight, is he? ... He's ay wanting something he never can get ... not even fighting ... He's too good at the running away, is Donald. *(She returns placidly to her work)*

MAIRI

But he's drunk, Auntie.

BELLE

Aye, he's ay drunk on Horse Fair night.

MAIRI

Oh, the door's shut now, and there isn't light enough. I can't see him any more: it's so dark.

BELLE

No, but you'll hear him all the same ... Come in and shut the window, or you'll get your death of cold. The night air's sharp. You'd better be off to bed.

MAIRI

But it's only eight o'clock, Auntie!

BELLE

Is it? ... I was judging from Donald Gorm. He's further on in drink this fair than usual.

MAIRI

(shutting the window). Auntie, do you remember saying that you never had any of my kind of adventures at the Inn? The knight in glittering armour, and the minstrel with his harp, you know?

BELLE

Aye, I mind some daft talk of yours about folk like that.

MAIRI

Well, fancy now! I've only been three days here, and already there have been challenges to duels, and elopements, and deserted brides, and all kinds of strange things.

BELLE

(drily). And now there's a Horse Fair. That will be adventure enough for me, Mairi.

(The shouting outside is renewed.)

Just listen to Donald Gorm! He'll be your minstrel, I suppose; and yon string o' tin cans his harp of gold, eh?

MAIRI

Oh, please don't laugh at me! Just think how fine it would have been if those splendid horses that came in for the fair to-day had been mounted by knights in armour and their men-at-arms ... Such horses too! Bay and roan and white and dapple-grey and piebald! And so wild and free, with their long manes and their tails streaming in the wind! ... But no knights at all! Only the lairds with their red toories, and the queer old men with the long beards from the outer isles!

BELLE

Aye, aye, it was a great to-do, and I wish it was all over. *(A Gaelic chorus rouses up below)* Hearken to that now! Aren't they the noisy ones!

MAIRI

(coming back to her work at the table). I think it's fine. Just like a gathering of the clans ... Roderick Vich Alpine Dhu and his men ... I wish Sir Walter could be here!

BELLE

Tuts! You and your Sir Walter!

(BETA enters by the door on the left.

BETA

Well, well! Wonders will never cease!

BELLE

(from her work at the sideboard). And what now?

BETA

The Captain! He's making up to Tostary and the other lairds as if they were bosom friends and he'd never quarrelled with any of them in all his life. They're as thick as thieves.

BELLE

They'll be drinking then?

BETA

Aye, and toasting each other. I cannot make it out at all, at all. Time was when he couldn't even bear mention of their names.

BELLE

Indeed, then, I'm glad to hear of something else than squabbling 'twixt him and them.

BETA

Och, what harm in the Captain showing some spirit! Tostary's just an old fool.

(ISHBEL *and* ANNA *suddenly enter on the gallery and come downstairs,* ISHBEL *has donned a riding-habit once more, and carries a riding-whip.* ANNA *is in indoor dress; she is pleading with* ISHBEL, *and carries some crochet-work in her hand as if she had been interrupted at it.*

ANNA

Be wise, lass, be wise!

ISHBEL

Let me be. I'm going, I tell you.

BETA

Well, thanks be! Somebody's going. There are too many people in this house. *(And she flounces out angrily on the left.)*

BELLE

Och, never mind her, Miss Ishbel. She never means half what she says, that one ... But, keep me! you're surely not for the road, and it so late? It's not safe at all, at all.

ISHBEL

Yes, I'm for home. And I quite agree with Beta. There are too many people in this place. I cannot bear the outcry that's in it. It's like a madhouse.

ANNA

But your father may turn you back! And the country is throng with wandering men and wild horses. Be wise and bide here till morning.

BELLE

Yes, it is indeed dangerous out-of-doors on a Horse Fair night.

ISHBEL

But you've surely a gillie who could ride with me? Anna will not come.

ANNA

Not I, lass.

BELLE

There's Murdo. But his hands are full with Donald Gorm and his like, drunk as usual. Stay you here till daylight, Miss Ishbel.

ISHBEL

I'm for home to-night. Get me a gillie, please.

BELLE

But there is no gillie for you this night ... Anna, cannot you bring her to her senses?

MAIRI

(suddenly). Oh, Auntie, couldn't I put on a man's cloak and be her gillie!

BELLE

You be quiet, or it's to bed you'll go.
(A crash and some more shouting from below. **DONALD GORM** *is evidently storming the Inn door again.*

ISHBEL

Listen to that! Savages! Has none of the lairds come yet?

BELLE

Yes, most of them.

ISHBEL

Is Carsaig there?

ANNA

Carsaig, lass!

ISHBEL

Yes, Carsaig. Is he below, Belle?

BELLE

He is that.

ISHBEL

Please ask him to come to me. *(She seats herself at the fire.)*

BELLE

(*foreseeing trouble*). Come you, Mairi. Off to your room. We'll be wanting this place for the lairds presently. Take your papers with you now.

MAIRI

Oh, but, Auntie ...!

BELLE

Come away! (*She takes her by the arm to the door at the back and sees her out. Then returning, she goes out on the left, saying:*) I'll see if I can find Carsaig for you.

ANNA

What daft thing is this you're for doing next! Carsaig of all men!

ISHBEL

He brought me to this pass ... Let him take me out of it ... I'm for home, I tell you.

ANNA

But Carsaig?

ISHBEL

At least I know the worst of him. I know nothing of any of the others.

ANNA

Nonsense. There's the Captain. Let me find him for you. He's old, but he's wise and strong.

ISHBEL

Let be, Anna ... let be. I'll have my own way in this.

(**CARSAIG** *enters with* **BELLE** *on the left.*

CARSAIG

Ishbel! To go out o' doors on such a night! ... Horse Fair night! No, no, you mustn't stir a step.

(**BELLE** *and* **ANNA** *steal out at the back. A fresh babel of angry voices is heard from below.*

ISHBEL

(*speaking with averted head*). I'll endure this uproar no longer. Better to face my father's rage. Those men are mad with drink. (*She turns to him.*) Oh, Alan, take me home!

CARSAIG

I'd gladly do that. But what kind of welcome will you have?

ISHBEL

We must try that. I cannot bear another night of this.

CARSAIG
I'm sorry, my dear!

ISHBEL
No more of that! I sent for you only because there was no one else.

CARSAIG
But if I come, you must let me speak to your father.

ISHBEL
You must not. You'd only inflame him further ... All I want is for you to take me to his door, even if he keeps it shut on me ... I'll shame him to his knees when he finds me asleep on his doorstep by morning.

CARSAIG
By Heaven! you'll never play so mad a game! I must see him and speak him fair.

ISHBEL
Let us be going out of this, whatever the end.

CARSAIG
My dear, I'll go. But say you forgive Daft Alan.

ISHBEL
Oh, lad!
(SHE *gives him her hand, and he kisses it. They look at each other.* SHE *smiles at his ardour, and suddenly he clasps her in his arms. But* SHE *breaks away and sits down by the table, sobbing.*

CARSAIG
(coaxing). But why home, Ishbel? A bootless journey.

ISHBEL
It must be home. Where else?

CARSAIG
(kneeling by her side). Where else but to the minister at Kilfinichen as first we planned?

ISHBEL
No, no, Alan. You are indeed daft.

CARSAIG
Aye, daft with love for you, my dear; but wise in this way of it ... I am a landless man, Ishbel, but I love you dearly.

ISHBEL
Oh, the wine-stoups, Alan, the wine-stoups! They'll be your undoing.

CARSAIG

I'm done with them; I swear it ... You'll come?

ISHBEL

(surrendering). My dear!
(*They kiss ardently, and just then the door on the left opens, and* **LINNELL** *enters. At first they do not see him, and his face is contorted for a moment with anger and amazement. But he controls himself when they turn in confusion as the door closes behind him. There is a pause; then* **LINNELL** *bows.*

LINNELL

Pardon. I am seeking Captain MacColl.

CARSAIG

Then you must seek him elsewhere.

LINNELL

I mean to. *(He crosses to the staircase, the least hint of a smile on his lips.)*

CARSAIG

(furious). Do you smile, sir?

ISHBEL

Insolence! *(She proffers her riding-whip to* **CARSAIG**.*)*

LINNELL

No, no, madam, not insolence, I assure you. Only nerves, madam ... only cowardice.
(*He goes upstairs quickly, and turns into his room on the right.*

ISHBEL

(angrily). Oh, why didn't you take my whip across his face?

CARSAIG

Because he fled, my dear. White blood and whole skin, you know.

ISHBEL

You'd let him make a mock of us! Even you fail me ... I'd best go home.

CARSAIG

Then your home will be Carsaig ... And I'll call Anna.

ISHBEL

No, no. I can't bide her tongue.

CARSAIG

A fig for that, or Belle's either. They must know sooner or later. *(He goes to the door at the back and calls:)* Anna! ... Belle!
(**ANNA**, **BELLE** *and* **MAIRI** *come in while* **ISHBEL** *sinks in confusion at the table, her back to them.*

CARSAIG

Miss Ishbel's for the road with me, Anna ... Will you also be coming?

ANNA

Her father will never open to her.

CARSAIG

No, but the minister at Kilfinichen will ... And I've no care whether her father knows that or not.... Get your cloak, Anna.

ANNA

Save us! And has she swung round again! ... No, I'm tired of the minister at Kilfinichen ... And she'll swing round once more, before you're an hour on the road ... I know her.

ISHBEL

(rising in anger). Anna MacDougall!

ANNA

(with spirit). Aye, that's my name.
(They try to outstare each other. Then **CARSAIG** *puts his arm around* **ISHBEL** *and leads her out by the door on the left.*

BELLE

(moving to the staircase). Well, well! I'd best be setting her room in order, for we'll be needing all the beds we have this night for the Horse Fair gentry.

ANNA

Och, be leaving her room as it stands. She'll be turning back before they're a mile on the road. She's a weathercock, that one!

MAIRI

(who has stolen to the window). Oh, I can see Carsaig at the stable with a lanthorn ... She's waiting for him outside.
 *(***BELLE** *and* **ANNA** *join* **MAIRI** *at the window.* **LINNELL** *comes downstairs.*

LINNELL

Is the Captain not yet come? He's not in his room.

BELLE

He's below-stairs, sir. He left a message you were to wait him here.

MAIRI

(excitedly, at the window). Oh, he's taking out the horses!

LINNELL

What's ado?

BELLE

It's Carsaig and Miss Ishbel ... Another elopement.

LINNELL

(coolly). Ah, this is the third time!

BELLE

It is indeed.

LINNELL

Well, it's said the third time's lucky, isn't it?

BELLE

Aye, so it's said, sir.
  (*The group of women at the window have turned to stare at him, half in curiosity, half in amazement, as he walks easily to the fireplace.*

LINNELL

Have you ever read Byron, Miss Anna?

ANNA

Indeed no, Mr. Linnell.

LINNELL

Well, don't. It's dangerous. Leads to elopements and all kinds of trouble. You ask the Captain. He knows.

ANNA

(merrily, as she nudges BELLE*)*. If he knows that, then it will not be from any experience of his own, I'm thinking. I've never heard of him being mixed up in an elopement.

BELLE

(giggling). Wheesht you, Anna!

MAIRI

(unheeding this levity and coming over to LINNELL *at the fireplace)*. I'm sorry.

LINNELL

(turning a smiling face on her). And why, my dear?

MAIRI

Well, Donaldina ... do you remember ... in my poem? ... And you're "the other man," aren't you? ... I only found that out this morning.

LINNELL

Then that will give you some fresh cantos for your poem, Mairi.

MAIRI

Oh, never mind that! What I wanted to say was that you mustn't grieve for Ishbel. She is unstable as water and shall not ... shall not excel.

LINNELL

Tilly-vally! I'm heart-whole. Keep your regrets for Carsaig.

(A sound of horses' hoofs is heard, and **MAIRI** *dashes off to the window again,* **BELLE** *and* **ANNA**, *join her.*

MAIRI

Hooray! They're off!

BELLE

(at last turning away, to find **LINNELL** *regarding the group with a smile of amusement).* Maybe I'd better find the Captain for you, sir?

LINNELL

Don't hurry, Miss Belle. Speed the parting guests, first of all.

BELLE

Och, them! ... I'll soon get the Captain, never fear. *(She moves to the door on the left, then halts.)* And ... and I trust you're comfortable at Callachly, sir?

LINNELL

Quite. But I'd rather be here, Belle

BELLE

Oh, thank you, sir. *(Flustered, she goes out.)*

MAIRI

(coming away from the window, as ANNA *closes it.)* Another adventure! *(She sighs luxuriously.)*

ANNA

(crossing and sitting down to her crochet work again). Poor Carsaig! What a life that woman leads him!

MAIRI

(taking some papers from her satchel). Do you know what I call my new poem, Mr. Linnell?

LINNELL

No. Something fine, I'm sure.

MAIRI

"The Inn of Adventure."

LINNELL

How exciting!

MAIRI

Isn't it! ... There's a man in it named Filippo.

LINNELL

Ah! Suspiciously like Philip, that.

MAIRI

Hush! *(She indicates* **ANNA** *with a warning finger. But* **ANNA** *seems too deeply engrossed in her crochet to take any notice; and* **MAIRI** *goes on in a lower tone:)* And a girl named Aurelia ... She's only sixteen.

LINNELL

Your own age? How remarkable!

MAIRI

Hush! ... And she has a fine passage with a man much older than herself, where she says, "Wait for me."

LINNELL

Really? I trust the fortunate man was Filippo?

MAIRI

Ah, that's a secret! *(She scribbles hastily)* But, if you're good, I'll show it you when I've finished.

(**BELLE** *enters on the left with the* **CAPTAIN**, *who — when he sees* **LINNELL** *— puts his finger to his lips and points downstairs.*

CAPTAIN

Plenty of the lairds about to-night, Anna. Every one of note is there. Even your great friend Ardow.

ANNA

(crocheting away quietly). Ardow's no longer any friend of mine.

LINNELL

All Anna's friends are leaving her, Captain. Even Miss Ishbel's taken wing.

CAPTAIN

Never! What's afoot?

LINNELL

Oh, the gallant Carsaig elopes once more.

CAPTAIN

Godsake! She's gone earlier than you thought.

LINNELL

Well ... but hadn't we better set the ladies an example in the way of abstinence from gossip?

BELLE

Heard you ever the like, Anna!

CAPTAIN

Pure effrontery, Belle. But I'll take him off out o' this till he's better behaved. We'll go up to my room, Philip, if you please.

(They go upstairs and to the right.

BELLE

And isn't Mr. Linnell the cool one!

ANNA

'Deed, yes. I cannot make him out at all. And yesterday he was fair out of his mind about Ishbel's carryings-on.

BELLE

Och, yesterday he hadn't seen through her. Today it's a different story.

MAIRI

(looking up from her writing). "Unstable as water she shall not excel."

BELLE

Come on, you, and excel out o' this, my lady! The lairds will be coming up instantly ... You take her ben with you, Anna.

MAIRI

(reading from her manuscript as she goes). "Aurelia blows Filippo a kiss."

BELLE

Tuts! Blow yourself ben the house at once. I hear them on the stairs.

ANNA

(rising). We'll be safer in the other end, Mairi. Come away now.

(ANNA and MAIRI go out at the back, as SILIS, the serving-maid, comes in with a tray containing decanters and glasses. She is followed by the lairds. TOSTARY enters in talk with ARDOW; after them come MOY and OOLAVA. The last is a hard-bitten, soldierly man of about fifty-five, clad in riding garb. BELLE goes to the sideboard and prepares drinks with SILIS, who hands them round. Both women then retire by the door on the left.

TOSTARY

(sipping his drink). Twenty-eight, Oolava? Do you tell me now! Twenty-eight!

OOLAVA

Yes, that was the price. Twenty-eight.

ARDOW

A Uist pony at twenty-eight pounds! Nonsense, Oolava! ... But leave horses and let's turn to something livelier. Will you play, Oolava?

OOLAVA

Yes, and gladly ... I'm your man.

(**ARDOW** *and* **OOLAVA** *sit down to cards at the big table. The others draw in to the fire.*

MOY

Twenty-eight! No, I'll not believe anyone was fool enough to pay that price for any pony.

TOSTARY

(with an air of great sagacity). Stop you, Moy. Fool, did you say? ... I'm not so sure of that ... *(To* **OOLAVA**.*)* How many would there be in the crowd at the bidding?

OOLAVA

Forty or thereby.

TOSTARY

(triumphantly). Just as I thought! Now, look you, Moy, did you ever see forty people in Aros Isle all gathered together, and not one fool among them?

(*All laugh at* **MOY**'s *discomfiture.*

OOLAVA

Hit, Moy, hit!

TOSTARY

(well-pleased, as he stretches himself expansively). Yes indeed, there are strange things happen at horse fairs anywhere, but the strangest of all in Aros, I'm thinking ... I saw another queer business to-day with Iain of the Glen and old Rob Campbell.

OOLAVA

I saw that too. It was real droll.

ARDOW

And what was it?

TOSTARY

Well, they met to-day for the first time in twenty years and more; living as they do with thirty miles between them, they couldn't see much of one another except at horse fairs or funerals, could they?

OOLAVA

Aye, they hadn't met for twenty years, they're saying, as luck would have it; being old men, you see, and not travelling far nowadays.

ARDOW

Yes, yes, but mind your cards, Oolava. Let Tostary tell us in his own way.

MOY

(to **TOSTARY***).* And what happened?

TOSTARY

Well, old Rob was told such a one was Iain of the Glen. So up he goes to him, and shakes hands ... Two old men of eighty, look you, trying to recall each other from memories of youth. Man, it was queer!

MOY

And was that all?

TOSTARY

No, sir, it was not. You're in a deuce of a hurry, aren't you? Let me tell the story. It's mine, not yours! ... And, says Rob: " How are you, Iain? ... And how's your father?" —" Well," says Iain, "death took him from us twenty-two years ago ... and we haven't heard a word of him since."

(There is general laughter, during which the **CAPTAIN** *and* **LINNELL** *appear on the gallery;* **LINNELL** *dragging the* **CAPTAIN** *downstairs while the* **CAPTAIN** *endeavours to restrain him.* **LINNELL** *appears to be drunk, and his looks are haggard. He stumbles even on the level as he crosses the room.*

CAPTAIN

(looking round apologetically). Too bad to intrude. You must excuse Mr. Linnell: he's a trifle tired. But we heard your merriment and thought we'd join you.

(**LINNELL** *disengages himself from the* **CAPTAIN***'s arm and staggers across to the fire, disturbing* **MOY** *from his seat,* **MOY** *finds another chair.* **LINNELL** *starts crooning to himself softly, and extends his hands to the blaze.*

ARDOW

(rising). The rest of the company can speak for themselves, Captain MacColl; but for myself I'll say this ... There's not a room in all Aros Isle big enough to hold Mr. Linnell and me at the same moment.

CAPTAIN

Indeed, sir?

ARDOW

Did he not agree yesterday to my demand that he leave this Inn at once?

CAPTAIN

He did, Ardow. And he has removed to the Inn at Callachly ... But he has returned here for this night as my guest.

ARDOW

Well, sir, I think you show questionable taste in your choice of guests.

CAPTAIN

(*coolly*). That's as may be, Ardow. *(He turns his back on* **ARDOW**, *takes a pinch of snuff, and signs to* **SILIS** *to bring him a glass of wine.)* My claret, lassie. *(He sits down beside* **LINNELL**, *and then turns to* **TOSTARY** *and* **MOY**, *as if done with* **ARDOW**, *who is still on his feet, scowling at the* **CAPTAIN**)

Well, well, and hasn't it been the fine day, Tostary! ... And the prices very good at the fair, I hear?

ARDOW

(*angrily*). You heard me, Captain MacColl?

OOLAVA

(*twitching* **ARDOW**'s *coat-tail*). Let be, man, let be! The Captain's not to blame. And I'm sure Mr. Linnell will give no trouble. If he does, well, then, we can see about it.

MOY

Yes, yes, he'll soon be dovering. Would you have us all go out into the night because of some special grievance of your own? Get on with your game, lad. Quietly's the word!

TOSTARY

Och, yes. There's no need for standing on ceremony on Horse Fair night. It's not as if he'd come into the club in Edinburgh, you see ... Let be ... let be!

ARDOW

(*muttering as he resumes his game*). 'Gad! if you all knew him as well as I do, you'd kick him downstairs, club or no club.

TOSTARY

(*turning away from* **ARDOW**). Aye, some fine beasts selling to-day, Captain.

CAPTAIN

But they'll sell better the morn, after a rest. They've been long journeying, most of them.

MOY

One or two good saddle-horse yonder. I saw Carsaig had his eye on some of them. Doubtless he'd be thinking they'd make fine ladies' mounts, eh?

ARDOW

(*cocking an ear*). And what if he did, pray?

TOSTARY.

Tush, man! Moy was but jesting.

ARDOW

Well, he'll jest none at my friend's expense while I'm by.

MOY

And aren't you touchy now! Quietly's the word to-night, I tell you. And I'll not quarrel, just to disappoint you. I can see you're spoiling for a fight, no matter with whom.

TOSTARY

Aye, he's the wild one.

OOLAVA

(*rising*). He's having bad luck this turn: that's what's wrong with him. Let's call a halt, Ardow. You've lost enough to me, I'm thinking. (*Some money is paid over by* **ARDOW** *to him.*) Draw in to the fire and have your dram, and better luck next time to you, my hero!

ARDOW

I'm near enough that fireside, the way it's ranged at present ... Come, Moy, will you try the rattlers? (*He holds up a dice-box and shakes it.*) Your revenge for our last game, eh?

MOY

Not I! I've but twenty guineas on me ... And I haven't got over that last game with you. It's you were fortune's favourite with a vengeance, yon night in London town.

ARDOW

Fortune's favourite? Well, God send I'm such a bit oftener ... And it's Oolava's had all the luck at the cartes this turn.

(**LINNELL** *is rousing from his doze as* **ARDOW** *speaks. He now stands up unsteadily.*)

LINNELL

Cartes? ... Who shays cartes? (*A dead silence.*) Cartes? I'll play cartes, Cap'n, shertainly. I'll keel-haul ye any day, Cap'n ... Navy and Army, eh?

CAPTAIN

No, no, Philip, nobody's playing cartes ... Sit down and be civil, man.

LINNELL

Plenty money, y'know. (*He stumbles over to the table and thumps down a handful of guineas before* **ARDOW**.) Where'sh cartes?

CAPTAIN

(*crossing to him, and putting a hand on his arm*). Come, come, sir! You disturb the company. Sit down by the fire and content yourself. There are no cartes spoken of. The gentlemen are about to dice.

LINNELL

Right! Want dice myself. Hazard's agin the law, but who cares! ... Nobody tell, eh? *(He scatters some more guineas on the table, and sinks heavily in a chair, facing* **ARDOW**.*)* You take other fellow's place, Captain *(He points to* **ARDOW**.*)*

CAPTAIN

Not I, Philip. I've no mind and less money for dicing. Come over here to the fire. You're upsetting the company. *(He goes back to the fireplace.)*

LINNELL

(rising and following the **CAPTAIN**, *halts before* **MOY**, *whose hand he grasps.)* No, no. Never upset a friend ... never. *(He then swings round and makes for the table again, plumping down as before, in front of* **ARDOW**.*)* Must really rattle a bit, y'know.

MOY

Oh, for Heaven's sake take the fool on, Ardow! Otherwise he'll be quarrelsome. Play him a few throws, and then it will be quicker to bed for all of us.

ARDOW

(sneering). Oh, by all means! Let the good Ardow sacrifice himself for the good of the company ... All right, I'll take him.

TOSTARY

That's a good fellow!

ARDOW

And let him pay his shot like the next man, eh?

MOY

Well, he seems to have guineas enough.

CAPTAIN

Oh, no. Without stakes, if you please. My friend's not himself.

ARDOW

Really, Captain MacColl, do you doubt me? It's hardly a game of skill where wits are needed.

TOSTARY

Hear, hear! It's all chance at hazard.

CAPTAIN

But wits are necessary when a man is to know when to stop, aren't they?

LINNELL

You stan' out o' this, Cap'n. See? That's where you stop, right away ... Plen ... plenty guineas here, y'know. Stakes are here, Cap'n. So rattle 'em up, I say. Five, eh? And here they are, sir.

(**LINNELL** *counts out five guineas clumsily and sets them against five of* **ARDOW**'s. **ARDOW** *rattles the dice.*

ARDOW

I call eight. *(He throws.)* Two sizes! I nick.

(He draws the guineas over to his side of the table; and they go on playing during the ensuing dialogue. The play is clearly in **ARDOW**'s *favour, and a file of guineas gradually accumulates on his side. The group by the fire watch the match for a little; then* **TOSTARY** *speaks:*

TOSTARY

Well, they're settling down to it. That should keep the Linnell lad out o' mischief for a bit, eh?

OOLAVA

Aye, I reckon he's safe for a while.

TOSTARY

Do you know, I saw Hugh of Kellan do a silly thing to-day.

CAPTAIN

Indeed.

TOSTARY

Yes, he had been like your friend over there, tilting his pinkie too much for his own good.

CAPTAIN

Aye, aye, poor Philip!

TOSTARY

Well, Hugh was trying to sell a brown gelding with a white forefoot; and at last he sold her for eighteen, just as he was on the way to getting quite soused.

OOLAVA

Wasn't that early in the day, now?

TOSTARY

Aye, in the late morning ... Then, in the afternoon, he was thoroughly fuddled, and soon had the same horse back in his hands, this time with no white forefoot.

MOY

Aha! Tricked?

TOSTARY

Just that. A Sassenach horse-couper had bought the beast for eighteen, painted out the white stocking, and sold it back to Hugh for twenty-five.

CAPTAIN

Man, man! Isn't the drink the great deceiver!

OOLAVA

It's deceiving your friend, anyway. Time he was stopping. Look how his guineas are passing over to the other side of that table.

ARDOW

I hear you, Oolava, I hear you. The luck's against him for the moment, that's all.

LINNELL

(sinking back sulkily in his chair). Yesh! Luck's bad ... bad ... bad!

ARDOW

Time to be stopping, my hero.

(The group by the fire now look on in silence.

LINNELL

No, no ... Must have 'nother go ... My call. Eleven. *(He throws.)* Mine, bully-boy! Hand over. *(He rakes the money to his side of the table.)* Aha! Luck's turning, you see.

ARDOW

And time too. *(He rattles the dice.)* Ten—*(He throws)* Cinque ... cinque ... Mine. *(He draws over the stakes.)*

LINNELL

(rattling.) Size ... (He throws) Trey.... Bad ... bad!

(**ARDOW** *draws over the money.*

ARDOW

(shaking the dice). Twelve ... *(He throws)* Two sizes! ... Now that's something like a throw! *(He again takes the stakes)* Hadn't we better call a halt, sir? The luck's all my way, it seems.

LINNELL

Right, we'll stop ... But s'pose we have a last shot ... a big one ... *He counts out some guineas)* Lucky number o' mine, eh? Thirteen's very good number at times ... Here y'are. *(He fumbles the coins.)* Eleven, twelve, thirteen ... Thirteen shiny boys against thirteen yours, eh?

ARDOW

As you like. Last shot ... thirteen. Your call.

LINNELL

My call? ... Then, eight. *(He throws.)* And eight it is ... Ha-ha bully-boy! *(He draws over a big pile.)* Too bad, though. Give you revenge ... Come on, 'nother shot, eh?

ARDOW

Oh, very well.

LINNELL

Tell you what ... I'll put down thirty against thirty o' yours. What say? *(He counts out the guineas, painfully slow.)*

ARDOW

I'll take you. My cast! And may my luck come back! ... Seven ... *(He throws.)* Cinque doubled ... that's fine! ... Chance to me, so I throw again. *(He throws.)* And it's double cinque once more. Hooray!
(He is raking over the money, when **LINNELL** *casts a sharp eye on the* **CAPTAIN***, who nods in return.* **LINNELL** *suddenly rises to his feet, very sober: he tosses* **ARDOW***'s hand away from the stakes.*

ARDOW

What's ado?

LINNELL

Cheat!
(The fireside group start to their feet, **ARDOW** *makes to throw himself at* **LINNELL***'s throat by an adroit move that will also overturn the table. But the* **CAPTAIN** *has come forward, and his right hand steadies the table instantly. Then, interposing between the gamesters, his left hand sweeps* **ARDOW** *back to his seat. The others crowd around.*

CAPTAIN

Leave the table untouched, gentlemen! ... Mr. Linnell has made a charge against Ardow.

ARDOW

(rising). And, by God! he'll answer for it!

LINNELL

Will someone of you test the dice, please? *(Nobody stirs)* Come! You all saw how often cinque was doubled in the last throws. I say that either of these dice will fall cinque at every throw ... They're loaded.

TOSTARY

Loaded! Nonsense, man! *(He steps forward, and, rattling the dice, throws.)* Cinque ... and cinque! ... Try again. *(He throws once more)* Double cinque again! ... Heavens, Ardow!

MOY
Surely not? *(He takes up the dice and throws.)* Double cinque! My God!

ARDOW
A trick! ... He's palmed them off on me!

LINNELL
Trickery? No ... Why, gentlemen, he has two other false dice in the left pouch of his vest. But they are different by a point: they fall double size.

ARDOW
A lie! ... Let me go, Captain MacColl!

LINNELL
Prove it a lie then. Empty that pocket, or I'll empty it myself.

ARDOW
(storming). Come and try! There's none here will empty pockets o' mine.

CAPTAIN
(clapping him on the back with his left hand as if to soothe him). Come, come, Ardow, there's nobody here wishing to do you an injustice. There's been a charge by Mr. Linnell; and now you make a countercharge. If the dice aren't in your pocket, then they aren't there, and that's an end of the matter. (*And suddenly his right hand dips into the left vest pocket of the young laird.* ARDOW *is as if mesmerised by the boldness and speed of the move, and has not time to stir, as the* CAPTAIN *nimbly extracts a pair of dice and tosses them on the table*) All the same, Ardow, the memory is a bit treacherous at times. So doubtless you forgot these fellows ... I see they fall ... double size!

TOSTARY
(leaning forward and noting the dice). Double size!

ARDOW
Damn you all for a set of tricksters! ... You'll hear more of this, Linnell!

(He ducks below the CAPTAIN*'s arm and rushes out by the door on the left. The lairds, pale-faced and shaken, regard each other blankly and in silence. After a pause the* CAPTAIN *tosses all four dice.*

CAPTAIN
Well, are you satisfied, gentlemen?

MOY
Good Lord, yes! The man's done for!

CAPTAIN
You've seen dice like these before, Tostary?

TOSTARY
You mean, at Alverca?

CAPTAIN
Aye, at Alverca. You remember, Moy? And you? *(He turns to* **OOLAVA**.*)* Yes, the dice there were just like these, green with age ... God knows how long they've been in that family at Ardow ... But I think this we've seen to-night breaks the succession of an heirloom so dangerous.

MOY
Godsake! You cannot mean it's the same set, father's and son's.

CAPTAIN
Ask Anna MacDougall. She tells me he had them from his father. They've been in the family for years most likely ... Yes, those are the Alverca dice without a doubt.

OOLAVA
(suddenly crossing to **LINNELL** *and shaking his hand)*. Well done, sir ... Damme, well done!

TOSTARY
(to the Captain). And you mean to say ...?

CAPTAIN
Yes. Like father, like son.

TOSTARY
Then you think old Ardow the cheat at Alverca?

CAPTAIN
Good God! Are you still as dull witted as you were then?

TOSTARY
Do you know what you are saying, sir?

CAPTAIN
I do. And if you don't like it, you have the remedy in your own hands ... I am saying that you are as dull witted as you were in the year 'nine when you doubted the integrity of this lad's father. Don't you remember? It was double cinque at Alverca, and it's double cinque here to-night.

TOSTARY
Well, well, here's a light on the past!

CAPTAIN

And is that all you have to say?

TOSTARY

(*going up to* LINNELL *impulsively*). My dear sir! (*He puts out his hand warmly, and* LINNELL *grasps it.*) I've been very blind ... Blind and foolish. Forgive me.

MOY

Fine, Tostary, fine. I'm sure Mr. Linnell will understand. (*He also shakes hands with* LINNELL)

OOLAVA

Understand be blowed, Moy. Say you're damned sorry and be done with it.

MOY

(*suddenly scared by* OOLAVA's *vehemence, and speaking parrot-fashion*). Mr. Linnell, I'm damned sorry.

CAPTAIN

There, there! Don't make too long a song about it all ... But you three had better pass the story of these dice to the other old fools of the Sixty-First, who thought Charlie Linnell was at fault at Alverca ... Like father, like son, say you. And you can add it's as true of the Linnells as of the Ardows, but with a difference, thank Heaven!

TOSTARY

(*turning away astounded.*) Yes, yes, we'll tell them that ... we'll tell them ... Cinque, cinque ... (*He wanders off to the back of the room, muttering: "Cinque ... cinque"*)

OOLAVA

And I'll have Ardow posted in every club in the land ... See if I don't! (*A fresh noise of shouting is heard out-of-doors.* TOSTARY *goes to the window and opens it. The others crowd round him.*

TOSTARY

That's Ardow. He's in some fresh trouble. Time he was out o' this. I'll go down to him.

CAPTAIN

Just a moment, Tostary. You'd better take those stakes with you. Their disposal might be left to Ardow's club in Edinburgh, I'm thinking ... What do you say, Philip?

LINNELL

I think they might well go to the regimental chest of the Sixty-First.

TOSTARY.

The very thing. I'll suggest that to the club. *(He picks up the money.)* But I'd best be after that fellow or he'll do murder down there.

(As he turns to go, MAIRI dashes in from the door at the back, followed by ANNA. MAIRI goes the window.

MAIRI

Oh, Anna, it's Donald Gorm again!

(TOSTARY goes out on the left, followed by OOLAVA and MOY. The women crane out of the window. The noise continues.

MAIRI

See! Donald's wanting to fight somebody... Oh, it's Ardow! There! In the light of the door! ... And, just fancy! Ardow's running away!

ANNA

Yes, and Donald after him. Saw you ever the like!

MAIRI

Ardow's up on his horse now. Donald will never catch him ... Yes, he's off! Tostary was too late!

(A clatter of horse-hoofs is heard; it dies away in the distance, accompanied by shouts from DONALD GORM.

MAIRI

Oh, didn't Ardow and Donald look funny!

ANNA

Come in, come in. It's all over now.

MAIRI

This is the place for adventures, isn't it! *(She comes away from the window.)* Oh, here's Mr. Linnell! ... Oh, Mr. Linnell, I want more advice about my poem very badly. *(She takes her scroll out of her satchel and sits down at the table to look over it.)*

ANNA

Och, never heed her or her poem, sir ... And you must excuse us running in on you as we did. It was such a noise, we quite forgot our manners, thinking it was some danger, you see; and there being no good view from the window ben the house ... Come you now, Mairi! Your aunts will be angry if they find you staying on here.

MAIRI

(reading her notes.) Oh, just one moment, Anna. There's something I want to ask ... *(Then to LINNELL)* How old are you, Mr. Linnell?

ANNA

Mairi MacDonald! What a question!

MAIRI

It's only for my poem that I want to know.

LINNELL

I'm twenty-four.

MAIRI

(sighing). And Aurelia's only sixteen! But I suppose twenty-four will just have to do. *(She makes a note and then continues.)* Do you think it would look strange if Aurelia married a man of twenty-four?

ANNA

Such manners!

LINNELL

Of course I haven't studied your poem as yet. After all, there are different kinds of people at sixteen and at twenty-four, aren't there?

MAIRI

Yes, yes ... And I think Aurelia's just the kind of young person that would cry, "Oh, Filippo, wait for me!"

ANNA

Tuts! Say good-night now, Mairi, and come off with you.

CAPTAIN

A very good advice, Anna. I'm deaved with her poetry and her nonsense.

MAIRI

Oh, fie! You know you're not. It's only that you're angry because I never asked you your age.

CAPTAIN

For any sake take her away, Anna! or I'll say something I'll regret ... My age! ... How dare you, you randy!

(ANNA *takes* MAIRI *by the arm, but* MAIRI *breaks away, trips to the door at the back, where she curtsies gracefully, and chants "Good-night" in a mock recitative. But before she can open the back door,* BETA *comes in on the left.*

Making for the stairs, BETA *crosses, holding up her hands momentarily to indicate her amazement at something she has seen downstairs. At sight of this* MAIRI *and* ANNA *immediately postpone their departure.*

CAPTAIN

What's this next, Beta? What's ado?

BETA

(briefly and grimly). She's back.

CAPTAIN

Who?

BETA

The weathercock. *(And without a word further she continues her progress upstairs, and so to the door on the left, where she disappears.)*

ANNA

Ishbel! ... Again!

CAPTAIN

Poor lass!

LINNELL

Let us all go.

ANNA

Wheesht! They're coming!

(**LINNELL** *and the* **CAPTAIN** *move hastily across to the window. The door on the left opens, and* **BELLE** *ushers in* **ISHBEL**, *who, holding her head high, crosses to the stairs followed by* **BELLE** *They go upstairs and enter the room on the left.*

CAPTAIN

(exploding). It's all that crazy fellow Byron's fault ... dammit! ... This countryside is going to the dogs because of him. Ever since his death they've made a martyr of the man, and treat his verse like the word inspired; and they're all Childe Harold or Don Juan or Marino Something-or-Other, or Haidee or Thyrza or The Maid of Athens ... Romantick nonsense that leads nowhere!

ANNA

Aye, and you seem to know more of him yourself than I would have credited, Captain, if he's so dangerous as all that.

CAPTAIN

I've read enough of him to be warned, Anna ... And I'm safe on the score of romance, you'll allow?

ANNA

I'll allow nothing of the kind ... Did you not see the look Ishbel gave you in the passing? ... Just you be taking care, or she'll be riding off with yourself some fine night before harvest.

CAPTAIN

(awkwardly attempting to fall into this humorous vein). I'm afraid Philip would have something to say to that ... And I'm rather old for the lists of love ... Eh, lad?

LINNELL

And I've no desire for further ventures in those lists.

MAIRI

(with a little moan). Oh!

ANNA

(startled). Come you, Mairi. It's long past our bed-time. *(She opens the door at the back.)*

MAIRI

Oh, Anna, my poem! *(She retrieves it from the table; then reads aloud from it as she returns to* ANNA.*)* "Oh, Filippo, wait for me! "

ANNA

Mairi, you baggage!

MAIRI

But I was only quoting, Anna ... See, there it is in black and white ... "Wait for me!" *(She points to the manuscript, and* ANNA *is speechless at the manoeuvre.)*

LINNELL

(suddenly and eagerly). By the Lord! Mairi, I believe I shall!
   (The CAPTAIN *and* ANNA *nod to each other, well-pleased and smiling. The young folks gaze at each other in wonder, transported into a new world.*

CAPTAIN

Wait, is it? ... Man, man! Waiting's the biggest venture of all ... Is it not, Anna?

ANNA

Well, Duncan, it's yourself should know.
   *(*ANNA *shakes her head at him reprovingly,* MAIRI *flourishes her scroll gaily to*
LINNELL.
And each of the quartette senses dimly that they are once more in the pose they had already held in those very surroundings not so long ago.

CURTAIN

Heather Gentry

The action passes at the estate of Drimfearn, in the West Highlands. The time is present day. It is August.

ACT I	The Study at Drimfearn	*Afternoon*
ACT II	The Study at Drimfearn	*Evening of Next Day*
ACT III	Scene One	
	"The Dispensary " at Drimfearn	*Afternoon: A Week Later*
	Scene Two	
	"The Dispensary " at Drimfearn	*An Hour Later*

PERSONS

CAMPBELL OF DRIMFEARN	A Highland Laird
MRS. CAMPBELL OF DRIMFEARN ------	Wife
MURRAY CAMPBELL	Their Son
DR. KENNEDY	The Local Doctor.
MARSALI MACALPINE	A District Nurse
MACNAB	A Gamekeeper
BRIDGET	A Tablemaid
JANET	A Housemaid
BORDEN	A Shooting Tenant
CRADDOCK	His Nephew
KELLY	A Profiteer
A CHAUFFEUR	

HEATHER GENTRY was first produced by the Scottish National Theatre Society, at the Lyric Theatre, Glasgow, on 24th December, 1927, under the direction of Tyrone Guthrie, with the following cast:

Campbell of Drimfearn	R. B. WHARRIE
Murray Campbell	ANDREW STEWART
Dr. Kennedy	MOULTRIE KELSALL
MacNab	JAMES ANDERSON
Borden	MORLAND GRAHAM
Craddock	GEORGE F. YUILL
Kelly—	T. P. MALEY
A Chauffeur	HAMISH SMITH
Mrs. Campbell of Drimfearn	MEG B. BUCHANAN
Marsali Mac Alpine	ELSIE BROTCHIE
Bridget	NELL BALLANTYNE
Janet	PEGGY MORTON

NOTE

MACNAB speaks with a Highland accent; BRIDGET and KELLY, of course, with Irish tongues—BRIDGET's brogue being very light. All the other Persons of the Play talk straight English.

NOTE

No reference is made to any living person in this play. The events described are imaginary.

ACT I

SCENE. *The Study at Drimfearn, West Highlands, on an afternoon in August: a large room, comfortably furnished, the walls lined with books on shelving but not so closely as to interfere with the display of an etching here and there.*

There are only two doors, one midway in the back wall and one in the left, well forward. The fireplace is set about the middle of the left wall. In the right wall are great windows through which are seen a ruined tower and the sunlit waters of a Highland loch.

Several easy chairs, a couch, and a library step-ladder are disposed about the room. A writing table and a chair are set close to the window in the right corner.

MARSALI MACALPINE, *a young woman of twenty-five in the dress of a District Nurse, is looking out of the window. Presently she turns away as if impatient, and it is seen that her face has a grave beauty.*

MURRAY CAMPBELL *dashes in by the door at the back. He is a young excitable man of twenty-six, clad in a kilt outfit of rough homespun tweed. He carries some papers in his hands—accounts, invoices and so on.*

MURRAY
Hillo, Marsali! Not away yet?

MARSALI
No. Waiting for your mother. Have to see her about cook.

MURRAY
I'd forgotten cook. How is she?

MARSALI
Nothing serious, I think. But just to make sure, we've sent for Dr. Kennedy.

MURRAY
(in a low voice, as he comes over to her). I say ... Nobody about ... Do you mind? *(He stoops as if to kiss her; but she evades him, and he contents himself with kissing her hand.)* All right: I'll be good ... Look here, Marsali, doing anything special this afternoon? I've got to cross the loch. Why not come for a sail?

MARSALI
Sorry. I'm busy. Some visits to do in the village.

MURRAY
Can't you put them off till evening? A blow on the briny will do you good.

MARSALI
No, I must run as soon's I've seen Mrs. Campbell.

MURRAY

You've never any time for me nowadays. What's wrong?

MARSALI

Nothing. I'm here for work, not play; that's all.

MURRAY

Oh, but I do work when it's working-time. But this is August, my dear ... You should see me in winter, swotting Agriculture in that old college in Glasgow ... Come now! It's really August, y'know. *(He draws her back to the window.)* What a day! You don't know what you're missing ... I say, doesn't the old tower look fine in the sun there?

MARSALI

Yes, great! Stark and dignified. Not like those pretentious shooting lodges all around.

MURRAY

Well, the shooting lodges are meant for the pretentious bounders who rent them ... By the by, have you heard the latest about our gem of a shooting tenant at Ben Veon?

MARSALI

Borden? No.

MURRAY

Well, he's God's worst fisher, and can't get a fish. Says the river's being poached, and swears he'll net it just to spite the poachers ... Ever hear the like?

MARSALI

That's bad.

MURRAY

He's going to net on Saturday; but we're meaning to forestall him. Having the Faolinnvore crofters over to-morrow night to net all the pools before he can get at them.

MARSALI

That's worse.

MURRAY

How worse?

MARSALI

It's poaching off a tenant.

MURRAY

Not at all, we're only getting in our punch before he gets in his. Father's quite keen on it.

MARSALI

Well, the Drimfearns that lived in that old tower would never have descended to such a trick.

MURRAY

No, they didn't have to. They carried dirks, and knew how to use them. Nowadays we've only stamped parchments, and chaps like Borden know more about using those than father. So we have to keep our end up some way or other.

MARSALI

Oh, the poor Highlands! what's to become of them!

MURRAY

Look here, Marsali. You'll have us both in the blues! Let's sail over to Faolinnvore. Get a sniff of the open sea, eh?

MARSALI

To Faolinnvore? To the crofters? About this poaching business?

MURRAY

Hush!

MARSALI

And you're going to help? Because Borden won't play the game, you won't? The laird's son a poacher!

MURRAY

But look here, Marsali ...
(**JANET,** *the housemaid, opens the door at the back. She carries a leather, brass-locked post-bag which she lays down on the table, as she announces:*)

JANET

Dr. Kennedy, sir.
(*She goes out after having shown in the* **DOCTOR,** *a fair-haired, breezy-mannered man of thirty. He wears a dark suit of Harris tweed and brown leather leggings.*)

MURRAY

Hillo, Doctor! How goes it! (*They all shake hands.*) Of course, you two have all kind of medical horrors to discuss, but I'm used to that; so I'll just stay on if you don't mind, and get these figures of father's into some semblance of sanity. (*He sits down at the table and starts work at his papers.*)

DOCTOR

I've seen cook.

MARSALI

Nothing serious?

DOCTOR

Not smallpox anyway.

MARSALI

I'm glad of that ... And now you're here I needn't wait to see Mrs. Campbell. I've so much to do; and you can tell her yourself about cook. It was chiefly that I wanted to see Mrs. Campbell about.

DOCTOR

Yes, you cut off. I know you're busy. And I'll calm her down about cook all right ... Oh, by the by, they've got a new maid here, haven't they?

MARSALI

(smiling). Yes. Why do you ask?

DOCTOR

A bit queer, isn't she?

MARSALI

A little. Didn't you see the rogue in her eye?

DOCTOR

Didn't get a chance. All I saw was her heels.

MARSALI

What's she been up to now?

MURRAY

(chipping in). Yes. What next?

DOCTOR

Well, when I arrived, Janet answered the door. Then, as I was taking off my coat in the hall, I caught a glimpse of this new maid at the end of the long corridor, and immediately she saw me she took to her heels and sprinted—positively sprinted right to the end of that passage; and you know how long it is. Next, round the corner in a skid that was masterly, and so out of sight.

MARSALI

Just like Bridget. Pretty, isn't she?

DOCTOR

I tell you I didn't get a chance to see. She was off before you could say knife. What's her trouble?

MARSALI

Oh, she hasn't got used to our out-of-the-way life here... Never been in the Highlands before ... She's Irish.

MURRAY

Double strong Irish, too!

DOCTOR

Irish? I'll bet she gets on the chief's nerves.

MARSALI

All do, poor girls! Irish or not Irish ... But I must really get off. Good-day, Doctor. Day, Murray.

(The **DOCTOR** *opens the door at the back for her, and just then* **MRS. CAMPBELL**, *a fussy old lady of fifty enters by the door on the left. She shakes hands with the* **DOCTOR** *and* **MARSALI**.

MRS. CAMPBELL

Oh, but you're surely not going already, Marsali? Sorry to have kept you waiting, my dear.

MARSALI

Well, Doctor will tell you all about cook. Good news: it's nothing serious. So I needn't wait. I've loads of work waiting me out there.

MRS. CAMPBELL

But I wanted all your home news. All well?

MARSALI

Yes, all well. But I'll be back as soon's I've done my round, and we'll have a talk then.

(She goes out by the door at the back, **MURRAY** *opening it for her, as they exchange smiles of something more than friendliness.*

MRS. CAMPBELL

Good of you to come so quickly, Doctor.

DOCTOR

Oh, it's my new motor-bike. She does fly.

MRS. CAMPBELL

So glad to hear cook has nothing infectious. Sure it isn't smallpox? Those pimples about the nose?

DOCTOR

Whisky.

MRS. CAMPBELL

Ah! Now, why didn't I think of that! I've always suspected cook. But it's so difficult to get servants here, we just have to take anybody ... You're quite sure now it's nothing infectious?

DOCTOR

Quite.

MRS. CAMPBELL

I'm so relieved. A great upset if it had been. We'd never have let another shooting this season.

DOCTOR

Yes, yes, but there isn't the least danger, I assure you ... Oh, talking of servants, you've a new maid, I see.

MRS. CAMPBELL

Yes, and that's another trouble. She's so outspoken. And she never will say "ma'am,' although I reprove her constantly. Always addresses me as "Mrs. Campbell". But I've just got to put up with her or go without.

DOCTOR

Yes, servants are always a bother anywhere, even in the cities, aren't they? ... And how's the chief?

MRS. CAMPBELL

Oh, quarrelling with his shooting tenants as usual. But this time I can't blame him. That man down at Ben Veon is positively the limit.

DOCTOR

Borden, the timber merchant?

MRS. CAMPBELL

Yes. The blackguard says the river's being poached. And by way of protecting himself he's going to net all the salmon there.

DOCTOR

But that's not done, is it?

MURRAY

(*intervening*). Of course it's not done. (*And he returns to his figures.*)

MRS. CAMPBELL

So Drimfearn told him. But Borden said if we made a fuss about it he'd advertise a sub-let in all the sporting papers—The Field, and so on, —and give his very small game bag up to date.

DOCTOR

Pretty slim dodge, that.

MRS. CAMPBELL

Yes. And the bag's so extremely small, an advertisement like that would ruin us.

DOCTOR

A bad lot, that chap.

MURRAY

You've said it, Doc. *(He rises, bundling up his papers.)* Finished at last, thank God! ... I'm off for Faolinnvore, mother. Back in the evening sometime.

MRS. CAMPBELL

Faolinnvore! ... Murray, you're surely not going on with that business after all I've said? Borden will have us in the law courts if you do.

MURRAY

Borden be hanged, little blighter! We'll show him how to net salmon!

MRS. CAMPBELL

But it's dangerous, Murray. And he'll say it's poaching. Please don't go!

MURRAY

But I've promised, mother. And the Faolinnvore men won't go without me. There's really no danger. All I've got to do is lie down inside their boat and be a watchman over it—see that nobody moves it away, so's our lot can get safely off after the raid's over ... Come now, don't worry! *(He kisses her.)*

MRS. CAMPBELL

Oh, Murray, I'm so afraid!

MURRAY

Nonsense! What is there to be afraid about, eh? *(He moves off to the door at the back.)* Please don't bother, I'll be all right ... Father's in the billiard room, Doctor. *(The door at the back opens, and* **DRIMFEARN** *enters.)* Oh, here he is!

DRIMFEARN

Hillo, Murray! You off already?

MURRAY

Yes. Got those figures all right at last. *(He hands* **DRIMFEARN** *the bundle of papers)* Off to Faolinnvore. Back in the evening.

(He goes out at the back
*(***DRIMFEARN** *is a stout, consequential man of fifty-five, slightly bald; his ruddy face is clean-shaven. He wears a kilt of Argyll Campbell tartan. A knowing smile frequently plays around his lips. When he sits he twiddles his thumbs, and his mind is evidently very often running on other subjects than that under discussion at the moment.*

DRIMFEARN

Hillo, Doctor! Well, how's cook? Is it smallpox?

DOCTOR

No.

DRIMFEARN

Ah, that's a pity.

MRS. CAMPBELL

Colin, what a thing to say!

DRIMFEARN

Well, some of those women would be better dead. The cook can't cook, and the housemaid can't house. And the table-maid...! *(He holds up his hands in horror.)* Doctor, have you seen the table-maid?

DOCTOR

In the distance only.

DRIMFEARN

Lucky man! She's like nothing on earth. Ab-so-lute-ly! ... You'd better get rid of her, Margaret, or there'll be murder done here before long. I'll poison that girl some fine day.

MRS. CAMPBELL

I wish you wouldn't say such things, Colin. She's the best I can get for a place so quiet as this, in the heart of the Highlands.

DRIMFEARN

The best! Then I wonder what the worst is like! ... And she's Irish, Doctor.

MRS. CAMPBELL

Well, she has a good heart, Colin, even if she has odd ways.

DRIMFEARN

If she has odd ways? ... If? ... If? ... What d'ye think, Doctor? ... Yesterday she addressed me as "Drim" ... "Drimfearn," I said. ... "Fearn?" says she; "I knew it was some kind of a flower." And off she went, grinning like a Cheshire cat ... What do you think, eh? *(The others smile.)* Oh, laugh, of course! *(Then suddenly to the DOCTOR.)* Look here, you're quite sure cook hasn't smallpox?

DOCTOR

Quite sure.

DRIMFEARN

Because, y'know, if there's the least doubt about it, I think we should pack off the whole menagerie.

DOCTOR

But there isn't any doubt.

DRIMFEARN

(plainly disappointed). Well, I suppose we must just put up with things as they are! ... Ah, the post! ... Excuse me, you people.

(He goes to the letter-bag on the table.

MRS. CAMPBELL

I do wish you'd be ... well ... more reticent, Colin. You're forgetting the harm you'll do to the estate if you go on talking and talking about smallpox and things like that.

DRIMFEARN

Oh, all right, all right, all right! ... Let's have a look at the letters ... Heard the news about Ardnish, Doctor? We're letting it to a friend of mine, a brother-officer in the old days. Not fixed ab-so-lute-ly, y'know, but almost. Colonel Merritt. North of India man. Good chap. *(He is unlocking the letter-bag as he goes on talking.)* Pony Merritt, we called him. Ten years since we met last.

MRS. CAMPBELL

It certainly was most kind of him to think of us.

DRIMFEARN

(sorting out the letters). Ten years! Dear old Merritt! Ah, no friends like the old friends! *(Then selecting a letter suddenly.)* Talk of angels! Here's Merritt's hand o' write! Aha! nothing like the old friends, Doctor! *(He opens the letter.)* Dear old Merritt! *(He reads)* What! ... The damned scoundrel! ... He's not coming!

MRS. CAMPBELL

Whatever's happened?

DRIMFEARN

Says he's heard there's a difficulty about the supply of coal at Ardnish, and that there's a rumour about infectious disease being rife round our way.

MRS. CAMPBELL

There! What did I tell you, Colin!

DRIMFEARN

Oh, blame it on me, of course! ... Well, Colonel Merritt, we'll see about this, my boy! ... We'll see about this coal supply libel, oh, yes! ... Also the rumour, my good man! (**JANET** *opens the door at the back.)* Well, what is it, woman?

JANET

(terrified at his shout). Oh, if you please, Drimfearn, it's MacNab.

DRIMFEARN

There, you see! *(He appeals to the* **DOCTOR**.*)* That's how they do things here. "It's MacNab." *(Then to the girl.)* Well, send him in, can't you, instead of staring like a mooncalf? ... I haven't got smallpox, have I?

MRS. CAMPBELL

Colin! Again!

DRIMFEARN

Oh, all right, my girl ... Sorry... Send him in, will you?

MRS. CAMPBELL

(as **JANET** *goes out).* All very well, Colin, but the damage is done. See if that girl doesn't spread the news that you've got smallpox all over the estate before the day's over.

DRIMFEARN

Well, you jolly well must see she doesn't. Tell her I was only joking.

MRS. CAMPBELL

I'll have to go now, Doctor. *(She extends her hand)*

DOCTOR

And I'm off, too. May I see you a moment, Mrs. Campbell? Just a word about cook.

(They move together to the door on the left.

DRIMFEARN.

Stay the night here, Doctor, y'know, if you find it convenient. Any night, my dear chap! No trouble, y'know. Delighted to have you.

DOCTOR

Not to-night, thank you. But to-morrow night, if I may. Suits my work better.

DRIMFEARN

Right. Your room's always ready— mean to say.

*(***JANET** *ushers in* **MACNAB** *at the back and then retires, just as* **MRS. CAMPBELL** *and the* **DOCTOR** *go out on the left.* **MACNAB** *is a man of sixty, straight as a lance, courteous and dignified in his well-fitting kilt outfit of crotal-coloured Harris tweed, over which—although it is a broiling day—he wears an Inverness cape of the same stuff. Under the cape he carries with difficulty several wooden boxes. He at once sets these down in a corner, and taking off his cape drapes it over them so as to conceal them completely.* **DRIMFEARN** *lifts one end of the cape and inspects the boxes hurriedly.*

DRIMFEARN

Got the birds at last, MacNab. Six brace, eh?

MACNAB
Six brace, sir. They're just out of the post-gig, half-an-hour ago; and I've been feeding them. As fine grouse as ever I saw.

DRIMFEARN
Well, see here, MacNab; these are for Mr. Borden's benefit.

MACNAB
Very good, Drimfearn.

DRIMFEARN
He's threatening me with all kinds of trouble because the birds are so few on his ground. Says he's had the smallest game bag he ever heard of for the two weeks after the Twelfth.

MACNAB
Well, well, what nonsense!

DRIMFEARN
Says they go the same way as the salmon ... Poachers, he says.

MACNAB
Just nonsense, Drimfearn. Neither him nor any of his people can handle a gun: that's all. Or a rod either, if the truth were told.

DRIMFEARN
Well, we'll show him some grouse ... and then hear what he has to say ... Now you get some soft soap out of the store—soft, you understand?

MACNAB
Yes, yes, soft soap, Drimfearn.

DRIMFEARN
And give these birds plenty of it along back and wings.

MACNAB
Yes, yes, Drimfearn ... Back and wings.

DRIMFEARN
Then set them along the march fence on the Ben Veon ground tonight after dark. The wind's west, and rain's sure before morning, isn't it?

MACNAB
Yes, yes, plenty of rain this night.

DRIMFEARN
That soap'll keep the birds pretty well where you leave 'em till morning. And by then it'll be a trifle washed off by the rain, but they'll not be too lively on the wing, eh? Look like young birds, you understand.

MACNAB
Isn't it wonderful, the inventions nowadays?

DRIMFEARN
Go on with you, MacNab! As if you'd heard of soft soap on a bird's back for the first time! (MACNAB *smiles broadly.*) Ah! Thought so, you old rascal! Now you know what to do?

MACNAB
Och, I'm understanding fine, sir.

(JANET *opens the door at the back.*

JANET
(*still scared*). If you please, Drimfearn, Messrs. Borden and Craddock would like to see you.

DRIMFEARN
Messrs.! What in all the world is this place coming to! ... No, no, my girl: it's Mr. Borden and Mr. Craddock. You mustn't say Messrs. Where in all the world did you pick that up?

JANET
If you please, sir, that's what Bridget calls them.

DRIMFEARN
Bridget be ... Well, never mind, never mind! Run away and tell them I'll see them in five minutes' time. And ask them to wait here, will you? Run off now like a good girl, and bring them up. And for goodness' sake don't call them Messrs.

JANET
Yes, Drimfearn. Thank you, Drimfearn.

(*She goes out, dubiously pondering.*

DRIMFEARN
Hurry, MacNab. He mustn't see those birds. Where can we plant them? ... There! outside the door there, for the present! (*He points to the door on the left,*) Come on ... I'll tell you the rest out of doors ... It's the only safe place in a house like this ... Congenital idiots all over the show!

(*They go out by the door on the left;* MACNAB *first of all depositing the boxes outside the door and carefully draping them with his cape. Presently* JANET *ushers in* BORDEN *and* CRADDOCK *by the door at the back.*

JANET
The chief will be with you in a wee meenit. (*She makes to retire, but suddenly returns.*) Oh, no, it was five!

BORDEN

Five? *(He looks at his watch.)* Five o'clock?

JANET

Oh, no: five wee meenits. *(And she goes out triumphantly, having remembered her lesson.)*

(BORDEN is a slight, dark-complexioned man, with a full forehead, and somewhat bald. His age is about fifty. He wears a shooting-kit of Burberry. CRADDOCK is similarly attired. He is fair-haired, lackadaisical, and wears a monocle. As the door closes on JANET, BORDEN turns eagerly to CRADDOCK.

BORDEN

Well?

CRADDOCK

Well?

BORDEN

Don't you recognise her?

CRADDOCK

Not the least bit, uncle. A bit daft, but has good legs ... What's the game?

BORDEN

Good Lord! I asked you to come with me and try to remember faces ... And all you can do is gas about the girl's ankles.

CRADDOCK

Surely no harm in a squint at an ankle, uncle? ... That's good! ... Ankle, uncle! .., Ankle, uncle!

BORDEN

I didn't rush you up from London just to listen to your limericks, y'know.

CRADDOCK

Sorry. It's the heather, I think. The air up here seems to knock everybody balmy. Even you are not the strong, silent man I know in town.

BORDEN

Less fooling. What do you think I brought you here for, this afternoon?

CRADDOCK

To squeeze a reduction of the rental out of old Drimfearn, I suppose.

BORDEN

Of course! But what was my special objective?

CRADDOCK

Surely not this flapper just gone out?

BORDEN

My God, no! The girl in the hall ... the one with the Irish brogue. Goes by the name of Bridget.

CRADDOCK

Then why on earth didn't you tell me you were looking for her?

BORDEN

Because I wished to see if you'd recognise her without any prompting.

CRADDOCK

Aha! Then we are sleuth-hounds, are we? ... Look here, uncle, I know you've shares in films, but I didn't know you wrote scenarios for them.

BORDEN

Oh, quit fooling! Drimfearn will be here in a minute ... Can't you remember that girl's face? Lively dark eyes, and a devilishly fascinating smile. Think, man, think!

CRADDOCK

The heather's got you too, uncle. I know the feeling. Romance in the air. Steady, now!

BORDEN

Well, put it that way, if you like. Have you any romance left in you, I wonder?

CRADDOCK

Aha! Confession! Who is this Bridget? Did you know she was here when you took the shoot at Ben Veon?

BORDEN

Not exactly. But I trailed her to within twenty miles of this before I took Ben Veon. And that was near enough for me.

CRADDOCK

Good! "Trailed" is a good film word.

BORDEN

Oh, damn the films! This is the real thing, I tell you.

CRADDOCK

What! You dotty on this slavey?

BORDEN

Slavey be blowed.

CRADDOCK

Not a fairy princess in disguise, surely?

BORDEN

You're getting warm at last. Now, think hard, please ... Did you never see that girl before? ... Say, somewhere in town? ... Eh?

CRADDOCK

No ... I'm stuck, really.

BORDEN

Well, think again ... Say, at the Wilburs ... at dinner one night?

CRADDOCK

(thinking hard). Sorry. Nothing doing in the memory line regarding the Wilburs' dinners.

BORDEN

Not even a table-maid there?

CRADDOCK

My God, no! Who's going to look at a table-maid when Jennie Wilbur's about. Pretty hot stuff, Jennie! ... You'd better tell me the whole tragedy, uncle. I was never good at this catechism business.

BORDEN

All right. You'll probably, however, recall the gossip columns of the evening papers of last spring, more readily than your dining-out, that season. There was a hash-up about a table-maid at the Wilburs then. No names mentioned, but it got into the Press all the same.

CRADDOCK

Sorry. I missed that. Tell me.

BORDEN

Well, Bridget — or rather Kate Kelly, as she called herself — a girl with pots o' money, signed on at the Wilburs as a table-maid.

CRADDOCK

Fairy-princess after all! ... But why a table-maid?

BORDEN

Lord knows! But there she was ... and getting along famously till her father gave the show away.

CRADDOCK

How?

BORDEN

Oh, he'd a habit of turning up on her days off with his big Rolls-Royce in a lane near the Wilburs' place and taking her out for a run, Henley or Oxford way. Back again at night, of course.

CRADDOCK

Fine. The stage is well set, uncle. But what about the hero of the romance? Where do I appear?

BORDEN

Not in this film, Philip. This is my show.

CRADDOCK

What! *(Then shaking his head sadly.)* No, uncle, I can't see you as a marrying man ... really can't. Think again, before it's too late.

BORDEN

Oh, chuck this nonsense. I'm in dead earnest, you understand.

CRADDOCK

All right. But, remember, I've warned you! ... And in any case you're not certain it's the girl, or you'd never have rushed me up, all the way from town, just to help identify her.

BORDEN

I'm practically certain. But I wanted to be doubly sure ... Yes, she has a turn of the head! ... Hang it all, man! Can't you remember! You were often dining at the Wilburs last spring.

CRADDOCK

Really can't recall a single thing at the Wilbur dinners, except Jennie Wilbur, I tell you ... But, never mind. What's the game?—I mean, what line will you take? How are you to get friendly with Bridget? ... I ought to know, if you're to have my support—moral and otherwise, oughtn't I?

BORDEN

Your support! Humph! ... But it's quite simple. My game will be that I knew a relative of hers away back in the distant past ... That will make for talk and confidences ... and the rest is easy ... See? ... And you keep clear, please.

CRADDOCK

But couldn't I also know the distant relative and confirm your fable? Every little helps, y'know.

BORDEN

No. Too many cooks, etcetera. *(A* **MOTOR-HORN** *sounds near at hand)* Hear that! Maybe old Kelly at his old game! Come to give her a drive, I'll bet!

(He runs to the door at the back.

CRADDOCK

Steady, steady! Think nobody in the world has a hooter except old Kelly?

BORDEN

But didn't you notice that when that girl opened the door she was in her going-away dress?

CRADDOCK

Going-away dress! Whatever are you saying, uncle! Y'know, you do haste to the wedding.

BORDEN

I mean her outdoor things. She wasn't in uniform, I expect it's her half-day off.

CRADDOCK

Well, you have got it bad! ... But I say, you can't run off and leave me to face old Drimfearn about that reduction.

BORDEN

Right! ... I'll do that, if you'll be a good chap ... Pop out and run that motor to earth ... See if that girl gets into it. And no fooling, or I cut down your next month's allowance.

CRADDOCK

You really serious, uncle? Sounds to me like an Edgar Wallace, y'know?

BORDEN

Well it sounds to me like a motor-horn, and that's all I care about for the moment ... Get off now.

CRADDOCK

Oh, well, if I must ... *(He turns to the door)*

BORDEN

Good man! ... If there's an old buffer with an Irish brogue in that car, we scoop the bank ... Wait a moment, I'll ring and see if we can get anything out of that silly of a housemaid, first of all ... I'll tell her I've rung to explain you have to go ... Then we can extract a little news from her about Bridget's movements perhaps, just before you start scouting. *(He rings.)*

CRADDOCK

All right, I'll wait ... But in the midst of these honeymoon raptures, don't forget to give it good and strong to Drimfearn about his rotten shooting at Ben Veon. A half-rent's all he deserves.

BORDEN

Don't worry. I'll open up that all right, or at any rate make preparation for a frontal attack on the rent later on ... Hush! here's the maid.

(The door opens, but it is not JANET *who presents herself:* BRIDGET *is there instead. She is not in uniform, however, but in a plain outdoor costume. Her face is that of a roguish girl of twenty-four, her manner confident, her colour and her spirits high.)*

BRIDGET
Did ye ring?

BORDEN
Oh, ah ... sorry. Thought the other maid was on duty.

BRIDGET
She should be, but she's busy helping cook catch a wee hen.

BORDEN
Indeed!

BRIDGET
Yes, for to-morrow's dinner.

BORDEN
And so you're on duty till the hen's caught?

BRIDGET
Divil a fear! They'll never catch that hen. It knows too much. I'm only deputising till they get tired chasing it.

BORDEN
I understand. So it's your afternoon off?

BRIDGET
Ye've hit it ... But what is't you're wanting? Not the history of the hen, surely?

BORDEN
What I wanted to say was that Mr. Craddock here has to leave. He has to go over to Ben Veon in a hurry, as he can't wait longer. And we thought he might take the short cut. You go past the big pines, don't you?
(They all move over to the window.

BRIDGET
Ye do that. And then. *(Pointing.)* Ye keep to the left of the big rock yander ... 'Tis as easy as goosey-goosey-gander.

CRADDOCK
Big rock yander ... Goosey-goosey-gander. Good rhyme. I'm in luck to-day.

BORDEN
(glaring at him and signalling he is to clear out). I think you'd better hurry, Philip.

CRADDOCK
All right. I'm off. *(He goes out huffily by the door at the back.)*
(BRIDGET makes to follow him.

BORDEN
Ah! ... Just a moment, please. Which of those tracks leads to the ferry for Faolinnvore?

BRIDGET
The low one: the narrow wee one with the twist in it.

BORDEN
Looks rather a climb. Ever go that way yourself?

BRIDGET
Not me. I do be too busy polishing silver and the like all day for any nonsense like climbing hills.

BORDEN
Oh, come now! Hill-climbing's not all nonsense. You should see the view from behind Ben Veon Lodge. I'll bet there's nothing finer in all Ireland.

BRIDGET
And who's talking of Ireland?

BORDEN
But you're Irish, aren't you?

BRIDGET
And who tould ye that?

BORDEN
Oh, well, you see ...

BRIDGET
Indeed and I don't then ... Did ye never hear of Michigan, U.S.A.?

BORDEN
Michigan! Pardon me! *(He turns away, as if much moved.)*

BRIDGET
And what's wrong with Michigan to upset ye like that? ... I was only born there, if that's any comfort; although 'twas in Ireland I was bred.

BORDEN
Yes, yes. I'm silly to be so much moved, but you stirred old memories, that's all. Ah! ... Michigan!

BRIDGET
And have you been there?

BORDEN

No, no. But I had a niece—the dearest girl! And she was born in Michigan. You are very like her ... And I wonder ...?

BRIDGET

Ye wonder what? You're surely not for making out there's two of us. My father says one Bridget's enough at a time.

BORDEN

Yes, but your face ... So like! *(He sits down, pretending to be much affected.)* She's dead, you see.

BRIDGET

Och, and is that the way of it? *(But she smiles behind his back, as she puts a comforting hand on his shoulder.* **BORDEN** *pats her hand, his head still bowed)* And it was long ago, was it?

BORDEN

Yes, long ago.

BRIDGET

Dear-a-dear, ye poor ould man!

BORDEN

(starting). Ah, yes, I'm getting old ... Forty-nine now. How the years fly!

BRIDGET

Ah, but grief does be a terrible thing for ageing us. And ye look sixty, if a day.

BORDEN

Michigan! She died there ... And you are so like! You might almost be her sister.

BRIDGET

And then, in a kind of a way, you might almost be my uncle?

BORDEN

(starting again, for he is not sure of her). Yes ... yes, I suppose so. Queer that! ... Ah, how your fresh young face brings her back to me!
  (He takes her hands and looks up into her eyes. A distant **MOTOR-HORN** *is heard, and* **BRIDGET** *starts visibly. The* **HORN** *sounds nearer still.*

BRIDGET

Och, there's the carrier's van; and Janet and cook are sure to be still chasing that wee hen ... I'll have to be going down for the parcels.

BORDEN

Well, go if you must; and leave me to my memories!

BRIDGET

Och, don't be taking on so! I'm sorry for you. Really I am. I'm understanding fine how you feel ... uncle.

(She goes rapidly to the door at the back. BORDEN *gazes after her, wondering if this is only gaucherie, or is it chaffing.* DRIMFEARN *comes in hurriedly on the left.*

DRIMFEARN

Sorry to have kept you waiting, Borden.

BORDEN

Oh, that's all right.

DRIMFEARN

(to BRIDGET, *who is just on the point of going out).* Stop! ... What the deuce are you doing here, and not in uniform?

BRIDGET

Sure, it's my afternoon off. And Janet couldn't attend to Mr. Borden, having to catch a wee hen.

DRIMFEARN

A hen! Good Heavens, what a house! You women will drive me mad! (BRIDGET *flounces off.)* Well, Borden?

BORDEN

Sorry Craddock couldn't wait ... Is MacNab about?

DRIMFEARN

In the gun-room ... Want him?

BORDEN

Yes, if you don't mind.

DRIMFEARN

All right. *(He opens the door on the left and calls.)* MacNab!

MACNAB

(in the distance). Yes, sir!

DRIMFEARN

Come here, please. *(Then, to* BORDEN.*)* Jolly day.

BORDEN

Not bad.

DRIMFEARN

How are you getting on with the wild goat?

BORDEN

Nothing doing. But it's not wild goat I've come about.

DRIMFEARN

Indeed?

(MACNAB *enters on the left.*

BORDEN

Afternoon, MacNab.

MACNAB

Good-afternoon, sir.

DRIMFEARN

Mr. Borden has some complaint to make, MacNab.

BORDEN

Several complaints would be a better way of putting it ... And first of all there's this. I saw something queer yesterday at Allt-Criche—at the deer-fence between your ground and Sir John's.

DRIMFEARN

And what was that?

BORDEN

A bank of turf leading from Sir John's side right to the top of the deer-fence. A couple of hinds were crossing to your ground by means of it, just as I came up ... A regular deer-trap.

DRIMFEARN

God bless my soul! You hear this, MacNab?

MACNAB

Maybe the woodcutters made it for a shortcut, Drimfearn.

BORDEN

Nonsense. Easy enough for them to climb over the fence without going to all that bother. You'll be suggesting next that the deer themselves made it.

DRIMFEARN

(*suddenly inspired*). And why not, sir, why not? What do any of us know about the limits of animal intelligence? ... A wonderful thing—animal intelligence!

BORDEN

Animal fiddlesticks!

DRIMFEARN

Quietly, sir, quietly! Here the scientific method comes in ... Have you never heard of beavers building dams? Why, don't you know they carry stones and mud in their forepaws to do that! Seen them myself out in Canada ... And if beavers can build dams, why not deer a fabric of the kind you describe, eh? Easiest thing in the world for a stag to shove up a pile of turf with its horns. Isn't it, MacNab? *(He makes movements of his hands and head, and succeeds in shovelling some cushions off the couch.)*

MACNAB

Oh, yes, sir, they might well do that.

DRIMFEARN

Might? They might? I'll bet they did.

BORDEN

Fudge, just fudge, my dear sir.

DRIMFEARN

Ah, but don't take this too lightly, Borden. We must examine this carefully. Have photographs made of this wonderful structure, and write to *The Field* about it. We may be on the eve of a great discovery.

BORDEN

Yes, and Sir John will make that discovery when he hears where his deer are going.

DRIMFEARN

I am surprised, Borden. After all, the matter is one between Sir John and myself, I suppose, and doesn't concern you ... You can go, MacNab. I'll examine this further myself.

BORDEN

And so shall I ... But I'd rather MacNab didn't go just yet. I've something else to discuss, and he can bear me out in what I say.

DRIMFEARN

All right. Sit down, MacNab.

BORDEN

Do you realise, sir, that in a ten-mile walk with the guns yesterday we only raised three brace? That so, MacNab?

MACNAB

Something like that, Mr. Borden. But there will be good days and bad days with everything, you'll understand.

DRIMFEARN

You certainly had bad luck then, for I saw six brace well within half-a-mile from where I sit, not ten minutes ago.

BORDEN

Nonsense!

DRIMFEARN

Ask MacNab. He also saw them.

MACNAB

I did that, sir. Six brace. As fine birds as ever I saw. Young birds they were, and not too strong on the wing.

BORDEN

Well, I'm glad to hear it, for—as I already told you—if I don't have better luck before the week's out, I'll advertise a sub-let of my shooting, and give exact details of my miserable bag so far.

DRIMFEARN

You wouldn't dare! I'll have you in court if you do.

BORDEN

Well, I'm warning you. So I hope, MacNab, we'll see something of that six brace to-morrow.

MACNAB

(*miserably*). I'm sure, sir, I hope we will.

BORDEN

All right then. And now I'll leave you to your study of Animal Intelligence, Drimfearn. Look up the encyclopedia. Try under "Beavers," and you'll think you're in Canada ... again ... Good-day to ye! (*He goes out by the door at the back.*)

DRIMFEARN

What an outsider! Ever hear the like, MacNab?

MACNAB

He's the wild man, yon one, sir.

DRIMFEARN.

Plenty of soft soap on those birds, remember. He must see them tomorrow, sure.

MACNAB

Very good, Drimfearn.

(*A* **MOTOR-HORN** *is heard.*

DRIMFEARN

That was another horn! This place is becoming infested with motors nowadays, damn them!

MACNAB

Och, it's just the children tootling at the Doctor's new bicycle. It's down beside my own house.

DRIMFEARN

Well get them to drop that sort of thing. I hate these horns going all day.

BRIDGET

(*opening the door at the back*). Nurse MacAlpine.
    (**MARSALI** *comes in.* **BRIDGET** *is about to retire, but noticing the cushions disarranged and lying on the floor—the sequence of* **DRIMFEARN***'s demonstration on Animal Intelligence—she comes in to tidy up.*)

DRIMFEARN

Hillo, Marsali! (*Then, to* **BRIDGET**.) Look here, I can't stand this out-of-uniform business!

BRIDGET

But it's my afternoon off.

DRIMFEARN.

Then why the devil aren't you off? Where's the other girl?

BRIDGET

Sure, she's still catching that wee hen. (*And she goes calmly on with her tidying up.*)

DRIMFEARN

That hen! You women'll drive me crazy! (*Then, turning to* **MARSALI**.) Well, Marsali?

MARSALI

Oh, I only wanted to leave a message from old Donald MacIver for Mrs. Campbell.

DRIMFEARN

Better deliver it yourself, my dear. She's in the garden ... But I'll send her in to you. Just going that way ... MacNab, please.
    (**DRIMFEARN** *and* **MACNAB** *go out by the door on the left.*)

BRIDGET

Isn't he the rare ould Tartar! And all because of a wee hen. (*She crosses to the window and looks out.*) Och, they'll never catch that hen! It's just having a game with them.

MARSALI

But you shouldn't be so off-hand with the chief.

BRIDGET

Well now, isn't everything off-hand in this place, even the poultry ... Och, will you just look at cook, tearing round after that hawk of a hen! And Janet after tumbling into yon big bush!

MARSALI

(*joining her at the window*). Not much smallpox about cook if she can run like that.

BRIDGET

Them and their smallpox! Sure, ye never see it in this country. It's as rare as a tinker's funeral.

MARSALI

But you've seen a good deal over in Ireland, I suppose.

BRIDGET

Devil a one in Ireland. But plenty out East.

MARSALI

Out East?

BRIDGET

Yes, in Yugo-Slavia it was.

MARSALI

Yugo-Slavia! Come now, no fairy-tales!

BRIDGET

No fairy-tales about it. 'Twas in Belgrade.

MARSALI

Really, Bridget! You're far-travelled, surely?

BRIDGET

Och, not much on that side of the world. Ragusa's the only other town I know out there.

MARSALI

But that's on the Adriatic, isn't it?

BRIDGET

It is just. A fine town. And it's there you'll get the finest people in all the world.

MARSALI

The finest? Now what on earth do you mean by that, Bridget?

BRIDGET

People like you and me, of course.

MARSALI

Oh, Bridget, you are quaint! And whatever were you doing so far from home?

BRIDGET

Hospitals. *(Then, excitedly, as she looks out of the window.)* There they go! Out of the garden and down to the shore! They'll never catch one feather of that wee bird! *(She comes away from the window.)* There was one hospital at Belgrade and another at Ragusa. You wouldn't think I had been a nurse myself, now, would ye?

MARSALI

Splendid! At Ragusa?

BRIDGET

Och, I had only two months there, more's the pity! But I had a whole year at Belgrade.

MARSALI

Wonderful. Among all those foreigners! What kind of a staff had you?

BRIDGET

Every kind. But mostly Scotch; for ye find them everywhere. 'Twas a place run by a kind of "Save the Children" Fund started in London years and years ago. And most o' the people there must have forgot what that Fund was for, but the Fund still kept on saving those children till they grew up and had children of their own. And there they go—tearing away at the good work, generation without end.

MARSALI

Splendid! But wasn't it strange so far away from home?

BRIDGET

It was and it wasn't. But I had the time o' my life! ... What do ye think? I had three proposals out there.

MARSALI

Bridget! Really!

BRIDGET

I'll not say they weren't all from the same man. But they were three anyway.

MARSALI

Whole three! The poor fellow! ... But fancy you a nurse, Bridget ... And now you're a table-maid!

BRIDGET

(returning to the window). You'd be safer to say an apprentice table-maid. I'm still only learning my job, according to ould Drim. *(Then, looking excitedly out of the window.)* Sure that hen's just laughing at them. Did ye ever see such an ould devil of a hen!

MARSALI

(crossing to her). They're spoiling that shrubbery no end. Drimfearn will be mad!

BRIDGET

This is only the second lap! Twice round the garden! But that bird has got its second wind by now, I'll bet; and cook hasn't a breath left in her ... Och, out of sight again!

MARSALI

All very amusing. But I wish Mrs. Campbell would come. Time I was at the Dispensary.

BRIDGET

And ye dispense as well as nurse, do ye? ... Well, ye're working at too many things for your own good, my girl. Ye'll get fired by the union if ye don't take care.

MARSALI

Oh, dispensing's only one of many things. I'm cataloguing this library as another extra. Like to give me a hand? Come in any night about nine. The place is quiet then, and your work will be over. We could have a talk ... Say a quarter to nine, eh? And you could tell me all about your cases at Belgrade!

BRIDGET

Well, I'd like the yarn all right. But will ould Drim not be popping in on us?

MARSALI

Oh, you can be tidying up if he does.

BRIDGET

Whisht, here's somebody! *(She sets about re-arranging the cushions once more.)*

(**MRS. CAMPBELL** *enters by the door on the left, then, holding the door ajar, turns to speak to* **MACNAB**, *who is seen stooping over the grouse-boxes just outside the door.*)

MRS. CAMPBELL

Where are you taking those things, MacNab?

MACNAB

To the store-room, ma'am.

MRS. CAMPBELL

Well, please wait for me there. And you'd better go through this way: it's quicker ... Now, don't forget to wait, MacNab ... I must have all your account of this affair before you go home. *(Then to* **MARSALI**.*)* I'm always keeping you behind, my dear! What's wrong with poor old Donald now? Come up to my room for a little and tell me all about him.

(**MRS. CAMPBELL** *and* **MARSALI** *go out by the door at the back.* **MACNAB**, *with his Inverness cape round his shoulders once more and the boxes concealed under it, crosses from the door on the left to that at the back.* **BRIDGET**, *at present making believe to tidy the hearth, rises as he enters.*)

BRIDGET

It's a warm day for an ould man to be wearing a petticoat round his neck.

MACNAB

I'm wishing it was over my ears when I hear that long tongue of yours, my woman.

BRIDGET

(*peeping at the boxes*). Some more of ould Drim's tricks, I'll be bound.

MACNAB

Whatever are you saying now!

BRIDGET

I'm saying you and Drim are as close as the hoofs of a Donegal donkey. You're a pair of dodgers, so you are!

MACNAB

My girl, it's to you I'll be giving the good advice. Say not a word of this to anyone, or I'll be saying plenty about yourself.

BRIDGET

And what would that be now?

MACNAB

I'd be saying you're too fond of riding about in big motor-cars for a girl of your position. I'm knowing quite a lot about you.

BRIDGET

Ach, go on with ye!

(**MACNAB** *goes out by the door at the back.* **BRIDGET** *crosses over to the window to watch the progress of the hen-hunt; and, forgetting the window is closed, begins to shout and jump about as if directing the chase.*

Hit her with the rake, cook! ... Nab her, can't ye! ... Get in front of her now, Janet! ... Come on the two of ye! ... Come on! ... Come on! Och, that wee hen can put rings round ye both! ... Missed her again! She's just laughing at ye!

(**DRIMFEARN** *enters by the door on the left, and advances to the window, unperceived by* **BRIDGET.**

DRIMFEARN

Great Scott! Is this a circus? . Woman, what in all the earth are you doing here?

BRIDGET

Just helping them catch a wee hen.

DRIMFEARN

Then, for God's sake! run out at once and help them to stop catching it, or my laurels will be ruined! Get out, I tell you, and chase these wild people back to their kennels.

(He sinks, exhausted by his fury, on a chair, and mops his forehead. **BRIDGET** *rushes out at the back, just as* **MRS. CAMPBELL** *enters then followed by* **MACNAB**.

MRS. CAMPBELL

Whatever's the matter with that girl! ... Colin, dear, are you ill? Whatever's wrong?

DRIMFEARN

That blasted hen! *(He rises and crosses to the window.)* Ah! Gone at last!

MRS. CAMPBELL

A hen, dear?

DRIMFEARN

Yes, a hen ... H—E—N ... Hen. ... But never mind, never mind! ... Only I warn you those idiotic servants of yours will be the death of me some day soon! ... What's MacNab doing here? What fresh tragedy is this?

MRS. CAMPBELL

Oh, dear! if only we could get the nice local girls we used to have!

DRIMFEARN

(loudly). But what's up?

MRS. CAMPBELL

Please don't shout, Colin! ... It's this ... You remember when I came back from London—last Tuesday week—I had to motor all the way from Torlochan, because the steamer had broken down?

DRIMFEARN

Yes, yes. But what's all this to do with MacNab?

MRS. CAMPBELL

Now don't be impatient, Colin. I'm coming to that ... But, first of all, do try to remember! ... Tuesday, two weeks ago come next Tuesday, didn't I say to you that a big Rolls-Royce passed my motor about ten miles from here?

DRIMFEARN

Well, yes, I do remember something about motors passing you at a scorching speed.

MRS. CAMPBELL

And didn't I say to you that there was somebody in that Rolls-Royce very like Bridget, our maid?

DRIMFEARN

No. Did you?

MRS. CAMPBELL

Oh, how tiresome! Surely, surely you must remember a thing like that. It's most important.

DRIMFEARN

My dear Margaret, I can't remember all the tittle-tattle I hear. Fancy Bridget in a Rolls-Royce!

MRS. CAMPBELL

But it wasn't tittle-tattle ... And it was Bridget ... Mr. Borden's chauffeur told MacNab he'd seen Bridget motoring all over Torlochan that same Tuesday, quite the lady ... And MacNab told cook ... And cook told me ... And when I questioned MacNab just now, he confirms it.

DRIMFEARN

Indeed? This so, MacNab?

MACNAB

It is just, Drimfearn ... It was Mr, Borden's own chauffeur that told me. A MacLachlan he is, and a nice lad who would tell no lies. He said she was all over Torlochan that Tuesday, in a fine motor-car, and sitting alongside a gentleman dressed like a ... like a ...

DRIMFEARN

Like a what, you fool!

MACNAB

Och, no, I'll not be saying what he said.

DRIMFEARN.

And why not? There's mystery enough about this girl already ... I insist, MacNab.

MACNAB

Well, if you will be forcing me, young MacLachlan said the man she was with was dressed like ... like a bloody earl.

DRIMFEARN

Good Heavens! ... Meg, you hear! ... Ring for that girl at once! (*A* **MOTOR-HORN** *sounds far away. They all start at the sound.*) Ring that bell, please, MacNab.

MRS. CAMPBELL

(*as* MACNAB *rings*). But she won't be in, Colin. It's her half-day off at three o'clock. And it's half-past now.

DRIMFEARN

(*testily*). I know it's her half-day off ... too well! But she was here not half-a-minute ago. She can't be far away, I'll bet.

(JANET *appears at the back in answer to the bell, She is somewhat blown, after her adventure with the hen.*

MRS. CAMPBELL

Please see if Bridget is anywhere about, Janet, and ask her to come here.

JANET

Yes, ma'am. (*She retires.*)

MACNAB

(*warily*). I can be going now, Drimfearn, I suppose?

DRIMFEARN

All right, all right! And, remember, plenty of soft soap, MacNab.

MRS. CAMPBELL

Soft soap, Colin? Whatever for?

DRIMFEARN

Bait.

MRS. CAMPBELL

How unusual! I never heard ... (*She is interrupted by the entry of* BRIDGET *at the back, as* MACNAB *goes out there.*) Ah, there you are, Bridget ... Sorry to trouble you when you're off duty; but I wanted to ask you about your half-days off: Tuesdays and Sundays, aren't they?

BRIDGET

Yes, Mrs. Campbell

MRS. CAMPBELL

And, may I ask, in what way do you spend them?

BRIDGET

Och, any way at all, as long's there's diversion.

MRS. CAMPBELL

(*in reproof of the mildest*). Oh, Bridget! ... Now, about ten days ago—a Tuesday, of course— you were, I hear, in Torlochan, and driving about in a motor-car with a man dressed like a ... like a ... like some kind of an earl?

BRIDGET

Me with an earl! Och, Mrs. Campbell, go on with you! ... No, no: it was only my second-cousin that's chauffeur to Mr. Kelly.

DRIMFEARN

Well—mean to say—who is Mr. Kelly?

BRIDGET

He's the gentleman that my half-brother is chauffeur to.

MRS. CAMPBELL

Now, now, Bridget! You said just a moment ago that it was your second cousin was Mr. Kelly's chauffeur. There wasn't a word about your half-brother.

BRIDGET

Did I that now? Did I mix the two of them up? ... I wonder now if it's Mr. Kelly, senior's, car, or Mr. Kelly, junior's, car, ye are meaning?

DRIMFEARN

(grimly). Whichever you like, my girl ... Proceed.

BRIDGET

Well, you see, I do be riding in both cars at times; and I was forgetting which car I was in that Tuesday. And the one is chauffeur to ould Kelly, and the other to young Kelly ... And sometimes the chauffeurs will be swopping places; the cars being in the family like. And it gets very mixing, minding who was driving, and which car ye were in, and all that.

DRIMFEARN

That will do, girl ... Return to your duties.

BRIDGET

But it's my half-day off!

DRIMFEARN

Well, anyway, clear out. *(Then, shouting.)* You can go!

MRS. CAMPBELL

Colin, please, don't shout.

BRIDGET

(to DRIMFEARN*).* And aren't ye as cross as a bag of cats! ... I hope ye've nothing against the Kellys.

(*A* **MOTOR-HORN** *is heard in the distance.*

DRIMFEARN.

Oh, damn those motors! Might as well be in Oxford Street! ... Girl, will ... you ... go?

BRIDGET

(*imperturbably*). Real nice quiet people, the Kellys. And they were talking of taking a let of some of your shootings, I was hearing ... At least, Kelly, senior, was.

DRIMFEARN

Oh?

MRS. CAMPBELL

(*gently but firmly*). All right, Bridget, you can go.

BRIDGET

And thank you kindly, Mrs. Campbell ... Kelly, senior, it was that talked of the shootings, you'll mind. Not the young one. (*And she goes out at the back.*)

DRIMFEARN

Kelly? ... By gad, Margaret! we were jolly near putting our foot in it that time! ... And so there's really a chance of letting this old place for the stalking after all! ... Kelly? ... Who the devil is he? ... I must write the Torlochan agents at once ... Well, old lady, it's an ill wind blows nobody good ... Mean to say—funny world! ... A bit of gossip exaggerated, and, hey presto! We let Drimfearn!

MRS. CAMPBELL

But, Colin, I'm sure that girl was prevaricating.

DRIMFEARN

Nonsense ... I must enquire about this Kelly chap right away.

MRS. CAMPBELL

My dear, I'm sure she was just pulling your leg.

DRIMFEARN

Well, I'll risk that ... Now, look here, Meg, you leave this to me ... And please don't fuss that girl with further questions. At present, all we can say is that she's a mystery ... yes, just a mystery. (*A* **MOTOR-HORN** *sounds very near at hand.*) By gum! that may be Kelly come to look at this place!

(**JANET** *opens the door at the back.*

JANET

It's MacNab, sir.

(**MACNAB** *enters breathless.*

DRIMFEARN

Hillo! What's up?

MACNAB

She's off again, sir.

DRIMFEARN.

Who's off?

MACNAB

Bridget.

MRS. CAMPBELL

Off?

MACNAB

Yes, ma'am ... In the big motor, with the earl.

DRIMFEARN

Earl be hanged! The man she was with that Tuesday was only a chauffeur.

MACNAB

But there was both a chauffeur and his master in the car ... And he kissed her!

MRS. CAMPBELL

What? Kissed her? ... Publicly?

MACNAB

Aye ... And it was not one kiss only!

DRIMFEARN

What!

MACNAB

Aye ... Two or five or more or so!

MRS. CAMPBELL

And his master looking on!

MACNAB

(perplexed). Whose master, ma'am?

DRIMFEARN

Look here, Meg, you've got this all wrong. Now, attend to me, MacNab ... Who kissed her? ... It wasn't the chauffeur, was it?

MACNAB

No, sir ... The bloody earl.

CURTAIN

ACT II

SCENE. *The Study at Drimfearn on the evening of next day.*
DRIMFEARN, *in a dress kilt and coatee, is looking over some books and comparing titles, etc., with catalogue-slips.*

MRS. CAMPBELL

(*entering by the door at the back*). Oh, there you are, Colin. I'm worrying dreadfully about this affair to-night. Is Murray really going out with these men from Faolinnvore, after all I've said? It's poaching, Colin—nothing else!

DRIMFEARN

Poaching! Nothing of the sort! It's simply a counter-move against Borden's threat to net the river for salmon he can't get with his rod ... We're surely entitled to protect ourselves against a bounder like Borden, eh? ... And Murray will be all right. All he has to do is to lie down inside a boat drawn up on the shore and act as watchman—give warning to the Faolinnvore men if any of Borden's people are about. Understand?

MRS. CAMPBELL

Of course, I understand. And I tell you I don't like it ... I'm afraid! (*She becomes tearful.*)

DRIMFEARN

Now you'll worry yourself into a headache if you go on like that! Come, come! Sit down and control yourself ... And tell me what you made out of Bridget this morning. Extraordinary business, that joy-ride! Brought off under our very noses, so to speak! Wish I could get to the bottom of this Kelly affair ... No letter yet from Torlochan ... Well, what did Bridget say? Who was the fellow in the car?

MRS. CAMPBELL

(*her face lighting up, as she passes quickly from tears to smiles*). Oh, she was so funny about it, Colin! ... The things she said! (*She laughs silently.*)

DRIMFEARN

Oh, do stop giggling! ... Well, what did she say?

MRS. CAMPBELL

She said her half-brother once had an old Ford, all tied up with string ...

DRIMFEARN

Yes, yes; but what was she doing in that Rolls-Royce yesterday?

MRS. CAMPBELL

Well, you see, I thought it best not to press the matter, because it might interfere with our chance of letting the shooting to this Mr. Kelly, or whoever he is.

DRIMFEARN

Of course, of course, but didn't you do a little fishing for a hint of what it all amounts to?

MRS. CAMPBELL

Well, I really meant to, Colin, but I clean forgot. She was so funny about that old car her half-brother used to run!

DRIMFEARN

Good Heavens! Do you mean to say she got round you? ... Never gave a word of explanation about ... the ... the ... earl!

MRS. CAMPBELL

Oh, but I don't think he was an earl, dear ... And really! I laughed so much about the carburettor on her half-brother's car...

DRIMFEARN

Oh, damn her half-brother and his car! ... But, of course, you laughed and she laughed ... And then you laughed together ... I know ... Women! ... Good Lord!

MRS. CAMPBELL

But I don't think there's really any harm in the girl, Colin.

DRIMFEARN

Oh, no ... oh, no! ... And yesterday you doubted every word she said.
(**MARSALI** *comes in by the door on the left. She doffs her cloak and cap.*

MARSALI

Good-evening, people!

DRIMFEARN

On the nick of time as usual, Marsali. Good girl! Here's the catalogue paper. *(He hands her some slips.)* Down to the first three lines of the letter D.

MRS. CAMPBELL

Take it easy, Marsali. Don't overwork yourself.

DRIMFEARN

If you see the Doctor, Marsali, tell him I'm checking the medical books of my ancestors. They're not many, and they're away back, but the calf bindings are a joy ... Perhaps he'd like to help catalogue them; and, if so, he'll find me in the spare room ... You'll give me a hand till he comes, Meg, won't you?

MRS. CAMPBELL

Surely, dear.
(*She goes out with* **DRIMFEARN** *at the door at the back.* **MARSALI** *ascends the library-steps and starts work on the slips. After a little* **BRIDGET** *peeps in by the door at the back. She is in uniform.*

MARSALI
Hillo, Bridget! Ready for a good yarn?

BRIDGET
I'm ready for anything but work. I'm tired cleaning everything that's clean already.

MARSALI
Well, I don't want you to do a stroke. So, just take this duster *(she brings one out of the drawer in the library-steps)*, and if anybody comes in you can begin to use it; but not unless somebody comes, y'know.

BRIDGET
(seating herself on the floor beside a bookcase). Dear-a-dear! What a power o' books! And I don't believe ould Drim reads one of them.
(She dusts a few volumes carelessly and glances at a page or two.

MARSALI
What makes you think so?

BRIDGET
Och, he's too busy scheming. *(She suddenly concentrates on a book.)* Well, well! "Gaelic Proverbs"! ... And they very kindly give you the English on the next line ... Much need too, for this is the queer Gaelic.

MARSALI
What! Do you really know Gaelic?

BRIDGET
I know real Gaelic, and that's Irish.

MARSALI
You're wonderful, Bridget! ... You know Gaelic, and you've been a nurse, and you've seen the Danube and the Balkans and all that! And now you're a housemaid at the Back o' Beyond!

BRIDGET
(too engrossed in the book to listen to her). Och, look at this now. If there isn't something here about yourself! You're a MacAlpine, aren't ye?

MARSALI
Yes. What is it?

BRIDGET
Sure, it says here: "Hills and waters and MacAlpines. But when did the MacArthurs come?" Now what's the meaning of that?

MARSALI
It means that the Clan MacAlpine is as old as the hills, of course.

BRIDGET

Well, they're as high and mighty, anyway ... Oh, and here's young Drim's hand o' write at the side of it!

MARSALI

What?

BRIDGET

He's written: "How true ... Proud Marsali!" And then his initials: "M. C."

MARSALI

I must rub that out at once.

BRIDGET

You'll not now. *(They struggle playfully for the book.)* Ye might as well try to put a blister on a hedgehog, as fight with me, my lady.
   (The door at the back opens, and **MURRAY** *appears. He is dressed in his everyday kilt suit—not in Highland evening wear.*

MURRAY

I say! ... Is this ju-jutsu? Which side do I take?
   *(***MARSALI** *and* **BRIDGET** *at once resume the appearance of work. Then* **BRIDGET** *hands him the book open at the page she had quoted from.*

BRIDGET

We were just cleaning off some pencil-marks.
   (He reads his scrawl, closes the book with a bang and looks up with a smile at **MARSALI***, who is now making notes on' her slips with express speed. Suddenly* **BRIDGET** *rises and makes for the door hurriedly.*

BRIDGET

Och, and didn't I forget to tell cook about them cauliflowers!
   (She goes out by the door at the back.

MARSALI

Now, you see!

MURRAY

Come down and talk to me, man to man ... See what?

MARSALI

See what your silly scribbling has done. Next thing, you'll be at the window-panes with a diamond.

MURRAY

By Jove! Why not?

MARSALI

Go away, please. This is no place for a poacher.

MURRAY

Right! The Faolinnvore men will be waiting. Thanks for reminding me. I'm off ... Oh, by the by, tell the Doctor when he comes that father's asking for him. He's cataloguing in the spare room. Be sure to tell him.

(He goes out by the door on the left. And as soon as he has gone, BRIDGET *enters cautiously at the back.*

BRIDGET

I'm always forgetting them cauliflowers.

MARSALI

Oh, you're tiresome!

BRIDGET

It's those ould books are tiresome. *(A* **MOTOR-HORN** *is heard.)* Isn't that the Doctor's bike?

MARSALI

Yes. And he's late ... But, of course this is the night he stays overnight.

BRIDGET

Tell me now ... Is he any good, the Doctor?

MARSALI

Good? Yes, I think he's a good doctor.

BRIDGET

Och, he always cut his flaps too short to my way of thinking.

MARSALI

Flaps?

BRIDGET

Yes. Amputation-flaps?

MARSALI

But you haven't seen him operate, have you?

BRIDGET

Och, many a time. Did I forget to tell you now? ... Wasn't he on the staff of that wee hospital out in Belgrade!

MARSALI

But how wonderful! ... And he never said a word to me about you! ... Surely he doesn't know you were there?

BRIDGET

Och, yes, but he does, too well ... The trouble is he doesn't know I'm here.

MARSALI

And did you know he was here when you arranged to come to this place?

BRIDGET

Are you suggesting I'd go running after any man?

MARSALI

Why not? I would ... That is, if I was desperately fond of him.

BRIDGET

And you'd be right too. But I'm not desperate for anybody ... All the same, isn't it funny how ye try to keep away from a place, and yet ye drift there in the end of all? ... Och, I wonder how I'll have the strength to face that boy!

MARSALI

Oh, Bridget, what a meeting that will be!

BRIDGET

(drily). You're very helpful, aren't ye? (Then, bitterly) Och, I wish I were dead!

MARSALI

I'm sorry. I shouldn't have said that ... But hasn't the Doctor seen you here?

BRIDGET

He has not then. I've kept well out of his way, else he'd be pestering the life out o' me.

MARSALI

Aha! The same as he did out in Belgrade? ... It was three times, Bridget, wasn't it?

BRIDGET

Never you mind, my lady. (And she makes a feeble attempt to dust a book.)

MARSALI

Splendid! ... And he was really a surgeon out there?

BRIDGET

He thought he was. But he couldn't surge much, as far as I could see ... Och, but a nice boy all the same.

MARSALI

But, Bridget, what I can't understand is your taking up a job like this after all your fine experience as a nurse out East.

BRIDGET

Och, well, it's always more experience, as the cow said when it ate the cobbler's apron.

MARSALI

Oh, Bridget!

BRIDGET

"Oh, Bridget!" ... As if ye didn't believe me? *(She sniffs a little and takes out a handkerchief.)*

MARSALI

(coming down the steps and petting her). I'm sorry. Hush, hush, now! I didn't mean anything, and I'm sure you don't care a snap of your thumb for him.

BRIDGET

And who tould ye that? ... I mean ... I don't know if I care for anybody at all ... And I only came here to learn the gentry's ways, so I did. Nothing else.

MARSALI

The gentry's ways?

BRIDGET

Just that. *(She is fibbing very carefully now.)* Ye see, Mary Donnelly was only a nurse, out at Belgrade, but she married a French general.

MARSALI

Yes; but who was Mary Donnelly?

BRIDGET

Just a small farmer's daughter, out from Donegal. And not much good at the nursing; but she married a general, all the same ... And then she couldn't run his big house ... So I said to myself: "When I marry a general, I'll be able to run the largest of all large chateaux." ... And here I am, learning my job.

MARSALI

Yes, you certainly want to know the ways of the nobs, if you're to housekeep for a general.

BRIDGET

Och, it's all foolishness, these big houses! But I just stay on for the fun of seeing the nobs strutting around like turkey-cocks ... Heather gentry, I call them.

MARSALI

Heather gentry? What's that?

BRIDGET

People like Borden and Craddock and the rest of the shooting lot. At home they're nobody; but up here they're the lords of creation ... And then ould Drim starts strutting too ... play-acting the noble Highland chief, just to keep up with their nonsense.

MARSALI

Now, now, Bridget! Drimfearn's a great friend of mine.

BRIDGET

Och, he's a friend of mine too. I really don't mislike him. And when he was from home a week ago, I missed him sorely ... I missed his lies!

MARSALI

Yes, he does draw the long bow, doesn't he! ... But about this big house of yours, Bridget— I do hope you'll get it some day soon, as well as your general.

BRIDGET

Och, the weest of wee houses is all I want, after having seen all the nonsense of the big ones ... And now you really know why I'm here?

MARSALI

Quite. Just for the fun you get out of it ... And, of course, I understand you didn't know the least bit about the Doctor being here.

BRIDGET

But I never said that.

MARSALI

Well, something very like it.

BRIDGET

I couldn't have. For I'd an idea he might be somewhere around this way, when I heard of the job first of all ... But that was no reason for not taking the place, was it? Am I to be having that man like a lion in my path, whenever I want to go anywhere?

MARSALI

(smiling to herself). Certainly not. Go where you like, and do what you like. And blow the men! *(Then, suddenly.)* And blow these old books! ... I'm tired.

BRIDGET

You've said it. *(She pushes a pile of books aside and stands up.)* Now, what call have you, the District Nurse, to be cataloguing ould Drim's library, when ye should be resting after a hard day's work?

MARSALI

Oh, he asked me so nicely. And he's my father's friend ... My father's a laird, you know, just like Drimfearn, and just as poor.

BRIDGET

And ye cut ould Drim's hair to save his barber's bill. And ye pull his stumps of teeth to save his dentist's bill. And ye massage his stiff leg! ... I'd not do one of them, if I were you! *(She is facing away from the door at the back, as is also* MARSALI; *and neither perceives* DRIMFEARN *enter quietly there, and listen. He has still the catalogue-slips in his hand.* BRIDGET *continues:)* I'd just say to him: "Look here, ould Drim," I'd say. "I'll pull your teeth, or cut your hair, or massage your stick of a leg, or catalogue your library ... but I'll not do all four, so I'll not ... I've patients to attend," says you, "and they're roaring out for me from every ben and every glen ... And I'm a nurse, so I am, and not a blooming cor ... nu ... cop ... ia!" *(She strikes a heroic attitude.)*

DRIMFEARN

(coming forward). Woman! leave off destroying those valuable books! And pack your trunks ... A week's notice! ... Understand?

BRIDGET

It's himself! And me shaking like a dog in a wet sack!

DRIMFEARN

(shouting). A week's notice! *(Then, turning to* MARSALI, *he says quietly:)* Looking for the Doctor, Marsali ... Seen him?

MARSALI

No, Drimfearn.

DRIMFEARN

He's very late, surely ... I'm stuck over those funny medical books until he comes. (BRIDGET, *replacing some of the books she has been dusting, tumbles them with a crash.)* Will you leave off, woman! Put down those books, and clear out!

BRIDGET

I'll go, I'll go. But you've frightened me out of a year's growth. *(She lifts the books.)*

DRIMFEARN

I must get out of this, Marsali. Let me look at your slips in the billiard-room, will you? . . , These servants will drive me crazy. Phew! What a dust!

(They go out on the left. BRIDGET *carefully replaces the fallen books. She finishes, sighs, and looks round the room. Her eyes fall on the cloak and cap of* MARSALI. *Roguishly, she lifts them up, admires, and then dons them. For a*

little she stalks about in these borrowed plumes, halting at times to look down at the sweep of the cloak; tries mincing steps, then long ones; and is thoroughly enjoying herself when the door at the back opens and DR. KENNEDY *enters.* BRIDGET *has her back to the door, but she senses who it is, and — without turning round — picks up some catalogue-slips as yet unused, and pretends to be working hard at checking these,*

DOCTOR

Well, Nurse, hard at work as usual. I'm looking for Drimfearn. (BRIDGET *turns full-face to him.*) Good Heavens! Sister Catherine! ... What in all the world are you doing here?

BRIDGET

Why, if it isn't Dr. Kennedy!

DOCTOR

I say it is good to see you again! ... I didn't know you were friendly with the Drimfearns.

BRIDGET

Well, it's Nurse MacAlpine that's my friend ... And she's making a catalogue here, ye see ... And I'm giving her a hand.

DOCTOR

Vile work, that catalogue! (*He can't keep his eyes off her now.*) ... But fancy seeing you in the heart of the Highlands!

BRIDGET

(*nervously*). Yes, it's strange meeting like this. Accident or the act of God, as the lawyers say ... And how are you, Doctor?

DOCTOR

Oh, all right, except for a bad jaw. Broken tooth, I'm afraid. A crash off my motor-bike. (*He nurses his chin.*) But it *is* queer to meet again, isn't it? (*He is now as nervous as she is.*)

BRIDGET

(*gasping a little*). Yes, it's what you would call ... queer ... wouldn't you?

DOCTOR

Yes, isn't it? Well, I hope you'll let me see more of you than I saw at Belgrade. Those confounded hospital restrictions were the limit!

BRIDGET

Och, they didn't restrict some people very much.

DOCTOR

Oh, come now! I wasn't bad.

BRIDGET

Little peace I had when you were around.

DOCTOR

But, Kate, my dear.

BRIDGET

Whisht! I hear ould Drim!
(She dashes off the cloak and the cap, and rushes to re-arrange the books once more. **DR. KENNEDY** *gapes in amazement at sight of the bib and apron now revealed.)*

DOCTOR

But what ... what's this?
*(***DRIMFEARN** *and* **MARSALI** *enter on the left, pencils and catalogue-slips still in their hands.)*

DRIMFEARN

Ah, Doctor, there you are at last! *(His eye now falls on* **BRIDGET**.*)* Will you leave those books alone! And clear out o' this. *(Then to the* **DOCTOR**.*)* Hillo, are you ill, Doctor? Man alive! You're like a ghost.

DOCTOR

Neuralgia. Broken tooth. *(He clutches his jaw, and his round eyes of amazement are fixed on* **BRIDGET**.*)*

DRIMFEARN

My dear chap, awfully sorry! Have a peg of whisky. Come into the billiard-room. *(He leads the way.)*

DOCTOR

(gaping over his shoulder at **BRIDGET** *as he goes).* Whisky ... yes ... whisky should do.

*(***DRIMFEARN** *and he go out on the left.)*

MARSALI

Whatever happened?

BRIDGET

Och, it's all up now ... it's all up! ... I'll have to go.

MARSALI

Nonsense! Drimfearn didn't mean anything. He doesn't really want to give you warning.

BRIDGET

I know that. Sure, he gives me warning every other day ... It's not Drim I'm heeding ... It's the boy ... Did ye see that look of his? ... He'll give me no rest, that man, till he gets me ... I'll have to go.

MARSALI

But don't you want him to get you, as you call it?

BRIDGET

And how do I know till I make up my mind?

MARSALI

Tuts, Bridget!

BRIDGET

All very well, but that man just sweeps ye off your feet; and you thinking hard will he do or won't he! ... Out in Belgrade he had his pockets stuffed full of marriage licences and things ... And it'll be the same here, I'm certain. He doesn't know how to take things easy. There's no shaking him off!

MARSALI

Bridget, I really can't make you out.

BRIDGET

I'll have to go ... I'll have to go!

MARSALI

Oh, it's surely not so bad as all that.

BRIDGET

But it is, I tell ye! ... He has no sense, that lad, although he's a nice boy. (*A* **BELL** *rings loudly.* **BRIDGET** *composes herself with a sniff or two, and smooths out her apron.*) And who's this now, so late? I'll have to answer that door, for Janet's in bed. Tired out catching hens, she is.
(*She goes out at the back.* **MARSALI** *puts on her cap and cloak, and prepares to leave. Presently* **BRIDGET** *ushers in* **CRADDOCK**. *He is in evening dress, with an ulster over it. He bows to* **MARSALI**.

CRADDOCK

Don't let me disturb you, Nurse. Sorry to intrude on these good people so late. I was to meet Mr. Borden here at nine-thirty. We want to see Drimfearn rather urgently.

MARSALI

Mr. Borden hasn't come yet. I was just going. Make my excuses to the chief, Bridget. Goodnight.

CRADDOCK

Good-night, Nurse.
(**MARSALI** *lays down her catalogue-slips carefully on the table, and goes out by the door at the back.*

BRIDGET
Will I tell the ould fella you're waiting, or will ye just wait?

CRADDOCK
"The ould fella"? Who's he?

BRIDGET
Ould Drim.

CRADDOCK
No, no, please. Wait till my uncle arrives. We want to see him together. What time is it? *(He jumbles with his watch.)* Hang these wrist-watches. Always off colour!

BRIDGET
Would a tin-opener be any good? We've one in the kitchen quite handy?

CRADDOCK
I say! You are a bit off-hand, aren't you? ... But, look here, your face seems familiar.

BRIDGET
Och, yes. You'd have a dear lady friend out in Michigan, just like me, I suppose.

CRADDOCK
Give it up. No good at conundrums.

BRIDGET
(making for the door on the left). I'll tell Drimfearn ye're waiting.

CRADDOCK
Please don't, till Mr. Borden arrives ... And, I say! ... Really now! ... Yes, you are an odd girl! *(He fixes his monocle and surveys her.)*

BRIDGET
Are ye out of the few senses ye ever had, young man?

CRADDOCK
Oh, I say! ... What!

BRIDGET
Ye're saying nothing. I'm only telling ye there's a great deal of sense in the world and none of it inside your head.

CRADDOCK
True. But I'm trying hard to get some inside. And meeting a girl like you makes it all the harder ... For things are not what they seem, are they? ... And I'm jolly well sure you aren't a table-maid ... Are you?

BRIDGET

Ye're smarter than I thought. Of course, I'm not.

CRADDOCK

Aha! Tell me all about it. There's a good girl.

BRIDGET

(*affecting shyness*) Och, it's a secret.

CRADDOCK

Come, now. Tell Philip.

BRIDGET

(*shyer still*). Sure, it's by no wish of mine that I'm put here in a place far below my station.

CRADDOCK

What a shame! And who put you here?

BRIDGET

'Twas my Auntie Morgan, so it was.

CRADDOCK

Oh?

BRIDGET

Yes. She says to me one day, says she, "Go out now among them mad English, and observe how they behave. There's nothing in them but wind and a few bones; but they're as God made them, and they've a way of getting on we haven't got."

CRADDOCK

Good for Auntie!

BRIDGET

"Get you out into the wide world," says she, "and learn some of their bits of tricks, and then we'll show Russia a thing or two."

CRADDOCK

Russia? Was your aunt a Russian?

BRIDGET

Divil a bit! She was a real ould Turk.

CRADDOCK

You pulling my leg?

BRIDGET

Och, I'm only telling you what Auntie Morgan said.

CRADDOCK

Well, if you don't mind me saying so, your Auntie Morgan seems to me a bit dotty.

(A **BELL** *rings in the hall.)*

BRIDGET

That'll be Mr. Borden at last. *(She turns to go.)* But ye'll not be telling him, will ye? ... Not one word now, about my Auntie Morgan.

(She goes out by the door at the back; **CRADDOCK**, *completely puzzled, staring after her, rubs his jaw as if to rouse his wits. After a few moments* **BRIDGET** *returns and ushers in* **BORDEN**. *His attire is similar to* **CRADDOCK**'*s.*

BRIDGET

I'll tell Drimfearn.

BORDEN

Do, please.

*(***BRIDGET** *goes out on the left, and* **BORDEN** *looks after her eagerly.*

BORDEN

By gum! if only I could be sure ... Pity you missed that motor yesterday. I'm certain it was old Kelly's car.

CRADDOCK

Well, she's a damn fine girl, Kate or no Kate.

BORDEN

Steady now. Let's get some real evidence.

CRADDOCK

When in doubt, don't. Is that it?

BORDEN

Yes, pity we can't tackle her just now. But we've enough on hand tonight with this poaching affair.

CRADDOCK

It's really poaching then? Have you got 'em?

BORDEN

Not yet, but they're down there all right—at the lower salmon-pool. A dozen crofters with nets.

CRADDOCK

Our fellows watching them?

BORDEN

All the men of the house-party. We'll hear the row presently. There'll be a shot or two, first of all, just to frighten them.

CRADDOCK
I see. And then we start squeezing the old boy?

BORDEN
Yes ... Get him to write off the whole season's rental to save exposure, don't you think? That too strong?

CRADDOCK
Not a bit. Let's leave it at that ... But, about this girl—I had a try tonight at finding out who she really was.

BORDEN
Well.

CRADDOCK
Oh, she mixed me all up about her Auntie, and a dear lady friend out in Michigan.

BORDEN
(anxiously). Didn't say anything about an ... about an uncle?

CRADDOCK
No, only her Auntie Morgan.

BORDEN
Here's the old chap!
(**DRIMFEARN** *enters by the left, while* **BRIDGET** *follows, and goes quietly out at the back.*

DRIMFEARN
Evening, Borden. Evening, Craddock.

BORDEN
Evening.

CRADDOCK
Evening.

BORDEN
Oh, before I forget ... Met your local doctor to-night. Seemed a bit stiff with me. Happen to know what's up?

DRIMFEARN
Oh, nothing wrong as far as I know. He's a bit off colour. That's all. Ran his bike into a gate. Hit his jaw. Broke a tooth.

BORDEN
Indeed? Was that at the new gate you've just put up across the public road, at Ben Add?

DRIMFEARN

Yes.

BORDEN

Well—mean to say—it's a public road, isn't it?

DRIMFEARN

Used to be — but I've taken it over. Arranged with the County Council. It's on my policies, and doesn't lead anywhere outside my policies, y'know. I pay for the upkeep of the road, so it's my affair nowadays.

BORDEN

But what's the use of it?

DRIMFEARN

Oh, only a little reminder of a family legend.

BORDEN

Well, it jolly near made a legend of me and my car, to-day, when we came round the bend there. Why didn't you give notice it was to be shut after dusk?

DRIMFEARN

Sorry. Thought the workmen wouldn't be finished for a day or two.

BORDEN

Family legend! It's some bally game, I do believe!

DRIMFEARN

Mr. Borden!

BORDEN

Oh, come off it! But that's not what I've called about. It's those damn wild goat.

DRIMFEARN

And what's wrong with the wild goat?

BORDEN

I paid for a kill of twenty head; but you knew very well I'd never get a single one. Might as well stalk chamois. Those cliffs are six hundred feet sheer, and the goats are never within range. Why didn't you make that clear when you let the shooting?

DRIMFEARN

My dear fellow, I told you, as I tell everyone it may concern, that the wild goat is extremely agile.

(*A* **GUNSHOT** *is heard.* **DRIMFEARN** *starts to his feet.*

DRIMFEARN

That was a shot!

BORDEN

Poachers, I suppose.

DRIMFEARN

Nonsense. No poaching hereabouts.

BORDEN

Oh, yes, there is. There are poachers at the Big Pool this very minute. Faolinnvore men.

DRIMFEARN

You're quite mistaken. Ab-so-lute-ly!

BORDEN

No, I'm not. Saw them getting ready with my night glass, just before I came on here. And I've plenty of witnesses.

DRIMFEARN

Never heard of such a thing!

BORDEN

Well, you've heard a gun, at any rate. And that belonged to one of my guests. All the men of my house-party are out; and there'll be dirty work at the cross-roads before we finish to-night.

DRIMFEARN

Look here, Borden. Call 'em off. No shooting. Good Lord, if anybody's wounded!

BORDEN

Oh, don't worry. That was only a shot to drill a hole in the poachers' boat, so they couldn't get off. Nobody'll be hurt.

DRIMFEARN

But, good heavens! they always have a watchman lying down inside the boat, you fool! ... Here, Meg! Meg!
 (*He dashes to the door at the back, just as* **MRS. CAMPBELL** *runs in there.*

DRIMFEARN

They're firing at the boat, Meg! Get a bed ready ... Hot water ... Bandages ... Dressings ... Send for the Doctor ... Send for Marsali ... I'm going down to the boat! (*He rushes out on the left.*)

MRS. CAMPBELL

(*sinking on the couch*). Oh, Murray, Murray!

BORDEN

(*to* CRADDOCK). By Jove, this looks serious. We'd better see ... We'll give the maid a shout.

(*They run out at the back; and* BORDEN'*s voice is heard calling on* BRIDGET *as they dash down to the hall. In a few moments* BRIDGET *enters at the back, and crosses hurriedly to* MRS. CAMPBELL

BRIDGET

(*petting her*). There, there, darling! And did they do it to ye! Whatever's the matter?

MRS. CAMPBELL

Murray! ... He's in the boat!

BRIDGET

What boat, my dear?

MRS. CAMPBELL

Poachers. Murray's with them. They're shooting at the boat ... He'll be killed.

BRIDGET

And where's Drimfearn, I wonder?

MRS. CAMPBELL

He's gone down to Murray ... . My boy, my boy!

BRIDGET

Well then, come you on to your room. Murray'll be all right if his father's there.

MRS. CAMPBELL

No, no ... I must wait for Murray.

BRIDGET

You'll wait in your own bed, then. You're not well at all. (*She puts her arm around the old lady, and leads her to the door at the back.*)

MRS. CAMPBELL

Let me go. I must find Drimfearn.

BRIDGET

Come on and lie you down, first of all. And then it's myself will find young Drim and ould Drim and all the other Drims ... Come on now.

(*As she leads* MRS. CAMPBELL *off at the back, the door on the left opens, and* MARSALI *appears supporting* MURRAY, *who looks deadly pale, and has his left arm bandaged and in a sling.* BRIDGET *signals to them to wait until she and* MRS. CAMPBELL *have gone.* MRS. CAMPBELL *has not seen them; and they wait to enter after she has been led off. Then* MARSALI *supports* MURRAY *to the couch.*

MARSALI.

Over here. *(She sits down with him, his head on her breast; then gets alarmed at his pallor, and leaves him for a moment as she rings the bell.)*

MURRAY

Marsali! Marsali!
(MARSALI returns to him quickly and supports his head again. BRIDGET bursts in excitedly by the door at the back.

BRIDGET

Whatever's wrong with him?

MARSALI

Bullet in the wrist. He was mixed up with the poachers.

BRIDGET

The poor lad!

MARSALI

I bandaged it. Bleeding's stopped. It's the pain makes him sick.

BRIDGET

Where's the brandy?

MARSALI

Try the store-room, *(BRIDGET makes for the door at the back.)* Stop! ... Say nothing to cook or Janet ... The laird's son a poacher! ... Wouldn't do, you know ... Too much talk!

BRIDGET

Right-oh! *(She goes out quickly at the back)*

MURRAY

You're a topper, Marsali. *(His eyes close.)*

MARSALI

You must lie down now. A bit faint, but you'll soon be all right. There's brandy in the dining-room, of course ... I'll get it, and make sure ... Keep still now. Back in a jiff.

(She goes out hurriedly by the door on the left. MURRAY lies still for a little, then slowly sits up, gets to his feet, pirouettes gaily, blows a kiss or two after MARSALI, re-arranges the cushions, and lies down again, sighing luxuriously. He does not know that BRIDGET has entered quietly at the back, and watched his capers cynically. She closes the door noisily. He starts to his feet and she confronts him.

BRIDGET

Go on with your dance now, for you'll drink none. *(She sets the glass she carries on a table)* You and your bullets!

(*He stands, shamefaced and irresolute.* MARSALI *enters on the left, also with a glass in her hand.*

BRIDGET

Out o' this, ye deceiver!

MARSALI

Bridget!

BRIDGET

Out ye go now!

(*He goes out in confusion at the back.*

MARSALI

Bridget! What's wrong?

BRIDGET

Didn't I see his poor wounded arm going like a Flanders windmill, and him making fun o' ye!

MARSALI

Oh! (*She sinks in distress on the couch.*) Surely not that!

BRIDGET

Nothing else but play-acting he was, that one! Wasn't he blowing ye kisses the moment ye were out the room? And myself standing like a pillar of salt at the door there, watching him; and him not knowing I was there.

MARSALI

But are you certain, Bridget?

BRIDGET

Och, maybe I'm blind ... He was just pretending he was hurt so's he could have you canoodling his poor head.

MARSALI

But he was really wounded ... Bleeding.

BRIDGET

Wounded my granny! Devil a bullet's in yon fellow. Just a scratch of the skin it must be.

MARSALI

(*dismally*). All pretence?

BRIDGET

What else? ... Wounded! Sure, there's not one of Borden's crowd could hit a hole in a ladder.

MARSALI

(*bitterly*). Oh, Bridget, Bridget! Aren't we a fine lot, we Highland folk! ... The lairds at foolish play! ... And their people a hungry flock that look up and are not fed!

BRIDGET

A hungry flock! Aren't some of them hauling in lashings of salmon this very night, and them never paid for!

MARSALI

Meanness! Decay! Yes, you're right, Bridget. Heather gentry! ... Play-actors, the whole gang of them.

(**MURRAY** *enters shamefacedly at the back. He has discarded his sling, but still wears his wrist-bandage. He goes up to* **MARSALI**.

MURRAY

I say, Marsali, I'm awfully sorry. Been a cad.

MARSALI

Bridget, I want a few words with him.

BRIDGET

A few thousand is what I'd give him.

(*She goes out at the back.*

MURRAY

Really sorry, Marsali. I don't know what came over me.

MARSALI

A Drimfearn! Stooping to that sort of thing! (*She adjusts the bandage on his wrist.*)

MURRAY

Don't be hard!

MARSALI

Oh, this place—this place! ... All make-believe! All sham, sham, sham! ... I think I'm through with you, Murray.

MURRAY

For God's sake, don't say that! ... You can't chuck me for a bit of harmless fooling, Marsali!

MARSALI

Fooling, yes ... And meanness ... And there has been nothing else here for many a day ... Harmless? ... Why, it's harming everybody, this trickery that is in the very air of the place ... You've got to put an end to it, my boy ... or fini!

MURRAY

No, no, you mustn't break with me, Marsali, or I'll go to the dogs. You're the only real person here! Do anything you like with me, but not that.

MARSALI

Let's come to an understanding then. We'll never get rid of this plague until we get to the root of it. And that's your father's dodging and what-not with his shooting-tenants and others. It's hard for you to hear it, but it's the God's truth ... His trickery infects everyone and everything at Drimfearn.

MURRAY

Oh, come now, Marsali!

MARSALI

(*passionately*). Yes, yes, yes! ... Oh, Murray, think of what the Highlands could be if we were really in earnest! I don't mean solemn-faced and go-to-meeting, but straight and healthy and jolly and friendly — above all, straight ... There's a cunning side to us, and we mistake it for the old Gaelic wisdom, but it isn't ... it isn't! ... And we lean to it because we think it will pay ... And we'll dodge and dodge, if we see money at the end of it all. We have no pride, no real old Highland pride, or we'd never stoop to these things. All we have is vanity. And a rag of tartan and a few old clan tunes and the memory of a long ancestry. That's all ... But they're nothing in the balance if our hands aren't clean ... if our ways aren't straight. Are they? ... Are they?

MURRAY

But father is straight! In his own way he's jolly decent. He may have a twist here and a twist there, but in the end ...

MARSALI

In the end there's a twist everywhere ... No, that kind of thing eats into you, Murray ... You must pull him up. Won't you try?

MURRAY

Poor old father! He does mess up things ... But I'll do anything, Marsali, if only ...

MARSALI

If only I'll not break with you ... No, you mustn't bargain about this. You must pull him up for the sake of himself ... and for the sake of the Highlands ... not for your own benefit, my boy.

MURRAY

But we'll be friends again? You won't throw me off, Marsali?

MARSALI

There you go again! I tell you I'm not bargaining over this. It's too serious ... Come on, be the real Highlander, not the other fellow.

MURRAY
All right! Although I'm hardly the kind to go plucking brands from the burning, am I?

MARSALI
That's the best word you've said to-day, Murray.

MURRAY
But what the deuce should I tackle him about? Dad's so elusive, y'know.

MARSALI
(smiling, in spite of her wrath). Oh, take him on any of his games ... The wild-goat shooting that people take, without knowing how difficult it is, and that they'll never bag one of them. And so on.

MURRAY
Golly! that will be a scene!

MARSALI
Tell you what. Take him on this new gate he's just had put up on the road at Ben Add. It's dangerous. But he doesn't care, as long as it draws people's attention to some old legend ... I'm sure it's just leading on to some other dodge with money at the end of it. A trick! So go in and smash it!

MURRAY
He's slippery as an eel. There's nobody's his match for cuteness hereabouts.

MARSALI
Oh, yes, there is.

MURRAY
(sceptically). Yourself, perhaps?

MARSALI
No. But Bridget.

MURRAY
Nonsense, my dear Marsali!

MARSALI
I'm serious.

MURRAY
Well, but ... well, there's social position and all that, isn't there? They can't ever meet in a trial of ... well ... wits, shall we say?

MARSALI

(smiling). They might.

MURRAY

No, I can't see them scrapping.

MARSALI

Oh, can't you? ... I can't see anything else ... Even your tackling of the chief fades into insignificance before my vision of Bridget's fight. Why, it's foredoomed, Murray! They were made for each other as far as scrapping goes. And, unless she gets the sack, a scrap is bound to be staged quite soon.

MURRAY

Well, if that's your feeling, there's no good ... or, at least, no urgency in my little fight with father, is there?

MARSALI

No, you don't, Murray! Your promise still holds. Bridget's fight will be an extra ... And what an extra! ... Oh, can't you see! Two such tigers in the same cage, and no jamboree? ... Impossible!

MURRAY

Oh, father will just gobble her up if she tries any such nonsense.

MARSALI

It's clear you haven't studied Bridget. What a fight that will be! ... Celt against Celt! ... Scotland against Ireland! ... And they're both dodgers!

MURRAY

I'm getting positively bloodthirsty, listening to your war-cries, Marsali. Also a bit jealous of Bridget ... I'll have a shot at father to-night as ever was, about this new gate ... And now, come out for a bit, and let's look for the moon.

MARSALI

What! You'll really go for him to-night. Good man! Shake! *(They shake hands.)*

MURRAY

Well, let's get out. There is no moon, of course. So I'd better see you down to your cottage.

(They move to the door on the left, but before they reach it, **BRIDGET** *ushers in the* **DOCTOR** *at the back, who carries some catalogue-slips, but finds himself embarrassed at discovering the room isn't empty.)*

BRIDGET

The Doctor's looking for Drimfearn, Mr. Murray.

MURRAY

Right-oh, Doctor! Have a perch. Father'll be around soon, I expect. Sorry I've to hurry ... hurry off, y'know.

(**MURRAY** *goes out with* **MARSALI** *on the left.* **BRIDGET** *attempts a retirement at the back, but* **DR. KENNEDY** *has his eagle eye on her.*

DOCTOR

Stop, please! You're Sister Catherine! ... I can't get this thing clear ... Sister Catherine! And yet here you are masquerading as a servant-girl, Bridget Something-or-Other?

BRIDGET

Och, no, it was only Bridget Something-or Other that was masquerading out in Belgrade as Sister Catherine.

DOCTOR

As you please. But who are you in reality? And why are you here?

BRIDGET

'Deed, ye may well ask! Myself, I'm asking every day who I am, and what I'm doing in a place like this, where I'm meeting so many ould friends.

DOCTOR

How many old friends?

BRIDGET

Let me count ... There's Mr. Borden, my long-lost uncle...

DOCTOR

Borden? Your uncle?

BRIDGET,

So he says ... And then, aren't you my long-lost brother?

DOCTOR

Don't, please! Don't begin that silly "I'll be a sister to you" business all over again!

BRIDGET

But, of course, I've no use for that Belgrade nonsense here. I draw the line even at brothers nowadays, so I do.

DOCTOR

And I at uncles! *(Then advancing, with outstretched hands.)* Oh, Kate, can't you see, it's different here?

BRIDGET

(retreating). I'll have to help cook peel the tatties.

DOCTOR

But Kate ...

BRIDGET

Wheesht! No more Kates, by your leave! I'm Bridget Gould in this place.

DOCTOR

But won't you tell me why there's all this mystery?

(**BRIDGET** *shakes her head solemnly.*

Well, never mind. You're here, that's the great thing! ... Bridget or Kate or any name under the sun, it's you!

BRIDGET

Och, ye wear well. And ye've the same wild tongue on ye as ye had in Belgrade ... But I'll have to get back to them tatties.

(She slips out at the back, just as **DRIMFEARN** *and* **MURRAY** *come in on the left. They are arguing volubly.*

DRIMFEARN

I won't hear of it, Murray! Not another word, please! ... Hillo, Doctor! Sorry I'd to run off so suddenly. Detained by that fool Borden. He's got the wind up about poachers and all kinds of nonsense. Tiresome little beast! ... Well, how's the jaw?

DOCTOR

Better, thanks ... You can have these catalogue-slips now. I think they're about right at last.

DRIMFEARN

Many thanks, Doctor. You're a brick.

DOCTOR

(tactfully, as he sees an angry glance pass between the chief and his son). Well, I think I'll knock a few balls about on the billiard-table before an early retiral. A bit fagged. Had a long round to-day.

DRIMFEARN

Do, my dear chap. Make yourself thoroughly at home. And if you've a few minutes after breakfast to-morrow, we'll have another look at those medical books, if you don't mind.

DOCTOR

(grimly). Oh, delighted, I'm sure. *(He goes out on the left.)*

DRIMFEARN

Look here, Murray, I'm sick of this badgering ... before guests too. The Doctor must have heard you ... That gate's not going to do anybody with any sense the least bit of harm.

MURRAY

So you say. But what about the Doctor's broken tooth?

DRIMFEARN

I said: "Anybody with any sense."

MURRAY

I see. If anyone gets hurt, he's a fool.

DRIMFEARN

Exactly.

MURRAY

(blazing). All right, I'll get Doctor. *(He makes for the door on the left.)*

DRIMFEARN

(gripping his arm). Here, where are you going?

MURRAY

I'm going to have you tell Doctor he's a fool.

DRIMFEARN

Now, now, my dear fellow! You know I spoke in heat. I'm sorry. I don't always mean all I say.

MURRAY

Did you mean what you said when you said the gate wasn't coming down?

DRIMFEARN

Not at present, at any rate. It will come down when it has served its purpose.

MURRAY

And what's that?

DRIMFEARN

Look here, my boy, I've never seen you so strung up. I expect it's that graze on your arm, and the scare you got when they fired on the boat.

MURRAY

Oh, never mind about the scare. That's all past ... It's not myself I'm scared about: it's you and your scheming I'm sweating over ... What purpose has that new gate? You must tell me!

DRIMFEARN

Really, Murray, you mustn't probe into this further, y'know. I'd rather you didn't.

MURRAY

(blazing again). It's nothing but some foul dodge to boost the shootings, I do believe.

DRIMFEARN

(also in a blaze.) But I can't for the life of me see what business it is of yours!

MURRAY

You mean you won't tell me? You won't trust me?

DRIMFEARN

I won't. And now for Heaven's sake, chuck it!

(**MARSALI** *enters suddenly by the door on the left.*

MARSALI

Mr. Borden's not here yet, is he?

DRIMFEARN

Borden? No ... Had enough of Borden for one night. What's up?

MARSALI

MacNab met up on me just after you went off with Murray. He says Borden's discovered some bloodstains in the boat, and thinks he's murdered somebody ... He mustn't suspect Murray! ... I didn't like to give MacNab the message, so came on myself ... MacNab says Borden has quite lost his head. *(A* **MOTOR-HORN** *is heard.)* There's Borden, I'm sure. He's certain to dash up here, if he's as bad as MacNab says ... Oh, do hide that bandage, Murray!

DRIMFEARN

And you ran all the way to warn us? Good girl! ... Run up to your mother, Murray, and tell her you're all right.

MURRAY

I'm not running away from Borden, sir.

DRIMFEARN

Well, hands in pockets, then ... That's it ... Steady! ... Everybody! At ease, at ease! ... Now! Prepare to receive cavalry!
(Humming to himself, he takes up a book, **MARSALI** *and* **MURRAY** *sit down in a corner.* **BRIDGET** *opens the door at the back.*

BRIDGET

Mr. Borden.

BORDEN

(entering in a state of high excitement). Sorry to rush in on you so late ... But, my God! Drimfearn, what are we to do! There's blood on the thwarts of that boat. Splashed all over it. The man may be bleeding to death somewhere out in the dark! Pah! It makes me sick to think of him!

DRIMFEARN

Well, I told you what to expect.

BORDEN

Yes, yes, excuse yourself, of course. You told me about the watchman in the boat when it was too late.

DRIMFEARN

You must make a search for the body. That's all I can suggest.

BORDEN

The body! You don't think? ...

DRIMFEARN

Oh, anything may happen when fools play round with guns on a dark night like this.

BORDEN

But can't you suggest anything? Where to look? ... What to do?

DRIMFEARN

Follow the drops of blood. Track 'em with a lantern. He may be only wounded, and hiding in the woods.

BORDEN

Of course, he's only wounded, or he wouldn't have got off so quickly.

DRIMFEARN

Anything's possible, Borden.

BORDEN

My God! I hope ... Look here, Drimfearn, you'll bear me out that I only meant to damage their boat.

DRIMFEARN

That's what you said, at least.

BORDEN

What, you don't believe me!

DRIMFEARN

Now, now, sir! Don't try to browbeat me.

(**BRIDGET** *comes in at the back.*

BRIDGET

MacNab would like to speak to Drimfearn.

DRIMFEARN

Aha! MacNab may be able to throw some light on the matter. Send him in, please.

(**BRIDGET** *retires and shows in* **MACNAB**.

MACNAB

They have all got away, sir.

DRIMFEARN

Who?

MACNAB

The men from Faolinnvore. That is, if they came from Faolinnvore. Myself, I've no idea where they came from.

BORDEN

But how did they get away?

MACNAB

In their boat, sir.

BORDEN

But there was a great gunshot hole in their boat. How could they?

MACNAB

Oh, no, sir. It was your own boat that got the hole in it.

BORDEN

Nonsense! There was a watchman in the boat that was holed.

MACNAB

There was that, Mr, Borden. But it was your boat, all the same.

BORDEN

The devils!

MACNAB

Och yes, no other boat. The poachers must have changed from their own boat to yours, because their own boat was too heavy of draught for the river. Just a wee loan of your boat, you'll understand.

BORDEN

And now they're off in their own boat, back to Faolinnvore, you think?

MACNAB

Back to where they came from. Myself, I'm not knowing anything about the ways of the people at Faolinnvore.

BORDEN

Damn them!

MACNAB

Whoever they were and wherever they came from, they left a big sack against the door of my house, without knocking or a by-your-leave. I fell over it, coming into my own porch. It's addressed to you,

Mr. Borden; and, as I did not like having a thing of the kind on my hands over-night, I was taking it up to your place just now. I have it in the gig outside.

BORDEN
And how do you know it's from the poachers?

MACNAB
Because it says so on the label, sir.

DRIMFEARN
(mischievously). Something in a sack? It isn't a dead body, eh?

MACNAB
Oh, no, sir, not the full size of a corp.

BORDEN
Stow that, Drimfearn!

DRIMFEARN
Best let MacNab have a look at it, Borden.

MACNAB
Oh, there's no need, sir. By the feel of it, I'm thinking it's a salmon of thirty pounds, no less. And it says on the label: "A present to Mr. Borden, from his fellow-sportsman at the Big Pool to-night". Thirty pounds if it's an ounce, sir! Weren't they kind now?

BORDEN
Kind be blowed! We'll see about this, Drimfearn!
(He rushes out at the back, followed by MACNAB, *smiling quietly.)*

DRIMFEARN
(chuckling). See away, my boy.
(A MOTOR-HORN *is heard, as* BORDEN's *car departs.)*

MARSALI
Off at last! What a man!

DRIMFEARN
You're a brick to have run all that way to warn us, Marsali. Don't know what we'd do without you.

MURRAY
(who has evidently been making progress in the good graces of MARSALI, *while the fuss with* BORDEN *was in full swing, puts his arm round her, and brings her forward).* My sentiments to a T, father. I can't do without her.

DRIMFEARN

What! ... Mean to say! ... Oho, oho! ... And is that how the land lies! ... My dear girl! *(He kisses her, and shakes hands with* **MURRAY**.*)* I couldn't have asked for better than your father's daughter! ... Murray, you lucky dog!

MURRAY

Glad you approve, sir.

DRIMFEARN

Daughter of an old brother-officer, like Ronald MacAlpine—what could be finer? ... No friend like an old friend—what! ... Where's your mother, Murray? ... This isn't my line, y'know!

MURRAY

I believe she's lying down, sir.

DRIMFEARN

So she is ... so she is! Best not disturb her. Bit jumpy to-night. We've had enough scenes ... Oh, yes, what was I going to say? ... She's nervous, yes ... mean to say, well—enough's as good as a feast, isn't it?

MARSALI

Yes, Drimfearn. I'll break it to her in the morning.

DRIMFEARN

"Break it to her!" Good! ... good! ... Oh, and I say, Marsali, do knock some sense into this chap. Talks of running away to fruit-farming in Tasmania and all that kind of rot, because I won't manage the estate in any way but my own ... Ever hear such nonsense?

MARSALI

I'm afraid I agree with him.

DRIMFEARN

What! You too! I believe you've been putting him up to bait me, you rogue! Talk of dodges! Allow women!

MARSALI

Yes, I did urge him on ... I won't deny it.

DRIMFEARN

Oho! And what do you young people know about the management of an estate, eh? Romance is all very well ... all very well, but—mean to say—has to be kept in its place, you know.

MURRAY

So has your way of managing estates, dad.

DRIMFEARN

Well, it's the way that gets the money to keep you at college, young man.

MARSALI

Money could be made in better ways. Come now, Drimfearn, you know it could.

DRIMFEARN

Oh, yes. I know! Forestry and that kind of humbug!

MURRAY

But short of forestry, isn't there some other method besides these dodges of yours?

DRIMFEARN

Dodges, Murray! Whatever are you talking about?

MURRAY

(*getting warm*). The same subject I took up with you half-an-hour ago.

DRIMFEARN

Oh, that stuff about the new gate...

(**BRIDGET** *runs in hurriedly at the back.*

BRIDGET

Quick, Nurse! An accident!

DRIMFEARN

Where's the Doctor!

BRIDGET

He's off, sir. I went for him first.

DRIMFEARN

But where ...?

(**MACNAB** *hurries in.*

MACNAB

It's Mr. Borden, sir! His head's smashed. They have taken him to the Dispensary. And the Doctor's gone to the Dispensary after him. And I was to tell the Nurse to go down there at once.

MARSALI

Right!
(*She goes out at the back and* **MURRAY** *with her; but* **BRIDGET** *does not follow. She is all eyes and ears for* **MACNAB** *as he continues his story.*

DRIMFEARN

But what on all the earth happened?

MACNAB

It was the new gate, sir ... It was closed for the night. And Mr. Borden, being upset and angry about the poachers, must have forgotten it. And his car just went smash.

DRIMFEARN

And, I'll bet, so did my new gate! The fool!

MACNAB

I'll be going down to see how the poor man is, sir.

DRIMFEARN (

(*grimly*). No fear, MacNab. You're going down to see how my poor gate is. Come on.

(*He crosses to the left, and* MACNAB *meekly follows him.*

BRIDGET

(*involuntarily, as she turns to go out at the back*). Poor ould Uncle Borden!

DRIMFEARN

(*halting, amazed*). Uncle? ... He's not your uncle, is he!

BRIDGET

(*going slowly out at the back, and still sorrowful*). Poor ould Uncle!

DRIMFEARN

(*his hand to his head, in perplexity, as he gazes after her and then turns to* MACNAB). Now, who the devil is that girl! (*But* MACNAB's *face is as full of blank amazement as his own.*)

CURTAIN

ACT III

Scene one

SCENE. *"The Dispensary" at Drimfearn, on a warm, sunny afternoon, a week later. This is a large hall generally used for concerts, dances and meetings — evening functions; in the day-time it sometimes serves the local nurse as a centre for dispensing medicines and doing dressings. In cases of urgency it has at rare intervals been converted into a temporary hospital.*

Only one angle of the place is seen, for the back wall slants from the right to meet the left wall; and, the left being the smaller, the floor-space shown represents a triangle with unequal sides.

There is a shelved cupboard midway in the left wall, open in its upper half, but shuttered below. In the upper section are bottles of medicine and pots of ointment; in the lower are stored splints, cotton wool, bandages and so on. Between the two sections is a drawer containing a few surgical instruments.

Further back in the left wall is a door leading to the kitchen.

The back wall has the big entrance door in its middle, and this is flanked by two large windows, through which the hills and the loch are seen in full sunshine.

Near the door is a plain deal table with a bandage roller at one end and a mortar and pestle on the other; some folds of calico lie between. Behind the table is an easel on which is hung an anatomical chart.

Several ten-feet fishing rods are propped against the corner of the window furthest back. A pile of benches and chairs lie higgledy-piggledy in front of the forward window; and to the left of the central floor-space there is a couch with some rugs and cushions.

The place is empty at first, but presently BRIDGET *enters by the main door. She is in outdoor dress, and is humming happily to herself.*

She looks round casually and then, as if at a loss for something to do, walks over to the medicine cupboard and inspects several of the bottles and pots. The drawer is next investigated, and the surgical tools handled gingerly; and after that it is the turn of the splints and bandages in the lowest compartment. Here she finds a large scissors, and with this she crosses to the table, cuts and tears several widths of calico, and sets to the rolling of bandages quite industriously, still humming. At last she breaks into song, and sings a verse of "Madelon" in very passable French.

CRADDOCK *comes to the main door and halts, looking in with an ingratiating smile.*

CRADDOCK
Good-afternoon, Miss Morgan. I forget your real name, y'know.

BRIDGET
Do ye really, now? It's so long since we met, of course.

CRADDOCK
A whole week. A week of anguish.

BRIDGET

Aye, ye're a week oulder and a week worse ... But Morgan will be doing for the time being.

CRADDOCK

May I come in? Just passing, you see.

BRIDGET

It's not my house; and I can't ask anybody in, or order anyone out.

CRADDOCK

(entering). They call it "The Dispensary", I believe?

BRIDGET

Yes. J'ever see such a rag and ruin of a place?

CRADDOCK

Kind of a public hall as well, isn't it? ... Concerts and dances for the villagers, eh?

BRIDGET

And at times it does be made into a wee hospital for people like your uncle.

CRADDOCK

Smashed heads? So that's where the bandages come in ... Can I help? *(He takes hold of a bandage which has become twisted.)*

BRIDGET

Hould it straight! *(She winds.)*

CRADDOCK

I say, what heaps of dressings!

BRIDGET

Maybe they're all for Uncle Borden. How is the poor man?

CRADDOCK

Getting on, thanks. But a nasty scalp wound, that. Leave a hefty mark, I'm afraid.

BRIDGET

Och, he'd be all the better of a wig, anyway. Is he out of bed yet?

CRADDOCK

Didn't you know? Been on his feet for the last three days, and comes round here for dressings now.

BRIDGET

And I reckon he thinks that'll be cheaper?

CRADDOCK

Aren't you cute! That's just it. Meeting the Doctor half-way should be something off the bill. Allow uncle!

BRIDGET

Well, if I were Doctor, I'd charge double for coming to a tumbledown old shack like this one.

CRADDOCK

Double? Some hope! ... But I say, you're off duty this afternoon?

BRIDGET

Yes.

CRADDOCK

Well, isn't it too hot for fooling around in this old Dispensary? What about a walk in the nice shady woods around here?

BRIDGET

But you surely wouldn't be seen walking with a slavey, Mr. Craddock!

CRADDOCK

Oh, go on! You're no slavey!

BRIDGET

Whisht! That was a secret.

CRADDOCK

No, it wasn't. It was just blarney. All the same, you're no slavey ... Come now, what's the little game?

BRIDGET

(*shyly*). Did Mr. Borden not tell ye?

CRADDOCK

Borden? No.

BRIDGET

The like o' that! ... And you his nephew! Didn't he tell you I was own sister to his niece that died out in Michigan?

CRADDOCK

Never! ... But, look here, if you were his niece's sister ... And I never heard of a niece in Michigan!

BRIDGET

Och, I'm only telling ye what he said.

CRADDOCK

But, don't you see, if you were his niece's sister, then you also would be his niece, wouldn't you?

BRIDGET

Och, I don't know. But she's dead, anyway. And he cried just lovely over her.

CRADDOCK

Over who?

BRIDGET

His niece.

CRADDOCK

But, see here ... *(A* MOTOR-HORN *is heard)* Who's this?

BRIDGET

(looking outside). The very man you want. My sister's uncle. And he'll explain every jot and tittle to ye.

(BORDEN *appears in the open doorway, his head swathed in bandages. He wears a plus-four suit of tweed.*

BORDEN

Hillo, Philip! ... Ah, good-morning, my dear. *(He takes* BRIDGET's *hand caressingly.)* Busy, I see. Whatever at?

BRIDGET

Making bandages for broken heads. It's the chief industry hereabouts.

BORDEN

You rascal!

CRADDOCK

(gallantly). And doesn't she do them well! Almost makes a chap wish he had a broken head to have his bandages wound by hands so fair.

BORDEN

(glaring at him). Yes, exactly. And you can have a smashed head any day at the new gate, my boy ... any day you like. Only don't take my car.

CRADDOCK

Thanks awfully for the hint.

BORDEN

(suavely). Not at all ... And, oh, Philip, would you mind running the car in question in the opposite direction from that gate just now ... down to the lower beat, and see how the fish are taking to-day? The gillie's there. I might try a cast or two in the evening ... And I have to wait here for the Doctor as usual. Beastly nuisance! He's always late.

CRADDOCK

(lounging off unwillingly). Oh, you won't find the time long waiting for Doctor. Not while your new niece is around.

(He goes off quickly, and rather angry... Presently the motor is heard to start.

BORDEN

My new niece?

(He regards **BRIDGET** *intently, and she hangs her head shyly.)* Hillo! what's my nephew been after?

BRIDGET

(still more shyly).
Och, maybe it was myself.

BORDEN

Nephew! ... Niece! ... Good Heavens! you're not married to him, are you?

BRIDGET

Och, no ... not as yet.

BORDEN

Not yet! Then he means to marry you, does he?

BRIDGET

And how can I tell what's in any young man's mind?

BORDEN

Good Lord, you witch! you'll drive me crazy! *(He seizes her hand.)* Bridget ... I'm no longer young ... but ... but ...

BRIDGET

Yes, Uncle?

BORDEN

Oh, you rogue, you rogue! ... Who are you? What are you?

BRIDGET

The slavey at Drimfearn. And it's my half-day off, and time I was going for my constitutional.

BORDEN

(beside himself with passion). Let me come with you, please. Out in the sun and wind with you, you lovely thing!

BRIDGET

Och, have sense! There's too much sun, and no wind at all, at all. *(She slips past him to the main door.)* And anyway, the sun's not good for a head like yours. *(She looks out to the left.)* And here's the Doctor coming, and the darlingest nurse that ever was.

BORDEN

Blast them!

BRIDGET

(*drawing back from the main door*). Easy now, Uncle. I'll just be slipping out by the back door. And they'll never know I was here, or what a fine time you've been giving your new niece.

(*She goes quickly out by the door to the kitchen, while* **BORDEN** *gazes in perplexity after her.* **MARSALI** *and* **DR. KENNEDY** *pass the window to the left of the door, and then enter.*)

DOCTOR

Ah, you've beaten us! ... What a scorching day! ... Sorry to have kept you waiting ... Well, shall we get to work at once. Sit here, please.

(*He sets a chair, and* **MARSALI** *unpacks her bundle of sterile dressings, while the* **DOCTOR** *removes the gauze bandages on* **BORDEN**'*s head,* **MARSALI** *brings the basins and hot water from the kitchen, and the* **DOCTOR** *and she scrub up before the rest of the work is done. This consists of the application of some spirit, and a simple changing of gauze pads. The gauze bandage is then reapplied.*)

BORDEN

How long till I'm healed now, Doctor?

DOCTOR

Oh, about two or three weeks. Trouble is there are, well, some rather dirty patches still to clean up,

BORDEN

Must be seen every day till then, I suppose?

DOCTOR

(*going on with the dressing*). Yes.

BORDEN

Well, I shan't grumble as long's it gets better all right. And it's not me that will foot your bill anyway. Drimfearn must see to that. If he will put up his silly old gates at the wrong places, he must take the consequences.

DOCTOR

You should have had your headlights on.

BORDEN

He should have had headlights on his gate, if it comes to that ... And what about your own crash at the same gate? Had you headlights on?

DOCTOR

No. It was full daylight when I crashed. My own fault. I'd been warned the workmen were at it in the day-time, but forgot.

BORDEN

And nearly broke your jaw ... If I were you I'd sue Drimfearn all the same.

DOCTOR

Oh, it's nothing. Only broke an old grinder that had seen its best days anyway. It'll have to come out soon, I expect.

BORDEN

Well I'd get at old Drimfearn nevertheless for the loss of a *good* tooth, if I were you ... But I must be going ... Thanks, Doctor ... Many thanks, Nurse ... Afternoon.

(He is about to go when DRIMFEARN *enters.*

DRIMFEARN

Hillo, Borden! How's the head? Just come round to ask for you. Looks as if the wild goat would get a rest for a bit; till the turban comes off your head, eh?

BORDEN

Oh, you're devilish cheerful, aren't you? ... By the way, you don't get the *Mail*, I think?

(He pulls a copy of a newspaper out of his coat pocket, and hands it to DRIMFEARN.

DRIMFEARN

Something of interest?

BORDEN

Only an account of my accident.

DRIMFEARN

(unfolding the paper). From your tone I guess you've been up to mischief, my friend.

BORDEN

Oh, I dunno. You read it; then you'll see ... And I've just been telling Doctor you'll pay his bill for my head.

DRIMFEARN

You send that bill to me, and you'll get a jolly sight heavier one for the repairs to my gate!

BORDEN

We'll see about that ... But just have a look at that paper ... And be sure you see next Wednesday's issue. Quite a good article on poaching, I hear. *(And he goes out, chuckling.)*

DRIMFEARN

He is the limit, that chap, isn't he? ... Let's see ... Where is it? *(All crowd round the paper, as he searches its pages.)* Aha! here we are! *(He reads.)* "Eccentric Highland Laird tries to keep out Ghost with Iron Gate." ..."The Headless Horseman of Drimfearn." ... I say, what good headlines, eh?

MARSALI

Little beast!

DRIMFEARN

Not at all, my dear. This is fine. My rentals must go up next season, after all this good publicity!

DOCTOR

What else?

DRIMFEARN

(reading again). "A recent motor accident in the Highlands has just made public one of those strange revivals of superstition... " And so on and so on. Ah, here we are! "A large Daimler car crashed into the gate, a substantial erection of wood and iron..." Yes, yes, yes ... "Mr. Borden states that the existence of the gate was unknown to him until the accident occurred." ... Well, by gad, he knows it now ... "Multiple injuries, but expected to recover ..." Indeed? ... Not if you get tetanus, my boy.

MARSALI

Oh, Drimfearn!

DRIMFEARN

Well, we don't know. He may. *(Reading again.)* "The Headless Horseman is said to ride around the house of Drimfearn on the eve of any calamity." ... Then Borden again! Why, it's all Borden, Borden, Borden. ... Not a single word of sympathy to the owner of the poor gate! *(He grins)*

MARSALI

But you seem pleased?

DRIMFEARN

And why not? Look at the boost the estate has got. Why, old Borden's done us handsome as a press-agent.

MARSALI

So that was the meaning of the gate? Press-notices to get Drimfearn shootings before the public?.

DRIMFEARN

Certainly. I wanted some fresh journalist to write up the Headless Horseman. Of course I'd no idea of smashing up the jaw of the good kind Doctor, or that little cad.

DOCTOR

Hear, hear!

DRIMFEARN

But, as I say, I did want shooting people generally to get to hear of the existence of a fine old Highland mansion, with a hefty historic ghost.

MARSALI

I don't like that way of doing things.

DRIMFEARN

Neither do I, my dear. I don't like advertising of any kind. But if you don't do it, the other chaps will. So where are you? The industrial age has us in its grip, Marsali, Highland though we be. Advertise, or get out ... That's the slogan for the Drimfearns as well as the Northcliffes: make no mistake about it. Regrettable, regrettable, but there it is. But I say, I quite forgot, with all that newspaper stuff what I really came for ... Any of you seen MacNab? ... I was to meet him here at three. *(He looks at his watch.)* Ten past already.

DOCTOR

Haven't seen him to-day ... A-a-ah! *(He clutches his jaw suddenly)*

DRIMFEARN

That tooth again?

DOCTOR

Yes.

DRIMFEARN

Well, you're a fine doctor! Toothache for a whole week, and no better yet! You should let Nurse have a go at it. She's a dandy with the forceps.

DOCTOR

Oh, but it's really improving, y'know ... *(He is plainly alarmed.)* I ... I ... I think I'll cut off now. I've got to see MacVicar: he's rather ill, y'know. *(He retreats in haste by the main door.)*

DRIMFEARN

(laughing, as he shouts after him) Coward!
(**MARSALI** *goes off to the bottles on the shelves and re-arranges them silently and moodily.*

DRIMFEARN

And what has given you the hump, may I ask?

MARSALI

Oh, it's so undignified all this scheming ... so un-Highland.

DRIMFEARN

Yes, yes! "The moon's on the lake, and the mist's on the brae ... Gregarach!"... Is that it? Rob Roy MacGregor, eh? ... Wasn't Rob Highland? And did Rob not scheme? Were his cattle liftings dignified?

MARSALI

All that was different. There was romance and adventure. And he had to take risks ... Hairbreadth escapes at times.

DRIMFEARN

Aye, aye. Risks and adventures. And do you think I don't get my share of them? There are nights I don't get a wink o' sleep, plotting and planning how to make ends meet; how to keep the old place together; how to keep up appearances on a reduced income ... It's not an easy kind of fighting—that, I can assure you. God! no! ... I'd as soon have Rob Roy's way of it.

MARSALI

I'm sorry, Drimfearn.

DRIMFEARN

Oh, don't be sorry for me, my dear. I rather enjoy my life, broken-winged as it is.

MARSALI

Broken-winged! What a fine word! If you see things that way, I believe you do get your share of romance, after all.

DRIMFEARN

'Course I do. *(Picking up the paper)* Fancy what the *Mail* is missing in head-lines! "A Modern Rob Roy," eh?

MARSALI

Yes, it's good when you look at it in that light. But really, Drimfearn, it could be so much better if you got beyond Rob Roy ... improved on him, y'know.

DRIMFEARN

But think of the gang I'm up against! All these business johnnies with their bucket-shop minds that I get as shooting-tenants. Look how they fake their balance-sheets at home. Look how many of them, almost millionaires, are doing time for that sort of thing. Look at Borden!

(**MURRAY** *comes in at the main door.*

MURRAY

Hillo, Marsali! Hillo, dad! Rehearsing an election address? ... Just looked in to ask for Borden. Is he off?

DRIMFEARN

Yes, and left me this billet-doux. *(He hands* **MURRAY** *the paper folded at the notice of the accident.)*

MURRAY

(reading). The gate! *(He glances rapidly through the paragraphs.)* Well, you've got some great publicity here ... So that was your game? What if Borden had been killed?

DRIMFEARN

Wish he had.

MARSALI

Isn't he terrible, Murray! He gets his press at the expense of poor Borden. And the Doctor's jaw still makes him squirm.

MURRAY

I say, dad, you must really chuck this sort of thing.

DRIMFEARN

Just been telling Marsali it's not so easy to fight dodgers without dodging in turn. And there's quite a lot of fun in it.

MARSALI

There you go, glorying in your shame!

DRIMFEARN

Ah! The next generation's going to be everything that's upright!

MARSALI

We'll have a shot at something better than dodges, anyway, won't we, Murray? ... Come now, Drimfearn. Give us a chance to start fair ... Promise us there'll be no more tricks this season.

DRIMFEARN

(ruefully.) Is this the thin end of the wedge? ... Well, this season won't be long till it's over. Yes, I think I can safely promise.

MURRAY

Fine, Marsali! Victory!

DRIMFEARN

(full of misgivings already). All right, all right. Let's drop it now. *(He looks at his watch again.)* Where the devil can MacNab have got to!

(A motor is heard to halt outside with the minimum of noise; then there are **VOICES***, and some people are seen to pass the window at the right of the main door. An* **OLD MAN** *enters, his coat torn, and a blood-stained wrapping around his head. He is followed by a* **CHAUFFEUR** *whose uniform is covered with dust, and who limps badly.)*

DRIMFEARN

Good heavens! I thought it was Borden once more!

THE OLD MAN
(halting in the doorway). I'm tould there's a doctor here. *(His accent is decidedly Irish.)*

MARSALI
Won't you come in and rest?

THE OLD MAN
Is there a doctor here? My head's spinning.

DRIMFEARN
Where did the Doctor say he was going, Marsali?

MARSALI
To MacVicar's. But this man is very ill ... He'd best rest here, and Murray will get Doctor to come round.

MURRAY
Right! I'll scoot over to MacVicar's. *(He runs out.)*

THE OLD MAN
Tell me where the doctor is and I'll go to him myself. I'm bad, and can't wait. I only escaped killing by the black o' my nail ... Oh, my head!

MARSALI
Yes, you're very ill. Come in at once and lie down on the couch here. *(She goes to him, and takes his arm.)*

THE OLD MAN
(shaking her off). I'll not, now. Only tell me where he is, and I'll go to him in my car.

MARSALI
(to the chauffeur). Do you know MacVicar's? *(She points to the left.)* The first cottage along the road there ... About half-a-mile off.

THE OLD MAN
He does not. He knows nothing, or he'd never have run into that gate.

MARSALI
What gate?

THE OLD MAN
The one the workmen are mending after the last week's accident. One of them said it was a gate against a ghost. And it nearly made a ghost o' me, so it did ... What's the matter with that fellow?
(He refers to DRIMFEARN, *who is stealing past him on his tiptoes, and has now halted just outside the main door, finding his attempt at escape discovered.*

DRIMFEARN

(re-entering, with all the airs of innocence). Have you ... ah ... have you had an accident?

THE OLD MAN

Do I look as if I'd had anything else? ... Oh, my head! *(He totters.)*

MARSALI

(helping him to the couch). Lie down at once!

THE OLD MAN

(subsiding). My head's spinning.

MARSALI

We'd best keep him quiet till Doctor comes. I only hope he hasn't been called to some fresh case twenty miles away!

THE OLD MAN

Twenty miles! Twenty miles. Then I'll not wait for him. I'll go after him, so I will.

MARSALI

But you should be lying down. Your skull may be fractured.

THE OLD MAN

(sitting up with difficulty). Skulls are doctors' work, not young girls'. We'll find a real doctor and see what he says. *(He breaks away from* **MARSALI**, *and staggers to the door where he turns to his* **CHAUFFEUR**.*)* Come on, you, and help me find him.

DRIMFEARN

But, my good sir, why not come up to my house and rest?

THE OLD MAN

Stand aside, will ye! *(Then, to his chauffeur.)* Help me out o' this.

MARSALI

(to **DRIMFEARN**). He is stubborn, isn't he. I'd better go with him. *(She picks up a packet of dressings.)*

(**MARSALI** *and the* **CHAUFFEUR** *assist the* **OLD MAN** *out to his car, while* **DRIMFEARN** *fusses around, watching them from the doorway.* **MACNAB** *enters by the main door.*

DRIMFEARN

Well, where the devil have you been? You're a quarter of an hour late, MacNab. *(While he speaks he is watching the trio who have just left, as they board the car outside.)*

MACNAB

I'm sorry, Drimfearn. But I heard there had been another accident at the new gate, and I just ran down there to see if I could help. But the people who were hurt had gone off in their car, and so ...

DRIMFEARN

Yes, yes, yes! I know, I know! Those are the people out there ... Now take a good look at that car, MacNab ... It's a Rolls-Royce ... Is that by any chance the motor you saw Bridget go off in last week?

MACNAB

Yes, indeed, it is, just. And it's the same driver.

DRIMFEARN

And the old fellow's the man who kissed her? ... Fellow you called the earl. Eh?

MACNAB

Well, sir, in his present condition, I could not say who he was ... Och, now, and hasn't he had the sore knock, yon one!

DRIMFEARN

(*as the motor is heard to move off*). By gum! I believe it's Kelly ... Ab-so-lute-ly!

MACNAB

Kelly, sir?

DRIMFEARN

Yes, yes. Didn't I tell you a Mr. Kelly was likely to want a lease of Drimfearn? And that's Kelly, I'll bet!

MACNAB

Indeed then, I'm very glad, and I hope the poor man will not die from that head of his.

DRIMFEARN

Die? Nonsense ... I expect the rest will do him good.

(**BRIDGET** *comes in by the kitchen door.*)

BRIDGET

I'm sorry. I thought there was no one here.

DRIMFEARN

Oh, come in, come in! ... And how are you, Bridget? ... Another day off, eh? Lucky girl!

BRIDGET

A half-day only ... I'm looking for Nurse.

DRIMFEARN

Oh, she's away at an urgent case, I believe.

BRIDGET

Then I'll just be taking another wee walk on the hill behind till she comes back. (*She makes to go.*)

DRIMFEARN

Oh, but she won't be long, I hope... , And I wanted a word with you, please. *(Then, to* **MACNAB**, *who is moving towards the main door!)* Don't go, MacNab. I want you. *(Turning to* **BRIDGET** *again)* About that second cousin of yours, Bridget—the chauffeur to Mr. Kelly?

BRIDGET

(bewildered) Och, that one!

DRIMFEARN

Yes, well, what I wanted to say was ... mean to say ... if your cousin could ... ah ... ah ... suggest ... ah ... to Mr. Kelly the desirable nature of the shootings at Drimfearn, before they are snapped up, he might ... ah ... be doing Mr. Kelly a good turn ... And a good turn to MacNab here as well ... MacNab gets down-spirited, y'know, when we don't let all the shootings here. He loves his work, does MacNab ... the hills ... the moors ... the guns! Eh, MacNab?

BRIDGET

Och, ye droll ould man. Are ye coming your games on me, too?

DRIMFEARN

Ah, humour! ... Irish humour! ... Good! ... Quite good! ... But possibly you know Mr. Kelly well enough to approach him personally?

BRIDGET

Indeed and I do. Didn't we both feed out o' the same tattie patch before he got among the gentry.

DRIMFEARN

I'm afraid I don't quite follow. But it's sufficient if you know him personally. Now you also know MacNab ... Couldn't you somehow let Mr. Kelly know what a fine keeper MacNab is?

BRIDGET

I could that. I could tell him he's that fond of the grouse he puts them under a petticoat on the warm days, just to keep them from having too much of the sun.

DRIMFEARN

A petticoat?

MACNAB

Och, never heed her, sir. It's my Inverness cape she's meaning. It's just her ignorance.

BRIDGET

Ignorance, yourself. And call it what you like, Inverness or anything, a petticoat's my name for it. And that's the name I'll give to it, when I explain how kind you are to Mr. Kelly.

DRIMFEARN

What on earth is all this about, MacNab?

MACNAB

Och, leave her alone. She's talking of the day the grouse came from Stirling.

BRIDGET

Yes, and weren't they in the nice comfortable boxes, and both o' ye hiding them?

DRIMFEARN

Oh, that's it, is it? Those were the birds we got to try the feeding-stuff on, weren't they, MacNab?

MACNAB

No doubt, sir. Yes, that would be the way of it.

BRIDGET

Well, it's the first time I've heard of feeding-stuff made out o' soft soap.

DRIMFEARN

Soft soap! Oh, come now! Nonsense, nonsense! You mustn't talk foolish stuff of that kind to Mr. Kelly, or you'll do me a grave injury.

MACNAB

Indeed, yes.

DRIMFEARN

I'm sure MacNab never made a mistake of that kind. Whatever made you think we'd do such a cruel thing! Feed birds on soap! Tut-tut! No, no!

BRIDGET

But I saw them. Sloshed all over them on back and wings it was that night, when I had to go into the store-room for candles. And if you'll not tell what it was for, maybe Mr. Kelly will.

DRIMFEARN

No, no, please, you mustn't speak of such a silly matter to Mr. Kelly .... I know what she's driving at, MacNab ... It's the lubricant ... the Norwegian lubricant ... Yes, you've got it all wrong, my dear Miss ... ah ... Miss ... mean to say, that was nothing but a special preparation we get from ... ah ... Norway. Said to be the best lubricant for the birds' wings. Gives them special powers of flight. And so the sportsmen get better sport. Birds are more difficult to get, you see. That so, MacNab?

MACNAB

Och, yes, they fly quite different. It's the lub ... lub ... what you said, sir.

BRIDGET

Well, ye'd do more good if ye left the birds alone, and rubbed it on the backs o' them that shoots ... They never hit anything.

DRIMFEARN

Ha! ... Irish humour again! Good! Very good! ... But seriously now, Bridget, since you do know something of Mr. Kelly, I'd be infinitely obliged if you'd do what you could to help me personally in this matter. I want very much to let Drimfearn ... May indeed be in serious financial straits if I don't ... And I'm sure MacNab will bear me out when I say that you'd also be doing Mr. Kelly a good turn in putting him wise to a really fine thing in the way of a shooting. As a matter of fact ... (*A* **MOTOR-HORN** *is heard.*) Hillo! (*He goes to the open main door.*) What! Back already?

(**MARSALI** *and* **DR. KENNEDY** *enter.*

DOCTOR

Yes, our patient very kindly put his very fast car and his partially damaged chauffeur at our service. A regular scorcher, that car! We came from MacVicar's in about forty-five seconds, I'll bet.

DRIMFEARN

All very well, but I don't want Marsali's life endangered by that sort of thing. (*Then, turning to* **BRIDGET**.) Well, my dear, I hope you'll have a nice half-holiday. (*He shepherds her to the main door.*) Get as much of the sun and the breeze as you can. A joy-ride even, if opportunity offers. Now there's someone in that car ... A chauffeur, isn't it? He may even be a relative, eh? ... And in any case, as I've said, what you want is a right good airing.

BRIDGET

And what about my life being endangered just like Nurse's?

DRIMFEARN

Oh, well, you would ask him to go carefully, of course ... (*A* **MOTOR-HORN** *sounds.*) Tuts! he's off ... Well, it can't be helped. But see and have a good time. Plenty of ozone, that's the thing ... (*Then turning to* **MARSALI**.) And now, Marsali, tell me all your adventures.

BRIDGET

The like o' that! Leaving me for the first that comes!

(*She goes out by the main door, but not before she has bestowed a grin on* **MARSALI**, *who is quite bewildered by* **DRIMFEARN**'s *affability to* **BRIDGET**.

DRIMFEARN

Well, Doctor, and how's the patient?

DOCTOR

Oh, sleeping sound at present. I had to give him some dope. Been badly knocked about, poor chap! ... Really time that gate of yours was down, sir. I know the road's through your policies. But it's the only road to the village, and I think you'll find the County Council have more to say in the matter than you think. They'll be down on your top, if you're not careful.

DRIMFEARN

(grimly). Let 'em try.

DOCTOR

In any case you should have notices put up half-a-mile on either side of it. And fancy the joiner closing it in the day-time, while he worked at it! You'd best take care! Look what's happened within a week. First, myself; then Mr. Borden; then this Mr. Kelly.

DRIMFEARN

(with a shout of joy). Kelly? ... Kelly? What did I tell you, MacNab! ... Where did you say he was, Doctor?

DOCTOR

At MacVicar's cottage. I was just clearing out when in he barged, dizzy as could be ... Had to put him to bed there, right away. The only safe thing with a man who's had a concussion. May have worse to follow, y'know.

DRIMFEARN

Yes, yes. But why not bring him along to my house?

DOCTOR

Because he's had enough moving around for one day. We really can't risk any more. He might start bleeding inside his skull, you see, and that would be almost fatal.

DRIMFEARN

But I don't see. Frankly, I don't. There are so many other things to consider, aren't there? A crofter's hut isn't the place for a man of his position, is it now? And we've plenty of spare rooms at Drimfearn ... Besides, who's going to nurse him?—nurse him night and day in a hole of a place like MacVicar's? And we've only one nurse here.

DOCTOR

Yes, your place would be much better. But for the first night at least he's got to stay where he is. And I'll sit up with him, myself to-night, and see how he does ... Ah! ... *(He clutches his jaw suddenly.)* Excuse me!

DRIMFEARN

Sorry that tooth's so bad. Hope it won't bother you to-night, Doctor ... Well, as soon's your patient can be moved, we'll be glad to relieve you, y'know. Yes, "The stranger that is within thy gates" ... and all that. "Take him in." Yes, yes ... "Take him in." (MARSALI *chuckles.*) Well, what are you sniggering at? Never knew such people as the young ones nowadays! ... All right, Doctor, I think I'll take time by the forelock, and see about a spare room for Mr. Kelly right away, in case you should want him removed to-day ... And, by the by, MacNab, you'd better run down to the village and see that his second cousin ... his chauffeur, I mean ... and his car, get housed somewhere, will you?

MACNAB

Very good, sir. (*He goes out.*)

DRIMFEARN

Well, I'll cut off now. Good-day to you both! You're a hard-worked pair ... Sorry about that tooth, Doctor.

DOCTOR

Then take down that gate, Drimfearn, and give us a rest from broken heads and broken teeth.

DRIMFEARN

All serene! We'll see what can be done. (*He goes out.*)

DOCTOR

And now, for Heaven's sake, Nurse, get me some carbolic jelly. I'd never have brought you away from old Kelly in such a hurry if it hadn't been that I can never find things here, (*He searches among the bottles on the shelved cupboard.*) Where is that carbolic?

MARSALI

(*at the bottles at once*). Here you are. I'll make you a fresh mixture.

DOCTOR

Gimme the stuff, and I'll do it .myself ... And some wool ... Is there a mirror in the kitchen?

MARSALI

Yes. (*She hands him two bottles, a small basin, and a tiny wisp of cotton wool. He is going to the kitchen, when* BRIDGET *enters by the main door.*)

BRIDGET

Afternoon, Nurse ... Afternoon, Doctor.

DOCTOR

(*halting*). Afternoon.

MARSALI
Afternoon, Bridget ... That tooth again. He's trying carbolic jelly.

BRIDGET
The poor man! He should have it out.
(**MARSALI** *pushes the* **DOCTOR** *into the kitchen.*

MARSALI
Don't heed her, Doctor. Get on with the good work ... *(Then, to* **BRIDGET**.*)* Thought you were going to spend your half-day in the hills.

BRIDGET
I was; but my friend didn't turn up.

MARSALI
How could he, with a toothache like that!

BRIDGET
Och, that one! No, no, this was another ... Not the Doctor.

MARSALI
Bridget! What a flirt!

BRIDGET
Och, there are other ways of passing the time besides that. *(The* **DOCTOR** *returns from the kitchen, looking much relieved.)* That gate'll kill ye yet, Doctor. Sure the jaw's not cracked?

DOCTOR
No, jaw's all right. And carbolic's wonderful stuff. Pain's gone from that tooth already.

BRIDGET
Well, that gate's just got to come down, or some fine night it'll murder ye. And where would we get another doctor so good ... or so handsome!

MARSALI
(melodramatically). Yes, where?

DOCTOR
Go on ... go on! Strike a man when he's down. *(He tests his jaw gingerly, as if expecting a recurrence of the pain.)*
(**MARSALI** *crosses to the shelves, and returns the bottles the* **DOCTOR** *hands to her.* **BRIDGET** *sits down at the bandage-roller, and gets to work there, singing "Madelon" again.*

DOCTOR
(turning in delight to **BRIDGET***).* "Madelon"! ... Your singing brings back old days.

BRIDGET

And would ye call that singing?

DOCTOR

I would ... The finest ... Come now, you know what I mean.

BRIDGET

I do ... too well! I can feel it in my bones.

MARSALI

(suddenly). Oh, I quite forgot. How stupid! *(She hastens to the main door.)*

BRIDGET

Here, my girl! Where are ye going?

MARSALI

Down to see cook about some cauliflowers.

(And she is off like a deer.)

DOCTOR

Cauliflowers? What has she got to do with cook?

BRIDGET

The Lord knows! But just wait till I get a hold o' her.

DOCTOR

(approaching). And what I say is: bless the cauliflowers.

BRIDGET

(alarmed). Stand away from me, now! I could never bear the smell of carbolic. And you're smelling like a chemist's shop!

DOCTOR

(retiring). Jolly good stuff for a bad tooth, all the same ... But do go on with "Madelon". It's a great song!

BRIDGET

It's all that. But it doesn't go well with the smell of carbolic.

DOCTOR

All right, I'll keep off ... But, I say, do you remember Christmas night, when the Serbians sang carols, and then scandalised Matron when they finished up with "Madelon"?

BRIDGET

(reminiscent of a sudden). Dear-a-dear! 'Twas a queer Christmas, that! *(The* DOCTOR *has again come near.)* Will ye stand off from me now! That carbolic's just terrible! Stand apart now, or it's out o' this I'll be running!

DOCTOR

(*again retiring*). Don't worry ... I'll be good ... Yes, a strange Christmas! ... Belgrade ... The city under snow, all white and still ... And the moonlight on the Danube!

BRIDGET

(*winding furiously at the roller*). None o' your moonlight, my boy! I've tould ye three times already! And it was "No" every time.

DOCTOR

But, Kate, it's different now, isn't it? This isn't Belgrade ... I never thought to see you again, but at last...

BRIDGET

Drop all that, for it's no use ... And stop dancing around like a daddy-long-legs, and go on out o' this ... That carbolic 'll suffocate me, so it will.

DOCTOR

Oh, you're heartless!

BRIDGET

Och, go on! ... I mean, don't go on! Stop all your foolishness and behave.

DOCTOR

My dear, I'll be foolish in this way to the end of time ... And I still have that marriage licence from the consul in Belgrade.

BRIDGET

And what's the use of a Belgrade licence in this country ... I mean, that just shows all the sense you have ... And I'm telling ye I don't care if ye had a hundred licences, and every one o' them international. (*In her confusion, she winds a bandage twisted.*)

DOCTOR

But Kate ...

BRIDGET

I'm not Kate any more. (*She puts a stretch of bandage before her face, and speaks from, behind it.*) I'm Bridget Gould, so I am ... Table-maid to ould Drimfearn, to earn my bread and butter ... And I'm poor ... And I'm no class ... So hould your tongue and have sense.

DOCTOR

Ah, but you'll always be Sister Catherine to me!

BRIDGET

And isn't that what I always said—that I'd be a sister to ye ... Keep away now! ... That carbolic's going to my head!

DOCTOR

But, Kate, dear ... Ah! ... *(He gives a little moan, and his hand goes involuntarily to his jaw once more.)*

BRIDGET

(concerned instantly, and rising from her task). Och, your poor tooth! ... And me making fun of it! ... Let me see it, darling.

DOCTOR

(gasping). Say that again! ... "Darling!"

BRIDGET

(grimly). Show me that tooth this minute.

DOCTOR

But, Kate ...

BRIDGET

Come on now! Show me that tooth, or it's out of this I go ... Here am I, that can't abide carbolic, shut up in this hole all alone with ye ... And this is how you'd go on? ... Let me see it this minute, ye bosthoon!

DOCTOR

Never mind the tooth, dear ... It's you I want ... not ... not ...

BRIDGET

Not the toothache ... I believe ye, my boy ... But I'll not hear another word from ye till I see that ruffian of a grinder ... Open your mouth, will ye? *(She puts her hands on his head, and—hypnotised by her touch—he opens his mouth)* ... I just thought as much. It's not a wife ye need: it's a dentist ... Where's the nearest ivory-snatcher in this wilderness?

DOCTOR

Torlochan, fifty miles from here ... But never mind the tooth, Kate. What I want to say is ...

BRIDGET

Say away as much as ye like, and want as much as ye like. It's myself that knows what you're in need of. And I know where you're going to get it ... And that's right here and now. *(She crosses to the cupboard and rummages in the instrument drawer.)*

DOCTOR

But, Kate, dear, you're surely not proposing ... proposing ...

BRIDGET

I am not, then. It's you that's proposing, ... And you've done nothing else ever since I set eyes on ye ... *(She rummages further)* Where, in the name of all the saints, does she keep them forceps! ... Aha! *(She discovers several dental forceps, and selects one)* We're in luck! Glory be! I've found the very one for you!

DOCTOR

But, Kate! ... Cocaine ...

BRIDGET

Cocaine, my granny! That tooth's as loose as a pea in a pod ... Come on, into the kitchen with ye, where we'll get hot water and things.

DOCTOR

But, really, Kate, it's better already.

(MARSALI *enters by the main door.*)

MARSALI

Whatever's wrong?

BRIDGET

He's come to his senses: he's having it out ... Get in there and put some wood under the kettle, and boil this gimlet ... You go, and I'll watch he doesn't escape. (MARSALI *goes into the kitchen.* BRIDGET *takes the* DOCTOR's *arm.*) Come on in, now.

DOCTOR

Oh, but look here, Kate!

BRIDGET

I'll give ye one more chance ... Are ye coming, or are ye not?

DOCTOR

(hesitating, but desperate). I'll come.

BRIDGET

Ye'd best, I'm thinking.

MARSALI

(coming out). It's boiling.

BRIDGET

(opening the kitchen door, and pushing the DOCTOR *in, closes the door firmly and turns to* MARSALI.*)*
Let it boil, then ... And now, Miss, what d'ye mean coming that cauliflower dodge over me, and leaving me all alone with a pursuer like that one?

MARSALI

A pursuer?

BRIDGET

Just that ... D'ye not see the hole ye've put me in? ... He's got a marriage licence in his pocket, and I can't frighten him off my doorstep ... And he'll let me pull his teeth or his toe-nails ... or ... or .. . anything ... And I'm lost entirely with a man like that, who'll take no denial ... And it's you and your cauliflowers and what-not that has done it on me ... But, wait you, my girl! I'll get even with you yet ... My turn's coming! *(She shakes her fist in* MARSALI's *smiling face.)* Come on, and hould his hands! *(She goes into the kitchen, but* MARSALI *is scared, and doesn't follow her.* BRIDGET *presently looks out of the kitchen door, saying:)* Will ye hurry now, and hould his little hand?

MARSALI

(unnerved). I ca ... ca ... can't!

BRIDGET

Well, then hould your ears! *(She enters the kitchen, and closes the door.)*
*(*MARSALI *holds her ears, but not a sound is heard. Presently* BRIDGET *rushes out, throwing up her arms in despair.)*

BRIDGET

Och, I've made a mess of it!

MARSALI

Never!

BRIDGET

The tongs slipped, and it's not out!

MARSALI

Oh, Bridget!

BRIDGET

The poor man! What he's suffering! ... And he'll never look at me again! My number's up, this time!

MARSALI

I'll see how he is! *(She dashes into the kitchen, and returns in a moment.)* Splendid, Bridget! It's out all right! And what a whopper!

BRIDGET

Och, let me hould his poor head!
(She runs into the kitchen, just as a MOTOR-HORN *sounds outside.* MARSALI *is about to follow her, but turns back at the sound of the horn and goes to the main door.* BORDEN *and* CRADDOCK *appear, supporting* KELLY *between them.* KELLY *is now minus his jacket and shoes; and his head is now properly bandaged.*

MARSALI

Oh, dear! whatever has happened? Has he escaped?

BORDEN

Do you know him, Nurse?

MARSALI

(*miserably*). Oh, yes, yes, yes! He is a case of Dr. Kennedy's. Bring him over here, please.

KELLY

Lay me down, boys ... I'm as tired's a dog that can't bark.
(*They take him to the couch, and* **MARSALI** *adjusts the cushions for him.*

MARSALI

I should never have left him ... He has had a concussion of the brain, you see! (*She is almost in tears.*)

BORDEN

So that's it! Couldn't think what was wrong with him. We found him wandering on the road, in front of our car ... Quite delirious ... Nearly ran him down.

MARSALI

Oh, dear! I should have stayed with him ... But he was so quiet ... And we thought Mrs. MacVicar could do all that was necessary till Doctor got back to him ... There, there, Mr. Kelly! ... Lie still now, and I'll get Doctor at once.
(*Marsali goes off into the kitchen ...* **BORDEN** *and* **CRADDOCK** *exchange significant nods at the mention of* **KELLY**'s *name.*

CRADDOCK

Suppose I run down the car to Drimfearn, and bring up that Irish girl at once. Then see what happens, eh?

BORDEN

Good man! Yes, that should settle it ... Off you go.
(**CRADDOCK** *makes for the door, but halts suddenly as* **BRIDGET** *and the* **DOCTOR**, *followed by* **MARSALI**, *enter from the kitchen.* **BRIDGET** *rushes at once to the figure on the couch.*

BRIDGET

Father!

KELLY

Kate!

CURTAIN

Scene two
SCENE. *"The Dispensary" at Drimfearn, an hour later.*
KELLY *is peacefully asleep on the couch. His clothes are on a chair beside it.*
BRIDGET *is leaning over him anxiously. Without awakening him, she takes his pulse; then moves to and fro between the bedside and the kitchen with various things—feeding-cups and the like.*
BORDEN *comes quietly to the doorway and enters.*

BORDEN
Glad he's asleep at last. Better, isn't he?

BRIDGET
And thanks to you, Mr. Borden.

BORDEN
Mister Borden? Come, come! It was "Uncle", last time.

BRIDGET
And so it was, now! And me forgetting!

BORDEN
Uncle, yes. But I don't like the title. Something futile about it, isn't there?

BRIDGET
Och, you have the big words, Mr. Borden! And me not understanding them at all.

BORDEN
Our talking won't disturb him, I hope?

BRIDGET
Not one bit. He's too sound with all the dope he's had, poor man!

BORDEN
Then, Miss Kelly, I may as well be brief; I'm a plain man, and mean what I say.

BRIDGET
And what's this now! Have I been doing something that's wrong?

BORDEN
On the contrary, my dear, you have been doing the happiest thing imaginable. You've softened a rather hard heart ... Quite simply, it comes to this. I'm deeply in love with you, and I've the great honour of asking you to become my wife.

BRIDGET
And you do it very nicely too. No beating about the bush, either ... But it's hardly decent in an uncle, is it?

BORDEN

You rogue! *(He attempts to kiss her. But just then the* **DOCTOR** *appears in the doorway.* **BORDEN** *is instantly in confusion, and says hastily:)* Well, of course, yes, you have your work to do ... Busy people ... Mustn't keep you back ... Ah ... Good-day, good-day! *(He goes out hurriedly.)*

DOCTOR

What did the fellow want here?

BRIDGET

Och, what does anybody want here?

DOCTOR

And what's that?

BRIDGET

Me, of course.

DOCTOR

Oh, why didn't I get in a kick before he left! *(He goes to the door, but she intercepts him.)*

BRIDGET

Ye'll not now. Ye'll get hurt, so ye will ... There's been enough scrapping here for one day ... How's the poor jaw?

DOCTOR

Splendid, thanks to you.

BRIDGET

Then ye'd best take a good look at father. He's not well at all.

DOCTOR

(taking **KELLY***'s pulse).* Very good ... He's all right.

BRIDGET

And ye think he'll get well?

DOCTOR

I do. And you ought to know enough, with all your training, that he's not too bad.

BRIDGET

Yes, but nursing Serbians is one thing; and your own father's another, isn't it?

DOCTOR

Of course. I'm sorry ... You see, there's no laceration, only a slight concussion ... He'll be fit's a fiddle in a few weeks' time if we can keep him quiet.

BRIDGET

Him that was never quiet all his life. There never was a more unquiet man from the centre all round to the sea ... You're sure he'll come all right?

DOCTOR

I'm sure.

BRIDGET

Well then, that's good ... And now you and me's got to have a word of explanation.

DOCTOR

But I want none, dear. I only want you not to worry.

BRIDGET

I'll worry as much as I like. And you keep still ... And listen to me ... That's my father over there.

DOCTOR

I know, my dear, I know.

BRIDGET

Ye don't know. All ye know is that I'm telling ye.

DOCTOR

All right.

BRIDGET

He's John P. Gould-Kelly of the Blue Cross Brandy Syndicate ... And, through no fault o' mine, he's a very rich man.

DOCTOR

Yes, yes, but don't excite yourself, Kate.

BRIDGET

I couldn't help his getting rich. And I misdoubt if he could help himself, the way the money just rolled in on him. All the same, there was a time when he was as decent a wee licensed grocer as ever ye met ... And look at him now ... And look at me!

DOCTOR

(*all eyes*). I'm looking at you, dear.

BRIDGET

Och, will ye stop your blatheration and listen!

DOCTOR

Sorry.

BRIDGET

It all came out o' this Prohibition business when he left America, and came home to trade in England. And how it all happened I don't know;

but he got in among the Restrictions of the Drink Traffic lot here, and now he seems to know too much ... And everyone else seems to stop in the way o' making money, but money just keeps rushing down on him, whatever he does ... And now, look at him ... A man that can't walk a mile, unless he has a big motor-car to do it for him ... And he wanted ...

DOCTOR

But all this money surely can't make any difference to you and me, my dear.

BRIDGET

Will ye whisht, and let me get in a word edgewise? And he wanted a big house in town ... And he got it ... And I couldn't run it ... And then he took a big country-house, away over in Perthshire ... And I couldn't run it either ... And he said to me: "You get out among the nabbery, and learn how they do it." ... And I knew it was no use me trying their Society capers; so I hired out as a slavey ... And I tried the town, but it was no good ... And then I came on here. And it's no good neither.

DOCTOR

All that kow-towing! That's not like my Kate.

BRIDGET

No, but it's like my father.

DOCTOR

Nonsense!

BRIDGET

And don't I know! He's my father, not yours.

DOCTOR

Not as yet.

BRIDGET

Well! Of all the brazen ones I ever met! ... Will ye keep quiet now, and let me tell it my own way!

DOCTOR

All right. Carry on.

BRIDGET

And here I am; and I've seen enough of high life to turn a regiment o' monkeys sick ... What use is it for me to know how ye eat celery with your fingers, and what drink goes with this course, and what drink with that? ... I'm only plain Kate Kelly at the end of all ... And my father half-killed into the bargain.

DOCTOR

What a time you've had ... Terrible!

BRIDGET

Terrible, says he! Terrible? ... Now don't you be misunderstanding ... Why, I've just had the time o' my life ... Don't ye know there are two kinds o' gentry—a right and a wrong, it seems ... And I've never struck the right kind yet. Most of my time's been spent with the wrong ones, God help them!

DOCTOR

But how could you have had the time of your life with the wrong ones?

BRIDGET

Och, just watching them fancying they were somebody that counted. Dear-a-dear! I just stayed on for the fun of it all ... Play-acting's not in it with that crowd, let me tell ye.

DOCTOR

Well, I'm glad you chose this place for watching the play.

BRIDGET

And who tould ye I chose it? I didn't ever say one word about choosing, so I didn't ... The conceit of ye! You're surely not thinking that your being here had anything to do with my being here.

DOCTOR

I never suggested anything of the kind.

BRIDGET

Did ye not, now? ... Well, ye'd maybe have had some little wee reason in thinking that same, after all ... For I knew the Highlands was a wild country, and not so handy for some things as the town. And knowing a little about nursing, my mind went out to hospitals and the like. And I knew they weren't exactly in abundance hereabouts; and I thought what would I do if I were ill at any time ... I'm not tiring ye, am I?

DOCTOR

Not in the least. Just my own feelings when I first thought of coming here.

BRIDGET

And at long last I said to myself, "Well, if there's a good doctor handy, what need to bother about hospitals?" ... And then I remembered you were about these parts, and I just said: "If I go anywhere in them wild Highlands, that's the place to go." ... But ye wouldn't call that choosing, would ye? *(She smiles broadly.)*

DOCTOR
(advancing on her joyously). You rascal!

BRIDGET
(avoiding him). It's what ye'd call a coincidence, isn't it?

DOCTOR
Call it what you like, it's brought us together again.

BRIDGET
"Brought us together again!" I like that!

DOCTOR
So do I.

BRIDGET
You'd best be careful … You're going too fast and too far.

DOCTOR
(thoroughly roused). I'll go farther still. *(He attempts to kiss her, but only succeeds in getting an arm around her waist.)*

BRIDGET
Keep off now!
(A chair is knocked over, and the sound of its fall arouses **OLD KELLY**, *who instantly sits up—a quaint figure.*

KELLY
Leave go of that girl, young man!

BRIDGET
It's the Doctor, father.

KELLY
I know it's the Doctor. But I didn't hire him to attend the whole family. It's me he's treating … not you.

BRIDGET
(coming over to him). Lie down, father … You're better, I can see. And the Doctor says so … Lie down at once, now, when your nurse tells ye… I'll have no mercy on ye, even if you're my own father, when it's for your own good.
*(***KELLY*** subsides meekly, murmuring protests, and after a short interval apparently dozes off. The* **DOCTOR** *and* **BRIDGET** *retire from his side and talk in low tones.*

DOCTOR
I think, you know, you're a bit hard on him.

BRIDGET

I'm none too hard ... I'm his daughter as well as his nurse. And it's as a daughter I was speaking ... And what business is it of yours, anyway? Am I to be lectured ...

DOCTOR

Don't raise your voice, please. I'm not lecturing you. I'm only suggesting, for your own good....

BRIDGET

You've no right with me at all.

DOCTOR

I've right of the man you care for most in all the world.

BRIDGET

But I'm not caring for ye.

DOCTOR

That's not true.

BRIDGET

When did I ever say I cared for ye?

DOCTOR

Never. But I know it.

BRIDGET

But how can ye, if ... if ... *(Tears in her eyes now.)* Och, ye'll break my heart, so ye will!

DOCTOR

(taking her in his arms, but with a watchful glance on **KELLY***).* My dear!

BRIDGET

(nestling to him). Let me go now, or I'll ...

DOCTOR

But, Kate ...

BRIDGET

Och, but you're the determined man! ... There, then! *(She returns his kiss.)* Let me go now.

DOCTOR

Call me Jim, first.

BRIDGET

I'll not. I'll scream the place down if you'll not behave.

DOCTOR

You'll waken your father if you do ... Say "Jim."

BRIDGET

Take care! There's somebody coming.

DOCTOR

Let them come. Say "Jim".

BRIDGET

Indeed, and I'll not.

DOCTOR

Say "Jim."

BRIDGET

I tell ye there's somebody outside!

DOCTOR

All right. But say "Jim."

BRIDGET

Jim!

DOCTOR

Thanks! (*He kisses her swiftly, and they both turn to the medicine-cupboard with every appearance of busy people, as* DRIMFEARN *enters by the main door.*)

DRIMFEARN

(*catching sight of* KELLY). Ah! So it's here he is! ... Heard he'd got out, but didn't know you'd collared him ... Well, Doctor, a day's march nearer home, so to speak, eh? ... Mean to say, quite close to Drimfearn House now ... only half-a-mile ... So what's to hinder us having him up there right away? We've got a suite of rooms, just the thing ... Quite safe at our place ... Couldn't escape from there, y'know ... By gum! I'd sit up with him myself.

(KELLY *hoists himself up and listens, unperceived by the others.*

BRIDGET

'Deed, and he'll not move out o' this till he's well enough to travel to town.

DRIMFEARN

(*irritably*). My good woman, what business is this of yours?

KELLY

(*excitedly*). Sir! Would ye dare call my daughter a woman!

DRIMFEARN

Your daughter? Good heavens!

KELLY

What else?

DRIMFEARN

My dear Miss Kelly! ... I'm so sorry.

BRIDGET

Och, go on with you. *(She turns her back on him, and tucks the rugs round her father, getting him to lie down again.)*

DRIMFEARN

Of course, I'd no idea ... well ... that we'd been entertaining angels unawares.

BRIDGET

Angels! ... Ghosts are more in your line, I'm thinking ... You, and your ould gate!

DRIMFEARN

I'm really very sorry, Miss Kelly, about that gate. And it's coming down at once, I assure you. Also, I'm anxious to make what amends I can to you all. So, if Mr. Kelly would care to accept any small hospitality that I can offer him at Drimfearn...

KELLY

Devil a bit! What would ail me not to get better after a day or two more of this place?

BRIDGET

There now, there now! Go to sleep.
   *(**MARSALI** and **MURRAY** appear at the main door; but only **MARSALI** enters, **MURRAY** saunters off.*

MARSALI

And how is he now, Bridget? *(She comes up to the couch, and casts a professional eye on **KELLY**.)*

BRIDGET

Och, he'd soon be well, if he hadn't too many kind enquirers. *(She turns a basilisk eye on **DRIMFEARN**.)*

DRIMFEARN

Well, I only called to suggest that Drimfearn might offer better nursing facilities than this place. That's so, isn't it, Marsali?

MARSALI

That's good of you. Yes, I think that would be fine. What does the Doctor say?

DOCTOR

Well, er ... er ...

BRIDGET

The Doctor's saying nothing. But I'm saying my father's staying here for a bit till he's some better. And you're going to do some of the nursing as well as me, aren't ye?

MARSALI

Of course, my dear.

BRIDGET

Well then, come on and do it. I'm going out for a turn.

MARSALI

Oh, do you mind if I see a patient in the village, first of all? I've just remembered I'm due there now.

BRIDGET

(with a glance outside at MURRAY, *pacing to and fro).* Drimfearn will be going soon, and ye can bring the patient in here. I've just remembered I've to see the Doctor about some poaching down at the Big Pool. *(She crosses to the fishing-rods and examines them.)*

DOCTOR

Poaching? At the Big Pool? Under Borden's very nose?

BRIDGET

Och, it's quite safe. Uncle Borden would never dream of shooting his own niece, would he? Come on, now. *(She hands him a rod.)* We'll get the flies from MacNab.

DOCTOR

But why not some of Drimfearn's beats? You don't mind, sir, do you?

DRIMFEARN

Not in the, least. Indeed honoured, Miss Kelly. *(He bows.)*

DOCTOR

There, you see!

BRIDGET

Och, what a man! ... Drimfearn's beat or Borden's beat, what does it matter! ... Come away with you, and bring that rod. *(At last her meaning dawns on his slow mind, and he shyly accompanies her to the door. As* BRIDGET *goes out with him, she turns to* MARSALI *and says:)* Cauliflowers! ... Didn't I tell ye my turn would come?

DRIMFEARN

Hum! Well, I'm not an expert in modern slang, but I strongly suspect those two young folk are about to 'click.' Is that the word?

MARSALI

That's the word, Drimfearn.

DRIMFEARN

A true word in this case?

MARSALI

Hope so.

DRIMFEARN

So do I. Good chap. Extraordinary girl.

MARSALI

I think she's a brick.

DRIMFEARN

And what a flow of language!

MARSALI

Yes, takes after her father.

KELLY

(*sitting up suddenly*). D'ye think I don't hear ye?

MARSALI

Sorry. Really didn't mean anything, Mr. Kelly. Just fun. Thought you were asleep.

KELLY

I had to pretend, or she'd have talked my head off ... So this is Mr. Drimfearn?

MARSALI

It's just Drimfearn we say in the Highlands. He is Campbell of Drimfearn, you understand?

KELLY

Well, well! Drimfearn let it be ... I wonder now, Drimfearn, if ye know what the man from Castlecary said to the man from Tipperary?

DRIMFEARN

Something about a drink, I believe. But I'm afraid you can't have any. You must wait till you're well again.

KELLY

Och, yes, when the sky falls we'll all catch larks.

MARSALI

You certainly can't have any liquor.

KELLY

Look at that now ... I that have spent my life drinking and dealing can have neither, eh? ... But maybe Drimfearn could have a drink, and I could look on at him having it ... And maybe him and me could have a wee deal ... What's your line, my boy?

DRIMFEARN

I'm afraid I don't understand, Mr. Kelly. *(But he draws forward a chair, and settles down as if to business.)*

KELLY

I'm asking what ye deal in? ... I deal in drink. What's the goods with you?

MARSALI

I really think you'd better lie down, Mr. Kelly. You mustn't put a strain on your mind, you know.

KELLY

The only strain here, young woman, is that I'm talking of drink, and tasting none.

MARSALI

Drimfearn, can't you make him see reason?

DRIMFEARN

Oh, he'll be all right. He'll worry if we don't talk; and that might do more harm than the talking.

KELLY

And ye never said a truer word, Drimfearn. I'd worry none at all if I'd a wee glass or two of something I know the name of too well.

MARSALI

All right. It's your pigeon, Drimfearn. Only I wonder what the Doctor will say!

KELLY

You leave the Doctor to Drimfearn and me, and we'll show him sense ... Come on, sir, what's your line, I was asking?

DRIMFEARN

Oh, deer-forests and grouse-moors and so on.

KELLY

And what, now, do ye consider a fair profit in your line o' business?

DRIMFEARN

Oh, I dunno. What I can get is usually what it amounts to.

KELLY

Leave it there! *(He shakes hands effusively.)* A shilling for a shilling! My own motto! ... And couldn't we do a deal now? ... I like ye, man! ... I like ye!

DRIMFEARN

Oh, you're hardly fit for business yet, Mr. Kelly, I fear ... A talk? Yes ... But business? No, no.

KELLY

It's equal to me whether I talk of business or anything else. But believe you me, I'm so used to business I find it easier talk than any other ... Have ye anything against that argument, Nurse?

MARSALI

I wash my hands of the whole affair. But both of you will hear some real good talk when I report to Doctor.

KELLY

Don't ye believe her, Drimfearn. The Doctor's a wise man ... And it's me that's paying him. *(He grins)* Come on now ... I'll deal in whisky; and you can deal in deer.

MARSALI

I'm warning you, Drimfearn!

KELLY

Come on! How much the gross for your deer?

DRIMFEARN

Oh, we don't go by the gross ... not so many as all that, y'know ... We only allow our tenants to shoot twenty stags in a season.

KELLY

And what's the price?

DRIMFEARN

Five hundred for three months and twenty stags.

KELLY

Five hundred for twenty beasts! ... The Lord forgive ye!

DRIMFEARN

Of course, you have the grouse as well ... But if you'd prefer wild goat instead of the deer, we'll allow you fifty wild goat at the same price.

MARSALI

Really, Drimfearn, the man's not well enough for all this bargaining.

KELLY

Yerra, girl! Will ye stand aside! *(Then, to* **DRIMFEARN**.*)* Ye were saying fifty wild goat?

DRIMFEARN

Yes.

KELLY

Well then, what about a half-season at the same?

DRIMFEARN

As you please.

KELLY

When does that begin?

DRIMFEARN

Fifteenth September. A little over a fortnight from now.

KELLY

Och, I'll surely be well enough in a fortnight ... Twenty-five wild goat. When do I pay?

DRIMFEARN

About the week of entry.

KELLY

Twenty-five. Make it thirty, and I'll give ye cash.

DRIMFEARN

(with alacrity). Certainly. *(He pulls out a pocket-book and extracts two forms.)* I just happen to have two provisional forms here. *(He fills in the papers hurriedly with his fountain pen.)*

KELLY

Gimme over that coat, girl.

(**MARSALI** *hands him over a coat from the chair, and he takes a cheque-book from it.*)

DRIMFEARN

(reading from his form). Half-season ... Fifteenth September to October the tenth ... Thirty wild goat ... Two hundred and fifty pounds ... That includes, of course, occupation of Drimfearn House, stalkers' wages, occupiers' rates and taxes, and so on ... Usual terms ... You sign both forms, Mr. Kelly ... Here ... And I sign ditto.

(**KELLY** *signs, and so does* **DRIMFEARN**, *who hands one form to* **KELLY** *and pockets the other.*)

KELLY

(*writing his cheque*). That's a real deal now! And it's done me more good than a power o' medicine, so it has ... But I caught ye napping on the cash down, eh? ... Allow Kelly! (*He hands over the cheque.*) But I did ye on the ready money, didn't I?

DRIMFEARN

I'm afraid you did, Mr. Kelly. (*He pockets his cheque, while* **KELLY** *reads his form carefully, and lays it down on the heap of clothes on the chair.*)

KELLY

And where now is that daughter o' mine, till; I tell her the good news?

DRIMFEARN

Ah! A fine girl, sir ... My wife and I have enjoyed her stay at Drimfearn so much! ... At first we were a bit puzzled finding a girl like her engaged in humble tasks ... But, there, it's the way of the young people nowadays! ... They're all for experience ... Haven't our early Victorian outlook on life ... staidness, and keeping one's station in life and all that, eh? ... Modern ... modern! ... And God knows where it will end! ... Quaint, these young people ... very quaint! ... And, damn it all, so very old-fashioned after all, although they don't know it ... But, where was I ... Oh, yes, my wife and I, yes! ... Yes, we did enjoy Miss Kelly's little play-acting ... The life and soul of the place, sir! ... Ab ... so ... lute ... ly!

KELLY

Och, she's not bad at all, at all, even if her tongue's a bit sharp ... A fine girl is Kate.

DRIMFEARN

Kate? ... Yes, yes, but of course we called her Bridget.

KELLY

Och, Bridget or Kate, it's all one. Catherine Bridget Gould-Kelly ... with a hyphen nowadays ... that's her full name. And I'll see that she lives up to it ... And when she and her father get among them nannie-goats, we'll give them the time of their lives.

DRIMFEARN

Well, I trust you will get among them, Mr. Kelly. They are very agile animals, you know.

KELLY

Agile? What's that?

DRIMFEARN

Oh, good at running and jumping.

KELLY
Och, but haven't I a Rolls-Royce?
(MURRAY *knocks and comes in, with a questioning eye on* MARSALI.

MURRAY
Hillo, Marsali! Didn't know you were on duty?

MARSALI
Sorry to have kept you waiting, Murray, but I just had to be on duty all of a sudden.

MURRAY
(*approaching* KELLY's *couch*). Thought I'd look in to ask for you, sir.

DRIMFEARN
This is my boy, Mr. Kelly.

KELLY
(*shaking hands*). Pleased to meet ye ... I'm doing bravely ... I'm just after having a real deal with your father.

MURRAY
Indeed? (*He glances interrogatively at* MARSALI.)

MARSALI
Wild goat ... He's at it again, after all his promises.

MURRAY
Father! At the old game?

MARSALI
Yes, but there's another hand to play, as you know.

MURRAY
Oh, Bridget, of course. Isn't she here?

DRIMFEARN
Miss Kelly? I confess I don't understand all these asides, Marsali?

MARSALI
Oh, Murray! won't it be a scene, when she hears her father has a wild-goat shooting this season!

MURRAY
The devil he has? ... Father!

DRIMFEARN
Well, only a half-season, as a matter of fact.

MARSALI
A half-season will make no difference to Bridget, I'm afraid! ... Murray! When Greek meets Greek!

MURRAY
When dodger meets dodger, father! ... I knew this was bound to come!

MARSALI
You didn't until I told you, Murray. It's my show!

MURRAY
So it is ... I remember ... When Gael meets Gael... Bridget against the world!

MARSALI
Irish against Scottish! ... Hooray!

MURRAY
Then comes the tug of war! ... Oh, poor father!

KELLY
Whatever is all the noise about? What's Bridget to do with the deal, anyway?

DRIMFEARN
(concerned). Yes, what? ... We need not trouble Miss Kelly with our ... ah ... business transactions, surely?

MURRAY
He scents the battle from afar!

MARSALI
The Laird against Bridget! Keep the ring!

MURRAY
Bridget will wash out that deal, father, believe me!

KELLY
Och, the deal, is it? ... No, no, Bridget's as fond of a deal as her father any day ... She'll give no trouble at all, once she knows how I bested Drimfearn. 'Twas a real bargain, so it was.

DRIMFEARN
(eagerly). A bargain! Yes, that's it ... Stick to that, Kelly, and I'm sure Bridget will see things in their true perspective ... And in any case Marsali can testify that the proposal came from Mr. Kelly.

MARSALI
Testify! Oh!

KELLY
Testify? Of course! I'll testify myself! *(He is now as nervous as* DRIMFEARN.*)* And Drimfearn can testify that I got the better of him ... Be sure ye say that, Drimfearn, or she'll have the ears off me!

DRIMFEARN

(now righteously indignant). Certainly! We have nothing to conceal, have we? Indeed, just to show my confidence in Mr. Kelly, I'm prepared to do another deal with him, here and now.

MARSALI

Yes, just on the principle of "In for a penny, in for a pound." Eh, Murray?

MURRAY

And, in haste, before Bridget arrives! Oh, father, you're the limit!

MARSALI

And he'll never give it up!

DRIMFEARN

(noting KELLY's *bewilderment, and explaining the situation to him).* They're referring to the deal, Mr. Kelly. They always think my terms are too generous.

KELLY

Generous? They don't know ye, my boy.
(BRIDGET's *voice is heard outside, and presently she comes in, followed by the* DOCTOR ... *But they have forgotten their fishing-rods.*

BRIDGET

(to the DOCTOR*).* Come on in, and talk to him yourself. He's waking again, I see; and entertaining visitors, no less. *(She goes up to* KELLY*.)* Lie down, father.

KELLY

D'ye hear her? A tongue that would clip a hedge.

BRIDGET

Quiet now. The Doctor wants a look at ye.
(KELLY *cringes at once, as the* DOCTOR *comes forward and takes his pulse.*

DOCTOR

Eighty-four. Much better ... much better.

DRIMFEARN

Good! Very good! Don't you think, Miss Kelly, he looks well enough to move into ... ah ... more suitable ... ah ... conditions for nursing? He's much improved within the last hour, y'know.

BRIDGET

(disregarding the hint, and speaking in a toneless voice). MacNab's asking for ye outside.

DRIMFEARN

Oh?

BRIDGET

Something about your prize bull.

DRIMFEARN

What's up?

BRIDGET

It's had an argument with your new gate. And there's not much left of either.

DRIMFEARN

My God! *(He goes out hurriedly.)*

BRIDGET

(turning to MARSALI). I'll relieve you now, my dear. *(Then, glancing at MURRAY.)* So I needn't keep ye from your patient any longer.

MARSALI

(tossing her head as she moves to the door, followed by a rather sheepish MURRAY). Oh, thanks awfully. But I wonder what happened to the fishing-rods!

(They make moues at one another, then smile. And MARSALI shakes a playful fist at BRIDGET; then goes out with MURRAY.

MURRAY

(as he goes). Yes, what about those fishing-rods, Doctor?

DOCTOR

(now rather nervous, as he takes KELLY's pulse once more). Yes, really a bit better ... Yes, I think so ... But I fancy it's a bit jumpy, this pulse, all the same ... Perhaps we'd best leave it till later ... He's still too excitable, y'know.

BRIDGET

(taking the pulse herself). Let me see it ... There's not much wrong there ... Go on ... Tell him.

DOCTOR

Oh, but I don't think there's so much hurry as all that.

BRIDGET

Tell him at once now, and have done. *(She walks off to the bandage roller, and plays about with it, leaving the DOCTOR still pawing nervously with KELLY's wrist.)*

DOCTOR

(clearing his throat). Mr. Kelly ... I ... I've something to say to you.

KELLY

(sitting up suddenly). And what now?

DOCTOR

Please lie down, sir, at once! (KELLY *subsides apprehensively.*) I ... ah ... as I said ... have something to say ... Your daughter is really ... really an old friend of mine, although you may not be aware of it ... We got to know each other about two years ago out in Belgrade at a hospital there... And ... and ... until a week ago I had not the pleasure of renewing that acquaintance, so full of happy memories. But then, under circumstances which were—to say the least—rather unusual ...

KELLY

(sitting up once more). By the hokey! Ye'd talk the teeth out of a saw ... Is this politics or what?

DOCTOR

(doggedly). Under circumstances which—to say the least —

BRIDGET

(crossing to them). Och, you're making such a palaver I can't hear my own ears ... It's this, father ... This man has a marriage licence in his pocket.

KELLY

Och, and is that where ye are? *(Beckoning* BRIDGET *closer.)* Come over ... And has he money?

BRIDGET

He has not then. But he has as much as yourself had ten years ago, which wasn't great ... And he's as good a man as you were then, and a deal better than ye are now ... You and your ould money!

KELLY

(subsiding once more). That settles it ... Ye can have her, young man ... And God help ye!

DOCTOR

We thought of running over to Belgrade for the marriage, Mr. Kelly. You see, the licence is a consular one, and can only be made use of in Belgrade. And we'd save time and worry.

KELLY

Well, ye'd save time anyway.

DOCTOR

You ... you ... you don't mind then?

KELLY

I do not. *(He speaks with conviction.)* I've no mind left, with the pair of ye! ... But ye'll hurry back and help me shoot some nannie-goats.

BRIDGET

Which?

KELLY

Nannie-goats.

DOCTOR

And what's that?

KELLY

(lifting the provisional agreement from his heap of clothes). Wild goat. I've taken a shooting from ould Drimfearn ... Thirty wild goat ... Reduction for cash.

BRIDGET

Wild goat! *(She takes the agreement and glances over it; then throws it down.)* And ye've paid him, ye poor innocent! ... Man, man! ye'll never get near one of them ... Ye know as much about sport as a cow knows about a holiday!

KELLY

Whatever are ye saying! 'Twas a grand deal.

BRIDGET

Grand deal! I'll be bound ye've paid for every hair on the tails of them.

DOCTOR

So Drimfearn's beat you after all, Kate!

BRIDGET

Has he that, now! I'll show him where the beating comes in.

DRIMFEARN

(entering hurriedly). The gate's in bits and pieces. But the bull's all right, thank God!

KELLY

(his hand to his head). But his head will be mortal sore, poor thing!

DRIMFEARN

Has Borden been here?

DOCTOR

Borden! Good Lord, no!

DRIMFEARN

MacNab says he's looking for me, and in a devil of a rage.

DOCTOR

What about?

DRIMFEARN

Well, it seems the bull went off very angry, after his ... ah ... his encounter with the gate. And Borden came across him in the road, and tried to shoo him off. Whereas the bull shoo-ed Borden off ... Gave him a good cross-country chase, in fact ... Gad! I wish I'd seen that ... And now he's been telling MacNab the bull must be shot, and swears he'll give me a bit of his mind.

BRIDGET

(*picking up the agreement and handing it to* DRIMFEARN). Well, there's more than Borden want to give ye a bit o' their mind.

DRIMFEARN

(*affecting nonchalance*). Ah, the agreement! (*He glances at it carelessly, and lays it down.*) Well, Miss Kelly, fancy you being shooting-tenant here, after all your escapades below-stairs!

BRIDGET

Yes, just fancy! Not to speak of my father's escapades at your famous ould gate!

DRIMFEARN

Aha! Humour again! ... Good! ... Quite good!

BRIDGET

What's good? ... My father's head?

DRIMFEARN

Of course, I feel dreadfully sore about all that, y'know.

BRIDGET

Where are ye sore?

DOCTOR

Drop it, Kate! This won't do at all!

BRIDGET

How do ye know it won't do? ... I don't see anybody sore except father.

KELLY

Yerra, girl! Will ye wheesht! ... I'm making no complaints. And I'm not so bad as the Doctor would make out.

BRIDGET

Lie ye down, now, and leave this to me ... (*Then, to* DRIMFEARN.) Ye say you're dreadfully sore ... Are ye sore in the place where ye keep your money?

DRIMFEARN

I'm afraid I don't quite follow.

BRIDGET

I'm asking, what damages are ye going to pay?

DRIMFEARN

Really, Miss Kelly ...

KELLY

Will ye leave the man alone! I'm putting no price on my head.

BRIDGET

No, but I'm doing it for ye. And my price is the price of thirty wild goat, reduction for cash. *(To* DRIMFEARN.*)* Hand me over that cheque.

KELLY

You take that cheque, my girl, and I'll give him another.

BRIDGET

Ye would, would ye?

KELLY

I would, surely ... Kate, can't ye see I'll not be at ease till I'm well again and having a bit o' sport, blazing away at them wild nannie-goats?

BRIDGET

Och, have done with your blarney!

KELLY

But I'm serious, girl.

BRIDGET

(suddenly). All right then. And you'll be wanting me to give ye a hand?

KELLY

Sure!

DRIMFEARN

The very thing, Miss Kelly! You'll look well in sporting kit ... No more bib and tucker, eh? Changed days ... changed days!

BRIDGET

Yes, it will be changed days when my husband and myself get back from Belgrade with an aeroplane and a machine-gun ... And Heaven help your ould wild goat then!

DRIMFEARN

Aeroplane! ... Machine-gun! For my wild goat?

BRIDGET

Oh, we won't kill more than the thirty allowed. But I think we could get them all in one day.

KELLY

(*to* DRIMFEARN). Never heed her. Nothing but talk, that. Only talk.

BRIDGET

We'll see if it's only talk ... Yes, Drim, ye can beat Borden, and ye can beat Kelly, but ye can't beat me! (*Then, to the* DOCTOR.) Come on out and show me how far a machine-gun can shoot.

DOCTOR

Steady, Kate! You're carrying this rather strong, aren't you?

BRIDGET

I'm not now. I know what I'm doing. And you keep out of it.

DOCTOR

Very well, I'll keep out. And you go in and scalp them good, and get it over ... But hurry now, for we've still to gather up those fishing-rods.

BRIDGET

(*more mercurial than ever, as she passes from wrath to smiles*). So we have, boy ... But, och, what a fine getaway ye've spoiled for us both!

DOCTOR

And don't you see that Drimfearn's taking you seriously. Go on. Tell him it's all bluff. He doesn't understand you.

BRIDGET

(*smiling*). And do you?

DOCTOR

Better than anyone in all the world. Go on now. Tell him.

BRIDGET

(*to* DRIMFEARN). And did ye think I was really in earnest! ... Och, I'm as tame as a tame doctor ... and that's saying a lot ... And if ye'll kindly be getting some rooms ready in Drimfearn, my father and I will be moving in to-night.

DRIMFEARN

That's very handsome of you, Miss Kelly ... Of course, I knew you were just humbugging me in that charming Irish way of which you have the sole secret in these desert solitudes ... Ah, if I were only young again! (*He sighs.*)

BRIDGET

Tach! ye ould dodger! ... Not that I'm blaming ye ... I'm a bit of a dodger myself.

DRIMFEARN

Do you know, I was beginning to suspect ... just beginning, you know ... just beginning!

(**BRIDGET** *gives him a handshake, then goes over and kisses her father.*

KELLY

D'ye know what that means, Drimfearn?

DRIMFEARN

I should think ... well, it looks as if you'd be writing a rather large cheque before long, Mr. Kelly.

BRIDGET

Ye've said it ... Father, the Doctor and I were talking over things, when we were down at the Big Pool...

KELLY

How much do you want?

BRIDGET

That depends on the size of the hospital.

KELLY

Which hospital?

BRIDGET

The one we want to build out in Belgrade or Ragusa or somewhere else out East.

KELLY

And ye're for leaving me?

DOCTOR

Not in the least, if you'll come too.

BRIDGET

It's for children, of course, but we'd put in an extra ward for head cases of all ages, if ye liked.

KELLY

Godsake! And aren't ye to have a home and childer of your own?

BRIDGET

I should hope so. A rare big house, and the finest of childer. Will ye come?

KELLY

I'll have a look at ye anyway. How much will ye want?

BRIDGET

As much as ye can spare.

KELLY

Would five figures do ye, Doctor?

DOCTOR

For a beginning? ... Yes.

KELLY

The Lord save us!

BRIDGET

And five for me, father. Nice curly ones, with six or a nine for the first of them, please.

KELLY

Do ye hear her now? All that money going foreign, too. Why, in the name o' the saints, can't ye be doing the thing in your own country, girl?

BRIDGET

Because they've more need out there. All those places out East are packed with brains, but they've little or no money. Whereas we've brains *and* money ... or hope to have money, if you're as good as ye look.

KELLY

Give us another kiss, and I'll think it over. A good one, now.
(**BRIDGET** *obliges gracefully, and just then* **BORDEN** *rushes in, followed by* **MARSALI** *and* **MURRAY**.

MURRAY

Don't heed him, father! It was really his own fault. He shouldn't have scared the poor beast.

BORDEN

Mind your own business, sir. I'd never have said a word to you, if I'd known you meant to follow me here ... Look here, Drimfearn, that bull of yours will have to be shot!
(**BRIDGET**, *the* **DOCTOR** *and* **DRIMFEARN** *are in the centre of the group, and the odd figures of* **KELLY** *and* **BORDEN**, *each with his head swathed in bandages, on either flank.* **MARSALI** *and* **MURRAY** *are a little in the rear.*

BRIDGET

Och, here's father on the one hand, and uncle on the other! ... J'ever see such a family for broken heads!

DOCTOR

(*his arm around her, and drawing her close*). Hush, dear!

BORDEN

(*in mingled amazement and dismay at sight of this gesture*). Ah! ... Pardon! ... An appointment! (*He wheels suddenly and dashes out.*)

BRIDGET

Och, these men o' business! ... Always in a hurry! ... But wouldn't we have been fine and complete now, if only he'd brought the bull! ... I'd have bandaged him rare and tight, so I would. *(Turning to* DRIMFEARN.*)* Would ye do me a favour, Drimfearn?

DRIMFEARN

At your service, my dear, ab ... so ... lute ... ly!

BRIDGET

Well, then, keep your eye on father, and see he has no more deals with anyone ... The Doctor and I are just going down to look for some fishing-rods and cauliflowers and things. *(She flashes a glance at* MARSALI.*)* And then we have to discuss whether that hospital's to be at Belgrade or Ragusa.

DOCTOR

Well, I'm all for Belgrade.

BRIDGET

And I'm all for Ragusa.

(They link arms and go out, smiling.

DRIMFEARN

I think I'll lay my money on Ragusa. Ten to one. Any takers? What say, Kelly?

KELLY

Nothing doing. I'll have to be on short commons now as long's I live. Me saving; and them two spending, hand over fist, on heathen childer!

DRIMFEARN

But I said ten to one, Kelly.

KELLY

In what?

DRIMFEARN

In single notes.

KELLY

Man alive, but you're very saving! What kind of a bet is that for a man of any consequence!

DRIMFEARN

Well, what do you suggest?

MARSALI

Isn't he dreadful, Murray! That's how he keeps his eye on father.

MURRAY

Let's quit, or we'll be blamed for this.

(They run out, laughing.

KELLY

There they go! Did ye hear them? No charity or loving-kindness at all in the young ones nowadays. They're all for devilment themselves, and for keeping it from us ould ones ... Whisper, man! ... Is there not by any chance a pack o' playing-cards in this rabbit-hutch?

DRIMFEARN

Now that's an idea. I remember ... Now, what was the occasion? ... Yes, a bazaar and whist-drive held here for the Nursing Association. *(He crosses to the instrument cupboard, and searches it.)* No, not there, not there, my child. *(He returns to* **KELLY**'s *bedside.)* I wonder where I saw cards the other day! ... Ah, of course! *(He plunges his hand into a hip-pocket and produces a pack of cards.)*

KELLY

Man, ye're the rare ould conjurer!

DRIMFEARN

Just remembered! Took them out for a hand after lunch on the hill yesterday, when the Hepburns came over ... Talk about luck, eh?

KELLY

Luck! ... It's more like Harrods stores! ... You're a right jewel of a landlord, so ye are ... Begob! I believe now, if I asked ye for a deer or a salmon or a nannie-goat, ye could be bringing it down one of your sleeves ... Lay them out, boy!

DRIMFEARN

(tossing the pack down on the couch). What shall it be?

KELLY

What about Euchre?

DRIMFEARN

Agreed.

KELLY

(seizing the pack and running rapidly over it to discard small cards). "No more deals," says she, Draw in your chair now, and we'll show them dealing! ... As if two grown men like you and me are ta be ordered about by a chit of a girl! ... And her with her Belgrades and her Ragusas ... And us not to have our diversions as well as her ... There's no reason in the young ones nowadays, as I was saying ... They're neither civil nor civilised, if ye ask me ... And what I want to know is ...

DRIMFEARN
(suddenly). Hush! I think I hear her!

KELLY
(sweeping the cards under the quilt). Och, I wish to God she was out o' this and away at Ragusa! *(He assumes his invalid attitude at once, creeping under the rugs.)*

DRIMFEARN
Wait a moment! *(He tiptoes to the door and peers out carefully, this way and that.)* All clear! ... No ... wait! ... Yes, I think ... Yes, a false alarm ... Sorry. *(He returns to* KELLY, *who pops up at once, and starts to retrieve the cards from under the coverings of the couch.* DRIMFEARN *assists by picking up some from the floor)*

DRIMFEARN
(as they settle down once more). Talking of Ragusa and the hospital—I can't help thinking that's a mistake, y'know ... Why not in our own country ... The children here are as much in need of hospitals and all that as children in foreign countries, as you very wisely pointed out to Miss Kelly.

KELLY
(assorting the cards). I'm with ye, man ... I'm with ye there.

DRIMFEARN
And if you want a site in the British Isles that offers the purest air, Mr. Kelly, what about the air around Drimfearn. Why shouldn't she build her hospital here, sir? Why should she not commemorate the greatest happiness of her life when she met the man of her choice here ... and, of course, your own rapid recovery from your accident, which was ... ah ... which was ...

KELLY
Not of my choice, if ye please.

DRIMFEARN
I was about to say "so regrettably serious." Anyway, I'll back Drimfearn against Ragusa or Belgrade ... back it against all comers. And I think she couldn't do better than commemorate all those happy consummations I referred to by building here ... Then there's the country produce to hand ... fresh eggs, the best butter in the Isles, and— most nourishing of all— goats' milk ... Goats' milk, sir, positively in torrents.

KELLY
Whisper, boy! Don't ever mention goats any more ... I know her...

DRIMFEARN

Well, perhaps ... yes ... perhaps, as you say.

KELLY

And now, for the Lord's sake, take another look around, and see if we're safe. *(He has the cards ready at last.)*

(**DRIMFEARN** *makes another reconnaissance, and is about to return smiling, but suddenly turns on his tracks and repeats his observations nervously.* **KELLY** *sits up eagerly watching him, and at length, becoming irritated beyond bounds by the delay, dashes the pack of cards on the floor in sheer exasperation.*

KELLY

Saints above! Two grown men ... and we can't stir hand or foot without waiting to hear what that slip of a girl will say about it all! ... Whisper, man! (**DRIMFEARN** *approaches.*) Come over! ... I like ye well ... And I like this place ... Think of the fine times we could be having here, if we only had peace to live! ... For the love o' God don't say a word about building that hospital anywhere but Ragusa ... D'ye get me? ... Not one word against Ragusa!

(They nod gravely to one another, and shake hands solemnly on the pact.

CURTAIN

www.ingramcontent.com/pod-product-compliance
Lightning Source LLC
Chambersburg PA
CBHW050157240426
43671CB00013B/2162